The Active Stylist

An Anthology of Canadian, American
and Commonwealth Prose

Edited by

W. H. New
W. E. Messenger

University of British Columbia

Prentice-Hall Canada Inc., *Scarborough, Ontario*

To the memory of
Roy Daniells

Canadian Cataloguing in Publication Data

The Active Stylist
This is an alternate edition of Active Voice.
ISBN 0-13-003632-3
1. College readers. I. New. William H., 1938.
II. Messenger, William E., 1931-

Prentice-Hall, Inc., Englewood Cliffs, New Jersey, U.S.A.
Prentice-Hall International, Inc., London
Prentice-Hall of Australia, Pty. Ltd., Sydney
Prentice-Hall of India Private Limited, New Delhi
Prentice-Hall of Japan, Inc., Tokyo
Prentice-Hall of Southeast Asia (Pte.) Ltd., Singapore

Production Editors: Anne Sinclair/Veronica Orocio
Designer: Gail Ferreira
Composition: Dimensions in DesignType Ltd.

ISBN 0-13-003632-3

81 82 83 84 85 WO 5 4 3 2 1

Printed in Canada by Webcom Limited

CONTENTS

A Note to the Reader

No book can answer all your questions about writing or tell you once and for all how to write, for people learn to write only by writing—by finding out what does reach readers and what does not. There are no rigid rules, no certain shortcuts, no guarantees of success, and for that matter, no inevitable pitfalls. But there are models. By reading attentively, and by responding—sympathetically, analytically, and inquiringly—to other writers' efforts to communicate, you can increase your understanding of the relation between writer and reader, and you can learn some of the practical strategies that successful writers use.

The Active Stylist gives you a cross-section of such models. It shows a variety of twentieth-century writers (Canadian, American, British, Australian, Trinidadian) dealing with a variety of subjects (science, history, language, medicine, politics, the arts, economics, psychology, race, personal experience) in a variety of styles and forms (formal, informal, experimental; personal narrative, journal, interview, letter, review, investigation, argument, explanation, entertainment). But the thematic and the technical are only the most obvious among the many avenues of approach offered you here. For example, asking if Americans write differently from Canadians, or women from men, or writers of the 1920s from writers of the 1970s, might lead to an informed discussion of the biases of culture, sex, and fashion that sometimes colour a writer's attitude or affect the premises on which an argument rests. Exploring the nature of rhythm might lead to a greater understanding of the importance of sound to an essay's effect on a reader. Seeking the relation between technique and meaning might lead to a greater understanding of the nature of literacy and a greater appreciation of the need for verbal accuracy in all kinds of communication. Examining expository essays alongside poems and narratives, and even beside prose forms conventionally considered nonliterary, might help develop an appreciation for literary endeavour in general. Much depends on your willingness to invest effort and imagination in the process of reading. The readings in this book, then, give you models to follow and places to begin learning about writing: by asking questions, suggesting possibilities, affirming the open-endedness of literary inquiry, and indicating something of the range of twentieth-century stylistic excellence.

The essays and categories isolated here are not meant to impose limits on your powers of invention. Whatever the examples in this collection might imply, not all letters have to be argument, nor all reviews humorous, nor all journals serious reflections on poverty, politics, or race. It is important to emphasize this flexibility of language, to assert again and again that the forms of composition overlap and that the categories by which we describe the varieties of prose form are not mutually exclusive. Many of the pieces in this book have more than one aim: to explain *and* persuade, for example, or to describe *and* amuse. And many, with some difference of emphasis, could be classified differently: Haig-Brown's essay could be considered explanatory, Orwell's essay persuasive, Woolf's letter humorous, and so on. Keep in mind that the organization of any anthology of essays is essentially an arbitrary structuring device, one which the good reader will both use and transcend.

The particular organization that we have adopted for *The Active Stylist* is meant to draw your attention to three features of the strategy of writing essays:

1. The large purpose that motivates a writer to write (to tell a story, to explain a problem, to convince someone of something). This element of form governs the division of the book into its six sections. Section I stresses the importance of observing closely, actively, and personally; all the essays show what the authors themselves see, hear, do, and remember. By focussing on the interview and the journal, section II considers two of the ways writers reveal their reactions to other people and invite reactions from them; it shows, further, how several writers have adapted the techniques of the interview and the journal to the essay form itself. Sections III and IV explore the tasks of persuasion, explanation, and instruction; they show how these apparently abstract enterprises can also be subjectively organized, sometimes deliberately and sometimes unconsciously—the art of persuasion being the most open to personal bias, and the art of explanation being the most neutral. The last two sections, V and VI, isolate particular formal problems—humorous writing and experimentation—for practical consideration, and encourage apprentice writers to experiment intelligently as they practise their way toward their own personal style.

2. The immediate purpose—the sense of audience—that governs the writer's choice of form (letter, recipe, review, feature article, research essay). These forms range across the general categories; you will find other kinds of form—advertisement, poem, anecdote—also used as examples in various parts of the book, and you may find it instructive to compare the conventions of prose with other, often more exclusively visual or aural, conventions of communication.
3. The specifics of technique by which writers develop and express their ideas.

The introductions to each section establish this triple context. Rather than analyze the essays that follow or prescribe procedures for reading them, however, they suggest some of the terms of reference within which different kinds of analysis and discussion can take place. They do this in part by definition and discussion, and in part by technical example. Direction, like meaning, often lies in form. The introduction to section IV, for instance, concerns the need for explanations to be clear, which is a commonplace that will raise little argument and little cheering. How actually to write clearly is another question. The essays in this section provide examples of some successful techniques: using a precise vocabulary, making comparisons between unfamiliar and familiar things, telling illustrative anecdotes, and adopting an informal, person-to-person tone. The introduction strives at once to generalize about these methods and to use at least some of them in the process of talking about them. Hence it begins anecdotally in order to discuss the effect of anecdotal beginnings, and uses the vocabulary of its own anecdote as part of its process of exploring the language of explanation. Meaning and method unite. You will discover analogous techniques in the other introductions as well: an ironic quotation, quoted ironically, forms part of the commentary on humorous writing; sentence fragments appear in a section that asks if it is acceptable to break standard rules of composition; rhetorical questions and other deliberate devices—litotes, chiasmus, simile, antithesis—appear both as strategies for argument and as examples for analysis.

Some of these terms and techniques—such as litotes (the "negative positive": "not unusual") and chiasmus (an X-shaped structure: "He had a talent for making the easy difficult and the difficult easy")—will not be familiar to all readers. Some of the essays, too, might seem unusually difficult. To add to what the introductions can do to illuminate them, therefore, some brief explorations of relevant terms and some suggestions for study, discussion, and composition are provided at the end of each section. Like the introductions, these study sections neither assert easy answers nor suggest that all answers come easily; part of the function of this book is to encourage a little overreaching, for no real learning takes place without it. Wrestling aimlessly with a difficult subject can be frustrating, of course, but returning to something challenging after having discovered the resources that can help one master it—resources both within oneself and in the form of external guidance—can prove far more stimulating than simply resting with the skills or knowledge one already has.

Throughout, *The Active Stylist* emphasizes the extent to which form embodies meaning. In particular, this idea is the central concern of the essays in the last section, which therefore constitutes a kind of formal and argumentative coda to the book as a whole. But, depending on one's approach, this section could provide as forceful a beginning as it does an end. The essays offer variety, and hence a variety of places to start. Most of all, they are enjoyable in their own right, whether as models for the apprentice writer or as inquiries and diversions for people who just like to read.

To conclude this introductory note, here are some terms that you should be familiar with at the outset:

Diction The choice and use of words. "Good diction" means the use of correct and specific words. The term "levels of diction" refers to formal, informal, colloquial, and slang usage.

Idiom A combination of words, peculiar to a specific language, in which the words work neither literally nor solely ornamentally. For example, consider the prepositions in the command "Sit down and sit up!" Or consider the *literal* meanings of the words in "Put up or shut up." The English language is full of idiomatic expressions like "taking the lion's share" or "go the whole hog." Idioms often consist of doublets, such as "high and dry" and "vim and vigour." And they are often metaphorical, as in "shipshape" or "bottle up." Clearly, such idioms can seldom be translated literally into another language. (And see Hornyansky's essay in section VI.)

Abstract, concrete Basically, an abstract word denotes something intangible, such as an idea, quality, or condition (honour, beauty, laziness, patriotism, sorrow), whereas a concrete word denotes something tangible (chair, fir tree, hyena, raindrop). Amateur writing is often weak because of a lack of concreteness.

Cliché A trite expression, one worn-out from overuse (a bolt from the blue, last but not least, pretty as a picture, nothing new under the sun, it's a small world).

Syntax The grammatical structure of phrases, clauses, and sentences. *Grammar* is simply the scientific study and description of the way a language works.

Active voice, passive voice Grammatical terms describing different ways some verbs (transitive ones) can be used. A verb in the active voice acts upon an object: A woman *bought* the car. When a verb is in the passive voice, what would normally be the object of the verb becomes the subject of the sentence: The car *was bought* by a woman. (The instrumental "by" phrase is not always present: The car *was sold* to a woman. The verb is nevertheless still in the passive voice.) Verbs in the passive voice are generally weaker than verbs in the active voice.

Fragment A group of words lacking a subject or a verb, or both. A fragment that is acceptable, that is satisfactorily complete because of context (as would be a brief answer to a question), is sometimes referred to as a *minor sentence*.

Point of view The angle or perspective from which an author writes, which governs the way a reader receives information.

Figurative language A deliberate departure from standard structure, order, or literal meaning for some visual or rhetorical effect. You will find more comment on various figures of speech and rhetorical devices below and in the "Terms and Topics" sections of this anthology.

Metaphor A figurative use of language in which things not usually thought of as alike are identified; that is, a word or phrase usually applied to one thing is applied to something quite different. A metaphor not only helps clarify meaning but also provokes a sharp reappraisal of the subject. Slang is a productive source of metaphor: "wet blanket," "square," "high," "coffin nail." So is the poet's imagination: such a phrase as "tongues of consuming fire" uses metaphor to imply the act of eating. And some metaphors are buried deep in the language: "daisy" is a collapsed form of "day's eye." A simile is a form of metaphorical language which states the comparison explicitly: "His voice was *like thunder*." A metaphor would phrase this comparison explicitly: "His voice thundered" or "In his thundering voice, he. . . ." An *extended metaphor* (or simile) is one in which the implicit (or explicit) comparison is continued beyond a single statement: "His voice thundered. When he spoke, the clouds parted and the lightning of his wit flashed through. The resulting deluge of information and entertainment floated the audience's spirits." Extended metaphors are dangerous in that they can easily get out of control.

Image A verbal representation, either literal or figurative, usually of something visual. Metaphors often create figurative images. An image can also be aural, olfactory, gustatory, tactile, or kinesthetic.

Symbol An image that not only represents a concrete, empirical reality but also makes that reality stand for something else, usually something more abstract. A flag, for example, not only represents a country but also symbolizes, for many people, their country's political or ethical virtues. The word *rose* not only represents an actual flower, but also, in many poems, symbolizes something like feminine beauty. And be careful not to confuse the verbs *symbolize* and *represent*.

Tone An author's attitude toward his or her subject and audience. Tone is manifested by various stylistic qualities of a piece of writing. Tone can be formal, informal, relaxed, playful, serious, condescending, insulting, ironic, sarcastic, bitter, questioning, matter-of-fact, and so on. It is related to point of view.

Rhythm The movement implicit in an arrangement of words; the movement one feels when reading the words (even if one is not reading aloud). Is there a regular beat from the patterns of stress on the syllables, or not? Is there a rising or a falling inflection to the words? Does a series of phrases move quickly, or slowly?

Style The overall arrangement of sounds, words, phrases, sentences, and paragraphs that go to make up writing. Style consists of everything having to do with the *way* a writer writes something. Styles do not fall into absolute categories; styles are as individual as good writers. Style is affected by fashion and taste, by regional and cultural variations, by changing standards of usage, by the development of new words and new meanings in the language, and by the fertility of an author's imagination. A good style is one that most aptly chooses and arranges words to convey the particular shade of meaning, to produce the precise effect, that an author intends.

If you want further explanation of these and other terms defined in this book, or if we have not provided definitions of terms you don't know, you should consult a good standard dictionary. Better yet, there are many technical dictionaries, dictionaries or glossaries of literary terms, that will help you even more. Here are the names of a few of them, just to get you started:

> M.H. Abrams, *A Glossary of Literary Terms*
> C. Hugh Holman, *A Handbook to Literature*
> Lee T. Lemon, *A Glossary for the Study of English*
> Harry Shaw, *Concise Dictionary of Literary Terms*

Once the terms are familiar to you, apply them to the essays and to your other reading, practise using the techniques yourself, and ask yourself how useful and effective they are for shaping your ideas in prose and for reaching your chosen reader.

Introduction: Audience and Purpose

To begin, here are six examples of how some people actually talk:

1. "How are *we* today?"
2. "It has come to a point where the Prime Minister must begin to face matters and recognize that an election must be called forthwith."
3. "You have *no idea* how difficult it's been to arrange everything for this afternoon."
4. "Cold out by the bluff today, eh?"
5. "There's still a real relationship between him and I, irregardless of what he done."
6. "The organization metatalk of this is offered in terms of the recognition that composition situations will be met down the road, and persons without a game plan, on the basis of the correlation interface between their multivalent experimental factors and their societal age-group factors, will be quantified institution-wise."

Each utterance conveys a message—though the sixth example deeply buries it—and each conveys clearly the character of the speaker. Interestingly, however, the message that the speaker intends and the public face that he or she wishes to display often differ from the message an audience actually hears and the face it perceives. Consider again the six examples:

1. The first is the classic utterance of the stereotypical primary school teacher. She—and one makes a biased, presumptive leap identifying the gender here—appears to want to assert her oneness with her class. But how effective is the utterance if she uses it with a group of fifteen-year-olds instead of five-year-olds, or with a group of parents or school inspectors? The adult audience merely cringes politely, with some degree of pity for someone who can no longer separate herself from "her" children. The fifteen-year-olds, by contrast, bristle, for they indignantly reject what they hear as condescension, what they identify as the speaker's refusal to recognize how much they have grown up. Given a difference in the age of the audience or a difference in milieu, this communication therefore breaks down.

2. The second utterance, clearly political, just as clearly comes from the mouth of someone not on the governing party's side. It will scarcely be effective. Compare it for a moment with the standard slogans of actual election campaigns: "Hold the Vote Now!" "Vote Them Out!" "Time for a Change!" The bluntly monosyllabic slogans appeal directly—hence personally—to the listener: "*You* vote them out." But any utterance that begins phrasally (*It has come to a point where*), continues with vague words (*matters, forthwith*), and closes with a passive evasion (*must be called*—by whom???) dooms itself. No one will take it seriously. No one will hear the overt message; they will hear a waffling covert message instead, something like: "I know this is futile but the party requires me to make a mechanical gesture." The emphasis falls, finally, on the futility and the sense of obligation.

3. The third example, too, offers a personal glimpse of the speaker. Ostensibly it's about *you* ("You have no idea"), but really it's about *I*, the speaker. "It's been *difficult*, for *me*," the speaker is sàying. "Admire *me* because *I've* done something difficult; *I've* put *myself* out." The message contains at least two further notions. The first—"I'm a martyr"—is a curiously perverse sort of self-aggrandizing. The second—"and it's *your fault*"—implies that the afternoon's event is less than successful. This last twist emerges because the message (*no idea*," "*difficult*") is essentially negative. It only occurs when there's a problem. And whose problem is it? The speaker's, perhaps—certainly not *yours*—but the speaker has difficulty admitting to it. In any case, an afternoon event that's proceeding well will call forth an utterance more like "There was a lot to do, but *we* had a *good* time doing it." It is at once less defensive and less shrill.

4. The fourth example reveals no problem of personality. It's a colloquial fragment of conversation, informal in tone, designed not so much to impart or to ask for information—despite the fact that it's cast as a question—as to give a kind of ritual voice to a chance encounter. "How do you do?" offers a more formal parallel. No one ever replies, "I do do well." The exchange is a social convention, varying according to the social circumstances. The speaker who says "Pleased to meet you" may in fact not be. The speaker who says "Charmed, I'm sure" conveys the distinct impression that he isn't, and that he's stuffy to boot. What we know of the speaker who uses *bluff* and *eh?* has more to do with his nationality than his social status. He's likely Canadian. But there's another geographic variable here, for if he's a prairie speaker, *bluff* means a *grove of trees*, not a *cliff*. Without a context, the utterance is ambiguous.

5. In a conversational context, a sentence fragment—as in example number four—is perfectly acceptable. Provided it grows directly out of a previous utterance, its meaning will usually be clear. But the fifth example contains a grating combination of plain and fancy mistakes. Among some occupations and in some environments, grammatical errors do constitute a norm, of course; in such settings, correctly spoken English would sound curiously stiff. But in an environment where grammatical correctness is valued, an ungrammatical speaker sounds either boorish or ill-educated. Whether the simple mistakes in this example (mistakes of diction: *irregardless*, and of grammar: *what he done*) derive from lack of education or from regional or cultural norms of usage would be hard to tell were it not for the presence of the more elaborate mistake (*between him and I*). The overcorrection here—which erases *me* even on the occasions when syntax demands it—suggests some acquaintance with grammar and a conscious desire to appear "proper." But the ultimate effect is the same as that of tawdry paintings: of elegance wanted, and elegance still wanting.

6. The final example shows what happens when inflated notions of elegance and preciseness take over. The result is inelegance and impreciseness. Long words do not intrinsically sound better than short ones, nor do they somehow mean better. Yet these assumptions seem to lie behind every outburst of such bafflegab. Relying on the passive voice allows the speaker to evade responsibility for everything he says; relying on clichéd stock phrases (*game plan*), vague reference (*this*), noun clusters (*composition situation*), long words and invented words (*multivalent*, *metatalk*) allows him to create the illusion of complexity and great intelligence even when both are lacking. A listener cannot just absorb a communication like

this one; he has to decode it. And the message he decodes is often crashingly pedestrian.

These examples draw attention to many of the points of connection between speakers and their audiences. Age, education, occupation, social standing, nationality, region, time, and taste can all bring speaker and listener together or irrevocably separate them. The speaker who condescends, either through the tone he adopts or by oversimplifying his subject, causes a listener to respond, at the very least, unsympathetically. Similarly, overestimating an audience's ability to handle the complexity of a subject or a certain level of vocabulary will estrange speakers from the people they are trying to reach. Waffling, evading the responsibility for thought, speaking too quickly, and speaking too slowly or quietly all interfere with the act of communicating. An audience distracted by a speaker's dress or gestures, by the pitch of his voice, by his failure to look at them (or at the television camera that is transporting him into their homes), or by a series of verbal tics (*er, um, y' know, like*) is not listening to the words. It is more likely counting the *ums*. Such speakers parody themselves, but may never realize it, nor recognize how much they are dissolving in their audience's eyes.

Other speakers, knowledgeable about body language, can cleverly manipulate their audience through their gestures rather than through their actual words. The earnest crease in the forehead, the expansively open gesture of the arms, the honest raising of the eyebrows or widening of the eyes: speakers can falsify their emotions as easily as they can leave them on display. The informed audience learns how to distinguish between the trustworthy and the deceptive, between the actual and the acted, between the event and the ad. The social psychology of the relation between speaker and listener is far more complex than this simple declaration suggests, but the ability to recognize some of the links between them is increasingly necessary as North American culture comes to rely more and more on pictorial and oral communication.

The relation between writer and reader is not the same as that between speaker and listener. It is similar, but the act of writing things down has the effect of limiting an audience in further ways. Education, whether formal or informal, remains an issue, for writers almost always write to an audience that values the act of reading. Writing for a person who can't read is self-contradictory; writing for a person who won't read is probably futile. One might argue, therefore, that writing is essentially a middle-class act, and that the spoken rhetoric of the street, the wharf, the hustings, and the television set would reach a greater range of people than books would, and would reach them directly. Whether or not this argument is defensible, writers, like speakers, face problems of reaching and holding their chosen audiences. And they are subject to many of the same variables of style.

Tone, directness, accuracy, level, and movement all matter acutely if a writer intends to win a receptive audience. Merely writing things down, in the first words that come into his head and in whatever order they occur to him, will not suffice. Writing an economic argument in current slang would not convince the people attending a businessmen's luncheon; producing a simile like "as barren as a plant sale reduced to its lowest common cactus" is not likely to amuse ardent cactus fanciers. Writers write; but they write with both a purpose and a reader in mind. They first make broad choices: to write a letter or an essay or a book, for children or adults, for a specialized group or the general public. Then, as they plan and write and revise, the fine rhetorical choices follow, and in making them, writers shape what they say until they are as sure as they can be that they have matched their intention with their audience. They have to consider the age, education, biases, ability, and expectations of their readers. They have to decide if they want to be funny or serious or neutral or sad. They have to decide whether they want to entertain or instruct or argue or describe or reveal. They have to decide if they want to announce their subject directly or to draw their readers into deducing conclusions. They have to know their subject and their grammar sufficiently to be accurate. They have to decide whether to be personal, informal, and conversational, or distant and formal and objective. And they have to decide how to shape their rhetoric: whether to make it flow grandly or step in staccato phrases, to ring eloquently or murmur laconically, to dazzle by eloquent metaphor or to convince by plain speaking. Only when they have made these decisions are they close to a strategy for writing capably.

Whether consciously or unconsciously, writers question their choice of words (are they monosyllabic or polysyllabic? abstract or concrete? easy or difficult? objective or slanted? formal or informal? general or precise?), syntax and structure (are the sentences short or long? simple or complex? varied or unvaried? fragmentary or whole?), and the organization of their whole work (is it coherent? unified? clear? do the paragraphs flow?). If they are true stylists they worry also about rhythm and sounds and the freshness of the arrangements they have devised. In short, they address themselves actively to their audience in their own voice and in a form they choose. The choices they make do not derive from some secret set of absolutes. There is no hidden writer's chart somewhere that reveals to a chosen few that polysyllables are "good" and informality "bad." Nor do writers usually set out, as textbooks often imply, to tackle as vague a project as a "comparison-and-contrast essay." They do not begin with a structural device; rather they have subjects to explore, and they know that substance and style are intrinsically related. They have audiences to satisfy, and they have particular tasks to do—letters to write, explanations to provide, stories to tell, arguments to deliver. In carrying out these tasks as articulately as possible, skilled writers can use an extraordinary variety of verbal techniques, even to the point of making deliberate errors to achieve particular effects. In the process they will demonstrate not only some of the many creative ways in which words work, but also the individuality that can invigorate all prose forms. Their work reveals the force of writing both for an audience and with a purpose in mind.

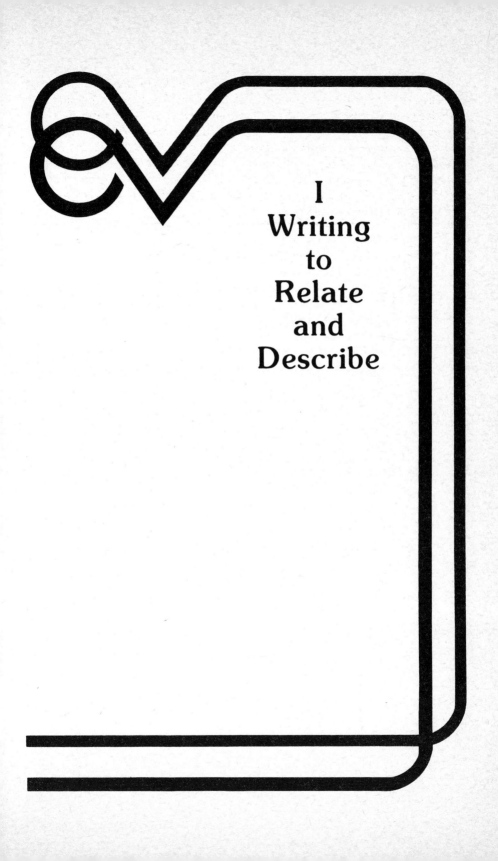

I
Writing
to
Relate
and
Describe

"Once upon a time..." and "Have you heard the one about..." are two of the most familiar ways in the language to begin a story. And they invite particular responses. The first, either part of a child's tale or else adopting the form of one, asks readers to suspend empirical judgments for the moment and to accept the possibilities of fantasy. The other nudges clearly toward the salacious bar-room jest or the simple corny joke. Like other preludes, they seize and settle the people in the tale-teller's audience and establish the likely mood of the story to follow. These particular preludes, moreover, invite audiences to expect an ensuing narrative rather than an explanation or an argument. Only a most sophisticated writer manages to use such an opening for a different end.

Story, or narrative, rarely appears in as undiluted a form as it does in joking anecdotes. Even when constructed with a careful plot, as in novels and short stories, narratives contain more than the basic narrative elements of event, time, and sequence. Stories can, however, also appear in contexts other than purely narrative ones. The personal narrative, for example, contains a story, or stories, and conveys an individual personality. But it is not plotted. White, Thomas, Haig-Brown, and Mukherjee, writing narrative memoirs and relating a variety of internal anecdotes, use an identifiable chronology and create individual characters. Plot, however, relies on causal relationships among episodes. One event makes another one happen, and part of the reader's task with a narrative is to unravel how and why. In these essays, the writers focus primarily on something other than cause and effect. The events they write about may join to achieve a consistent single effect, therefore, but they do not connect into a plot. Further, the narrative essayist characteristically employs descriptive as well as narrative techniques, and it sometimes becomes a moot point whether the essay that results should properly be called narrative or descriptive. In the long run, naming a proper category matters less than appreciating the essay itself, with its blend of techniques and the skilful balance which each author individually contrives.

Description, like narration, usually appears as an "impure" form. Narrative emphasizes temporal sequence but incidentally observes settings and records dramatic conversational exchanges; description emphasizes visual placement—direction, size, texture, and general appearance—but often for other than simply pictorial purposes. Hence in personal memoirs—and even in much fiction—descriptive passages frequently occur. They can heighten a reader's sense of both the place and the event a writer is recreating, intensify the mood that the writer is striving to convey, and often illustrate or epitomize, concretely and clearly, the writer's ideas. This excerpt from an 1883 feminist novel, Olive Schreiner's *The Story of an African Farm*, employs descriptive details for just such purposes:

It was eight o'clock when they neared the farm-house: a red-brick building, with kraals to the right and a small orchard to the left. Already there were signs of unusual life and bustle: one cart, a waggon, and a couple of saddles against the wall betokened the arrival of a few early guests, whose numbers would soon be largely increased. To a Dutch country wedding guests start up in numbers astonishing to one who has merely ridden through the plains of sparsely-inhabited karroo.

As the morning advances, riders on many shades of steeds appear from all directions, and add their saddles to the long rows against the walls, shake hands, drink coffee, and stand about outside in groups to watch the arriving carts and ox-waggons, as they are unburdened of their heavy freight of massive Tantes and comely daughters, followed by swarms of children of all sizes, dressed in all manner of print and moleskin, who are taken care of by Hottentot, Kaffir, and half-caste nurses, whose many-shaded complexions, ranging from light yellow up to ebony black, add variety to the animated scene. Everywhere is excitement and bustle, which gradually increases as the time for the return of the wedding party approaches. Preparations for the feast are actively advancing in the kitchen; coffee is liberally handed round, and amid a profound sensation, and the firing of guns, the horse-waggon draws up, and the wedding party alight. Bride and bridegroom, with their attendants, march solemnly to the marriage chamber, where bed and box are decked out in white, with ends of ribbon and artificial flowers, and where on a row of chairs the party solemnly seat themselves. After a time bridesmaid and best man rise, and conduct in with ceremony each individual guest, to wish success and to kiss bride and bridegroom. Then the feast is set on the table, and it is almost sunset before the dishes are cleared away, and the pleasure of the day begins. Everything is removed from the great front room, and the mud floor, well rubbed with bullock's blood, glistens like polished mahogany. The female portion of the assembly flock into the side-rooms to attire themselves for the evening; and reissue clad in white muslin, and gay with bright ribbons and brass jewellery. The dancing begins as the tallow candles are stuck up about the walls, the music coming from a couple of fiddlers in a corner of the room. Bride and bridegroom open the ball, and the floor is soon covered with whirling couples, and everyone's spirits rise. The bridal pair mingle freely in the throng, and here and there a musical man sings vigorously as he drags his partner through the

Blue Water or John Speriwig; boys shout and applaud, and the enjoyment and confusion are intense, till eleven o'clock comes. By this time the children who swarm in the side-rooms are not to be kept quiet longer, even by hunches of bread and cake; there is a general howl and wail, that rises yet higher than the scraping of fiddles, and mothers rush from their partners to knock small heads together, and cuff little nursemaids, and force the wailers down into unoccupied corners of beds, under tables, and behind boxes. In half an hour every variety of childish snore is heard on all sides, and it has become perilous to raise or set down a foot in any of the side-rooms lest a small head or hand should be crushed. Now, too, the busy feet have broken the solid coating of the floor, and a cloud of fine dust rises, that makes a yellow halo round the candles, and sets asthmatic people coughing, and grows denser, till to recognize any one on the opposite side of the room becomes impossible, and a partner's face is seen through a yellow mist.

To create the effect she wants, Schreiner chooses precise terms, often in Afrikaans (*kraal, karroo, Tantes*), specific numbers and colours (*one* cart, *brass* jewellery), exact and evocative details (*half-caste* nurses, *artificial* flowers, *bullock's blood*, and *John Speriwig*), and a whole array of verbs, both active and passive. The variety of adjectives lends colour and texture to the scene, but it is the verbs that give the passage its life. Schreiner marshalls the active verbs to contrive an illusion of speed and commotion: riders *appear, add, shake,* and *drink,* the wedding company *flock, reissue, mingle, sing, drag, shout,* and *applaud;* mothers *rush, knock, cuff,* and *force.* Such verbs help her to perceive and define movement exactly and therefore to describe scenes effectively. She uses static verbs (*is, seem, appear*) sparingly. But somewhat surprisingly, she does use a number of verbs in the passive voice (coffee *is handed round,* the dishes *are cleared away,* everything *is removèd* from the table), which ordinarily would have a dampening effect on the action; here, under creative control, they manage to generalize from the specific event, to imply that the events and relationships described never change in this society: the women, who are doing the work, disappear into the passive structures. It is not difficult, then, to see the relation between form and meaning, to see how the author makes the activity itself inherently misleading, and how she makes the paragraphs form part of her novel's general attack upon the static roles and relationships which society opens to women.

Essayists, like novelists, can use prose rhythm and precise detail evocatively. Thomas's attempt to capture the Welsh vernacular, Mukherjee's anecdotal representations of Indian speech, and MacLennan's choral invocation of the Québécois *ouais* all illustrate the effectiveness of rhythmic control. Forster's, White's, Eiseley's, and Moorehead's mastery of simple verbs, their talent for metaphor, and their eye for significant detail all contribute to their transformation of experience into art. Good writers know, of course, that not all details are significant; much of the art of good writing is bound with knowing when to leave things out. The wrong details, or too many or too few, will evoke either an undesired response or no response at all. Nor are all metaphors valid. Many are inappropriate, clichéd, irrelevant, and unnecessary; and no good writer would be drawn into writing a mixed metaphor—as in the sentence "He's buttered his bread, and now he must lie in it"—without being totally aware of the ludicrous image it is likely to create. If the writer's intended mood is humorous or the established situation a little bizarre, the mixed metaphor's incongruity might reinforce the effect; but otherwise it will jolt a reader abruptly out of an essay.

Perhaps most important, because narrative tries above all else to interest and entertain, good writers know that not every personal experience intrinsically fascinates every reader; it is the *telling* of a story that is fascinating. When a writer subtly transforms experience, the process may appear effortless, but behind the subtle transformations lie his skill and his understanding of the kinds of choices that good writers know consistently how to make.

Once More to the Lake*

E.B. White

(August 1941)

One summer, along about 1904, my father rented a camp on a lake in Maine and took us all there for the month of August. We all got ringworm from some kittens and had to rub Pond's Extract on our arms and legs night and morning, and my father rolled over in a canoe with all his clothes on; but outside of that the vacation was a success and from then on none of us ever thought there was any place in the world like that lake in Maine. We returned summer after summer—always on August 1st for one month. I have since become a salt-water man, but sometimes in summer there are days when the restlessness of the tides and the fearful cold of the sea water and the incessant wind which blows across the afternoon and into the evening make me wish for the placidity of a lake in the woods. A few weeks ago this feeling got so strong I bought myself a couple of bass hooks and a spinner and returned to the lake where we used to go, for a week's fishing and to revisit old haunts.

I took along my son, who had never had any fresh water up his nose and who had seen lily pads only from train windows. On the journey over to the lake I began to wonder what it would be like. I wondered how time would have marred this unique, this holy spot—the coves and streams, the hills that the sun set behind, the camps and the paths behind the camps. I was sure that the tarred road would have found it out and I wondered in what other ways it would be desolated. It is strange how much you can remember about places like that once you allow your mind to return into the grooves which lead back. You remember one thing, and that suddenly reminds you of another thing. I guess I remembered clearest of all the early mornings, when the lake was cool and motionless, remembered how the bedroom smelled of the lumber it was made of and of the wet woods whose scent entered through the screen. The partitions in the camp were thin and did not extend clear to the top of the rooms, and as I was always the first up I would dress softly so as not to wake the others, and sneak out into the sweet outdoors and start out in the canoe, keeping close along the shore in the long shadows of the pines. I remembered being very careful never to rub my paddle against the gunwale for fear of disturbing the stillness of the cathedral.

The lake had never been what you would call a wild lake. There were cottages sprinkled around the shores, and it was in farming country although the shores of the lake were quite heavily wooded. Some of the cottages were owned by nearby farmers and you would live at the shore and eat your meals at the farmhouse. That's what our family did. But although it wasn't wild, it was a fairly large and undisturbed lake and there were places in it which, to a child at least, seemed infinitely remote and primeval.

I was right about the tar: it led to within half a mile of the shore. But when I got back there, with my boy, and we settled into a camp near a farmhouse and into the kind of summertime I had known, I could tell that it was going to be pretty much the same as it had been before—I knew it, lying in bed the first morning, smelling the bedroom, and hearing the boy sneak quietly out and go off along the shore in a boat. I began to sustain the illusion that he was I, and therefore, by simple transposition, that I was my father. This sensation persisted, kept cropping up all the time we were there. It was not an entirely new feeling, but in this setting it grew much stronger. I seemed to be living a dual existence. I would be in the middle of some simple act, I would be picking up a bait box or laying down a table fork, or I would be saying something, and suddenly it would be not I but my father who was saying the words or making the gesture. It gave me a creepy sensation.

We went fishing the first morning. I felt the same damp moss covering the worms in the bait can, and saw the dragonfly alight on the tip of my rod as it hovered a few inches from the surface of the water. It was the arrival of this fly that convinced me beyond any doubt that everything was as it always had been, that the years were a mirage and there had been no years. The small waves were the same, chucking the rowboat under the chin as we fished at anchor, and the boat was the same boat, the same color green and the ribs broken in the same places, and under the floorboards the same fresh-water leavings and débris—the dead helgramite, the wisps of moss, the rusty discarded fishhook, the dried blood from yesterday's catch. We stared silently at the tips of our rods, at the dragonflies that came and went. I lowered the tip of mine into the water, tentatively, pensively dislodging the fly, which darted two feet away, poised, darted two feet back, and came to rest again a little farther up the rod. There had been no years between the ducking of this dragonfly and the other one—the one that was part of memory. I looked at the boy, who was silently watching his fly, and it was my hands that held his rod, my eyes watching. I felt dizzy and didn't know which rod I was at the end of.

We caught two bass, hauling them in briskly as though they were mackerel, pulling them over the side of the boat in a businesslike manner without any landing net, and stunning them with a blow on the back of the head. When we got back for a swim before lunch, the lake was exactly where we had left it, the same number of inches from the dock, and there was only the merest suggestion of a breeze. This seemed an utterly enchanted sea, this lake you could leave to its own devices for a few hours and come back to, and find that it had not stirred, this constant and trustworthy body of water. In the shallows, the dark, water-soaked sticks and twigs, smooth and old, were undulating in clusters on the bottom against the clean ribbed sand, and the track of the mussel was plain. A school of minnows swam by, each minnow with its small individual shadow, doubling the attendance, so clear and sharp in the sunlight. Some of the other campers were in swimming, along the shore, one of them with a cake of soap, and the water felt thin and clear and unsubstantial. Over the years there had been this person with the cake of soap, this cultist, and here he was. There had been no years.

Up to the farmhouse to dinner through the teeming, dusty field, the road under our sneakers was only a two-track road. The middle track was missing, the one with the marks of the hooves and the splotches of dried, flaky manure. There had always been three tracks to choose from in choosing which track to walk in; now the choice was narrowed down to two. For a moment I missed terribly the middle alternative. But the way led past the tennis court, and something about the way it lay there in the sun reassured me; the tape had loosened along the backline, the alleys were green with plantains and other weeds, and the net (installed in June and removed in September) sagged in the dry noon, and the whole place steamed with midday heat and hunger and emptiness. There was a choice of pie for dessert, and one was blueberry and one was apple, and the waitresses were the same country girls, there having been no passage of time, only the illusion of it as in a dropped curtain—the waitresses were still fifteen; their hair had been washed, that was the only difference—they had been to the movies and seen the pretty girls with the clean hair.

Summertime, oh summertime, pattern of life indelible, the fadeproof lake, the woods unshatterable, the pasture with the sweetfern and the juniper forever and ever, summer without end; this was the background, and the life along the shore was the design, the cottages with their innocent and tranquil design, their tiny docks with the flagpole and the American flag floating against the white clouds in the blue sky, the little paths over the roots of the trees leading from camp to camp and the paths leading back to the outhouses and the can of lime for sprinkling, and at the souvenir counters at the store the miniature birch-bark canoes and the post cards that showed things looking a little better than they looked. This was the American family at play, escaping the city heat, wondering whether the newcomers in the camp at the head of the cove were "common" or "nice," wondering whether it was true that the people who drove up for Sunday dinner at the farmhouse were turned away because there wasn't enough chicken.

It seemed to me, as I kept remembering all this, that those times and those summers had been infinitely precious and worth saving. There had been jollity and peace and goodness. The arriving (at the beginning of August) had been so big a business in itself, at the railway station the farm wagon drawn up, the first smell of the pine-laden air, the first glimpse of the smiling farmer, and the great importance of the trunks and your father's enormous authority in such matters, and the feel of the wagon under you for the long ten-mile haul, and at the top of the last long hill catching the first view of the lake after eleven months of not seeing this cherished body of water. The shouts and cries of the other campers when they saw you, and the trunks to be unpacked, to give up their rich burden. (Arriving was less exciting nowadays, when you sneaked up in your car and parked it under a tree near the camp and took out the bags and in five minutes it was all over, no fuss, no loud wonderful fuss about trunks.)

Peace and goodness and jollity. The only thing that was wrong now, really, was the sound of the place, an unfamiliar nervous sound of the outboard motors. This was the note that jarred, the one thing that would sometimes break the illusion and set the years moving. In those other summertimes all motors were inboard; and when they were at a little distance, the noise they made was a sedative, an ingredient of summer sleep. They were one-cylinder and two-cylinder engines, and some were make-and-break and some were jump-spark, but they all made a sleepy sound across the lake. The one-lungers throbbed and fluttered, and the twin-cylinder ones purred and purred, and that was a quiet sound too. But now the campers all had outboards. In the daytime, in the hot mornings, these motors made a petulant, irritable sound; at night, in the still evening when the afterglow lit the water, they whined about one's ears like mosquitoes. My boy loved our rented outboard, and his great desire was to achieve single-handed mastery over it, and authority, and he soon learned the trick of choking it a little (but not too much), and the adjustment of the needle valve. Watching him I would remember the things you could do with the old one-cylinder engine with the heavy flywheel, how you could have it eating out of your hand if you got really close to it spiritually. Motor boats in those days didn't have clutches, and you would make a landing by shutting off the motor at the proper time and coasting in with a dead rudder. But there was a way of reversing them, if you learned the trick, by cutting the switch and putting it on again exactly on the final dying revolution of the flywheel, so that it would kick back against compression and begin reversing. Approaching a dock in a strong following breeze, it was difficult to slow up sufficiently by the ordinary coasting method, and if a boy felt he had complete mastery over his motor, he was tempted to keep it running beyond its time and then reverse it a few feet from the dock. It took a cool nerve, because if you threw the switch a twentieth of a second too soon you would catch the flywheel when it still had speed enough to go up past center, and the boat would leap ahead, charging bull-fashion at the dock.

We had a good week at the camp. The bass were biting well and the sun shone endlessly, day after day. We would be tired at night and lie down in the accumulated heat of the little bedrooms after the long hot day and the breeze would stir almost imperceptibly outside and the smell of the swamp drift in through the rusty screens. Sleep would come easily and in the morning the red squirrel would be on the roof, tapping out his gay routine. I kept remembering everything, lying in bed in the mornings—the small steamboat that had a long rounded stern like the lip of a Ubangi, and how quietly she ran on the moonlight sails, when the older boys played their mandolins and the girls sang and we ate doughnuts dipped in sugar, and how sweet the music was on the water in the shining night, and what it had felt like to think about girls then. After breakfast we would go up to the store and the things were in the same place—the minnows in a bottle, the plugs and spinners disarranged and pawed over by the youngsters from the boys' camp, the fig newtons and the Beeman's gum. Outside, the road was tarred and cars stood in front of the store. Inside, all was just as it had always been, except there was more Coca Cola and not so much Moxie and root beer and birch beer and sarsaparilla. We would walk out with a bottle of pop apiece and sometimes the pop would backfire up our noses and hurt. We explored the streams, quietly, where the turtles slid off the sunny logs and dug their way into the soft bottom; and we lay on the town wharf and fed worms to the tame bass. Everywhere we went I had trouble making out which was I, the one walking at my side, the one walking in my pants.

One afternoon while we were there at that lake a thunderstorm came up. It was like the revival of an old melodrama that I had seen long ago with childish awe. The second-act climax of the drama of the electrical disturbance over a lake in America had not changed in any important respect. This was the big scene, still the big scene. The whole thing was so familiar, the first feeling of oppression and heat and a general air around camp of not wanting to go very far away. In midafternoon (it was all the same) a curious darkening of the sky, and a lull in everything that had made life tick; and then the way the boats suddenly swung the other way at their moorings with the coming of a breeze out of the new quarter, and the premonitory rumble. Then the kettle drum, then the snare, then the bass drum and cymbals, then crackling light against the dark, and the gods grinning and licking their chops in the hills. Afterward the calm, the rain steadily rustling in the calm lake, the return of light and hope and spirits, and the campers running out in joy and relief to go swimming in the rain, their bright cries perpetuating the deathless joke about how they were getting simply drenched, and the children screaming with delight at the new sensation of bathing in the rain, and the joke about getting drenched linking the generations in a strong indestructible chain. And the comedian who waded in carrying an umbrella.

When the others went swimming my son said he was going in too. He pulled his dripping trunks from the line where they had hung all through the shower, and wrung them out. Languidly, and with no thought of going in, I watched him, his hard little body, skinny and bare, saw him wince slightly as he pulled up around his vitals the small, soggy, icy garment. As he buckled the swollen belt suddenly my groin felt the chill of death.

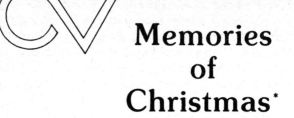

Memories
of
Christmas*

Dylan Thomas

One Christmas was so much like another, in those years, around the sea-town corner now, and out of all sound except the distant speaking of the voices I sometimes hear a moment before sleep, that I can never remember whether it snowed for six days and six nights when I was twelve or whether it snowed for twelve days and twelve nights when I was six; or whether the ice broke and the skating grocer vanished like a snowman through a white trap-door on that same Christmas Day that the mince-pies finished Uncle Arnold and we tobogganed down the seaward hill, all the afternoon, on the best tea-tray, and Mrs. Griffiths complained, and we threw a snowball at her niece, and my hands burned so, with the heat and the cold, when I held them in front of the fire, that I cried for twenty minutes and then had some jelly.

All the Christmases roll down the hill towards the Welsh-speaking sea, like a snowball growing whiter and bigger and rounder, like a cold and headlong moon bundling down the sky that was our street; and they stop at the rim of the ice-edged, fish-freezing waves, and I plunge my hands in the snow and bring out whatever I can find; holly or robins or pudding, squabbles and carols and oranges and tin whistles, and the fire in the front room, and bang go the crackers, and holy, holy, holy, ring the bells, and the glass bells shaking on the tree, and Mother Goose, and Struwelpeter—oh! the baby-burning flames and the clacking scissor-man!—Billy Bunter and Black Beauty, Little Women and boys who have three helpings, Alice and Mrs Potter's badgers, penknives, teddy-bears—named after a Mr Theodore Bear, their inventor, or father, who died recently in the United States—mouth-organs, tin-soldiers, and blanc-mange, and Auntie Bessie playing 'Pop Goes the Weasel' and 'Nuts in May' and 'Oranges and Lemons' on the untuned piano in the parlour all through the thimble-hiding musical-chairing blind-man's-buffing party at the end of the never-to-be-forgotten day at the end of the unremembered year.

In goes my hand into that wool-white bell-tongued ball of holidays resting at the margin of the carol-singing sea, and out come Mrs Prothero and the firemen.

It was on the afternoon of the day of Christmas Eve, and I was in Mrs Prothero's garden, waiting for cats, with her son Jim. It was snowing. It was always snowing at Christmas; December, in my memory, is white as Lapland, though there were no reindeers. But there were cats. Patient, cold, and callous, our hands wrapped in socks, we waited to snowball the cats. Sleek and long as jaguars and terrible-whiskered, spitting and snarling they would slink and sidle over the white back-garden walls, and the lynx-eyed hunters, Jim and I, fur-capped and moccasined trappers from Hudson's Bay off Eversley Road, would hurl our deadly snowballs at the green of their eyes. The wise cats never appeared. We were so still, Eskimo-footed arctic marksmen in the muffling silence of the eternal snows—eternal, ever since Wednesday—that we never heard Mrs Prothero's first cry from her igloo at the bottom of the garden. Or, if we heard it at all, it was, to us, like the far-off challenge of our enemy and prey, the neighbour's Polar Cat. But soon the voice grew louder. 'Fire!' cried Mrs Prothero, and she beat the dinner-gong. And we ran down the garden, with the snowballs in our arms, towards the house, and smoke, indeed, was pouring out of the dining-room, and the gong was bombilating, and Mrs Prothero was announcing ruin like a town-crier in Pompeii. This was better than all the cats in Wales standing on the wall in a row. We bounded into the house, laden with snowballs, and stopped at the open door of the smoke-filled room. Something was burning all right; perhaps it was Mr Prothero, who always slept there after midday dinner with a newspaper over his face; but he was standing in the middle of the room, saying 'A fine Christmas!' and smacking at the smoke with a slipper.

'Call the fire-brigade,' cried Mrs Prothero as she beat the gong.

'They won't be there,' said Mr Prothero, 'it's Christmas.'

There was no fire to be seen, only clouds of smoke and Mr Prothero standing in the middle of them, waving his slipper as though he were conducting.

'Do something,' he said.

And we threw all our snowballs into the smoke—I think we missed Mr

Prothero—and ran out of the house to the telephone-box.

'Let's call the police as well,' Jim said.

'And the ambulance.'

'And Ernie Jenkins, he likes fires.'

But we only called the fire-brigade, and soon the fire-engine came and three tall men in helmets brought a hose into the house and Mr Prothero got out just in time before they turned it on. Nobody could have had a noisier Christmas Eve. And when the firemen turned off the hose and were standing in the wet and smoky room, Jim's aunt, Miss Prothero, came downstairs and peered in at them. Jim and I waited, very quietly, to hear what she would say to them. She said the right thing, always. She looked at the three tall firemen in their shining helmets, standing among the smoke and cinders and dissolving snowballs, and she said: 'Would you like something to read?'

Now out of that bright white snowball of Christmas gone comes the stocking, the stocking of stockings, that hung at the foot of the bed with the arm of a golliwog dangling over the top and small bells ringing in the toes. There was a company, gallant and scarlet but never nice to taste though I always tried when very young, of belted and busbied and musketed lead soldiers so soon to lose their heads and legs in the wars on the kitchen table after the tea-things, the mince-pies, and the cakes that I helped to make by stoning the raisins and eating them, had been cleared away; and a bag of moist and many-coloured jelly-babies and a folded flag and a false nose and a tram-conductor's cap and a machine that punched tickets and rang a bell; never a catapult; once, by a mistake that no one could explain, a little hatchet; and a rubber buffalo, or it may have been a horse, with a yellow head and haphazard legs; and a celluloid duck that made, when you pressed it, a most unducklike noise, a mewing moo that an ambitious cat might make who wishes to be a cow; and a painting-book in which I could make the grass, the trees, the sea, and the animals any colour I pleased; and still the dazzling sky-blue sheep are grazing in the red field under a flight of rainbow-beaked and pea-green birds.

Christmas morning was always over before you could say Jack Frost. And look! suddenly the pudding was burning! Bang the gong and call the fire-brigade and the book-loving firemen! Someone found the silver three-penny-bit with a currant on it; and the someone was always Uncle Arnold. The motto in my cracker read:

> Let's all have fun this Christmas Day,
> Let's play and sing and shout hooray!

and the grown-ups turned their eyes towards the ceiling, and Auntie Bessie, who had already been frightened, twice, by a clockwork mouse, whimpered at the sideboard and had some elderberry wine. And someone put a glass bowl full of nuts on the littered table, and my uncle said, as he said once every year: 'I've got a shoe-nut here. Fetch me a shoe-horn to open it, boy.'

And dinner was ended.

And I remember that on the afternoon of Christmas Day, when the others sat around the fire and told each other that this was nothing, no, nothing, to the great snowbound and turkey-proud yule-log-crackling holly-berry-bedizined and kissing-under-the-mistletoe Christmas when *they* were children, I would go out, school-capped and gloved and muf-flered, with my bright new boots squeaking, into the white world on to the seaward hill, to call on Jim and Dan and Jack and to walk with them through the silent snowscape of our town.

We went padding through the streets, leaving huge deep footprints in the snow, on the hidden pavements.

'I bet people'll think there's been hippoes.'

'What would you do if you saw a hippo coming down Terrace Road?'

'I'd go like this, bang! I'd throw him over the railings and roll him down the hill and then I'd tickle him under the ear and he'd wag his tail. . .'

'What would you do if you saw *two* hippoes. . .?'

Iron-flanked and bellowing he-hippoes clanked and blundered and bat-tered through the scudding snow towards us as we passed by Mr Daniel's house.

'Let's post Mr Daniel a snowball through his letterbox.'

'Let's write things in the snow.'

'Let's write "Mr Daniel looks like a spaniel" all over his lawn.'

'Look,' Jack said, 'I'm eating snow-pie.'

'What's it taste like?'

'Like snow-pie,' Jack said.

Or we walked on the white shore.

'Can the fishes see it's snowing?'

'They think it's the sky falling down.'

The silent one-clouded heavens drifted on to the sea.

'All the old dogs have gone.'

Dogs of a hundred mingled makes yapped in the summer at the sea-rim and yelped at the trespassing mountains of the waves.

'I bet St Bernards would like it now.'

And we were snowblind travellers lost on the north hills, and the great dewlapped dogs, with brandy-flasks round their necks, ambled and shambled up to us, baying 'Excelsior.'

We returned home through the desolate poor sea-facing streets where only a few children fumbled with bare red fingers in the thick wheel-rutted snow and cat-called after us, their voices fading away, as we trudged uphill, into the cries of the dock-birds and the hooters of ships out in the white and whirling bay.

Bring out the tall tales now that we told by the fire as we roasted chestnuts and the gaslight bubbled low. Ghosts with their heads under their arms trailed their chains and said 'whooo' like owls in the long nights when I dared not look over my shoulder; wild beasts lurked in the cubby-hole under the stairs where the gas-meter ticked. 'Once upon a time,' Jim said, 'there were three boys, just like us, who got lost in the dark in the snow, near Bethesda Chapel, and this is what happened to them . . . .' It was the most dreadful happening I had ever heard.

And I remember that we went singing carols once, a night or two before Christmas Eve, when there wasn't the shaving of a moon to light the secret, white-flying streets. At the end of a long road was a drive that led to a large house, and we stumbled up the darkness of the drive that night, each one of us afraid, each one holding a stone in his hand in case, and all of us too brave to say a word. The wind made through the drive-trees noises as of old and unpleasant and maybe web-footed men wheezing in caves. We reached the black bulk of the house.

'What shall we give them?' Dan whispered.

'"Hark the Herald"? "Christmas comes but Once a Year"?'

'No,' Jack said: 'We'll sing "Good King Wenceslas." I'll count three.'

One, two, three, and we began to sing, our voices high and seemingly distant in the snow-felted darkness round the house that was occupied by nobody we knew. We stood close together, near the dark door.

> Good King Wenceslas looked out
> On the Feast of Stephen.

And then a small, dry voice, like the voice of someone who has not spoken for a long time, suddenly joined our singing: a small, dry voice from the other side of the door: a small, dry voice through the keyhole. And when we stopped running we were outside *our* house; the front room was lovely and bright; the gramophone was playing; we saw the red and white balloons hanging from the gas-bracket; uncles and aunts sat by the fire; I thought I smelt our supper being fried in the kitchen. Everything was good again, and Christmas shone through all the familiar town.

'Perhaps it was a ghost,' Jim said.

'Perhaps it was trolls,' Dan said, who was always reading.

'Let's go in and see if there's any jelly left,' Jack said. And we did that.

Behind
the
Salmon*

Roderick Haig-Brown

When the salmon turn into the estuary of a small stream one has a right to expect that some big cutthroat trout will be near them. Often they are, but often, too, they can be quite hard to find. Then, particularly if it is late in the season, one is likely to get an uneasy feeling that they have all moved up into the creek and that fishing the estuary may be a waste of time.

I know much better than to go up into the lower reaches of Cedar Creek and try to fish them, even though there are several pools that hold both cutthroats and steelheads really well. These pools are long and slow, for the most part too deep to wade and with steep slippery clay banks that support tangled crab-apple thickets on one side and over-hanging alders on the other side. Any kind of a backcast is out of the question and even a roll or spey cast is grossly inhibited by the precarious stance and crowding brush; it must also find a way into the water between the overhanging limbs. Inevitably one accepts all this and makes a cast or two. Just as inevitably, all goes well at first, one falls into easy admiration of the accurate and tidy way in which the fly settles close under the hazards of the far bank, its cunning search of likely places, the precariously smooth roll that sets it out again to search again. Then, and it can happen in various ways, from a slip on the clay bottom that fills waders to a hang-up in a high branch that catches the peak of the roll, all the ease and smoothness goes out of things and one recalls the forsaken resolve to stay away from such places.

As recently as last fall I found things too slow in Cedar Creek estuary

° From *Fisherman's Fall* by Roderick Haig-Brown, Wm. Collins Sons & Co. Canada Ltd. 1964.

and decided to take a quick look up the creek in the hope of finding a good fish or two to round out the day. It was well on in October and I knew that a strong run of humpback salmon had moved in, so it was reasonable to suppose the estuary cutthroats had all moved up behind them.

The head of the long pool is not too bad a place to get at. After a wild struggle with the crab apples I found myself in the water at the head of the pool, fairly securely placed and with a nice space between the alder limbs inviting my fly to a strongish run on the far side. The creek was flowing well with good fall water, dark but clear, and past experience suggested I should find the first fish twenty or thirty yards further downstream, probably near my own bank where the current spread. I had put up a Harger's Orange, one of several I had tied with claret-colored hair in the wing instead of orange a few years before and a fly I like particularly well for fall cutthroats as well as steelhead. It rolled out nicely, settled into the water and was immediately chased and taken by a fine cutthroat of about three pounds.

At this stage I wasn't really fishing—just getting my fly out. I did set the hook, but then I stood like a particularly dull-witted sheep while the fish ran off downstream. There was an impressive tangle of brush against my bank about forty yards downstream; before I came to and started to move, the line was well tangled in it and the fish was jumping below.

I had sense enough to forget him and work my way carefully downstream—after all, he could only break the leader and if he chose instead to lie quietly I might even be able to disentangle the line and tighten up on him again. The tangle was worse than I had expected, but I struggled with it in admirable calm, freed the worst of it with no more harm than my right arm wet to the armpit and saw my empty fly trailing in the current below. It was a mild disappointment, because it is always satisfying to free a mess of this sort and find that the fish has waited through one's patient efforts, but I knew very well I had earned nothing better—that recovering the fly was a good deal more than I deserved.

For a moment I considered working on down the pool from the brush pile, but that seemed wrong since I had made only one cast at the head of the pool, so I worked my way back up again to where I had started. I placed myself carefully, repeated my first cast exactly, watched my fly settle again nearly between the alder branches and began to think of the next cast and the next after that, when I might reasonably expect to find another fish. Then I saw the fish shouldering across behind the fly, an exact double of the one I had just lost. He took, I tightened; two minutes later my line was tangled in the same brush pile and I was floundering down, by no means calmly, to free it again. And again the fish was lost but the fly was there. In the end I did hook and kill a good fish far below the brush pile, almost at the tail of the pool, but I solemnly renewed all my resolutions about avoiding the crab apples and clay banks and other humiliations of Cedar Creek's most productive pools.

The next day I went about forty miles down along the coast of Vancouver Island to look at several small creeks and their estuaries, among them Sedge Creek. The sensible way to Sedge Creek estuary is to wade down the gravel bed of the creek itself from the highway bridge. It is clear and comfortable going, and one can make an occasional cast to where the creek deepens on a bend or under a root.

Just below the highway bridge the creek bed has been deepened by a bulldozer for several hundred yards to give the flood water an open, easy channel. To break the flow still more and prevent washing of the gravel there are heavy cross logs set into the high gravel banks at intervals of fifty or sixty yards. Behind these, long shallow pools of gently flowing water with a few deeper spots make good lying places for dog and coho salmon—and sometimes cutthroats.

On this particular day there was a school of some twenty or thirty dog salmon in the upper pool, big fish, moving a little, calm and lazy. There was every possible chance that a few cutthroats were lying somewhere amongst them, so I kept as well back from the water as I could and began to drop my Harger's Orange as nearly as I could behind individual members of the scattered, shifting school. Every so often a fish would move up under the swing of the fly and I would feel the fly or the leader scrape against him, but I slacked carefully at such times and for a while all went well. Then the inevitable happened. A fish moved up under the fly almost as it landed. For a moment of time Harger's Orange was swinging freely across the current, a moment later it had stopped, securely set in the dorsal fin of a fifteen-pound dog salmon.

At first neither I nor the fish was greatly concerned. I thought I should get my fly back without too much difficulty, he didn't think the slight restraint of the line was particularly significant. He began to swim slowly upstream. I left the line slack, hoping the fly would come free. Near the head of the pool he turned and began to swim, still quite slowly, downstream. I decided to tighten, again in the hope that the fly would come free. My fish resented this and swam a little harder, taking line nicely and stirring up the other fish in the pool. By the time he turned, just above the cross log at the tail, most of them were following him. By the time he had swum his majestic way back to the head of the pool they were tightly schooled around him, sympathetic or curious or both or neither.

The next trip down the pool was a lot faster and at the tail he broke with some violence, the school all about him still. He liked it down there and I had some difficulty in persuading him to come back up. In the end he came, the whole school still with him. And so it went on, up and down the pool, the school so closely together that it seemed I had hooked twenty fish at once on my single poor little fly. And my one fish felt like twenty. I had to accept that he was not tiring in the slightest and that my little eight foot rod was not going to bring him to beach or to hand within the foreseeable future. I tried my best, because I was really quite fond of that fly. I could direct him a little, turn him at the tail of the pool, even force him to break water, but that was about all. In the end I pointed the rod at him and broke.

Although I had kept fairly well back from the edge of the water throughout the performance, it seemed certain that the pool must be completely disturbed, so I climbed the high gravel bank on the left and started down it. I kept back in the shade of the timber, though, and watched curiously, because I wanted to see how the salmon settled down and how the fish behaved with my fly still in his dorsal fin. I found him easily, with the claret of hackle and wing in the fly showing up nicely, and he seemed just as calm as the others still schooled around him. They were already beginning to spread out through the pool and their movements were slow and lazy. As I turned my eyes from them to search the lower part of the pool I found the quiet, still shapes of two good cutthroats under the overhanging limbs of a small fir, some sixty feet up from the cross log.

These were the fish I had hoped to find among the salmon. They were flat on the bottom now, unmoving and apparently uninterested in anything about them. But it was not the sort of chance one passes up without a try of some sort. I drew farther back into the brush and circled carefully around to the tail of the pool.

My first guess was a good big floating fly. The larger fish of the two was lying a little farther out and a little downstream, so I put it over him, accurately and carefully, with a right-hand curve cast that kept the leader upstream of the drifting fly. Neither fish made the slightest move and though I repeated the cast a dozen times I could not detect even the quiver of a fin to give me encouragement.

My next thought was a nymph, but I discarded this in favor of an orange fly with a weighted body. I aimed for the same right-hand curve cast, but forgot to allow for the reduced air resistance and greater weight of the new fly. It overshot badly and whipped round into a left-hand curve that dropped it in midstream, at least eight feet over from where the fish was lying. He moved like a flash the second it touched the water and took perfectly. I tightened, held him for a second or two, then the fly came away. To my surprise he returned at once to his old position, though the second fish had disappeared.

It seemed a safe assumption that I had mistimed the strike in the surprise of seeing him come so far for the fly. To expect him to take again was totally unreasonable, but I threw the fly up anyway. It landed about six inches to his left and a foot upstream of him, and again he was on it the second it touched the water. This time I was certain of my strike. He was a strong, very fast fish of rather over two pounds, but I controlled him after two or three good runs and moved to a favorable spot to beach him, just above the cross log. As I brought him in there, the fly came away. This time I looked at the fly and found that the point and barb were broken off, no doubt by touching the rocks of the high gravel banks on a backcast.

The lesson is, I suppose, that if you are as careless a fisherman as I seem to be you should stay away from the upstream reaches of the small creeks. If you do not, they will certainly temper your pride, test your vocabulary and perhaps humiliate you in other unforeseen ways. But in the fall they hold some very good fish and the slightly larger ones like Cedar Creek and Sedge Creek may present some very pretty and interesting situations. Any resolve to stay away is only good for a few days. One can so easily make a counterresolve to be careful, respectful, far-sighted and extremely skillful. Beside this the frustrations of entangling brush, slippery banks and limited casting room fade into insignificant memory. Pride is completely restored and all is ready for the next fall.

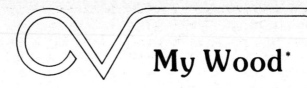

My Wood*

E.M. Forster

A few years ago I wrote a book which dealt in part with the difficulties of the English in India. Feeling that they would have had no difficulties in India themselves, the Americans read the book freely. The more they read it the better it made them feel, and a cheque to the author was the result. I bought a wood with the cheque. It is not a large wood—it contains scarcely any trees, and it is intersected, blast it, by a public footpath. Still, it is the first property that I have owned, so it is right that other people should participate in my shame, and should ask themselves, in accents that will vary in horror, this very important question: What is the effect of property upon the character? Don't let's touch economics; the effect of private ownership upon the community as a whole is another question—a more important question, perhaps, but another one. Let's keep to psychology. If you own things, what's their effect on you? What's the effect on me of my wood?

In the first place, it makes me feel heavy. Property does have this effect. Property produces men of weight, and it was a man of weight who failed to get into the Kingdom of Heaven. He was not wicked, that unfortunate millionaire in the parable, he was only stout; he stuck out in front, not to mention behind, and as he wedged himself this way and that in the crystalline entrance and bruised his well-fed flanks, he saw beneath him a comparatively slim camel passing through the eye of a needle and being woven into the robe of God. The Gospels all through couple stoutness and slowness. They point out what is perfectly obvious, yet seldom realized: that if you have a lot of things you cannot move about a lot, that furniture requires dusting, dusters require servants, servants require insurance stamps, and the whole tangle of them makes you think twice before you accept an invitation to dinner or go for a bathe in the Jordan. Sometimes the Gospels proceed further and say with Tolstoy that property is sinful; they approach the difficult ground of asceticism here,

* From E.M. Forster, *Abinger Harvest*, London: Edward Arnold (Publishers) Ltd. (1936).

where I cannot follow them. But as to the immediate effects of property on people, they just show straightforward logic. It produces men of weight. Men of weight cannot, by definition, move like the lightning from the East unto the West, and the ascent of a fourteen-stone bishop into a pulpit is thus the exact antithesis of the coming of the Son of Man. My wood makes me feel heavy.

In the second place, it makes me feel it ought to be larger.

The other day I heard a twig snap in it. I was annoyed at first, for I thought that someone was blackberrying, and depreciating the value of the undergrowth. On coming nearer, I saw it was not a man who had trodden on the twig and snapped it, but a bird, and I felt pleased. My bird. The bird was not equally pleased. Ignoring the relation between us, it took fright as soon as it saw the shape of my face, and flew straight over the boundary hedge into a field, the property of Mrs. Henessy, where it sat down with a loud squawk. It had become Mrs. Henessy's bird. Something seemed grossly amiss here, something that would not have occurred had the wood been larger. I could not afford to buy Mrs. Henessy out. I dared not murder her, and limitations of this sort beset me on every side. Ahab did not want that vineyard—he only needed it to round off his property, preparatory to plotting a new curve—and all the land around my wood has become necessary to me in order to round off the wood. A boundary protects. But—poor little thing—the boundary ought in its turn to be protected. Noises on the edge of it. Children throw stones. A little more, and then a little more, until we reach the sea. Happy Canute! Happier Alexander! And after all, why should even the world be the limit of possession? A rocket containing a Union Jack, will, it is hoped, be shortly fired at the moon. Mars. Sirius. Beyond which... But these immensities ended by saddening me. I could not suppose that my wood was the destined nucleus of universal dominion—it is so very small and contains no mineral wealth beyond the blackberries. Nor was I comforted when Mrs. Henessy's bird took alarm for the second time and flew clean away from us all, under the belief that it belonged to itself.

In the third place, property makes its owner feel that he ought to do something to it. Yet he isn't sure what. A restlessness comes over him, a vague sense that he has a personality to express—the same sense which, without any vagueness, leads the artist to an act of creation. Sometimes I think I will cut down such trees as remain in the wood, at other times I want to fill up the gaps between them with new trees. Both impulses are pretentious and empty. They are not honest movements towards money-making or beauty. They spring from a foolish desire to express myself and from an inability to enjoy what I have got. Creation, property, enjoyment form a sinister trinity in the human mind. Creation and enjoyment are both very very good, yet they are often unattainable without a material basis, and at such moments property pushes itself in as a substitute, saying, 'Accept me instead—I'm good enough for all three.' It is not enough. It is, as Shakespeare said of lust, 'The expense of spirit in a waste cf shame': it is 'Before, a joy proposed; behind, a dream.' Yet we don't know how to shun it. It is forced on us by our economic system as the alternative to starvation. It is also forced on us by an internal defect in the soul, by the feeling that in property may lie the germs of self-development and of exquisite or heroic deeds. Our life on earth is, and ought to be, material and carnal. But we have not yet learned to manage our materialism and carnality properly; they are still entangled with the desire for ownership, where (in the words of Dante) 'Possession is one with loss.'

And this brings us to our fourth and final point: the blackberries.

Blackberries are not plentiful in this meagre grove, but they are easily seen from the public footpath which traverses it, and all too easily gathered. Foxgloves, too—people will pull up the foxgloves, and ladies of an educational tendency even grub for toadstools to show them on the Monday in class. Other ladies, less educated, roll down the bracken in the arms of their gentlemen friends. There is paper, there are tins. Pray, does my wood belong to me or doesn't it? And, if it does, should I not own it best by allowing no one else to walk there? There is a wood near Lyme Regis, also cursed by a public footpath, where the owner has not hesitated on this point. He has built high stone walls each side of the path, and has spanned it by bridges, so that the public circulate like termites while he gorges on the blackberries unseen. He really does own his wood, this able chap. Dives in Hell did pretty well, but the gulf dividing him from Lazarus could be traversed by vision, and nothing traverses it here. And perhaps I shall come to this in time. I shall wall in and fence out until I really taste the sweets of property. Enormously stout, endlessly avaricious, pseudo-creative, intensely selfish, I shall weave upon my forehead the quadruple crown of possession until those nasty Bolshies come and take it off again and thrust me aside into the outer darkness.

Intimations*

Bharati Mukherjee

My life, I now realize, falls into three disproportionate parts. Till the age of eight I lived in the typical joint family, indistinguishable from my twenty cousins, indistinguishable, in fact, from an eternity of Bengali Brahmin girls. From eight till twenty-one we lived as a single family, enjoying for a time wealth and confidence. And since twenty-one I have lived in the West. Each phase required a repudiation of all previous avatars; an almost total rebirth.

Prior to this year-long stay in India, I had seen myself as others saw me in Montreal, a brown woman in a white society, different, perhaps even special, but definitely not a part of the majority. I receive, occasionally, crazy letters from women students at McGill accusing me of being "mysterious," "cold," "hard to get to know," and the letter writers find this mysteriousness offensive. I am bothered by these letters, especially by the aggressive desire of students to "know" me. I explain it as a form of racism. The unfamiliar is frightening; therefore I have been converted into a "mystery." I can be invested with powers and intentions I do not possess.

In a life of many cultural moves, I had clung to my uniqueness as the source of confidence and stability. But in India I am not unique, not even extraordinary. During the year, I began to see how typical my life had actually been, and given the limited options of a woman from my class and from my city, how predictably I had acted in each crisis. And I see how, even in the West, I have acted predictably. My writing is a satellite of my marriage and profession; I have chosen, or fallen into, the role of bourgeois writer, limited to a month of writing in a year, or one year of writing for every seven of teaching. The American alternative, *Mama Doesn't Live Here Anymore*, remains unthinkable.

Only the first eight years were spent in Ballygunge, in a flat crowded with relatives, and friends of relatives who needed a place for sleeping and eating while they went to college in the city, and hangers-on, whose connection with my family I did not have the curiosity to determine. I was not happy in that joint family. Perhaps some of my mother's frustration seeped down to me. People say that I look very much like her. Certainly I am, like her, a collector of resentments and insults, and am stubbornly unforgiving. I suspect that in those early years, it was more important to me to retain my position as my father's favorite daughter (he had written a poem about me, titled "Treasure of the Heart") than it was to imitate, in proper fashion, the personality of my mother. But I am sure that from her I learned only to feel relief when we could close the door of our bedroom and shut out the forty-odd relatives.

It was a small room after the corners and sides had been filled with the bulky furniture of my mother's dowry. Two beds—one was the bridal four-poster, the other was a simple *chowki*—were pushed together for the five of us, two adults and three daughters. I recall that because of shortage of space, my father used to store an untidy pile of scientific books and journals on the bridal bed itself and that we children had to be careful not to kick the books in our sleep. In a household where no one kept his opinions to himself, this room was our shrine of privacy.

Sometimes there were invasions by cousins or younger uncles. Once my mother, sisters, and I returned from our customary afternoon visit to Southern Avenue to find that my eldest sister's British-made painting book and paintbox, which she had won as a school prize, had been vandalized. Another time, the lock of the wooden cabinet in which my mother kept her jewelry and small cash savings had been forced open, and some money was missing. I was taught to think of these episodes as an assault on our desire to maintain slight separateness within the context of the joint family, rather than expressions of mischief by relatives.

Within the small perimeters of that room, it became clear to me that if I wished to remain sane I should not permit myself to squander my affections on too many people or possessions. With over-population of that sort, possessions and relationships could at best be fragile. I learned also to be always on my guard, and because I was small, shy, and the second youngest in the family, to stay in the background, out of danger's reach. During communal meals, when all the children sat on the floor of the corridor surrounding an inner courtyard, I did not demand the prized items—eyes and brain of carp—because I knew that if I set myself no goals, there could be no defeat. I had, I felt, an intimate knowledge and horror of madness. There was a mad aunt in the family, and during a long stay that she, her husband and four children inflicted on us (because there was some natural disaster, probably a flood, in the part of East Bengal where they lived), I had seen her chase her husband with an ugly piece of firewood. I cannot recall if I had actually seen her hit her husband on the head with the firewood before I was hustled off by my mother into the privacy of our bedroom, or if the aunt had only been standing, weapon poised, about to hit him. I did not think of the uncle, whom I disliked, as the victim. But I thought of madness as grotesque, and as shameful, for I had been told by my parents that if too many people came to know about the craziness in the family, it would be hard to marry us daughters off. I resolved immediately to fight in myself the slightest signs of insanity.

I was released from all that terrifying communal bonding by a single decisive act of my father's, shortly after my eighth birthday. Because of certain circumstances in the pharmaceutical company that he and his partner, a Jewish immigrant from the Middle East, had set up, circumstances that he did not explain to his daughters though he probably did to his wife, he brought home colorful brochures one day of an all-first-class boat on the Anchor Line, and within weeks we left the joint family, and Calcutta, in order to make a new start in London.

We were happy in Britain and Switzerland where my father worked on his research projects, and where we went to school and were remarkable for our good manners as well as our intelligence, and where my mother took night courses in flan baking and basket weaving. But my parents did not make for themselves a new life. The partner followed my father to London, for a while installed us in a company flat at the corner of Curzon and Half Moon streets, vacationed with us in Montreux, and was, I suspect, persuasive about his plan for the pharmaceutical company in Calcutta. And so, after almost three years abroad, we returned to Calcutta, not quite where we had left off, and certainly not to Ballygunge and the joint family.

That period abroad is the only time I have felt perfectly bilingual. It was a time of forgetting Bengali and acquiring English until I reached an absolute equilibrium. But that gradual erosion of the vernacular also contained an erosion of ideas I had taken for granted. It was the first time I was forced to see myself not reflected in people around me, to see myself as the curiosity that I must have seemed to the majority—a skinny brown child, in stiff school uniform and scarred knees, who could not do cartwheels. The sense that I had had of myself in Ballygunge, of being somehow superior to my cousins, was less destructive than this new sense of being a minority on account of my color. I felt I was a shadow person because I was not white. We were an extraordinarily close-knit family, but since I had been brought up to please, I felt I could not burden my parents with these anxieties. It would have made them unhappy, and I could not bear to do that. I could count only on myself for devising strategies of survival in London, our adopted city. I became less passive than I had been among relatives and friends in Ballygunge: I began to regard facility in English as my chief weapon for bending my own personality and for making friends among the British.

In sacrificing a language, we sacrifice our roots. On returning to Calcutta, we found that our image of ourselves had changed radically. It was not at all a question of money. *Jethoo*, my father's oldest brother, owned rice mills and lumber mills in Assam, but he would not be comfortable outside of Ballygunge. But to us, the thought of re-entry into that closed, conspiratorial joint-family world was unbearable. So we sublet a flat in fashionable Chowringhee, the break from the joint family being facilitated by a quarrel between my mother and another relative. We changed schools too, from the Anglicized Bengali school on the edge of Ballygunge to the most renowned girls' school on Middleton Row, a school where, it was rumored, Indian children had for a long time been denied admission. And in our new school, the foreign nuns treasured us for our faintly British accents which had survived the long homeward journey.

From our return to Calcutta after the false start in Europe until the middle of 1959, we lived in the compound of the pharmaceutical factory which my father and his partner had set up in Cossipore, on the outskirts of the city. My parents now refer to that phase of our lives as "the good days." I thought of the compound walls as the boundaries of a small constitutional monarchy in which my sisters and I were princesses. We presided at factory functions, such as sports events, religious celebrations, variety shows for workers, and looked on that as our necessary duty.

The pharmaceutical company had bought out the garden house and estate of a refined Bengali gentleman after whom a street had been named in happier times, but whose fortunes had now declined completely. His botanical gardens—full of imported rarities—were cut down and cleared, the snakes scared away, the pools filled, the immense Victorian house converted into a production plant for capsules, syrups, and pills. I saw the conversion as a triumph of the new order over the old, and felt no remorse. Nothing would return me to the drabness and tedium of Ballygunge.

For me, being part of the new order meant walking under arches of bougainvillaea with my sisters and a golden spaniel we had acquired immediately after moving in, while neighbors gawked at us from their rooftops. We were inviolable and inaccessible within our walled compound. To our neighbors, we were objects of envy, and probably freaks. There were screening devices to protect us: gates, guards, internal telephones. We were at home to only those we wished to see; others could be sent away from the front gate. Having been deprived of privacy in early childhood, I carried my privacy to an extreme; I did not even learn the names of the streets around the factory.

Every day we shuttled between this fortressed factory compound and the school compound in an old gray Rover, once owned by a British executive who had decided independent India was no longer the best place for him. Our privacy was guaranteed on these trips by a bodyguard who looked like Oliver Hardy. The ride from Cossipore to Middleton Row and back is very long, and the cityscape unusually unpleasant. I learned very quickly, therefore, to look out of the window and see nothing. During those rides, my sisters and I talked endlessly about the kinds of men we wanted to marry, and memorized passages from Shakespeare or from the Gospels for the morning's quizzes. My older sister, who is four years older than I and currently is a childless, working wife in Detroit, was the most romantic among us. She said that she did not care about money, but that the groom would have to have excellent table manners and be perfect at ballroom dancing. My younger sister and I knew what she meant by that: She wanted a "Westernized" groom who had studied abroad, and who could command for her a "Westernized" life-style in a pretty flat on Park Street or Chowringhee. Like us, she did not want to lapse into the self-contained vernacular world of Ballygunge.

During this period we were once visited by some female relatives of Mr. D. Gupta, former owner of the garden house that we had converted into a factory. My father arranged for the visiting women to be taken on a guided tour of the plant and then to have tea with us. It was intended by my father to be, and therefore was, an amiable occasion. We sat on the Georgian and Jacobean imported furniture that my parents had extravagantly selected from auction houses on Park and Free School streets, and we listened to the niece of the former owner describe how pretty the chute of colored syrups and capsules had been. It was amiable because the old and new orders had treated each other courteously. Confrontations would come later, and my sisters and I would one day not long after that tea, on our return from school, have to walk through a crowd of striking employees who had blocked our car and who carried placards we were too well-brought-up to read. This tea among the women of the former and current owners was an acknowlegment of another sort: the vulnerability of individual heroes or families in the face of larger designs. Having a street named after oneself was no permanent guarantee of dignity or survival.

That is why, on this 1973 trip back to India, when a newer order has replaced us within the walls of that same compound, I chose not to visit the factory, nor to walk once more under the flowering arches where my sisters and I dreamed about our "Westernized" grooms and "Westernized" life-styles. On this latest trip, I was told that the neighborhood around the factory had become dangerous, and that during the recent Naxalite agitations, workers had been beaten up and that a chemist I recalled well had been knifed in the head a block and a half from the factory gates.

For me the walled factory compound, the guards at the gate office, the bodyguard inside our Rover, the neighbors staring at us from the rooftops, are now emblems. We were typical of a class in the city. There was surely nothing ignoble in our desire to better our condition. In a city that threatens to overwhelm the individual who is passive, there was nothing immoral in self-protection. But we had refused to merge with the city; we had cleared the snakes and shrubberies; we had preoccupied ourselves with single layers of existence—getting ahead, marrying well—and we had ignored the visionary whole. And now, years later, those of us who left and settled in far-off cities like Detroit and Montreal, as well as those of my school friends who stayed and who now live in flats on Park Street or own houses on Rawdon Street, are paying for having scared the snakes and gutted the shrubberies.

My parents moved out of Calcutta long ago. But the impulse to erect compound walls, to isolate and exclude, appears all around me in Calcutta in 1973. My friends live in mansions that the British had built in less volatile times to separate themselves from the bazaars and settlements of the natives. These mansions, even now, are fronted by spacious lawns, gravel driveways, enormous gates with wooden watch posts, and one or more uniformed guards. The guards are not always alert on the job. One rainy July morning as we swung into the driveway of the home of a managing director of a former British firm, we caught the guard urinating against the compound wall.

The cry these days is more for protection than for privacy, and this cry is more shrill than I have ever heard. The women who live in these mansions and whom I meet very regularly for lunch and charity work, study groups and cocktails on the lawn, tell me about the "troubled times" when everything was "topsy-turvy" because the Naxalite gangs took over. With manicured nails jabbing the air, they describe to me how the Naxals scared the guards, sometimes invaded the compounds, threw gravel against the bathroom windows, tore up the lawns by playing soccer. One elegant young woman wearing a delicate pink nylon sari and Japanese pearls (it is hard for me to adjust to this new image, for I had last seen her as a pig-tailed schoolgirl with socks that kept sliding into her shoes) wants me to know that "the troubled times" are not over yet, that what I am seeing is simply a lull before the coming class confrontation. I do not disbelieve her; it is a common conviction all over Calcutta. A woman I had met a week before is now hiding out with her family in the house of another friend in order to avoid what she calls "mischievous acts"—acid bombs? sieges? kid-napings—by striking employees in her husband's firm?

Here in Calcutta, my friends go out into the city in groups, beautiful women in well-waxed cars, and they pack pills for lepers for Mother Teresa. They supervise sewing workshops for destitute women, even clean streets in front of photographers and journalists in order to save and beautify Calcutta. "CALCUTTA IS FOREVER" announces a billboard on Ballygunge Circular Road, paid for by the Beautification Committee. "KEEP YOUR CITY CLEAN AND DESCENT" mocks a less-professional effort near Free School Street. They have made their commitment to this decayed and turbulent city. In exchange, they want protection for themselves and their children.

To protect oneself is to be sensible, I am told. It is a city-wide obsession. Even the Scholar's Guest House where Clark and I stay and which is run by the Ramakrishna Mission, a religious Hindu order, is set apart from the street by high walls. Outside the walls are the accouterments of Ballygunge life: hawkers, beggars, loiterers, squatters, sleepers, cows and pariahs, cars, taxis, buses, mini-buses, cycles, rickshaws, bullock carts, and heedless pedestrians. Inside there is greenery, flowers, a studied calm. The *durwan* at the gate sits on a stool and separates the two worlds. He has a register and pencil to keep track of all visitors. But still the brutal world invades the mission, and brass gas rings disappear from the secondary kitchen, and dissatisfied employees demonstrate on the edge of the judiciously kept lawn.

We do not seem to have heeded the message of the anonymous sculptor from Deoghar. We have confined ourselves to single obsessions. We have protected our territory, and posted uniformed servants to keep out the confusions of the city. We have forgotten that the guard himself is in an ambiguous position and that his loyalties may be fragile. In a city like this, an elderly relative tells me as he chews an endless mouthful of betel nuts, *You just can't be too careful. If you relax for a second, someone will snatch your gold necklace or your purse.* He advises me against certain doctors—there have been stories about nearly any doctor that I mention. *That man is too black, That man is unmarried, Never go to a doctor alone.* But to be so wise, I would like to answer, is also to distort.

Out there beyond our walled vision is a reality that disgusts and confounds the intellect, and a populace that is too illiterate, too hungry, too brutish, to be gently manipulated. Or, just as confounding, a populace too gentle to be brutishly commanded. The odds against survival for an individual are enormous, and rewards, at best, are uncertain.

Merge, commands the Deoghar sculptor, *there are no insides and outsides, no serpents, no gods.*

But at this time, we who consider ourselves more intelligent, more politically conscious, more sophisticated, more charming than the ancient stoneworker, know that to merge, to throw in our lot with Calcutta, is also to invite self-destruction. If we take down the compound walls and remove the ceremonial guard who relieves himself in the street and picks his nose while opening the gates to visitors, what will happen to our children?

It is at this point that I separate myself from the chorus of my old school friends in Calcutta. My sons will return to Montreal at the end of the year, study very little, ski a little more, watch Saturday cartoons on TV, and inherit the promises of the New World.

For the children of my friends who have chosen to remain in Calcutta, the range of future possibilities is infinitely more frightening. Though we never discuss it, we all know that this city will yield its rewards only to the strongest, the smartest, or the most powerful.

Bombay: May-June 1973

For me, 1973 was a year of luxurious nostalgia. This nostalgia could be triggered by the smallest objects, such as a Venetian liqueur glass bought at Staynor's auction house during the "good days" and transported with love during the reluctant move from Calcutta to Baroda and Bombay. Nostalgia could overtake me anywhere and transform the immediate surroundings until my parents' carelessly furnished Chembur living room become once more the room stocked with Jacobean sofas that I had lolled on as a teenager.

But for many Indians, 1973 was a year in which nostalgia gave way to bewilderment and anger. The papers and periodicals were full of stories of misunderstandings. I read that an eighteen-year-old pregnant woman who had been cooking supper on the platform of a clean, new railway station was kicked to death by an outraged railway official. And that a starving mother threw her four daughters and herself into a well but succeeded in killing only two.

Then there were the standard stories of rage and frustration, of men killing each other in movie house queues, of knifings among street sleepers because a child had cried too loud and too long or one man had made a pass at another man's wife. The time for good humor seemed about to disappear. There were endless complaints about endless shortages, and short fierce strikes all over India, but no one had yet taken radical, irrevocable measures.

In Chembur, where we spent the first month and a half seeing my family and preparing for the trip farther east to Calcutta, I learned that fear is not an affliction; it merely is a way of ordering a confused world. The wives I met in Bombay relied on fear to give meaning to lives that might otherwise have seemed, even to them, banal. Like my mother, these women lived in compounds of factories in which their husbands worked, in executives' quarters which were considered luxurious. The compounds had the usual paraphernalia of security: walls, sometimes topped with barbed wire and always with wicked shards of glass, check posts, emergency "hot lines" to the general manager, uniformed and ununiformed guards. These executives' wives thrilled to the lazy salute of the watchmen as they drove in and out of the main gate on their way to the bazaar: The salute was reassurance of status. These women were valuable while the millions out-side the gates were not. The compound literally isolated them from the world of unassorted passions. The factory walls gave them their corporate identity, loyalty, and self-respect, created a calming communal village in a chaotic industrial zone. The women were grateful for the rigid security and for the group privacy, relieved to be cut off from the other Chembur in which degenerate or starving people burgled, murdered, cheated, used dirty words. They had intimations of danger each time they went to the bazaar in groups of two and three in private cars, or (because of gasoline prices) mostly in the factory's bus. More often than not the buses that bumped them along the narrow highways and city roads had windows covered with wire mesh to deflect any projectiles hurled by unhappy laborers.

Inside the compound, they lived in neatly kept houses, set in hierar-chical rows, and separated from the noisy, smelly work site by trees or hill slopes or at least a bamboo grove. Their children watched television in the company's recreation room, and sometimes if there was a really good movie being run, the women joined the children for an hour or two, fighting mosquitoes that preyed on all the viewers. There was also a Ping-Pong table, and though none of the women played themselves, they took secretive, unacknowledged pride in the Ping-Pong skills of their husbands and sons. They did not worry that there were no telephones, except in the houses of perhaps the general manager and the managing director. Their husbands handled all their serious relationships with the outside world; all they needed was the factory intercom so that they could call each other to set up visits and call their husbands home for lunch.

The women I met in that preparatory period before Calcutta were friendly, anxious to let me know that they did not hold my eccentric mar-riage against me, though, when pressed, they admitted they did not want their daughters or younger sisters to marry outside their state and caste. Their friendliness took the form of solicitous advice to Clark and myself. They found us naive, helpless, untutored in strategies of self-defense. So they became our eager tutors.

"Don't let Bart and Bernie go off to the park with the servant. You never know what gets into servants' heads. They should post a guard there."

"Did you read about that murder? After six and a half years, a servant goes crazy and murders the lady when her husband is at work. I tell you, you simply can't trust anyone."

"Chembur is one of the worst areas, one of the very worst," agrees another.

"Chembur is nothing compared to Calcutta. I don't know why you want to go to Calcutta. It's so nice here."

"Never ride a taxi in Calcutta. Tell your old friends to send cars if they want to see you."

"Make sure Clark gets in first. . . ."

"Have you told them about that European who lost his passport? Don't ever leave your hotel room for a visitor downstairs—make him come up."

"During the troubles people would just walk up to you on the street in broad daylight and snatch your gold necklace. They would cut off your fingers to get your rings."

"Things are better now, I must say. Hats off to Siddhartha Shankar Ray. He's been good and tough."

"Maybe a little bit better for the local people, but Bharati and Clark won't be able to manage. They are too trusting. I see Clark and I say to myself he is so open, always laughing, what will he do in Calcutta? He'll take his big Nikon camera to New Market and the *goondas* will beat him up. You tell him to be careful."

They told more stories. A niece whose earrings had been torn from her ears, shredding the flesh. An old widow whose gold chain was clipped from her neck in plain view of fifty people on a tram. For her complaints, she'd been lectured to by fellow passengers for having provoked the attack by wearing gold.

"Bharati, you better not wear *two* gold chains like that in Calcutta. It looks very nice—you have a very nice throat and collarbone area for necklaces—but in Calcutta that's an open invitation to burglars."

"There are so many gold smugglers around and they'll do anything."

"I'll tell you a story that happened to relatives of a friend of mine."

"Is this the one about prostitute rings?"

"No, this one is much worse."

She began the story; Clark was nearby, reading. It was all in Bengali, with a cluster of executives' wives hanging on every word.

"These people were quite young and the husband had a good job. One day they went to New Market to shop. They had an infant daughter who also went to the market with them. She was fast asleep, so the parents—and this is fate—left the baby locked in the car while they went in for a second to buy something, I've forgotten what—"

"They have *very* nice petticoats in New Market," my mother said. "It was probably petticoats."

"Anyway, they went to the store, and when they came back, there was no sign of the baby."

"It is fate," suggested another neighbor.

"Car was locked you said?"

"Completely locked. So there is absolute pandemonium. They informed the police, interrogated those Muslim chaps who hang around New Market acting as porters and touts, but no trace."

"They are absolute *goondas*—Mex, you hear that?"

"So, anyway these people had some important connections, and a real serious search was made, but still nothing turned up."

"That is good. These days in our country unless you have connections nobody will care."

"Nobody cares, that is right. It is terrible."

"Never let Bart and Bernie out of your sight for a minute."

"Every day, they had to drive here and there and everywhere to look at babies, but it was always the wrong baby. It gives you an idea how many stolen babies there are. Meanwhile the poor mother was so upset that she was almost mad, unable to eat or sleep. Then they got a call from the police to come out to the airport where a suspicious-looking mother and child had been detained. The husband and wife rushed out there, and sure enough, the mother recognized her daughter, and threw herself on the kidnaper—"

"Oh, thank God!" the women exclaimed.

"No, no—here comes the worst part. It was their baby all right, but she was dead."

"No! *Baapré-ba!*" They touched their foreheads.

"*Yes*. The smugglers—they were Muslims trying to get back to Abu Dhabi to get more gold—had taken out the baby's intestines and stuffed the cavity with gold bars, then sewn the stomach flaps back. Go ahead, translate it for Clark." He raised his head at the mention of his name. "*That's right, Clark, Calcutta no good. Calcutta full of goondas and very bad behavior.*"

My mother likes to lock doors. Also windows, safes, cupboards, closets, trunks, valises. Her closest friend in Chembur has installed a padlock and chain around the door of her refrigerator. Foodstuffs such as sugar, gram flour, cloves, cardamom, and cigarettes that cannot be fitted with locks are poured into plastic canisters and placed in neat rows inside lockable cupboards. Keys to locked cupboards are stored in other locked cupboards. My mother carries only one key on her person; it is frail and black and hangs limply from a knot in her sari, just below her left shoulder. Heavier rings of keys, the ones that issue insolent challenges to potential burglars—for example, the ring of keys to get to the purse that contains the key to another cupboard and to another purse which holds the key to a steel cabinet with a safe fitted with a double lock where my mother has stowed my scratched German leather purse full of passports, health certificates, and the children's photographs—these remain out of sight.

Clark considers this paranoia. He tells me that since the gate office of the factory compound screens all those who try to enter, this elaborate security system is designed to discourage only the live-in servant and part-time maids who come to wash the dishes, do the laundry, and to clean floors and toilets. I know, of course, that Clark is wrong. He does not understand the apocalyptic vision of my mother. He is annoyed that he cannot get to his tape recorder without having the women unlock several cupboards, or that when he is ready and waiting in the car for the long drive downtown it takes my mother and me several extra minutes of co-ordinated effort to give him his traveler's checks and identification cards. I explain to him that if the servant wanted to burgle or murder, he could easily do so during the siesta hour. My mother, though heavy, is not at all strong. She is totally at the mercy of any sinister intruder. Locking is her way of integrating belief in karma and belief in individual resourcefulness. She is alert to the conditions of modern India; she assumes that disaster, which in her childhood had seemed to lie in some unrealizable future, is now about to occur in her lifetime. Perhaps she remembers those wooden cupboards back in the joint family, when the forcing of a door was an attack upon all her defenses. She will not set herself impossible goals about reversing her fate or the country's; she will simply use her common sense to minimize the personal effects of disaster.

We suffer an unacknowledged crisis over Bernie's electric train, which we bought in Geneva en route to India and which we cannot permit him to play with guiltlessly in Chembur because of the factory's policy of "voluntary" power restraint. Bernie, who is obsessed by trains and planes, lies on the cool floor of his room and pushes his locomotive with his finger. My mother would like us to store the train set in a locked wall cabinet whenever Bernie is not playing with it. Clark refuses to do that.

"But that *chokra*-boy will wreck it in no time," my mother objects (to me, never to Clark). "He's a very curious and careless boy."

"It's a toy, for God's sake," Clark explodes with undue passion.

He is correct; he wins the round. We leave the electric train set out, and in a matter of weeks, the monsoon deposits rust flowers on the tracks, stealthily adventurous fingers leave dents on the underpinnings of carriages (it is Rajan who encourages Bernie to pry the tops off the passenger cars; it would not surprise me if Rajan had expected miniature people inside, reading their German newspapers), and the locomotive seems clogged with fluff and hair balls. And so my mother and Bernie conspire to save the train from further damage. They wrap the broken set in an old cotton sari and place it on the top shelf of a cupboard; it is transformed from a toy that functions to a souvenir of a nearly perfect visit by the family of a favorite daughter. I try once more to explain the episode of the train to

Clark. I paint him a middle-aged woman with an overwhelming sense of doom. A middle-aged woman who no longer reads, sews, goes to parties, sees films or television, visits friends, and whose children now lead independent lives in far-off cities or continents. Locking out hazard, locking in happiness. To deprive her of that would be brutal.

My mother has raised precaution to a high art. She has not only experimented with locks of various sizes and brands—on trips abroad to visit me or my sister, she has spent meticulous half-days at the key and padlock counters—but she has also extended the range of items to be locked out. In Chembur she locks out sunlight, insects, bats, toads, pariah dogs, servants' chums, and cobras. She is full of cautionary tales about the cobra that had slithered into the neighbor's bathroom because a window had been left unlatched. All her windows are still covered over with the heavy black paper that had been given out to all residents of the compound to block out house lights during the Indo-Pakistan war. During the war, she had supervised the cutting and pasting, making sure the servant did not let a single sliver of light slip through. You could develop film in some of those rooms, even in tropical daytime. Now when she shuts her windows during the day— and she does that by nine o'clock to keep out industrial soot and smells, heat, undesirable creatures—the house is peaceful, dark, and cavernous. With doors and windows battened down, and with her hands on the panel of fan and light switches, she can control her universe. Manipulation of breezes and light, she construes as a triumph of will over chaos. Each time she bars a window, causing the papered-over panes to cut off the sun, she sees it as a stalling of a future disaster.

The wartime paper, as it turns out, is destined to go. Clark does not like the paper; he cannot work behind closed windows. He likes to work, and he is more self-reliant than anyone else in the compound. Also, he has allies in the servant and the chauffeur, whose full names he, rather than my parents, has been the first to find out. After three weeks of writing longhand in bed under a ceiling fan that scattered his writing materials without cooling him, he has the chauffeur drive him out to the bazaar, where, without engaging in acrimonious and exhaustive comparison shopping, he buys a metal desk and a metal chair, and installs them himself in front of windows in our bedroom. Then, with Rajan's help, he rips aside the company curtains, unlocks the windows, peels off the black paper, takes a long gulp of the outside air, and writes uninterruptedly for five hours.

My mother looks in now and then and says in the direction of the servant, "Don't interrupt, *Sahib* at work here."

But to me she says, "Are you sure he'll be all right? All that black stuff from the factory chimney will make his eyes sore. Ask him, does he need anything? Shall I bring him some mangoes or sweet lime? Or how about tea? He needs to eat more."

Over the next few days, the servant continues with the paper-removing work that Clark began. The curtains in all the bedrooms start to bleach in window-sized rectangles. Those of us who suffer from nervous sick headaches in the sun suffer them more than usual. Clark, whose desk looks out over the rise and the chimney, develops itchy eyes and has to return to his original writing position on the bed under the fan. The children suffer continuous hay fever. Dust from the open window covers his desk, typewriter, arms, hands, and papers; he can't erase without smearing the page. The servant mops a great deal more than he has before. A window has been opened and a foreign element permitted indoors. Clark does not yet understand an Indian's relationship to "nature"; he still suffers from the American myth of nature's benevolence.

When it is time for Clark and me to fly from Santa Cruz Airport to Calcutta, I am not afraid to leave Bart and Bernie with my mother. She will, of course, be even more overprotective when she is their sole guardian. My father will be at his office until the boys' supper hour; so she will see herself as their principal custodian, and love will make her more fearful than usual.

I hear her shout as I pack my bags, "Bertie, don't play in the puddle. Hookworms will get you." And five minutes later, "Barnie, come back here darling, big, big cobras outdoors." These, I know, are her ways, and perhaps her only ways, of expressing affection to her stranger-grandsons. To love is also to minimize the beloved's exposure to danger. And, having been brought up in monsoon country, I know that hookworms and snakes slither in and out of maladied, middle-aged imaginations. Bernie has already shown me, five yards from our front door, six dead baby vipers (he called them "fat worms, Mommy"), washed down the hillsides by the heavy seasonal rains. So I do not shout out counterinstructions to the boys to go out into the rain and find their own adventure, to be resourceful and independent and not bother the grown-ups. I do not whisper to my mother to disguise or restrain the force of her love. This will probably be the last time that the boys, my hardy North American boys, will experience familial affection and not consider it burdensome.

But for many Indians, the excellent balance between fear and love is part of nostalgia. Extravagant, unrestrained love can no longer be expressed and extravagant fear has come to replace it. Only partially hidden under the stiff Indian-English of newspaper journalism, I see the spurts and flares of private terror in this year of threatened famine and deteriorating nerves.

Mr. Suprio Das, in *The Statesman* of August 1, 1973, writes
that while out on the V.I.P. Road for his customary evening
constitutional stroll, he had stumbled upon a decomposing
corpse bearing obvious knife wounds, and that though he
had done his civic duty by calling the police, he had not been
able to arrange for immediate corpse removal. Three days
later the corpse had disappeared, thanks to the efforts (he
believed) of neighborhood pariah dogs and vultures. And
now, the writer wants to know of the editor of that respected
newspaper, what should he do if during another evening
stroll, he happens on another corpse full of knife wounds?

In Habibur area, in the district of Malda, sixty-five-year- old
landlord (*jotedar*) wins posthumous notice by becoming
North Bengal's first fatal casualty during the crop-cutting and
harvesting season. He is rumored to have been shot full of
arrows by a tribal group who did not want him harvesting in
that area.

Hungry or simply immoral youths, in large gangs, attempt to
hijack loaded trucks in the Siliguri area, by blockading the
highway with boulders, then by throwing stones at the wind-
shield of the stopped truck in order to injure the driver and
his guard. This results in an organized protest by truck
drivers who tie up traffic on Highway 31 and demand better
protection. The protesters are finally persuaded to cease
their demonstration in time for the motorcade of West
Bengal's Chief Minister, Siddhartha Shankar Ray, who is
making an official visit to Kalimpong.

In India, then, for some people at least, it is a year of eroding faith in inevitable destinies. The daily newspapers, still uncensored, publish scorch-
ing indictments of official pronouncements and heap abuse on ministerial
fiats. The workers at Calico go out on strike. It is to last only a week, but it
drags on and on, sharpening into a show of force. Six months later, after a
death and several beatings, the workers will return, accepting the company
offer. Force alone still carries the greatest respect.

The Street-Car Conductor*

Hugh MacLennan

The street-car rattling westward was almost empty, for it was the slack hour of the early afternoon. The conductor was half-sitting, half-standing in his cage at the back of the car. On his cuff were six tarnished service stripes. On his face was an expression of unfathomable calm.

A bell buzzed. A passenger rose, moved down the aisle to the rear of the car and stood by the conductor's cage. This citizen was short, square, elderly and decisive. He carried a worn brief-case in his left hand; the fingers of his right drummed firmly on the polished steel rail of the conductor's cage. His grey face was stern and his wide mouth had formed itself into the thin straight line of a man who has waited too long to buy a set of false teeth. He fixed the conductor with accusing eyes and spoke in a harsh, clear voice.

"*La situation internationale est terrible!*"
"*Ouais,*" the conductor said, not turning his head.
"*L'Angleterre est finie!*"
"*Ouais.*"
"*La France est manifestement finie!*"
"*Ouais.*"
"*La troisième guerre vient pour sûr!*"
"*Ouais.*"
"*Nous sommes donc tous finis!*"
"*Ouais.*"

* Excerpt from *Thirty and Three* by Hugh MacLennan. Reprinted by permission of The Macmillan Company of Canada Limited.

The car stopped, the doors opened, the citizen stepped out, the doors closed, the car jerked forward, and as I looked at the conductor's quarter-profile from where I sat near the end of the long bench at the back of the car, I wondered why most of us take conductors for granted, seeing them but not seeing them, as though they were mechanical fixtures of their cars.

For thirty years, perhaps longer, this man had been half-sitting, half-standing in the sterns of street-cars in such a posture that he had always to watch the world recede from him as the car advanced. Summer and winter, fall and spring, millions of citizens had jostled him as his trams carried them to and from their work, to and from their sports and business *coups* and parties and love affairs. Girls with shining eyes had stared into the rapt faces of boys. Young married men with pay cheques in their pockets had stood cheerfully in the jam beside him thinking how happy they were going to make their wives that evening. Desperate men had plotted suicide and women in middle age had wondered how much longer they could stand it. The mothers of two generations had pushed children past him while they fumbled for tickets, and behind him old ladies had smiled when young men had risen to offer them seats. Billions of loves, hates, lusts, fears, hopes, boredoms and little private amusements had cavorted through the busy brains surrounding this man. And always *la situation internationale* had been *terrible*.

For thirty years, perhaps longer, this man had lived in the midst of it. In the headlines of newspapers tucked under arms or crunched before faces the epic of the twentieth century had been displayed in all editions and in both languages of the city. But because the papers were usually folded in the middle he had seen only half the headlines recording fires and floods, murders and rescues, rising and collapsing governments, and the land, sea and air battles of three wars. In the splintering anxieties of an apocalyptic epoch he had remained half-sitting, half-standing at his post in the stern of his car. On the morning in 1940 when France fell he was passing out his transfers. When the Third Reich dissolved in smoke and bomb-bursts he was calling out *Ghee—Guy—Côte des Neiges*. When the Chinese invaded Korea the world was still receding from him. Through all the tempests of his century he had ridden the street-cars of Montreal, half-sitting, half-standing, with an expression as mysterious, as remote, as profound as that of a Buddha in the jungle-infested ruins of Ankor Vat.

The car began to sway as it ran the straight passage of Sherbrooke Street past Westmount Park; it staggered a little as it took the curving slope towards Decarie; then it settled down for its run through Notre Dame de Grâce. Fifteen to twenty years ago this district had been loud and gay with the voices of children and adolescents, for it was the part of the city where young couples had moved to raise their families after the Old War. Now several thousands of those who had grown up in the nineteen-thirties had been killed in the Second War, and most of their brothers and sisters had married and moved away. The people on the sidewalks seemed to be in late middle age. For Notre Dame de Grâce *la situation internationale* had indeed been *terrible*...

We get into the habit of steeling ourselves for bad news, I thought, with the echo of the dour citizen's words still in my mind. The moment we stop worrying about something, we suspect we are losing our grip on reality. Troubles will arise—what would we do without them? but whatever evil we see in the near future can hardly rival the evils this conductor has been carrying about in the headlines of the papers his passengers have been reading over the past thirty years.

It was fashionable during the nineteen-thirties to talk of the death-wish that ruled the world. By feeding it with the incense of our fears we fattened it into a monster more frightening than Hitler's armies. Today we no longer consider it our master. Today we are tired of its company, and scorn ourselves for having invited it into our homes. But its strange and ghastly reign during the first forty years of the twentieth century will give historians of the future an opportunity to say some pretty nasty things about us.

When we first became aware, through Freud, of this thing in all of us which he called the death-wish—this thing which caused the dour citizen to assert with such relish *nous sommes tous finis*—it seemed romantic and exciting. In 1914 Rupert Brooke, most innocent of twentieth-century poets, sang of giving the world away and pouring out "the red, sweet wine of youth". The first of our wars gave many millions the opportunity of doing so. In the nineteen-twenties the face of the death-wish was painted with a false, bright gaiety, and young novelists like Ernest Hemingway began to glorify bullfights and hangovers, while older poets like T.S. Eliot chanted of the wasteland and hollow men with a loving eloquence which proclaimed that it was only in corruption and impotence that we could discover the seeds of beauty. The mask of the death-wish was weary and sophisticated in the first days of the depression when the blonde in Noel Coward's *Cavalcade* swung her pretty legs from the piano top and crooned "Twentieth Century Blues", asking what there was to strive for, love or keep alive for. By the late nineteen-thirties the death-wish had lost both its charm and its sophistication. Now it wore the mask of staring fear. It was distorted with fear on the day Chamberlain and Daladier flew back from Munich, when the populations of the two most civilized nations in the world cried out in rejoicing for the deal Hitler had made to destroy them.

The death-wish did more than make us act like cowards. It hypnotized us as though we were birds cowering before snakes. It sucked potency from our men and charm from our women. (Remember, those of you who can, the styles of the 1920's?) It made the old and rich ask only to be let alone. It persuaded the young and poor that every man in authority was their enemy. It made us pray for security instead of for courage. And when we discovered that we had courage nevertheless, we no longer talked about the death-wish, for by that time another generation had come along, and they took Freud for granted. But the old slogans glorifying security still had enough power to win elections. Worst of all, they persuaded Stalin, as they had persuaded Hitler, that we were ripe to be picked...

The tram began swaying again as it left Royal Avenue with the additional freight of three small boys who had been let out early at Lower Canada College. The conductor, half-sitting, half-standing, was concerned with his own cavernous thoughts as he watched the brick apartment buildings and small shops move away to his rear. From the folded front of my newspaper half of Winston Churchill's face stared upward. He looked older, but his expression was not much different from what it had been fifteen years ago when so many of us called him irresponsible merely because he was brave. The tendons in his neck were more prominent, but not much more than they had been in the days when he took the death-wish by the throat and choked it, and then turned and breathed some of his own courage into us as God breathed life into Adam.

"Were you working on this same route fifteen years ago?" I asked the conductor, wondering if he would know that my question was addressed to him.

"*Ouais.*"

Fifteen years ago Hemingway, our hero among the novelists of that time, had written that he was always embarrassed by words like "sacred", "glorious" and "sacrifice", for "the things that were glorious had no glory and the sacrifices were like the stockyards of Chicago if nothing was done with the meat except to bury it". Hemingway had written these words and we all knew that he himself was a brave man. We thought we knew everything in those days. We knew that Hitler and Mussolini had to be stopped and at the same time we knew that wars decide nothing. So we voted to stop Hitler and Mussolini and at the same time we voted to reduce the budget for armaments. *La situation internationale?* Today we shrug our shoulders and say, "But what do you expect?" Or merely, "*Ouais.*"

The tram and its impassive guardian continued to sway onward and I got up as I saw my stop a few blocks ahead. The acres of apartments on the old Benny Farm slid past and sunlight glinted on snow in open spaces. Again we were in a district filled with children.

In Red River suits they played in the snow or were drawn on sleds by their mothers (younger mothers these days than when we were married, young enough to enjoy their families vigorously and to remain young when their children grow up, so that in their early forties they will be free to make full use of what the world has taught them). The tram was nearing my stop and I reached up to press the bell. I stood beside the conductor and spoke to him again.

"Things aren't so bad these days."

"*Ouais,*" he said.

The car stopped, the doors opened and I stepped out into the street. The doors closed, the car jerked forward and I stood watching the conductor, half-sitting, half-standing, his image blurred behind the glass, riding off into the west.

A Pleistocene Day[*]

Alan Moorehead

Nairobi is the safari capital of Africa. This is the base where most of the hunters, the photographers and the ordinary run-of-the-mill sightseers assemble their vehicles and their equipment before they set off into the blue. You can travel very simply if you like, driving your own car and stopping for the night at country inns along the way. Camping, on the other hand, is more complicated and expensive and involves problems over petrol, water and food. Quite a number of people, however, get about with caravans or hunting cars that are fitted with beds, tents and cooking gear, and usually they take a couple of African boys along with them. Finally, you can go to one of the safari companies and travel *en grande luxe* complete with a white hunter and a regular entourage of servants. The East Africa Tourist Travel Association recently put out a booklet about these trips, and it contains some revealing passages.

'He (the hunter),' it says, 'can have radios, refrigerators, electric light, air mattresses, and every comfort. Well-cooked five-course meals are served attractively; hunting clothes are laundered each day and soft-footed servants wait on his every need...

'In general, it may be said that with every luxury possible, a safari for one person costs approximately £27 a day inclusive, except for alcohol and tobacco. As very little extra equipment is needed to handle two persons, the price drops to about £21 a day each.

'The normal routine of camp life is to rise about 5.30 a.m., breakfast on fruit, cereal, bacon and eggs, and coffee, at 6, and leave camp when dawn

[*] From *No Room in the Ark* by Alan Moorehead. London: Hamish Hamilton Limited. Reprinted by permission of Laurence Pollingel Limited.

is breaking about 6.30 a.m.; this period of the morning is fresh and crisp, the animals are grazing freely in the open and the light is still soft.

'After 10 or 11 a.m. the game disappears for a rest, and the sun is too warm for exercise to be pleasant, so, unless following an elephant or tracking some elusive and rare species, the hunters themselves usually return to camp for a rest and lunch. After which they again go out to be ready to greet their quarry about 4 p.m., at which time the game wakes up and grazes towards the waterholes.'

Women are advised to stick to neutral colours in their clothes or they will agitate the game. If you don't happen to have a rifle you can rent one for around £15 a month; on top of that there is the hunting licence. A full game licence in Kenya in recent years cost £50 and entitled you to 3 bushbuck, 3 duiker, 1 Grant's gazelle, 1 gerenuk, 2 Coke's hartebeest, 3 impala, 1 klipspringer, 1 oribi, 1 beisa oryx, 2 pigmy antelope, 2 common reedbuck, 1 serval cat, 1 steinbuck, 2 topi, 6 Thomson's gazelle, 1 defassa waterbuck, 2 wildebeest and 4 common zebra.

Additional licences must be obtained if you want to go after elephant (£75 for the first one, £100 for the second), rhinoceros (£40 each), leopard (£40), hippopotamus (£10), buffalo (5s.), Lion (£25), ostrich (£2-10), the blue monkey (£1).*

Since the war lion and leopard have become increasingly rare, and it is practically unheard of for a man to shoot out his full licence (which he has to pay for anyway whether he kills the animals or not); still, he is pretty well certain of bagging a dozen or more specimens of different species, and in the course of a month he will cover about 1,500 miles and see a number of remarkable things. Even if you prefer to photograph rather than hunt (and an increasing number of people do nowadays), it can be just as exciting; you have to get rather nearer the game. A safari, in fact, is probably the most rewarding adventure you can buy anywhere, and although a three months' trip for four clients and two white hunters may cost as much as £6,500 (including a fairly stiff tip to the staff at the end), there is no shortage of customers. Some of the larger safari firms in Nairobi are booked a year in advance. Americans are the chief clients.

In normal circumstances I do not think that my wife and I, on our journey through Africa, would have dreamed of going on a full-dress safari of this kind; we usually travelled by train or by ourselves in hired cars, and in any case we were not interested in shooting. In Nairobi, however, one of the best-known white hunters, Donald Ker, invited us to go out with him on a month's trip as his guests. Ker, a small compact man now in his early fifties, is an interesting case. Having spent half a lifetime hunting in the

---

* The game laws alter from year to year; the prices quoted may have risen since the above was written.

bush—at the age of sixteen he was already out on his own, sometimes for months at a time, shooting elephant—he cannot now bear to destroy a wild animal of any description, except for food; and even that he does with reluctance. His chief interest now is the study of wild life in its natural surroundings, and with this end in view he proposed a fascinating trip to the extreme south-western corner of Kenya. Here is an area of some six thousand square miles which for a long time has been a kind of island in the centre of the continent.

This is some of the finest land in all Africa, a network of forested rivers and great open plains that slope gently down to Lake Victoria, but there are no roads and because of the tsetse fly no one has ever lived there. Wild animals are not affected by the fly, and so they have been left to roam the country pretty well undisturbed except for occasional hunting parties coming down from Nairobi in the dry season, and gangs of African poachers who operate along the shores of the lake.

When the Mau Mau emergency began in 1952 this region became doubly remote; some of the Kikuyu tribesmen were in hiding there, and orders were issued by the British authorities forbidding anyone to go near the place. By the time we got there, however, things had quietened down considerably, and Ker had been given permission to visit the forbidden area. A few of the Mau Mau were still hanging about in the forest, Ker said, but they were known to be without ammunition, and in any case the authorities had arranged for a couple of native police to go along with him in addition to his own boys. He proposed to wander about through this virgin territory for two or three weeks before moving northward towards the Abyssinian border.

By early January the safari was assembled in Nairobi and everything was ready. It was not, Ker explained regretfully, like a safari in the old days. Then everyone in town turned out to see you off. No cars of course; the client riding on a mule and a hundred boys with bundles on their heads strung out down the main road in front of the town's one hotel. A squad of soldiers or askaris went first, and a sort of jester with a musical horn moved up and down the line to lead the singing and keep the porters happy. Every twenty miles or so they dropped off a group of men to form a camp, and in the end these camps might be stretched across several hundred miles of country. Like ants the porters kept up a constant come and go along the route, some of them bringing back trophies from the shooting party in the wilds, others coming up from Nairobi with supplies. Sometimes sportsmen would stay out in the field for six months or more and never see another white man. That was the way President Theodore Roosevelt, one of the greatest of hunters, had done it when he came out to collect specimens for the Smithsonian Institute in 1909.

Ker's outfit was not so impressive as this, and no one came to see us off; still, we were probably better equipped than the Roosevelt party. Ker and my wife and I rode in front in a hunting car with Saidi, his head boy, and a five-ton lorry followed on behind. The lorry was loaded with sleeping and dining tents, food and fuel supplies for a month, a good deal of heavy equipment for making repairs and getting across rivers and swamps, and of course a medicine chest. Such of the ten boys who could not get into the cabin of the lorry were perched on top of the baggage. The sun was shining and morale was high.

It was Ker's idea to take a roundabout route to our objective, travelling southwards first to the Tanganyika border and then moving westward across the Serengeti Plains towards Lake Victoria. We were to stop just short of the lake at a place called Ikoma, on the Grumeti River, and then strike northwards into the unmapped and uninhabited country. All this first part of the journey has been pretty well known to travellers for the past thirty years, and the roads and the well-worn tracks give you a sense of familiarity and security. It is a vast space, but space that has been tamed and civilized. Yet it is impossible to travel far in this part of Africa without something outlandish happening. On our first night, for instance, when we were camping under Kilimanjaro, I was introduced to a special breed of leather-eating hyenas. Hyenas, heaven knows, are capable of anything, and their own flesh is said to be so repulsive that even vultures will reject it if they can get anything else. Hyenas prey upon the young, the weak, and the dying, and no carcass is too rotten for their taste. Here around this camp there was no shortage of food; we had seen a dozen different varieties of antelope moving around the waterholes just as the daylight was fading, and the baboons were in hundreds. Yet this particular breed of hyenas around our camp was said to have a special predilection for good solid tanned boot leather. I did not altogether believe this, but when I went to my tent that night I tucked my own shoes (a thick-soled pair bought just a month before in London) well under my camp-bed.

Sleeping under canvas in the African bush is a special experience until you get used to it. The leopard coughs in the darkness. The hyenas grunt and snarl and whoop as they prowl about. A faint flicker of rose light from the camp-fire strikes the canvas above your head, and you hear, or think you hear, the first distant throaty roar of a hunting lion—though of this you cannot be quite sure because the noise is very similar to the deep voices of the African boys who sit on, hour after hour, around the fire telling endless stories to one another, and pausing only, when the leopard comes near, to throw another log on the flames. One thing at least is tolerably certain: wild animals loathe and fear the human smell, and although they may approach quite close out of sheer curiosity they will not come into the camp itself. Often in the morning you will see the tracks of some large animal, a rhinoceros perhaps, not fifty yards from your tent. The tracks, a series of large rosettes in the dust, come on very steadily until suddenly the animal has picked up the hateful scent in the air, and you can see where he has wheeled sharply away into the bush.

It seemed therefore incomprehensible to me on this night that I should have been woken by a strange presence in the tent. It was not so much a presence as a smell; a smell so vile, so absolutely sickening, it appeared for an instant to be an imaginary thing, part of a particularly bad dream perhaps. I groped for a flashlight and something an inch or two away from my face vanished into the darkness. All this was a great joke in the morning when the boys searched everywhere and found not so much as a trace of a hobnail from my shoes. Even the rubber heels had been eaten. After that I slept with my second pair of shoes inside my bed.

Hyenas have amazing savagery and determination. One alone will drive away a cheetah, the great spotted cat which is the fastest thing alive. (When some years ago cheetahs were raced against greyhounds in England the cheetahs jumped clean over the greyhounds' backs to get to the front.) Two hyenas will force a leopard to abandon a kill; a dozen of them will defeat a lion. Once Ker and I in our car headed off a hyena that was about to pounce on a baby Thomson's gazelle, and we chased it for upwards of six miles at twenty miles an hour, round and round in circles on open ground. It was not even breathing hard when we stopped at last. And when it turned its dark muzzle over its shoulder towards us, looking at us without rage or fear, simply accepting, as wild animals do, the instant prospect of death, we were a little ashamed.

Part of Ker's aversion to shooting is tied up with this matter of pursuing animals in cars. In earlier times—and not so far back as Roosevelt either—you tracked your quarry sometimes for scores of miles and for days or weeks on end. In a certain sense you earned the trophy. Now you drive along in comfort until you find your buffalo or your rhinoceros and the law requires you to walk only five hundred yards away from your car before you shoot. Very little exertion and not much danger is involved. Neither hunger nor any great skill in tracking brings you to the kill; and somewhere in all this the true excitement dies away.

I began to see Ker's point quite unexpectedly a day or two after we had left Kilimanjaro behind us and were moving west through cultivated country on the edge of the Great Rift Valley. We were six thousand feet up and a cold rain was falling. Across the muddy soil a stray gazelle buck came running, and a young African tribesman, naked except for a cloth around his waist, started up in pursuit. Normally the man would never have had a ghost of a chance of catching the buck, but perhaps he thought the mud would slow it up and anyway this meant a month's supply of meat. Man and animal went flying across the skyline at tremendous speed, bounding from one tussock to another, and they must have gone half a mile or more when the buck took an unlucky turn towards a group of native huts. A woman came out with a spear in her hand, and as he rushed past the young man grabbed it out of her hand like a runner in a relay race. He disappeared finally, his spear held high and a barking dog at his heels, over the curve of the hill. The buck was still going well and I don't think the young man ever caught up. Yet he was a real hunter, almost a figure from a classical frieze with that straining back, and one wished him luck, one would have liked to have seen him launch the spear and the kill would have been a good kill at the peak of a concentrated excitement.

All this country—the Great Rift Valley around the Ngorongoro crater mountain and the Serengeti plains that stretch away to the west—has been the scene of immemorial hunting, possibly the earliest hunting anywhere on earth. A German scientist, a man with the engaging name of Professor Kattwinkel, appears to have been the first to have discovered this. He walked up from Dar-es-Salaam on the coast somewhere about 1911, and having made his way out on to the Serengeti Plains, came on the deep watercourse which is now known as the Olduvai Gorge. Looking up from the dry bed of the river to the three-hundred-foot cliffs on either side the Professor found himself confronted with fossils of immense antiquity. There were the remains of the *deinotherium*, a huge elephant with tusks in the lower jaw pointing downwards like a walrus, the *metaschizotherium*, a creature with five-toed feet related to the rhinoceros, the *sivatherium*, a giraffe with a short neck and antlers that branched out to a distance of six feet, the *bularchus*, a giant ox, and the *pelorovis*, a sheep the size of a modern buffalo with a twelve-foot spread of horns. All these beasts, which have long since become extinct, had been hunted by stone-age men. (Their sharpened stones and stone axeheads can still be picked up in the gorge by the dozen.)

Kattwinkel's discovery caused something of a sensation when he returned to his home in Munich, and with the backing of the Kaiser a German called Dr. Hans Beck organized an expedition to Olduvai. Beck's work was cut short for a time by the First World War, when British and German forces were engaged in battles close to Olduvai for the possession of Tanganyika, but in the early thirties Dr. L. S. B. Leakey, the Curator of the Corydon Museum in Nairobi, returned to the site, and he has been making excavations there ever since. Leakey, a scientist of world repute, has made some startling discoveries, and he firmly believes that here or hereabouts will eventually be found the very earliest traces of mankind. Quite apart from the prehistoric animals there is evidence that human habitation in the region goes back at least 250,000 years. These early men hunted in packs like wolves. It was their practice to drive the animals into defiles and swamps, where they became bogged in the mud and easily killed. Later the *bolas* was invented, a weapon that is still used by the Eskimos and the Patagonians. It consists of three or more rounded pebbles, which are attached together by thongs. These were flung at the quarry, and when its legs became entangled it was brought to the ground. Then it was a simple matter with a sharp stone to skin and quarter the carcass, which was eaten raw. (When this theory was challenged on the ground that the animals were too fleet for a man to catch, and their hides too tough to be cut with a stone, Leakey, a former footballer, responded by giving a personal demonstration; he chased a Grant's gazelle on foot one day, and after a short run brought it down with a flying tackle. He then skinned the animal with a stone in a matter of fifteen minutes.)

Later again the hunters began to depict their exploits in drawings and paintings on the surfaces of overhanging rocks where they would be secure from the weather. In Tanganyika there are dozens of these decorated rock-shelters which have not been fully explored as yet. They contain drawings which are not unlike those in the caves at Lascaux in France—the same free outline and spirited movement, the same warm colours made from such mixtures as red ochre and grease. Many of these sketches are very gay and charming. Hunting is the persistent theme, and it seems possible that there was a certain superstition here; if a wounded animal got away in the darkness the hunter might well have wished to fix its image in a drawing, believing that thus it would stop its flight, and that its tracks would be easily picked up again in daylight on the following morning. The practice of sticking pins into the wooden or clay images of one's enemies appears to have come later.

The special charm of Olduvai is that nothing very much has happened there in the last few hundred thousand years, at any rate as far as man is concerned. As the Ice Age receded the ground thawed out, the sivatherium and the other monsters died, but the lion, leopard, hyena, wild dog and serval cat lived on (and incidentally they have not changed much in size or shape since prehistoric times). In Northern Africa the ancient Egyptian civilization came and went, but nothing was recorded here, and right up to the start of this century the local tribes had made very little advance beyond the stone-age. For some reason, perhaps the lack of water and the sparseness of the population, the Arab slave routes did not pass through the Serengeti, and the early explorers like Burton and Thomson tended to keep either to the south or the north of Olduvai Gorge. Theodore Roosevelt, who turned up in East Africa a good twelve months ahead of Professor Kattwinkel, was much struck with this enduring primitiveness. At the end of one of his early marches into the wilds he exclaims in his diary, 'A Pleistocene day!'

Leakey's view is that the drying up of the Sahara has had much to do with the isolation of Africa and the consequent backwardness of animal and native life there. Once the Sahara swarmed with all kinds of wild game, and the lions which were captured by the Romans (Pompey once paraded no less than 600 of them in the Colosseum), surely came from northern Africa as well as the Middle East. The Roman elephants too were African elephants, and it is something of a wonder that they could have been trained in battle, or that Hannibal could have induced them to cross the Alps, since today it is the hardest thing in the world to tame the African elephant, and very few people ever attempt it.

All this region around the Olduvai Gorge is wonderfully unspoiled country, mostly scrub and open grassland, and except for a few mud huts of the Masai tribe it is uninhabited. It is the essence of Africa. At midday the flat-topped acacia trees stand in absolute stillness on the empty land, and the horizon becomes lost in a floating mirage. Then, in the softer light of the evening, the distant hills take shape, and a blue haze gathers on every rock and cliff that juts above the plain.

It is said that in every country there is one particular thing which is so commonplace that no one speaks about it, and for me in Africa it is this blue haze. It haunts the early morning and the evening, and it gives one an intense feeling of liberation, of immense uncharted distances through which one would like to go on moving indefinitely, and without object, simply letting the time go by.

But the really spectacular thing at this eastern end of the Serengeti Plains is the Ngorongoro Crater mountain. Its circular rim rises 8,000 feet above the sea, and on the day we arrived heavy rain clouds were hanging about. Presently, however, the sun broke through, and from the top of the rim we were able to look down over the other side on to the bright green floor of the crater, 2,000 feet below. At first sight this crater floor does not seem to be very big—it is not unlike an ordinary circular football field seen from a seat high up in the grandstand—and it is difficult to believe that the actual area is 200 square miles. Nothing appears to move down there; it is as calm and silent as a mountain lake.

Ker decided to camp on the top for the night, and then go down into the crater on the following day. We could not make a direct descent— there was a gang of African convicts working on a motor-road but it was not finished yet—and so we had to make a twenty-mile journey round the rim of the crater to a point on the opposite side where there was a rough track leading downwards. With chains fixed to the wheels of the vehicles we set off in the first light of the morning. The convicts, I noticed, were already at work.

'No trouble about keeping them in at night,' Ker said; 'With so many elephant and rhinoceros about they don't even have to guard them.'

Yet there was no elephant or rhinoceros. Their tracks were clear enough on the sodden ground, but the forest was very thick and we saw nothing much except an occasional francolin, which is a queer little bird that runs with a rolling nautical gait like a man with his hands in his trouser pockets. There was no sound or sign of movement anywhere. A couple of hours went by like this and it was all rather disappointing.

But now we turned down along a steep and rocky track, and a few minutes later our car suddenly emerged from the trees into the bright sunshine on the floor of the crater. And there, spreading out before us, was a stupendous field of grass on which, at a guess, some ten thousand wild animals were roaming.

Nothing in Africa quite prepares you for this apparition. It is as though a curtain has been suddenly lifted on a brightly-lit stage; the eye falters for a moment and you must look again, a second and a third time, before you begin to comprehend what is happening. The wild animals don't take much notice of the vehicles. It may be as you drive quietly over the grass you may start the wildebeest off on one of their many gallops, that the baboons will bark at you and the elephants will fan out their ears suspiciously at the sound of the car. But here you are no more than one in a multitude, and you are as secure as Noah in his ark. The animals are engrossed in their own lives, and if the hyena, with his curious sloping walk, gives you a look of hate that is because he probably hates all living things. Even here the hyenas have a skulking air that suggests the whole world is against them— which it probably is.

Ker stopped the car on a patch of rising ground for a while, and we just sat there, looking. The sun was still shining. I fancy that, like a good and successful showman, Ker was just as pleased with my astonishment as I was myself. With a matter-of-fact air he let in the clutch and drove off across the plain, saying that we ought to come across a lion or two; there were about thirty in the crater.

It was the first lion that we met that I particularly remember. He was a huge, black-maned beast, and he was stretched out comfortably on the grass on his four paws like a monumental statue. Evidently he had just eaten, for when we approached to within twenty yards he did nothing more than favour us with a slow and casual stare. Then the yellow eyes closed, the jaws opened in a wide yawn, and in a deep daze of weariness the animal rolled over on his back. All around him in the sunshine herds of zebras and gazelles were quietly grazing. The hyenas sat and waited.

It was a little later in the morning that we saw the other side of this picture. We were driving along a watercourse on the opposite side of the crater when another lion got up suddenly in front of us, a younger beast with very little mane as yet, but he looked very fine as he lifted his head and made the air vibrate with a deep short throaty roar. Ker stopped the car at once. 'Now watch,' he said, 'he's hunting.' Over to the left, some two hundred yards away from the lion, a mingled herd of zebra and wildebeest were grazing, and they were now standing very still with their heads turned towards the point of danger. But for the moment the lion did nothing more. He sank down on his haunches and gently sniffed the breeze. Then again he got up in full view of his quarry, moved forward with a few slow paces, and again emitted his awful threatening growl. This time the zebras and the wildebeest bolted. They ran full tilt for fifty yards or so and then turned uncertainly and faced the lion again. Ker explained what was happening.

'You feel the breeze? It's blowing directly over the herd towards that gully over there; and in that gully somewhere a lioness is waiting. She is the one that will make the kill. She will wait until her mate has driven the zebras on to her hiding place and then she'll spring out on the nearest animal.'

'But don't the zebras know what is happening? Don't they ever learn from experience?'

'No, they never learn.'

It was obviously going to be a long business—perhaps a couple of hours or more—and we did not wait for the kill. In any case Ker explained that our chances of seeing the lioness spring were not very good. Up to the last minute one never knew exactly where to look, and it would all be over in an instant; just that one quick bound on to the victim's back and that terrible cat-claw reaching down to the zebra's eyes and mouth. Then probably the lion would come loping across the plain to join his mate and settle, roaring, on to the dying beast.

We missed all this, but we saw the aftermath when we came back in the afternoon, and that was fascinating. The victim—it turned out to be a wildebeest and not a zebra—had not long been dead, and two lions were squatting side by side on their haunches and tearing at the meat. All around us, in the sky as well as on the ground, the immemorial pattern of a kill was forming. There was a ring of jackals round the carcass, and from time to time one of them would dart in and seize a titbit from under the lion's jaws. The lions did not seem to mind this particularly; just once the female rose abruptly and made a tremendous swipe at one of the jackals that had grown too bold. But she soon settled down again. Beyond the jackals there was a second ring around the kill, the hyenas. In no circumstances, Ker said, would the lions permit them to approach the carcass until they themselves had finished. The hyenas, however, were getting at any rate an *hors d'oeuvre* in another way; every jackal that came away from the kill was immediately set upon and chased across the plain until it dropped the morsel in its mouth—unless of course it succeeded in gulping down the meat in time.

Meanwhile the vultures were arriving. In open country like this it does not take them very long to sight a kill. Each bird, ranging high above the crater, watches the flight of its neighbours, and directly one bird dives, the others follow. They came down in twos and threes, necks thrust forward, and with a frantic beating of their brown wings as they touched the ground.

Then they trotted forward and made still another outer ring around the kill.

And so for an hour or more things continued in this way in the bright peaceful sunshine until the lions were gorged at last and moved away. They sat down heavily at a little distance licking their red mouths in the grass. Instantly the hyenas passed through the ring of jackals and set upon the carcass. They fed noisily, snapping and snarling at one another, and like dogs they grabbed the biggest hunks they could get and ran away. It was the turn then of the jackals. The vultures continued to sit and wait; they would wait all night if necessary. In the end nothing would be left except the skin, the hooves, and the wet bones, and upon these the ants would soon be at work.

I found it absorbing too to watch the other animals all through this time. Once the dreadful act of murder had been committed the zebras, the wildebeest and the antelopes quietly resumed their grazing as though nothing had happened. Now that one of their number had been sacrificed they knew that they were safe for the next two or three days, at all events from these two lions, and all their fear had disappeared. They grazed right up to and around the bloody mess of their dead companion in the same way as a traffic stream will make an island of an accident and continue indifferently on its way.

In other words, there is no real anger in these dramas, and the death of the weak is accepted as part of the natural, unsentimental order of things. If there is anger in animals at all it seems to be reserved for their conflict with human beings, and the occasional fights between evenly matched rivals; the buffalo lunging at his neighbour in the mating season, the mother elephant driving off the lion from her young. And it is the special quality of the Ngorongoro crater that all these things can be observed so easily, almost as though you were sitting at some spectacle in the Roman Colosseum, and against the background of the sun shining so brightly on the close-cropped grass.

Lions, when mating, do not eat as a rule. For a week or more a couple will retire into the long grass or some shady valley and the devotion of the male is extreme: when the female turns her head he turns his too. Wherever she moves he follows. But it is very different when they return to the world again and the female makes a kill. With a forbidding roar the male drives his mate from the prey and she sits waiting a dozen yards or so away until he has finished his meal.

When the cubs are born the family groups tend to split up. The males go off to hunt by themselves often in groups of two while the females (sometimes assisted by an unmated lioness who acts as a kind of cubs' nurse) remain with the young.

We camped for four days inside the crater, and then moved west again across the Serengeti Plains. It was exactly the right time of the year to make the journey. The moon was full, and the great January migration of animals was on their long trek out towards Lake Victoria before the rains began. At a guess we must have passed in the space of two days a million gazelle and perhaps half as many wildebeest and zebra. The animals were calving early this year, and it was a marvellous thing to see a young gazelle, hardly a few hours old, get up to trot all day beside its mother. The wildebeest went forward in long columns like squadrons of cavalry, and although apparently no command was given, they kept closing their ranks when gaps occurred. They wheeled together to the left or right, and out on the flanks the sentinels kept their place. The sentinels do not graze like the others as they go along: they keep looking out in all directions across the wide plain, on the watch for lions, no doubt, until they are relieved by some other animal trotting out from the herd to take their place. But how this is organized and who decides just which animal is to go on duty at a certain time no naturalist has yet explained.

The Creature from the Marsh*

Loren Eiseley

I

The only thing strange about me is my profession. I happen to be one of those few persons who pursue the farther history of man on the planet earth, what Darwin once called "the great subject." But my business is not with the formal art of the history books. Take, for example, today.

Today I have been walking in the ruins of the city. The city still moves, it is true, the air drills ring against iron, and I am aware of laughter and of feet hurrying by at the noon hour. Nevertheless the city is in ruins. This is what the trained eye makes of it. It stands here in the morning sun while rust flakes the steel rails and the leaves of innumerable autumns blow mistily through the ribs of skyscrapers and over the fallen brick work lies a tangle of morning glories. I have seen this before in the dead cities of Mexico—the long centuries wavering past with the curious distortion of things seen through deep sea water. Even the black snake gliding down the steps of the cathedral seems a repetition, past and future being equally resolvable in the curious perspective of the archaeological eye.

But it was not for this that I hurried out to walk in the streets of the city. I wanted to find a symbol, something that would stand for us when the time came, something that might be proud after there was no stone upon another—some work of art, perhaps, or a gay conceit that the rains had not tarnished, something that would tell our story to whatever strange minds might come groping there.

I think I must have walked miles in those ruins. I studied a hundred shop windows. I weighed with a quarter century of digging experience the lasting qualities of metal, stone, and glass. I hesitated over the noble inscriptions upon public buildings, while the rain dissolved in the locked containers the files of treaties and the betrayal of all human trust. I passed by the signs of coruscating heat and the wilted metal of huge guns. I found the china head of a doll in the metal of a baby carriage that my mind took hold of and considered carefully, though later I realized I stood by a living nursemaid in the Park.

I looked at tools, and at flowers in the windows of tenements. (They will creep out and grow, I thought.) And I heard a dog howl in the waste streets for the comforting hand of man. I saw the vacant, ashy leaves of books blow by, but I did not pick them up. There were dead television screens and the curious detached loneliness of telephone receivers whose broken wires still thrummed in the winds over the Sierra.

It will never do, I thought; there was more to us than this—with all the evil, with all the cruelty. I remembered an inscribed gold ring in a pawnshop window. "From Tom to Mary," it had read, "for always." It is back there, I thought; that might be it—there was love in us, things we spoke to each other in the evening or on deathbeds, the eyes frank at last. It might be there. I turned and hurried back.

But the little shop was gone, and finally I came up short at a place where stones had tumbled in a peculiar way, half sheltering a fallen window. There were bones there, and at first this made no sense because bones in exposed places do not last well, and there are so many of them finally that the meaning escapes you.

There was a broken sign LED—Fi—Av—. And among the bits of glass, a little cluster of feathers, and under a shattered pane, the delicate bones of a woman's hand that, dying, had reached wistfully out, caught there, when the time came.

Why not? I mused. The human hand, the hand is the story. I touched one of the long, graceful bones. It had come the evolutionary way up from far eons and watery abysses only to perish here.

There was a little restless stirring beside me.

So it died after all that effort, I thought on. Five hundred million years expended in order that the shining thread of life could die reaching after a little creation of feathers in the window of a shop. And why not? Even my antique reptilian eye had a feel for something, a kind of beauty here.

The tugging at my sleeve continued. The slow, affectionate voice of my wife said to me, "Wait here. I want to go in."

"Of course," I said, and took and squeezed her slender hand as I returned from some far place. "It will look becoming," I said. "I will stand here and watch."

"The gloves to match it are of green lizard skin," she exulted.

"That will look just right," I ventured, and did not quite know what I meant. "I will stand here and watch."

A swinging light like a warning at a railroad crossing began flashing in the darkness below consciousness. A bell began jangling. Then it subsided. My wife was pointing, for the benefit of an attentive clerk, at a little cluster of feathers in the window. I came forward then and beckoned hastily. "But why—?" she said. "Another day," I said, wiping my forehead. It was just that—"Another time," I promised and urged her quickly away.

It is the nature, you see, of the profession—the terrible *déjà vu* of the archaeologist, the memory that scans before and after. For instance, take the case of the black skull, a retreat, some might say, in another direction.

II

The skull was black when they brought it to me. It was black from the irons and acids and mineral replacements of ice-age gravels. It was polished and worn and gleaming from the alterations of unnumbered years. It had made strange journeys after the death of its occupant; it had moved with glacial slowness in the beds of rivers; it had been tumbled by floods and, becoming an object of grisly beauty, had been picked up and passed from hand to hand by men the individual had never seen in life.

Finally it was brought to me.

It was my duty to tell them about the skull.

It was my professional duty to clothe these bones once more with the faint essence of a personality, to speak of a man or a woman, young or old, as the bones might tell the story. It was my task to read the racial features in a forgotten face, stare deep into the hollow sockets through which had once passed in endless procession the days and seasons and the shed tears of long ago.

The woman had been young. I could tell them that. I could tell them she had once fallen or been struck and that after a long time the bone had mended and she had recovered—how, it was difficult to say, for it had been a dangerous and compound fracture. Today such a wound would mean months of immobilization in a hospital. This woman had survived without medical attention through the endless marchings and journeyings of the hunters' world. Even the broken orbit of the left eye had dropped by a quarter of an inch—a serious disfigurement. Nevertheless she had endured and lived on toward some doom that had come fast upon her but was not written in the bones. It was, in all likelihood, a death by violence. Her skull had not been drawn from a grave. It had come from beneath the restless waters of a giant river that is known to keep its secrets well.

They asked me for the time of the events, and again, obediently, I went down that frail ladder which stretches below us into the night of time. I went slowly, by groping deductions and the hesitant intuitions of long experience that only scholars know. I passed through ages where water was wearing away the shapes of river pebbles into crystalline sand and the only sound in the autumn thickets was the gathering of south-flying birds. Somewhere in the neighborhood of the five thousandth millennium—I could place it no closer than that—the ladder failed me. The river was still there but larger—an enormous rolling waste of water and marshes out of which rose a vast October moon.

They interrupted me then, querulously, asking if archaeologists could do no better than this, and was it not true that there were new and clever methods by which physicists could call the year in the century and mark the passage of time by the tick of atoms in the substance of things. And I said, yes, within limits it was true, but that the methods were not always usable, and that the subtle contaminations possible among radioactive objects sometimes defeated our attempts.

At this point they shook their heads unwillingly, for, as I quickly saw, they had the passion of modern men for the precision of machines and disliked vagueness of any sort. But the skull lay there on the table between us, and over it one man lingered, fascinated in spite of himself. I knew what he was thinking: Where am I going? When shall I become like this?

I heard this in his mind for just an instant while I stared across at him from among my boxes of teeth and flint arrowheads that had grown chalky and dull with the passage of long centuries in the ground.

"Thank you," the visitor said finally, moving after his party to the door. He was, I saw, unsure for what it was he thanked me.

"You are quite welcome," I said, still returning slowly from that waste of forgotten water over which the birds of another century cried dolefully, so that I could hear them keening in my head. Like the man who asks a medium to bring back some whimpering memoryless ghost and make it speak out of a living mouth for the amusement of a group of curiosity seekers, he may have felt remorse. At any rate, he nodded uncertainly and fled.

I was the instrument. I had made this journey a hundred times for students who scrawled their initials on my skulls, a hundred times for reporters who wanted sensational accounts of monkey-men, a hundred times for people who came up at the end of lectures and asked, "How much money are the bones worth, doctor? Are they easy to find?"

In spite of this I have continued to make these journeys. It is old habit now. I go back into the past alone. I would do so if I fled my job and sought safety in some obscure room. My sense of time is so heightened that I can feel the frost at work in stones, the first creeping advance of grass in a deserted street. I have stood by the carved sarcophagi of dead knights in a European cathedral, men seven hundred years away from us with their steel and their ladies, and from that point striven to hurl the mind still backward into the wilderness where man coughs bestially and vanishes into the shape of beasts.

I cannot say I am a student of the dates in the history books. My life is mostly occupied with caves filled up and drifted over with the leaves of ten thousand thousand autumns. My speciality is the time when man was changing into man. But, like a river that twists, evades, hesitates through slow miles, and then leaps violently down over a succession of cataracts, man can be called a crisis animal. Crisis is the most powerful element in his definition. Of his entire history, this he understands the least. Only man has continued to turn his own definition around upon his tongue until, in the end, he has looked outside of nature to something invisible to any eye but his own. Long ago, this emotion was well expressed in the Old Testament. "Oh Lord," exclaimed the prophet Jeremiah, "I know that the way of man is not in himself." Therefore, I would add, as a modern evolutionist, "the way" only lies through man and has to be sought beyond him. It was this that led to a very remarkable experience.

III

"The greatest prize of all," once confessed the British plant explorer F. Kingdon Ward, "is the skull of primitive man." Ward forgot one thing: there are other clues to primitive men than those confined to skulls. The bones of fossil men are few because the earth tolerated them in scant numbers. We call them missing links on the road to ourselves. A little less tooth here, a little more brain there, and you can see them changing toward ourselves in that long historyless time when the great continental ice sheets ebbed and flowed across the northern continents. Like all the students of that age, I wanted to find a missing link in human history. That is what this record is about, for I stumbled on the track of one.

Some men would maintain that a vague thing called atmosphere accounts for such an episode as I am about to relate, that there are houses that demand a murder and wait patiently until the murderer and his victim arrive, that there are great cliffs that draw the potential suicide from afar or mountains of so austere a nature that they write their message on the face of a man who looks up at them. This all may be. I do not deny it. But when I encountered the footprint in the mud of that remote place I think the thing that terrified me most was the fact that I knew to whom it belonged and yet I did not want to know him. He was a stranger to me and remains so to this day. Because of a certain knowledge I had, however, he succeeded in impressing himself upon me in a most insidious manner. I have never been the same since the event took place and often at night I start up sweating and think uncannily that the creature is there with me in the dark. If the sense of his presence grows, I switch on the light, but I never look into the mirror. This is a matter of old habit with me.

First off, though, we must get straight what we mean by a missing link.

A missing link is a day in the life of a species that is changing its form and habits, just as, on a smaller scale, one's appearance and behavior at the age of five are a link in one's development to an adult man or woman. The individual person may have changed and grown but still the boy or girl of many years ago is linked to the present by a long series of steps. And if one is really alive and not already a living fossil, one will go on changing till the end of one's life and perhaps be the better for it. The term "missing link" was coined because some of the physical links in the history of man as a species are lost, and those people who, like myself, are curious about the past look for them.

My album is the earth, and the pictures in it are faded and badly torn and have to be pieced together by detective work. If one thinks of oneself at five years of age, one may get a thin wisp of disconnected memory pictures. By contrast, the past of a living species is without memory except as that past has written its physical record in vestigial organs like the appendix or a certain pattern on our molar teeth. To eke out what those physical stigmata tell us, we have to go grubbing about in caves and gravel for the bones of very ancient men. If one can conceive of the trouble an archaeologist might have in locating one's remains a half-million years from now, supposing they still existed, one will get an idea of the difficulties involved in finding traces of man before his bones were crowded together in cities and cemeteries.

I was wandering inland along a sunken shore when the thing happened—the thing I had dreamed of so long. In other words, I got a clue to man. The beaches on that coast I had come to visit are treacherous and sandy and the tides are always shifting things about among the mangrove roots. It is not a place to which I would willingly return and you will get no bearings from me. Anyway, what it was I found there could be discovered on any man's coast if he looked sharp for it. I had come to that place with other things in mind, and a notion of being alone. I was tired. I wanted to lie in the sun or clamber about like an animal in the swamps and the forest. To secure such rest from the turmoil of a modern city is the most difficult thing in the world to accomplish and I have only achieved it twice: once in one of the most absolute deserts in the world and again in this tropical marsh.

By day and night strange forms of life scuttled and gurgled underfoot or oozed wetly along outthrust branches; luminous tropical insects blundered by in the dark like the lamps of hesitant burglars. Overhead, on higher ground, another life shrieked distantly or was expectantly still in the treetops. Somehow, alone as I was, I got to listening as if all that world were listening, waiting for something to happen. The trees drooped a little lower listening, the tide lurked and hesitated on the beach, and even a tree snake dropped a loop and hung with his face behind a spider web, immobile in the still air.

A world like that is not really natural, or (the thought strikes one later) perhaps it really is, only more so. Parts of it are neither land nor sea and so everything is moving from one element to another, wearing uneasily the queer transitional bodies that life adopts in such places. Fish, some of them, come out and breathe air and sit about watching you. Plants take to eating insects, mammals go back to the water and grow elongate like fish, crabs climb trees. Nothing stays put where it began because everything is constantly climbing in, or climbing out, of its unstable environment.

Along drowned coasts of this variety you only see, in a sort of speeded-up way, what is true of the whole world and everything upon it: the Darwinian world of passage, of missing links, of beetles with soldered, flightless wings, of snakes with vestigial feet dragging slowly through the underbrush. Everything is marred and maimed and slightly out of focus—everything in the world. As for man, he is no different from the rest. His back aches, he ruptures easily, his women have difficulties in childbirth—all because he has struggled up upon his hind legs without having achieved a perfect adjustment to his new posture.

On this particular afternoon, I came upon a swamp full of huge waterlilies where I had once before ventured. The wind had begun to rise and rain was falling at intervals. As far as I could see, giant green leaves velvetly impervious to water were rolling and twisting in the wind. It was a species of lily in which part of the leaves projected on stalks for a short distance above the water, and as they rolled and tossed the whole swamp flashed and quivered from the innumerable water drops that were rolling around and around like quicksilver in the great cupped leaves. Everything seemed flickering and changing as if in some gigantic illusion, but so soft was the green light and so delicate the brushing of the leaves against each other that the whole effect was quite restful, as though one could be assured that nothing was actually tangible or real and no one in his senses would want it to be, as long as he could sway and nod and roll reflecting water drops about over the surface of his brain.

Just as I finally turned away to climb a little ridge I found the first footprint. It was in a patch of damp, exposed mud and was pointed away from the water as though the creature had emerged directly out of the swamp and was heading up the shore toward the interior. I had thought I was alone, and in that place it was wise to know one's neighbors. Worst of all, as I stood studying the footprint, and then another, still heading up the little rise, it struck me that though undoubtedly human the prints were different in some indefinable way. I will tell you once more that this happened on the coast of another country in a place where form itself is an illusion and no shape of man or beast is totally impossible. I crouched anxiously in the mud while all about the great leaves continued to rotate on their stems and to flash their endlessly rolling jewels.

But there were these footprints. They did not disappear. As I fixed the lowermost footprint with every iota of scientific attention I could muster, it became increasingly apparent that I was dealing with some transitional form of man. The arch, as revealed in the soft mud, was low and flat and implied to the skilled eye an inadequate adjustment to the upright posture. This, in its turn, suggested certain things about the spine and the nature of the skull. It was only then, I think, that the full import of my discovery came to me.

Good Lord, I thought consciously for the first time, the thing is alive. I had spent so many years analyzing the bones of past ages or brooding over lizard tracks turned to stone in remote epochs that I had never contemplated this possibility before. The thing was alive and it was human. I looked uneasily about before settling down into the mud once more. One could make out that the prints were big but what drew my fascinated eye from the first was the nature of the second toe. It was longer than the big toe, and as I crawled excitedly back and forth between the two wet prints in the open mud, I saw that there was a remaining hint of prehensile flexibility about them.

Most decidedly, as a means of ground locomotion this foot was transitional and imperfect. Its loose, splayed aspect suggested inadequate protection against sprains. That second toe was unnecessarily long for life on the ground, although the little toe was already approximating the rudimentary condition so characteristic of modern man. Could it be that I was dealing with an unreported living fossil, an archaic ancestral survival? What else could be walking the mangrove jungle with a foot that betrayed clearly the marks of ancient intimacy with the arboreal attic, an intimacy so long continued that now, after hundreds of thousands of years of ground life, the creature had squiggled his unnecessarily long toes about in the mud as though an opportunity to clutch at something had delighted his secret soul.

I crouched by the footprint and thought. I remembered that comparisons with the living fauna, whenever available, are good scientific procedure and a great aid to precise taxonomy. I sat down and took off my shoes.

I had never had much occasion to look critically at my own feet before. In modern man they are generally encased in shoes—something that still suggests a slight imperfection in our adaptations. After all, we don't normally find it necessary to go about with our hands constantly enclosed in gloves. As I sat contemplating and comparing my feet with the footprints, a faintly disturbing memory floated hazily across my mind. It had involved a swimming party many years before at the home of one of the most distinguished comparative anatomists in the world. As we had sat on the bench alongside his pool, I had glanced up suddenly and caught him staring with what had seemed unnecessary fascination at my feet. I remembered now that he had blushed a deep pink under his white hair and had diverted my inquiring glance deftly to the scenery about us.

Why I should have remembered the incident at all was unclear to me. I thought of the possibility of getting plaster casts of a footprint and I also debated whether I should attempt to trail the creature farther up the slope toward which he appeared to have been headed. It was no moment for hesitation. Still, I did hesitate. The uneasy memory grew stronger, and a thought finally struck me. A little sheepishly and with a glance around to see that I was not observed, I lowered my own muddy foot into the footprint. It fitted.

I stood there contemplatively clutching, but this time consciously, the mud in my naked toes. I was the dark being on that island shore whose body carried the marks of its strange passage. I was my own dogging Man Friday, the beast from the past who had come with weapons through the marsh. The wind had died and the great green leaves with their rolling jewels were still. The mistake I had made was the mistake of all of us.

The story of man was not all there behind us in the caves of remote epochs. Even our physical bodies gave evidence that the change was not completed. As for our minds, they were still odd compounds of beast and saint. But it was not by turning back toward the marsh out of which we had come that the truly human kingdom was to be possessed and entered—that kingdom dreamed of in many religions and spoken of in many barbarous tongues. A philosopher once said in my presence, "The universe is a series of leaping sparks—everything else is interpretation." But what, I hesitated, was man's interpretation to be?

I drew a foot out of the little steaming swamp that sucked at it. The air hung heavily about me. I listened as the first beast might have listened who came from the water up the shore and did not return again to his old element. Everything about me listened in turn and seemed to be waiting for some decision on my part. I swayed a moment on my unstable footing.

Then, warily, I stepped higher up the shore and let the water and the silt fill in that footprint to make it, a hundred million years away, a fossil sign of an unknown creature slipping from the shadows of a marsh toward something else that awaited him. I had found the missing link. He walked on misshapen feet. The stones hurt him and his belly sagged. There were dreams like Christmas ornaments in his head, intermingled with an ancient malevolent viciousness. I knew because I was the missing link, but for the first time I sensed where I was going.

I have said I never look into the mirror. It is a matter of old habit now. If that other presence grows too oppressive I light the light and read.

Terms
and
Topics

TERMS

1. *Formal, informal, colloquial, slang* These so-called "levels" of diction
   or style can more usefully be understood as occurring on a continuous
   spectrum. One point on the spectrum is not intrinsically better (or
   worse) than another; rather each is right, or appropriate, for a given
   subject, audience, and purpose. Try to sharpen your sense of the distinctions between them as you read and write. Most writing today uses a
   more-or-less informal style. But for what kind of occasion would a
   relatively formal style be most appropriate? or a colloquial style? Can
   you think of any occasion where it would be desirable to mix formal diction and slang? Can you find any instances of this in the essays in this
   book?

2. *Allusion* An indirect or casual reference to something, usually something outside of a given context. By alluding to the Bible, for example,
   Forster calls up in the reader's mind a whole array of associations which
   the reader is then expected to bring to bear on what Forster is saying.
   What allusions can you find in the other essays in this section?

3. *Paradox* A statement that is seemingly illogical, self-contradictory, or
   otherwise absurd, but that is somehow actually or at least possibly true.
   Many proverbs, for example, express paradoxes: slow but sure wins the
   race; the shortest way round is the longest way home; he who cannot
   obey cannot command. Shakespeare's "Sweet are the uses of adversity" *(As You Like It)* is another. It is paradoxical, yet true, that the best
   person for a particular job might be the one who knows least about it, or
   that a difficult task often makes one do better work than if the task were
   easy.

4. **Subject, thesis** A *subject* or *topic* is what is being written about; a *thesis* is a proposition about a subject which governs what a writer says about it. For example, a subject such as "modern travel" could have any number of theses: "Travel by ship is more romantic than travel by air," "Travel is safer today than it used to be," and so on. But a thesis need not be so explicitly argumentative—for example, "Travel is broadening." A good writer will almost always state his thesis in some way, usually near either the beginning or the end of an essay—and often in both places. Note, for example, how Forster states his thesis in his first paragraph, once in general terms and once in more specific terms—and both times in the form of a question. Try to find the thesis in each of the other essays. Are there any essays in which the thesis is left implicit, not stated directly? Practise by picking several subjects and then constructing several possible theses for each.

5. **Subjective, objective** These adjectives, as they apply here, designate opposite qualities of a piece of writing or of a writer's attitude. *Objective* means independent of the mind, free of any influence by the attitudes, emotions, or special interests of the writer; *subjective* means just the opposite. An objective writer could be said to be writing from a detached point of view. Subjectivity or objectivity is almost always a matter of degree: one is relatively subjective or objective at any given time. Even a camera can lie.

TOPICS: On Individual Essays

E.B. WHITE "Once More to the Lake"

1. What are some of the significant details White uses, and how and why does he use them? Do any details seem *not* significant?

2. The next to last paragraph is almost pure description. What is its function in the essay?

3. Try to decide what proportions of the piece are description and narration. Are some parts impossible to call one or the other? Is the overall purpose of the piece primarily narrative? Descriptive? Neither?

4. White's diction and syntax are basically simple. When he departs from a simple level, he does so for a purpose. Find instances where the level of diction or sentence structure shifts, and discuss the reasons for these shifts.

5. How does White establish and maintain the parallel between (a) himself and his father, and (b) his son and himself? What is the function of the parallel in the essay as a whole?

6. Why does White repeatedly refer to "time"? In what different ways does he introduce the idea of time?

7. What is the point of the passage (paragraph 6) in which he says, "the lake was exactly where we had left it"?

8. Write a narrative of personal experience focussing on the effects of time on someone or something. Try to avoid merely stating or asserting your point, but use as much description as necessary to make your point clear.

DYLAN THOMAS "Memories of Christmas"

1. Analyze some of the ways in which Thomas achieves the tone or outlook of a child without sounding merely childish. Consider, among other things, the sentence structures he uses.

2. Analyze and discuss the several metaphors in the first four lines of the second paragraph. How do they work? Thomas, primarily a poet, was fond of unusual metaphors. Discuss some of his more striking uses of metaphor elsewhere in the essay.

3. Does Thomas's essay have any "meaning" beyond evoking a past in a pleasant, nostalgic way? If so, how does he bring it out?

4. See if you can discover any principle of form or structure in this essay. Why are things related in the order they are? Is it simply chronological, or haphazard?

5. To what extent does Thomas realize the various characters he mentions? Can you visualize them? Is it important?

6. Thomas was fond of compound adjectives. Find several of these and note how much he achieved with how few words. Does he anywhere seem to you to overdo it? Are there any places where you feel that the style calls too much attention to itself? Or do even the more striking turns of phrase contribute to the effect in justifiable ways?

7. Describe some setting that you remember from your childhood. Use as much metaphor and be as "poetic" in other ways as you feel the prose will bear. Use as much narration as you need, and put as many people in the place as necessary to create the effect you want.

RODERICK HAIG-BROWN "Behind the Salmon"

1. For the uninitiated, are specialized terms like "Harger's Orange," "humpback salmon," "set the hook," "shouldering," and "leader" unnecessarily confusing, or do they add an air of authenticity? For a reader who doesn't fish, what is there here to hold the attention? Is the essay more likely to appeal to a fisherman?

2 Haig-Brown's piece is straightforwardly chronological in organization. Would any other scheme have worked as well or better?

3. How would you characterize the purpose of this essay? On what is one's interest focussed?

4. What is the tone of the essay? Point out some of the stylistic features that create the tone.

5. Write an essay about your engagement in some pursuit that you believe is not an interest shared by many—some unusual hobby or sport or other pastime—in which you try to convey your enthusiasm to the reader.

E.M. FORSTER "My Wood"

1. Analyze fully the metaphor in the fourth sentence of the second paragraph. Here Forster is using a biblical allusion, as he does again at least twice. Find and identify these and the several other kinds of allusions he uses, and explain their functions.

2. Is there any point to Forster's reference to his novel *A Passage to India*, or is it just a convenient anecdotal opening?

3. How would you characterize the tone of this essay? Is it consistent throughout, or are there shifts? If there are shifts, do they jar, or is there a pattern and purpose to them?

4. Forster has made the structure of his essay unusually obvious. How has he done this, and why do you think he did it? Does it work, or do you think it is obtrusive? What is the rationale for the order of the four parts? Is there a progression of any kind?

5. Does the short sentence "My bird," in part two, seem to you a deliberate echo of the title of the essay? If so, what is the point of the similarity?

6. Write an essay that indicates how some attitude (hatred of or affection for someone or something?) or possession (a car? a dress? a swimming pool?) affects you. Model the structure of your essay as closely as possible on that of Forster's, and be just as obvious about it as he is.

BHARATI MUKHERJEE "Intimations"

1. In the chapter preceding the one printed here, Mukherjee writes: "In Deoghar several time sequences coexist in what appears to be a single frieze." In the chapter printed here she writes: "We do not seem to have heeded the message of the anonymous sculptor from Deoghar." What is the relation between this allusion and the way she handles time? Is time rendered in a simple narrative or historic line? through retrospect and prospect? Are there several "layers" of time? If so, is one more important than the others? Is time itself in any way a subject of her essay?

2. Near the end of "My Wood" Forster refers to walls around a garden. Is Mukherjee's frequent reference to walls at all similar? Analyze the short paragraph that begins, "Out there beyond our walled vision...." What does she mean by "walled vision"? Is it a simple metaphor? Explain the paradox in the paragraph's first two sentences.

3. Nostalgia, along with associated feelings, is an idea both explicit and implicit in Mukherjee's piece, but it is far from being the simple nostalgia we commonly indulge in. Point out some instances where nostalgia is qualified and complicated in various ways.

4. How does Mukherjee force us to see various things through eyes other than her own? What is the point of view? Does she succeed in juggling subjectivity and objectivity so as to make you see things through your own eyes?

5. Try writing a brief personal narrative and description about some event or condition requiring a similar adjustment of more than one point of view for full understanding.

HUGH MACLENNAN "The Street-Car Conductor"

1. Would you call MacLennan's essay "plotted," or not? Explain its organization and movement.

2. Are you less likely in future to take for granted such an individual as this conductor? Has MacLennan made you "see" him? Or is he not even the real subject of the essay? If not, what is?

3. Analyze the essay's final sentence for everything you can find out about it and how it works.

4. What is the point of the final exchange, "Things aren't so bad these days," followed by the customary *"Ouais"*? Is this the beginning of the essay's conclusion? How has MacLennan prepared for it, led up to it?

5. Do you think MacLennan means to blame Freud for the ills of the twentieth century?

6. Analyze the paragraph beginning "It was fashionable..." (p. 54) for rhythm, sentence length and structure, coherence, parallelism, diction, metaphor, and any other stylistic matter you think worth mentioning. Discover everything you can about the way this paragraph works.

7. Write a piece which focusses on some "little person" of your experience, perhaps even a parent or other relative, but which is only nominally about that person, using him or her as a peg on which to hang other matter.

ALAN MOOREHEAD "A Pleistocene Day"

1. In writing about such vast and exotic things as Africa and its animals and so on, how does Moorehead nevertheless manage to make his essay seem a very personal one?

2. Does the reference in the essay's second sentence to setting off "into the blue" make sense without the further mention, two thirds of the way through, to the characteristic "blue haze"? Or are the two even related?

3. About halfway through the essay, Moorehead writes for two or three pages about the Olduvai Gorge and its history and significance. Does this section seem to you at all a digression? If so, how do you account for his taking his title, "A Pleistocene Day," from the middle of it? Has the title any relevance to the rest of the piece?

4. Discuss Moorehead's descriptive techniques. What kinds of things is he intent upon making us sense? What senses does he appeal to?

5. Write an essay about some specific place or event or experience; use the concrete subject as a stepping-stone to explore or reveal more abstract subject matter. Move from concrete to abstract by way of analogy or metaphor.

LOREN EISELEY "The Creature from the Marsh"

1. Would you describe the way Eiseley begins his essay as "bizarre"? Why has he chosen to begin that way? What effect, or effects, do the opening pages have? How long was it before his purpose became clear to you?

2. The whole opening passage is a kind of metaphor. Examine some of Eiseley's other metaphors, especially extended ones.

3. Eiseley doesn't clearly announce his subject until part III. Can you justify so long a delayed beginning? What is the function of part I? of part II?

4. This piece is written almost like a mystery story. Does that seem appropriate to its subject and purpose? What internal justification can you find for such a technique?

5. If you haven't done so already, re-read the essay, and note how several things that were probably puzzling the first time are now clear. Do you think Eiseley intended the essay to need two readings, or could a reader, with sufficient care, have understood all the points the first time through?

6. Write a short essay that doesn't reveal its subject until about half-way through and doesn't state its thesis until the very end. But don't be too obviously mysterious about it, and try to make sure that the reader will be, though somewhat in the dark, interested enough to read on.

TOPICS: General and Comparative

1. Consider the effects that writers can achieve by using adjectives carefully. Do they ever overuse adjectives? Are there occasions when more precise nouns and active verbs are preferable to adjectives and adverbs? Examine your style in light of this distinction.

2. Take a representative passage from each of the essays and list and classify its verbs (as was done with the passage from Schreiner in the

preface to this section). Try to justify what you find out about these verbs in terms of the purpose of the different essays.

3. Compare and discuss two or more of the essays in terms of some of the following features: sentence length, sentence structure, level of diction, frequency and length of metaphor, proportion of concrete detail, handling of chronology. You can probably think of still other ways to make useful comparisons.

4. If you should see a traffic accident, would you make a good witness? Try to record exactly a sequence of events that you observed or overheard this morning, or to describe exactly a person you saw several hours ago.

5. Taking one of the writers in section I as your stylistic model, attempt to write a paragraph or two of personal narrative. Think about your subject first. What incident do you wish to focus on? Why? What purpose or purposes do you want the incident to serve? Why do you want to share this particular incident with a reader? Which reader? How will you engage the reader? With details? a certain tone? an anecdote? metaphoric language? transcribed conversation?

6. Try writing a few sentences to describe exactly some of the following items or circumstances:

> a red frisbee, a screen door, the sound of moving water, warts, ice, a clear glass window, dirt, safety pins, escalator steps, sore feet, hair, a running shoe, wheat, porridge, dogs' noses, a car tire, a glove compartment, fish scales, a soccer ball, a dime, night, oil, lemons, linen, a cup of tea, bees, dancing, moustaches, the income tax department, people waiting for a bus, a row of houses, lipstick, the 42nd floor, spaghetti sauce, gargling, blue, happiness, a chess piece, an orange, anger, a blade of grass, bare feet, a hamburger, a tightrope walker.

What are the difficulties of description in each case? Finding the words to convey the appropriate sense impression? making an abstract notion concrete? avoiding clichés? What else? Where does the force of your description lie? In the verbs? adjectives? nouns? sentence rhythms? In some combination of these?

Try writing advertising copy for some of these same items (see section IV). How does your language differ?

7. Does history impose its own order on essays about historical subjects? Write an essay about some historical event, such as a battle, a journey of discovery and exploration, or an election. How does the chronology of the event affect the structure of your essay?

8. How does a knowledge of history benefit a reader of MacLennan, Mukherjee, and Moorehead?

9. Note how the writers in this section use the active voice in their essays. Try rewriting an effective paragraph in the passive voice. What is the difference in effect?

10. The writers in this section all make excellent use of *details*. What is the force of the opening paragraph of White's essay, for example? How does Haig-Brown's knowledge of the specifics of fly-fishing add visually or descriptively to his essay? How does Moorehead integrate his observations of African animals with his observations of human behaviour, and how does the integration serve to structure his reflections on the process of human inquiry?

11. *Rhythm* can derive from repetition (see MacLennan's essay) or from the use of voice patterns (see Thomas's essay). How does a writer's choice of monosyllabic words affect rhythm? How does rhythm affect meaning? How else does a writer control the rhythm of prose? Point out some examples of these things happening.

12. Consider the effectiveness of the structure of the essays by White, Mukherjee, Forster, and Eiseley:

   (a) Note how White relies on a shift in tone. What is the force of the reference to "ringworm" in the first paragraph? What does the last paragraph add to the essay? How does it alter the tone and the effects of the essay?

   (b) Note how Mukherjee shifts from commenting on the ordinary to reflecting on the extraordinary, the unusual, the insane. How does she use anecdote to alter a reader's perception of what constitutes ordinariness? How does ordinariness relate to political, cultural, economic, or philosophical matters? What is the point of this memoir?

   (c) Note how Forster controls and alters the image of the wood. Does he succeed in elevating the image into a symbol?

   (d) Note how Eiseley suspends the identification of his "discovery." What does this add to his inquiry? Why is point of view important in this essay?

II
Writing
to
Reveal

On bookstore shelves a few years ago, there appeared a work with a brief conversation for a title: *Where Did You Go? Out. What Did You Do? Nothing.* Parents and children alike will recognize this exchange. Whether used in conversation to express deliberate evasiveness or frank absent-mindedness, when used as a title it serves as a witty reminder of all the failures of communication between generations. But one can argue that the failure is only superficial, that the speakers are in fact communicating, and that lodged in the very indirectness of the replies is a message. It might be that the child leaves a key word unspoken and the parent actually understands it: "Nothing *unusual.*" Or it might be that the child is actually declaring, as psychologists suggest: "I'm busy now—ask me later" or "Leave me alone—let me have some privacy." Either way, the child is probably revealing more than he or she realizes.

One of the intentions of an interview is to provoke such self-revelation. In contact with others, and when relaxed or nervous or upset or inflamed, people show sides of their character that are not always on display. (Whether such traits should be on display is another question.) Anyone with a television set or a garden fence is familiar with the nosy chatterer, the patronizer, the inquisitor, the idle gossip, the invader of privacy. Equally familiar are some other encounters between people: political and legal cross-questioning, where an investigator does or does not push hard enough to uncover the facts; informed discussions, where the interviewer responds intelligently to the person being interviewed and so contributes to the illumination of his ideas; and monologues of many shades: dramatic and consequential revelations, boring and trivia-riddled expressions of ego-centredness, flights of rhetoric, verbal sighs, maunderings. They differ in attraction. Some turn into newspaper human-interest stories, some do not. But all potentially offer candid portraits of human experience, and in this promise of openness—of the exposure of behind-the-scenes truth— lies the essential fascination of revelatory forms of address.

The master of the dramatic monologue as a poetic form was Robert Browning. His 1842 poem "My Last Duchess" is a well-known example of unwitting self-disclosure:

FERRARA

That's my last Duchess painted on the wall,
Looking as if she were alive. I call
That piece a wonder, now: Frà Pandolf's hands
Worked busily a day, and there she stands.
Will't please you sit and look at her? I said
"Frà Pandolf" by design, for never read
Strangers like you that pictured countenance,
The depth and passion of its earnest glance,
But to myself they turned (since none puts by

The curtain I have drawn for you, but I)
And seemed as they would ask me, if they durst,
How such a glance came there; so, not the first
Are you to turn and ask thus. Sir, 'twas not
Her husband's presence only, called that spot
Of joy into the Duchess' cheek: perhaps
Frà Pandolf chanced to say, "Her mantle laps
Over my lady's wrist too much," or "Paint
Must never hope to reproduce the faint
Half-flush that dies along her throat": such stuff
Was courtesy, she thought, and cause enough
For calling up that spot of joy. She had
A heart—how shall I say?—too soon made glad,
Too easily impressed; she liked whate'er
She looked on, and her looks went everywhere.
Sir, 'twas all one! My favour at her breast,
The dropping of the daylight in the West,
The bough of cherries some officious fool
Broke in the orchard for her, the white mule
She rode with round the terrace—all and each
Would draw from her alike the approving speech,
Or blush, at least. She thanked men,—good!
      but thanked
Somehow—I know not how—as if she ranked
My gift of a nine-hundred-years-old name
With anybody's gift. Who'd stoop to blame
This sort of trifling? Even had you skill
In speech—(which I have not)—to make your will
Quite clear to such an one, and say, "Just this
Or that in you disgusts me; here you miss,
Or there exceed the mark"—and if she let
Herself be lessoned so, nor plainly set
Her wits to yours, forsooth, and made excuse,
—E'en then would be some stooping; and I choose
Never to stoop. Oh sir, she smiled, no doubt,
Whene'er I passed her; but who passed without
Much the same smile? This grew; I gave commands;
Then all smiles stopped together. There she stands
As if alive. Will't please you rise? We'll meet
The company below, then. I repeat,
The Count your master's known munificence
Is ample warrant that no just pretence
Of mine for dowry will be disallowed;
Though his fair daughter's self, as I avowed
At starting, is my object. Nay, we'll go
Together down, sir! Notice Neptune, though,
Taming a sea-horse, thought a rarity,
Which Claus of Innsbruck cast in bronze for me!

Listening between the lines, the reader can interpret what the Duke of Ferrara is saying here, and come quickly to understand him better than he might wish. The reader glimpses an egocentric and powerful man, for whom people and art matter only as personal possessions. Power and his public position matter more. He needs to be admired. He thinks himself grand and needs to feel that others think so, too. So he boasts, seeks praise, ensures that his power is known about, and yet pretends to be elegant, civilized, fastidious, and perhaps even humane. But how does Browning make sure that the reader knows better? And does the listener in the poem know the Duke as well as the reader does?

Interviews and journal entries are scarcely as compact or as finely organized as this poem, but they have their own shape and also demand skilful structuring. Silver Donald Cameron's talk with Robertson Davies shows how a simple conversational gambit can provoke wide-ranging reflections on literature and society; it reveals Davies's oral articulateness and perhaps also an authorial mask of his own. Margaret Lane addresses herself more directly to the problem of masks and to interviews that have gone awry—which nonetheless still reveal features of personality. And in the other four essays—by Ludwig, Woodcock, Huxley, and Orwell—the voices of people who have been interviewed, observed, and overheard combine creatively with the voices of the authors doing the recording. The effects are subtly varied. Each writer, in the form of personal journals, notes down fragments of conversation; each sets about to connect, weigh, and interpret them. But the revelations he perceives, thus filtered through his own consciousness, inevitably become part of a process of self-revelation as well. It is a mark of their craftsmanship that the essays also demonstrate how a personal and initially private record can turn into a forceful act of persuasion.

Interview with Robertson Davies:
The Bizarre and Passionate Life of the Canadian People*

Silver Donald Cameron

Walking into the porter's lodge of Massey College in the University of Toronto, I was frightened. Robertson Davies, the Master of Massey College, is not only a sensitive and urbane novelist, but also an accomplished playwright, an exceptional journalist, a penetrating critic, a professional actor, a scholar, and an astringent wit. "Mr. Davies," A.J.M. Smith once wrote, "brings the virtues of urbanity, sophistication, good humour, and a certain consciousness of superiority to bear on books, food, wine and social behaviour." I greatly admired Davies' 1957 essay on Stephen Leacock, but I felt his Leacock anthology, Feast of Stephen, *was a waste of time; Davies in turn considered my* Faces of Leacock *altogether too earnestly academic; and both of us had published these opinions. I knew, too, that Davies was at the top of his powers: at fifty-eight, he had just published* Fifth Business, *by any standard the best novel he had ever written. I expected an ironic and uncomfortable afternoon.*

Inside Davies' study—a room so elegantly comfortable can hardly be called an office—I encountered someone considerably more rumpled, more round, and more quiet than the tall, suave, saturnine figure I had prepared for. I began asking questions suited to the man I thought he was, and got disconcerting answers. Was he a connoisseur of wine and cheese? No, he didn't know much about wine and didn't greatly enjoy cheese. Didn't the Salterton novels assume the reader and author agreed on the

* Excerpt from *Conversations with Canadian Novelists* by Silver Donald Cameron. Reprinted by permission of The Macmillan Company of Canada Limited.

primary importance of social reality? No: consider the use of sermons, music, fantasy.

Confused, I resorted to the basic principle of good interviewing: when in doubt, shut your mouth and really listen. I heard Davies saying that he was very different from his public image, and as I reshaped my view of him I found myself experiencing a deeply personal, almost confessional conversation.

Cameron: As I read them, the Salterton novels show a very strong feeling for the Western cultural tradition, and specifically the English tradition.

Davies: Well, I am interested in a lot of cultural traditions, as many as I can experience, really, but what is apparent in the Salterton novels is a Canadian cultural tradition which I don't think gets the kind of attention in Canadian fiction that it might expect: a sort of delayed cultural tradition. About the period that I was working on the Salterton novels, just after the 1945 war, there were still people living in places like Salterton whose tradition was directly Edwardian, and who saw nothing wrong with that. They weren't even conscious that their ideas were not contemporary. I remember driving with my wife from Peterborough to Cobourg to see a production of Chekhov's *The Cherry Orchard*, and in that very beautiful little theatre was an audience which contained a considerable number of people in evening dress, which I thought was very curious. They had come from that district, and they felt that that was the way that they ought to dress for a theatrical production. After the first act I wandered around in the corridors listening to the people talk, and they were talking about the play as if it were a brand new play—because it *was* a brand-new play to most of them, and yet they were people of some education, of a very considerable amount of tradition; they had the kind of dress clothes that suggested that they were well accustomed to wearing them and had indeed been wearing them for a very long time. Suddenly it broke in upon me: these people don't know that the play is about *them*—and yet there it was. I knew who some of them were: they were descendants of people who'd come to this country in the middle of the nineteenth century or earlier; they had homes in which they used silver which their families had brought with them, they had pictures of Great-grandfather in his Bengal uniform, they had connections with England, cousins that they wrote to, and they still hadn't grasped the fact that an entirely new Canada had come into being, and that their sort of person was really almost dinosaur-like in its failure to fit into the modern scene. You could see what happened in *The Cherry Orchard* happening around there, because all kinds of places were having to be bought up, and people didn't quite know why, but somehow the money had run out. Canada is full of these people, and very rarely do they get written about, but I write about them, and they're *real*. I could lead you out on a walk within a mile of where we sit which would uncover a great many of them. This is something in Canada which people on the whole don't recognize: we've got a fantastic sort of fossilized past here. We always talk about ourselves as a country with a great future, but we never talk about ourselves as a country with a sort of living past.

Cameron: Don't those novels show a fairly strong current of sympathy for some aspects of that tradition?

Davies: It is sympathy for the people—not, I think, the tradition—because they *are* people. They're not caricatures, they're not oddities, they're not cardboard. They bleed when you stick them and they weep when they are miserable, and their sorrows and their distresses are made sometimes more poignant by the fact that they don't know why things are happening to them.

Cameron: The shape of the novels themselves is rather in the tradition of English domestic comedy, like Jane Austen or Henry James, in a way.

Davies: No. No, I've never read a novel by Henry James in my life, and I don't like Jane Austen. I agree with Max Beerbohm that the novels of Jane Austen are a marionette opera. I have no use for them whatever.

Cameron: I'm becoming convinced I've misread you—but I thought there was an assumption in the Salterton novels of a kind of accepted social reality.

Davies: The people in the novels agree that there is a certain kind of reality; I don't think that should be taken as the *author's* opinion. In *A Mixture of Frailties* there are things which a lot of people who'd like the previous two novels disliked very much indeed, because it suggested that I and they had not agreed upon a kind of little provincial city which they could be cozy about it. *They* may have reached some such idea—but *I* never did.

Cameron: You must have surprised them even more with *Fifth Business*.

Davies: Yes, and I hope to go on surprising them.

Cameron: Are you working on a novel now?

Davies: Yes, and a great many people, I think, will find it uncongenial. Some people wrote to me and said that they liked *Fifth Business*, but it wasn't as funny as the other books. I'm grateful that they found the other books funny, but I am a little dismayed that they thought that funny was *all* they were. I think it is the writer's duty to be as amusing as he can manage, but not to sacrifice everything to that. That was what happened to Leacock: he eventually got so that he'd rather be funny than honest or sensible or intelligent, and that's bad.

Cameron: Isn't it true that the comedy of the Salterton novels is a rather anguished comedy, too? That the reader is invited to feel for the character who is the butt of the comedy, as well as laughing at him?

Davies: Yes, he is the victim as well as the sort of originator. One of the things I was interested in doing when I wrote those novels was to try and find out whether such novels about Canada were possible, because I don't know of any others that deal with Canadian situations in quite that way—and yet they *are* Canadian. Many people said, Oh, I was trying to write as if Canada were England or as if I were an Englishman—but I'm *not* an Englishman, and Canada is *not* England, and English people found the books quite peculiar.

Cameron: The play you mentioned in Cobourg was Russian. I've talked to novelists who've said that if some things that go on in Canada were written about accurately, the only parallel would be in Russian literature.

Davies: Exactly; I agree a hundred per cent. In fact sometimes I get irritated with people who complain that Canada has no drama. The two great Canadian dramatists are Chekhov and Ibsen. The Ibsen and Chekhov situations can be paralleled in Canada twenty times over—the same sort of rather uncomprehending clinging to the past on the part of a certain group of people, and the same sort of self-satisfied littleness of mind that you get savagely dealt with in so many of the Ibsen plays. What do the trolls tell Peer Gynt is their philosophy? Troll, to thyself be self-sufficient: now that's *Canadian.* We make modest faces sometimes to the rest of the world, but the hopeless self-satisfaction of a large number of Canadians is a marvel to behold.

Cameron: I sense a good deal of Freudianism in your thinking. Is Freud someone you've read seriously and thought about a lot?

Davies: Yes, I have, as a matter of fact. I am, I guess, one of the very few people I know who has read Freud's collected works from end to end. Freud was an enormous enthusiasm of mine before I was forty; after forty I came to examine the works of his great colleague Carl Gustav Jung, and I have been, over many years, reading and re-reading and reading again the collected works of C.G. Jung.

Cameron: What gave you that serious an interest in psychoanalytic thought in the first place?

Davies: Well, I had been interested in the notion that this line of thought existed even when I was a schoolboy; when I went to Queen's University there was a remarkable professor of psychology there, Dr. George Humphrey, a notable man who later on became Professor of Psychology at Oxford and wrote a great book on the theory of learning. Humphrey talked a great deal about Freud, about whom he knew a lot, and so I was led to read some Freud. One of the things that enchanted me was that Freud was saying explicitly things which I had vaguely apprehended as possibilities. This whetted my appetite enormously, so on I went. Later on I discovered the same thing in Jung: he had the intellect and the ability to go into very deeply, and to talk about superbly, things which I had dimly apprehended, and so I was eager to follow.

Cameron: Was there something that you became unsatisfied with in Freud?

Davies: Yes, there was. It was Freud's reductive train of thought, which is very welcome to the young mind but becomes, I find, less welcome to the older mind. Freud didn't indulge in this kind of thing, but a great many of his disciples do: you're afraid of thunder because when you were little you heard your father fart and then he spanked you, or something of that sort. Well, this seems to me unworthy of the human race. It's not the kind of cheap wares in which Freud dealt, but it's a thing that people have rather developed from his line of thinking, and much of his thought *is* violently reductive—the tendency to feel that the sexual etiology of neurosis explains everything, and that sort of thing. As Jung pointed out, a surprising number of people seemed to turn up in Jung's consulting room with manifest neuroses which were not primarily related to any sort of sexual hangup. As Jung also pointed out, Freud was an extraordinarily brilliant and very, very successful young man—the darling of his doting mother—who had always lived a city life. Jung had led much more the kind of childhood I myself had had—going to country schools, living with country children, knowing country things, being quite accustomed to animals and the sort of rough and rather sexually oriented—but in an ordinary, daily way—life of the country person.

Cameron: Robert Kroetsch, who lives in the States, feels that Freudianism had great success there because it really appeals to something in American experience, in American ideology: the stress between the good guy and the bad guy, the id and the ego, a kind of Manichean view of the psyche.

Davies: That's extremely interesting.

Cameron: And he felt that Canada was a much more Jungian society.

Davies: Ooooh, this is music to my soul! I think we're a much softer-focussed country. In the intellectual life of the United States, there seems to be such a very, very strong Jewish strain—I would not for an instant suggest that that was a bad thing, but it is an intensely *condition-ing* thing. This intellectual ferocity and sort of black/white quality is very strong there. We're fuzzier, but I think we're more humane, and that's what I think about Jung, too.

Cameron: Kroetsch thinks that instead of seeing polar oppositions all the time, we tend to see two sides of a conflict as aspects of the same thing.

Davies: Yes, and tending to run into one another. You know, we had a very extraordinary evidence of that, in something which I think of as enormously important and significant about Canada: in the character of Mackenzie King, who was our Prime Minister for longer than any other man in any British country in the world. Mackenzie King seemed to be the quintessence of dullness. When you read in his diary that when he met Barbara Ann Scott, the skater, it seemed that he was expected to kiss her, and he "acquiesced"—a duller, more pedantic, dreary man you could scarcely think to find. But what was he in reality? A man who communed with the portrait of his dead mother to get political advice; a man who never set the date of a general election without consulting Nan Skinner, the Kingston fortune-teller; a man who could—and I know this from my father, who knew Mr. King quite well—burst into the most highly coloured and inflammatory kind of blasphemous, evil language when he was discussing certain topics; a man who wooed and sort of managed to keep peace with Québec, but who could talk about French Canadians in a way that would take the paint off a barn door—this was Mackenzie King, this was the opposites running into one another, and this is very Canadian. We now blackmouth him and pretend that we knew about him all the time, but he got elected over and over again; he knew this country marvellously, because he was essentially one of us. We're great withholders, Canadians. This is the sort of thing that my Australian-born wife has pointed out to me. Accept the bland, quiet, rather dull Canadian for what he seems to be: it's just like putting your hand into a circular saw, he'll have the hand before you know what's happened. I think this is very characteristic of our country, and when we really come to ourselves, we're going to be a very formidable people. We're going to be as formidable, I would say, as the Norwegians, or the Swedes, who are very formidable nations indeed; perhaps as formidable as the Russians. I was asked in connection with *Fifth Business* to say what I was trying to do, and I said that I was trying to record the bizarre and passionate life of the Canadian people. Well, I was dropped on by some Canadian critics who said, There I was again, trying to make an effect and talking silly so that people would look at me and think what a fancy fellow I was. *They* were the ones who didn't see what it was. I was speaking the exact truth, but they didn't see it. They *will* not see it.

Cameron: As you spoke, I thought, This is the theme of *Fifth Business*, the contrast between—

Davies: —the appearance and the reality, the grey schoolmaster and the man who was burning like an oil gusher inside.

Cameron: Yes, and at a place much like Upper Canada College, which many people consider the epitome of all that is dull and Edwardian.

Davies: You see, they don't know anything about it. I went to Upper Canada College, and I know what a tempest of passion can go on in there. I'm not saying it's individual to that college; it would be so in any school in Canada, I would think, if you just look. Some very rum things indeed go on in them. Every once in a while a teacher commits suicide, and everyone says, "Poor old Joe, you wouldn't have thought it of him, would you? He seemed to be the most level-headed fellow there ever was." But if you knew old Joe, you knew old Joe had been nutty as a fruit cake for years. I went to a collegiate institute for a while where there was a mathematics teacher who used to break down in the class sometimes; he would burst into tears and say, "Children, I don't want to die of cancer, I don't want to die of cancer." He eventually did—he wasn't doing it at that moment—but we just thought, well, that's the way old Scotty is. The goddamndest things go on in schools.

Cameron: How on earth did you get that astonishing report of the experience of a foot soldier in the First World War? You were all of one year old when the war broke out.

Davies: I wish I could give you some helpful and illuminating answer, but I can't. I just remember when I was a very little boy what some men who were in the war had said. They weren't very eloquent, but it was like that. But I will tell you something which is not dissimilar. In *Fifth Business* I mentioned that the Bollandists, and particularly Padre Blazon, wrote in purple ink. Well, I've never seen a Bollandist, and I think I've only met one Jesuit, and I've never visited the Bollandist Institute in Brussels, or anything of that sort, but I did meet a man in New York called Israel Shenker, who knows the Bollandists very well and is, as far as a layman and a visitor can be, a familiar there. And he said, How on earth did you know that they wrote in purple ink? I said, Well, I divined it—and he nearly fell out of his chair with indignation, because this was a bad answer. But it seemed to me very probable that they would write in purple ink, and apparently they do.

Cameron: But you didn't check.

Davies: How would you check? Would you write to them and say, Please, do you write in purple ink? It isn't a matter of importance, really. I could have just said that they wrote in ink. But it seemed to me—welllllll, *purple* ink. And they do.

Cameron: That's quite a chance to take. Certain kinds of reviewers would be very indignant if they were to find out that in fact it was green ink.

Davies: Yes, they would. They'd be very cross.

Cameron: The religious theme that emerged so strongly in *Fifth Business* had been seen primarily in social terms, I would have thought, in the Salterton novels.

Davies: Yes, but not entirely in social terms. In *Leaven of Malice*, the Dean makes it pretty clear what his view is about what has been going on, and puts in his ten cents' worth in a way I hoped was of some significance. Only a very few people have ever commented on the Dean's sermon at the very end of *A Mixture of Frailties*, which is going on contrapuntally to what the girl Monica is thinking when she's trying to make up her mind whether she'll marry Domdaniel or not. The Dean is preaching a sermon on the revelation of God to man in three forms: a revolution of nature for the shepherd, a penetration by wisdom for the wise man, and a sort of natural grace to Simeon. I think most people look at the italics and say, Oh yes, this is the sermon, and hop to where it gets to be roman type next, to see whether the girl's going to marry the old man or not. But it's there, and it's vital to the book.

Cameron: Has religion something to do with your interest in Freud and Jung?

Davies: Yes. One reason I was drawn to the study of Freud and of Jung was my religious interest, because I very quickly found that for my taste, investigation of religion by orthodox theological means was unrewarding. You never got down to brass tacks, or at least nothing that I ever read did so. You started off by assuming that certain things were true, and then you developed all kinds of splendid things on top of that. I wanted to see about the basic things, so I thought that I would have a look at people who had had a wrestle with these very, very basic things, and Freud was one of them. Freud decided that religion is essentially an illusion: well, I read that, I studied it and chewed on it and mulled it over for quite a long time, but it never fully satisfied me, because it seemed to me that brilliant as Sigmund Freud was, there have been men of comparable brilliance or even greater brilliance who had been enormously attached to this concept which seemed to him to be nothing better than an illusion. One of the figures which bulked very large in my ideas was St. Augustine. I was very interested as a very young boy to discover that I was born on the day of St. Augustine, the 28th of August, and also on the birthday of Tolstoy and Goethe; and I thought, Oh, that's great stuff, splendid! This is an omen. But St. Augustine was a man of the most towering intellectual powers, and if he was willing to devote his life to the exposition of this thing which Freud called an illusion, I felt that the betting couldn't all be on Saint Sigmund; some of it conceivably ought to be on St. Augustine. And there were other figures whom I thought intensely significant. I thought a great deal about it, and then I gradually began to look into the works of Jung and found a much more—to me—satisfying attitude towards religion, but it was not an orthodox Christian one. Orthodox Christianity has always had for me the difficulty that it really won't come, in what is for me a satisfactory way, to grips with the problem of evil. It knows an enormous amount about evil, it discusses evil in fascinating terms, but evil is always the other thing: it is something which is apart from perfection, and man's duty is to strive for perfection. I could not reconcile that with such experience of life as I had, and the Jungian feeling that things tend to run into one another, that what looks good can be pushed to the point where it becomes evil, and that evil very frequently bears what can only be regarded as good fruit—this was the first time I'd ever seen that sort of thing given reasonable consideration, and it made enormous sense to me. I feel now that I am a person of strongly religious temperament, but when I say "religious" I mean immensely conscious of powers of which I can have only the dimmest apprehension, which operate by means that I cannot fathom, in directions which I would be a fool to call either good or bad. Now that seems hideously funny, but it isn't really; it is, I think, a recognition of one's position in an inexplicable universe, in which it is not wholly impossible for you to ally yourself with, let us say, positive rather than negative forces, but in which anything that you do in that direction must be done with a strong recognition that you may be very, very gravely mistaken. This is something which would never satisfy the humblest parish priest, but I live in a world in which forces are going on which I am unable to tab and identify so that the tickets will stick. I just have to get on as well as I can. Various kind people in writing about my books have called me an existentialist, and they won't believe me when I tell them I don't know what an existentialist is. I've had it explained to me many times, but the explanation never really makes enough sense to me to cling. But I have tried to state for you what my position is, and I fear that I've done so clumsily and muddily—but if it comes in clumsy and muddy, it's just got to be that way. Better that than slick and crooked.

Cameron: Perhaps people find it difficult to believe that you don't know what an existentialist is because of your public *persona*, your image, to use the ad-man's word, which—

Davies: —my image, if I've got an image—I suppose I have—has been made for me by other people. Nobody wants to listen to what I want to say. They want to tell me what I think.

Cameron: Well, the image presents you as a man of formidable learning, formidable intellect, and fearsome wit, a man who *would* know about things like existentialism.

Davies: I am not of formidable learning; I am a very scrappily educated person, and I am not of formidable intellect; I really am not a very good thinker. In Jungian terms I am a feeling person with strong intuition. I *can* think, I've *had* to think, and I *do* think, but thinking isn't the first way I approach any problem. It's always, What does this say to me?

And I get it through my fingertips, not through my brain. *Then* I have to think about it, but the thinking is a kind of consciously undertaken thing rather than a primary means of apprehension. Also intuition is very strong in me; I sort of smell things. As for this wit business, it's primarily defence, you know. Witty people are concealing something.

Cameron: What are you concealing?

Davies: I suppose I'm concealing—hmmm. Well, you see, if it were easy for me to tell you, I wouldn't be concealing. I think I am concealing a painful sensitivity, because I am very easily hurt and very easily rebuffed and very easily set down; and very early in life I found out that to be pretty ready with your tongue was a way of coping with that. You know that is a thing which is attributed to Dunstan Ramsay in *Fifth Business*. He was always "getting off a good one". If you can get off a good one once or twice a day, people don't rasp you as much as they otherwise might. They'll do it enough, however defensive you are.

Cameron: Humour does fend people off.

Davies: It's defensive and it's diverting. You know, you suddenly send the dogs off in that direction, instead of straight ahead.

Cameron: One can't talk about these things as a dispassionate interviewer, you know. I've been known in some circles as a person of fairly savage humour myself, and I've always felt that in my case it had to do with profound feelings of insecurity and inadequacy, the sense that I was surrounded by people who knew their way around the world and were at home in it in a way that I wasn't.

Davies: Yes, there's that, and there's also a thing which I expect you have experienced, and which certainly I've experienced: the narrow outlook, and limited sympathies, and want of charity, and general two-bit character of what is going on under your very eyes, which drives you to the point of great extravagance. It comes out in terms of savage, bitter humour, just because you don't quite want to go to savage denunciation, but you want to blast them like an Old Testament prophet. Instead you just swat them around with the jester's bladder. But the impulse is the same.

Cameron: Isn't the effect actually more powerful through humour, and isn't that something else one easily learns?

Davies: Yes, but you haven't learned enough. If you blasted them like a prophet, they might forgive you; if you mock them like a jester, they'll *never* forgive you.

Cameron: That's true, but it's because making a joke of them is a more powerful thing to do.

Davies: Yes, I guess it is, in a way. Oh, it hurts, it stings, and they never forgive it. Now this is interesting: you have made a confession and I've made one. That's why one makes jokes, very often.

Cameron: To make confessions—?

Davies: No, to keep things at bay. It's a sort of distancing thing very often. Not always: I mean, sometimes you do it out of sheer lark.

Cameron: There's a very interesting interplay in your work between theatre and fiction. I suspect that for you theatre is a metaphor of some dimensions.

Davies: It's the element of illusion in life, the difference between appearance and reality. In the theatre you can be in the know about what makes the difference, and it is fascinating that you can know what creates the illusion, know everything about it, be part of it, and yet not despise the people who want the illusion, who cannot live without it. That's important, you know. So frequently it is assumed that if you know how something's done you despise the people who don't. You don't do that in the theatre. You respect them; you know that they know a good thing when they see it.

Cameron: You were with the Old Vic at one point, weren't you?

Davies: Yes, not for very long. For three years, until the war broke out and there was nothing further to be done there or anywhere else in England, so I came back to Canada.

Cameron: You are very strongly Canadian, aren't you, in that you have a very clear sense of who you are and which national community is yours.

Davies: Yes, indeed, and this became very very clear to me within the last two or three years. I've always felt strongly Canadian, which doesn't mean complacently or gleefully Canadian, but Canadian; and my father, who was a Welshman, had always, during the latter part of his life, spent all his summers in his native country, in Wales. My mother was Canadian and her family had been here for a very long time—since 1785 as a matter of fact—but my father always had this extraordinary pull back to his home country. Living in this college, I live in a house which is attached to the college, which is not mine, and when I retire I will not, of course, continue to live there. So my wife and I thought the time had come when we ought to have some place where we'll be able to go when we retire. Distant though that time may be, now is the time to get on with doing it, because when you're retired you don't want to plunge right into the business of finding a dwelling or building one. So we thought, what'll we do? Will we acquire some place in England and retire there? Now this would have been comprehensible because there was this very strong pull of my father's towards the old land, and my wife's family, who were Australians, were always drawn back to England as the great, good place in which all important things happened. We talked it over and decided that my wife had been a Canadian far longer than she'd been an Australian, and that I was really a Canadian, and that to leave this country would be like cutting off my feet. So we built a house in the country in Canada. That was a decision which went far beyond a matter of bricks and mortar. It would be impossible now to leave with the feeling that you'd left for good. We like to travel, we like to get around to see what's doing, we're both terribly interested in the theatre, which means we like to get over to England where the theatre is most lively, and to the continent. But to live, to have your being, to feel that this is where you're going to get old and die, that's another thing—and that's *here*.

Cameron: That doesn't surprise me now, but it might have before I met you.

Davies: Well, as we've said, the popular notion of what I am and why I do things is very wide of the mark. The mainstream of what I do is this sense which I can only call a religious sense, but which is not religious in a sectarian, or aggressive, or evangelistic sense. And also, you know, I really think I've now got to the age where I have to consider what I am and how I function, and I can only call myself an artist. Now people hesitate very much in Canada to call themselves artists. An extraordinary number of authors shrink from that word, because it suggests to them a kind of fancy attitude, which might bring laughter or might seem overstrained—but if you really put your best energies into acts of creation, I don't know what else you can call yourself. You'd better face it and get used to it, and take on the things that are implied by it.

Cameron: What sorts of things are implied?

Davies: A duty to be true to your abilities in so far as you can and as deeply as you can. I think this is where Leacock didn't trust himself, didn't trust his talent. He never thought of himself as an artist, which he started out, I'm sure, to be; his early work has a lot of that quality about it. He decided he was going to be a moneymaker instead, so he didn't become the writer he might have been, and I think that's what you've got to do if you have a chance. I couldn't have said this until fairly recently—you know, you step out in front of the public and say, I am an artist, and they shout, Yeah? Look who's talking, and throw eggs. If you step out in front of them and say, I am a humorist, they say, All right, make us laugh. You can do that fairly easily, but if you say, I can make you feel; I can maybe even make you cry, that's claiming a lot.

Cameron: And do they want you to do it?

Davies: They really do, but they want to be sure that they're in safe hands before they let you do it, because you might be kidding them: you might make them cry and then say, Yah, yah, look who's crying; I did that as a trick—and that's what would hurt them. They're sensitive too. It's an awareness of approaching and retreating sensibilities that is not very easy to acquire.

Cameron: W. O. Mitchell refers to the reader as a "creative partner".

Davies: Yes! Exactly! And you've got to find the way to make it possible for him to create without being ashamed of himself afterwards. Only an artist can do that.

November 9, 1971

The Ghost of Beatrix Potter*

Margaret Lane

Most of the hallowed books of childhood lose something of their magic as we grow older. Beatrix Potter's never. She even, to the mature eye, reveals felicities and depths of irony which pass the childish reader by; the dewy freshness of her landscape recalls Constable; her animals, for all the anthropomorphism of their dress and behaviour, show an imaginative fidelity to nature, a microscopic truth that one finds in the hedgerow woodcuts of Thomas Bewick.

It would be unwise to say any of this if she were still alive. She died in 1943, her brief creative period (thirteen years in all) having come to a close some thirty years before, since when she had evolved into a rather crusty and intimidating person, interested mainly in acquiring land and breeding Herdwick sheep, and whom nothing annoyed more than to have her books appraised on a critical level.

Graham Greene was sharply rebuked when he wrote an essay (a more or less serious one, though Miss Potter took umbrage at what she interpreted as mockery) in which he discussed the period of the 'great comedies'— *Tom Kitten, The Pie and the Patty-Pan, Tiggy-Winkle*—and the subsequent 'dark period' of *The Roly-Poly Pudding* and *Mr. Tod*, the 'near-tragedies', using the tone of a sober scholar discussing Shakespeare. 'At some time between 1907 and 1909,' he wrote, 'Miss Potter must have passed through an emotional ordeal which changed the character of her genius. It would be impertinent to inquire into the nature of the ordeal. Her case is curiously similar to that of Henry James. Something happened which shook their faith in appearances.'

* From Margaret Lane, *Purely for Pleasure*, London: Hamish Hamilton Limited (1966).

Miss Potter was affronted. Nothing, she told him in a 'somewhat acid letter', had disturbed her at the time of writing *Mr. Tod* save the after-effects of 'flu, which had not altered her so-called genius in any way. She sharply deprecated any examination of her work by the 'Freudian school' of criticism. Yet the essay, despite its Gioconda smile, was a flattering one, and anybody but the author of *Peter Rabbit* would have been pleased. She had become, indeed, curiously ambivalent about the whole of her *œuvre*. On the one hand, though she enjoyed the matter-of-fact acceptance of children, she was irritated to fury by any considered appraisal of her work; yet at the same time she could not have enough of the adulation which came to her in her latter years from America. Though she would see no others she would welcome reverent strangers from America, and the two or three poor-quality children's books of her late middle age all went to American publishers and were not in her lifetime allowed to be printed in this country. The reason for this, I believe, was that she was privately aware that they showed a sad falling-off, and while she was fairly confident of praise from the professional priestesses of 'kid lit.' in America she was unwilling to expose herself at home. Though she was impatient of serious attention from her compatriots, any hint of criticism exasperated her still more.

Miss Janet Adam Smith fell into this thorny trap in 1942 with an article in *The Listener*. 'Great rubbish, absolute bosh!' Beatrix Potter wrote to her publishers, who had thoughtfully sent her a copy, thinking she would be pleased to see herself placed, within her limits, in the 'same company as. . . Palmer, Calvert, Bewick and a host of earlier English artists'. To Miss Adam Smith she also wrote that she had read the article with 'stupefaction'. Her wrath was increased by a humourless misconception, since she plainly thought she was being accused of copying these artists. Much taken aback, Miss Adam Smith hastened to reassure her, explaining that 'your illustrations often give the reader the same kind of pleasure as the pictures of these earlier artists', and quoting a relevant passage from one of Constable's letters. Worse and worse. Miss Potter (or Mrs Heelis as she was in private life) now thought she was accused of copying Constable, and replied with a long expostulatory letter, ending with the tart postscript, 'When a person has been nearly thirty years married it is not ingratiating to get an envelope addressed to "Miss".' (An observation which would pass without comment in any of the several books about Tabitha Twitchet.)

I could, if asked, have warned anybody that it was unwise to meddle at all with Beatrix Potter, having nearly done so myself in 1939, when I was very sharply sent about my business. Like most people who have been wholly entranced by her little books in infancy, I had long believed that Beatrix Potter was dead. The occasional new production that one came across in bookshops (*A Fierce Bad Rabbit*, for example) was so egregiously bad compared with the early masterpieces as to strengthen the suspicion that they were written by somebody else. The bookshops denied this, and were not believed. It was no good asking questions about Beatrix Potter, because at that time nobody knew anything about her.

It was in the early days of the war that I first discovered that she was still alive, and living in the Lake District. My step-daughter was at school near Windermere, and brought home tempting scraps of some local legends that were current about her. She was very old. She was very rich. She was a recluse. She was a little mad. She drove round the lake on Sundays in an open carriage, wearing black lace and sitting very stiffly behind the coachman. (This, it turned out, was a memory of her mother, Mrs Rupert Potter, who had done exactly that.) Or alternatively, and this was the most popular legend of all, she did labourer's work in the fields, wearing sacks and rags.

It was very puzzling, but at least it seemed undeniable that she was still alive, and I fell, like Graham Greene and Miss Adam Smith soon after, into the innocent folly of wishing to write about her. Clearly, if she were as reclusive as people said, one must approach with care, and since it seemed desirable to go to the fountain-head as a precaution against inaccuracy or offence, I decided to write to her.

The sensible approach, indeed the only one, since I did not know where she lived, was through her publishers, and I wrote to Frederick Warne and Co. for her address. They replied with ill-concealed horror that on no account, in no possible circumstances, could her address be given. She lived in close retirement, she never saw anybody, they had her express instructions that nobody must ever be allowed to write her a letter.

This could have been final, but it was also rather a challenge to ingenuity, and since my intentions were of the most serious and respectful description I could not see why they should refuse to forward a letter. They did not refuse, though they clearly shrank from the impertinence, and in due course an extremely polite missive was forwarded to Sawrey. I told her of my lifelong pleasure in her books (addressing her, I am thankful to remember, as Mrs Heelis), expressed my admiration and my wish to write an essay on her work, and asked if I might one day call on her to check some facts and submit what I should write for her approval.

Back came, in a few days, the rudest letter I have ever received in my life. Certainly not, she said; nothing would induce her to see me. 'My books have always sold without advertisement, and I do not propose to go in for that sort of thing now.' Her reply could hardly have been more offensively worded if I had asked her to sponsor a deodorant advertisement.

Well, that was that, I thought. It would be impossible to write anything in the face of such hostility, a snub so out of proportion to the occasion. I tore up the letter in indignation, not knowing that I was only one of innumerable people who had had the breath knocked out of them by her acerbity.

And then, in 1943, she died; and Raymond Mortimer, at that time literary editor of *The New Statesman*, asked if I could write him an article on Beatrix Potter. I did my best but it was a poor best, for nobody seemed to know anything about her and the crumbs of fact I could gather were contemptible. I knew only that she had lived and farmed for years in the Lake District and was the wife of a country solicitor. I had to confine myself to an appreciation of her work, and even this contained some sad inaccuracies.

It soon became apparent, from the meagre obituary notices which followed, that I was not the only one who had failed to find out anything. The tone, everywhere, was one of surprise that she had been so recently alive, and it was suddenly borne in on me that what I wanted to do was to write her biography. Alas for such optimism! Here was a life so innocent, so uneventful that one would have supposed the only difficulty would be in finding something to say. Yet, when I approached her widower, the gentlest of men, who received me with a trembling blend of terror and courtesy, it appeared that he considered himself under oath to conceal the very few facts that he had in his possession. He knew remarkably little about her life before their marriage, which had taken place when she was approaching fifty, and what he did know he was unwilling to divulge. He impressed me as a man who for thirty years had lived under the rule of a fairly dominant feminine authority, and whenever, reluctantly, he imparted a scrap of information or a date, he would glance apprehensively over his shoulder, as though *every* moment expecting the door to open.

The house was indeed palpably haunted by her. She had not long been dead, and the imprint of her personality, clearly the more dynamic one in that marriage, was on every chair and table. Her clothes still hung behind the door, her geraniums trailed and bloomed along the window-sill, her muddles lay unsorted at one end of the table while he took his meals at the other, even a half-eaten bar of chocolate with her teeth-marks in it lay whitened and stale among the litter of letters on her writing-table.

Yet he had expressed himself willing, after much patient argument, that a biography should be written, and as a man of honour truly believed that he was doing his best. He had been, it is true, quite implacable at first, and had been at pains to explain, with the most considerate politeness, why such a project was impossible. She would not have wished it, he said; what was more, she would never have allowed it; and here he looked over his shoulder again and blew his nose in a large and dubious handkerchief. The argument which finally convinced him, in spite of his obvious misgiving that agreement was treachery, was that sooner or later, either in England or America, a biography would be written, and it was perhaps better to have it written while he was still alive and could presumably exercise some control over the biographer. He seemed relieved to think that by this means he might escape the attentions of some frantic American, but I had to promise that every word of every line should be subject to his inspection, and left the cottage after that first interview with my point gained, in the deepest possible dejection.

I knew exactly what he had in mind; the sort of biography he had at last brought himself, after the most scrupulous searching of conscience, to consider. It would be about a quarter of an inch thick, bound in navy blue boards with gilt lettering, and would be called *A Memoir of the late Mrs William Heelis*. We did not discuss the point, but I am sure he took it for granted that it would be for private circulation.

Then began a series of evenings which we spent together and which I look back on with misery. Every question, however innocuous, was met with the frightened response, 'Oh, you can't mention *that!*' Any detail of her parents, the date of her birth, even the fact of her marriage to himself fell under this extraordinary prohibition. Night after night I stretched my tact and ingenuity to breaking-point, feverishly changing from subject to subject, retreating at once when I saw his poor eyes watering in alarm, creeping back each night to my cold bedroom at the Sawrey inn to sleepless hours of knowing the whole thing to be impossible.

And then, after many evenings and by the merest accident, I changed my tune. Some tremulous negative, some futile protest over a harmless question, produced that sudden trembling which I have experienced only two or three times in my life and associate with the crisis known as losing one's temper. I found myself banging the table with clenched fist and crying 'Mr Heelis, you *must not obstruct me in this way!* ' The moment it had happened, in the petrified silence, I was overcome with embarrassment. But the effect was magical. He jumped, looked over his shoulder again as towards a voice he knew, pulled himself together, blew his nose, apologized, and suddenly seemed to feel remarkably better. I had never meant to do it, but the inference was plain. Tact, compliance, the yielding deviousness that had cost me so much effort, were things he was unaccustomed to and could not deal with. With decision, with firm opinion, he felt at home, and responded in the most eager and obliging manner. Pleased at last to be able to express his pride in his wife's fame he brought out his boxes of letters, rummaged in the bottoms of wardrobes and at the backs of drawers for photographs, produced such addresses and names as from time to time crossed his uncertain memory. The thing was started; I breathed a sigh of relief; though not without foreboding that my difficulties were only begun.

They were indeed, for over his eager compliance, which even extended to giving me two of her water-colours, hung the cloud of that final inspection of the manuscript which I knew would mar all. Left to himself, with typescript before him, I knew how his trembling hand would score it through, how little, how very little would come back unscathed, how in despair I would fling that little into the wastepaper basket.

Outside the precincts of Castle Cottage there was no such reticence; there were many people living who had known her well, Potter cousins, the niece of her last governess, Miss Hammond, innumerable farm and cottage neighbours who thought of her only as the eccentric little figure that the Lake District remembers—the odd bundle of country clothing, clad in innumerable petticoats, full of good humour, of authority, of sudden acerbities which could flash out quite brutally and inflict hurts where she probably never intended them. 'I began to assert myself at seventy', she wrote to one of her cousins a few months before she died, but this was an understatement. She had been asserting herself for thirty years, and the Lake District had come to respect her as a person it was dangerous to oppose, but very safe to love.

Those who spoke of her with the most feeling were the shepherds and farmers with whom she was most akin in temperament, and to the poetry of whose lives she had always responded, almost with the nostalgia of an exile. On her deathbed she had scribbled a note of indecipherable farewell to her old Scottish shepherd, the 'lambing-time man' who had come to her every spring for nearly twenty years, and with whom she had kept up a long and affectionate correspondence. He had preserved all her letters, dated and wrapped up in little parcels in the recesses of his cottage, and he sent them to me as an act of piety, for love of her memory.

I took innumerable journeys, sometimes with Mr Heelis, more often (and more fruitfully) alone, over the fells and along the valleys, to cottages and farmhouses that she owned, talking to the people who had known her. She had been a workmanlike landlord, most practically interested in fences and gates, the felling and planting of timber, the repairing of walls. As a sheep-breeder she was knowledgeable and shrewd, and the farmers round about thought of her principally as a dangerous rival at sheep fairs and ram shows, an enigmatic and authoritative presence in the Keswick tavern where the Herdwick Sheep Breeders' Association held its meetings.

At the same time I embarked on a sea of correspondence, which ebbed and flowed for more than a year. Beatrix Potter, for all the crowded busyness of her later years, when she was managing a number of farms and doing important work for the National Trust in the Lake District, possessed that last-century sense of leisure which permitted her to write long and frequent letters to a great many people—sometimes even to people she had never met, but whose personalities, when they wrote to her, had taken her fancy. Now, these letters began to flow into my hands, not only from English senders, but from places as far afield as America and New

Zealand; and the task of deciphering and sifting them for their shreds of biographical interest was for a time quite heavy.

To me, the series of letters which Warne's, her publishers for more than forty years, had kept without a gap since the day when they first accepted *Peter Rabbit*, was the most interesting of all, for they reflected her slow and painstaking development as an artist, her emotional growth from girl to woman, her emergence from unhappy and respectable nonentity into the kind of personality about whom biographies are written. The Warne family had played an important, and more than professional, part in her life, and without their help and confidence the book could never have been written.

But however much help I had from her publishers, relations and other friends, there was still to be faced the final confrontation with Mr Heelis, when, as I privately guessed, he would bring up reinforcements of prohibition and his mandate would fall on everything I had written.

I remember that on my last evening in Sawrey, returning from a walk with which I had tried in vain to recruit my spirits, I found a penny lying at the foot of a stile and decided to toss for it; whether I should give it up there and then or write the book as I saw it and be prepared to forget it for years in a locked drawer. The penny said heads, and I put it in my pocket as a charm. The drawer was the thing. I did not know how old Mr Heelis was, nor how I should explain my curious delay; but I was resolved I would not expose myself, or him, to the long-drawn agony of his excisions.

As it turned out, the penny proved a true oracle, for the poor widower, left alone and at a loss without the mainstay on which his thoughts and decisions had so long depended, died a few months after, before the book was finished, and I never paid that final visit to Sawrey. I do not believe he turns in his grave, honest man, nor that the stout little ghost which haunts the place would still, after all this time, find it necessary to be angry.

The Calgary Stampede*

Jack Ludwig

Start with its end, a July Saturday night, the Stampede cowboys pack-rolled, moving on, the rodeo pens and chutes empty, the chuckwagon races over. No race horses parade the track, people in the grandstand want broad-spectrum entertainment, "good fun," "real enjoyment." By 9 P.M. the Calgary Stampede has changed utterly. Now it's all tent show and provincial fair. Western sunset opens its sensational act, turning the uppermost third of the Ferris wheel into a burnished bridge, blinding the roller-coaster cowboys as, whooping up, they slingshot out of the shadowy lower depths. Gears mesh, lock, unlock, release, ratchet a coaster car slowly upward with the sound of a wooden stick rippling a picket fence, electronically augmented, a hundred times magnified, exploding then in a rush of screams and ooh's as subterfuge and centrifuge counterpoint the cry of "Come in, have your pitchur taken—hey, lady, take his pitchur so when he gets older he can see how much fun he had today."

But the barkers are bored, and the shills. That's the way it is at the fag end of any carnie stand. In these closing hours even the suckers may get an even break. A child losing at ringtoss is thrown a huge chartreuse hound dog with cerise tongue and pasted paper goo-goo eyes. A local hardball star has triumphed over the weighted milk bottles, and he and his woman friend walk off swathed in fuzzy Sicilian-tinted snakes and turtles luminous with purples, pinks, greens neither nature nor man ever expected or intended. Five bucks' worth of gaming has pecked out two bits' worth of kewpie dolls for the passing pigeons. Yet they come. Lines everywhere, ten, twelve deep for every blackjack seat at the Frontier Casino, as many or more waiting for a "color" of chips at the roulette tables. Those who never play from anything but "the farthest seat on the dealer's right" in blackjack will take any available place now; and those who never play any color but "blue" or "green" at roulette find all chips grey in the gathering dark. In only a matter of hours the Stampede will close, and who has the patience to wait till next year to lose a winter's stash of coins and bills?

Under canopies, in the few places one may sit and nurse a soft drink or beer without ransoming away an arm and a leg, the older folk stake claims to a seat, sip slowly, sagged and wilted. Arm in arm, leather-jacketed and blue-jeaned couples, parties, gangs, sweep through the crowd, in a great hurry to do it all before the chuckwagon horses change back to mice. Anyone dreaming of "one big break" must make his hit in the next few hours. So it's *hurry hurry, hurry scurry*, the rhythm on the midway, *click shuffle, scrape curse* in the casino, while in easy contrast, the young people space themselves out in front of the Sun Tree, make one joint service a dozen unhurried smokers while tired rock music ekes out its wobbly decibels. From time to time a pot-fogged dreamer floats off in the direction of food and finds lines—lines and lines here as elsewhere, sullen lines, giggly lines, crying lines (where the children wait for their last Stampede ride). The masses mass to pay out what was saved from bread to spend on circuses. In the Stampede's waning moments there are no good rides and bad rides, only short-line rides. If standards existed for what one eats, they're gone too. Soggy corn-on-the-cob turned sodden being served is sloshed over with watery butter, then devoured as if it were the manna. Cotton candy shows bald spots, iced drinks are warm, hot dogs clammy cool, ice cream runny, candy apples adhesive—the standard ingredients of "enjoyment." A massive burned onion cloud hangs over the spielway, memorializing every singed hamburger of Calgary's ten-day blow.

Calgary's a city on the tilt, sloping up from foothills to the Rockies, cowboy country, half cowboytown, and, eastward, flat as Saskatchewan, farmer country, half farmertown. Farmers and cowboys—even without the oil people—were never that easy to tell apart. Now, of course, the Western craze shrouds woman, man and child in blue denim. Farmboys regularly spruce up in boots, cowboy hats, string ties. To resemble their fathers, they part slicked-down hair just over the ear, then lay what's gained right across the forehead to look as up-to-date as dad's wig. Cowboys, farmers, oilmen still hang tight with Elvis sideburns. Women, to save the Stampede from going snooty, wear a metal clip on side curls, but, to prove the Stampede's a night out, forgo plastic rollers and curlers. The inevitable bikers loom up, black leather and studs, studded wristbands, silver zippers, black sunglasses, buckle boots, wartime/peacetime issue, worn by all male members of the enlarged nuclear family, the women in black leather, and democratically studded, everything but the receiving blankets a few have wrapped around infants.

These are the night people. In the morning and afternoon crowds summer was the dominant theme—short shorts, tank tops, cotton dresses, wash-and-wear dude shirts. What's ominous at night—the anachronistic freak show on the midway—in bright sunlight is only absurd. The flack for the Royal American Shows says that complaints "about bad taste from local patrons" persuaded the firm to cut out its "two-headed baby act," stout fellow! *And* its "chamber of horrors." Still, it offers midwayniks a Palace of Illusions featuring such nonbad taste items as Madam Twisto, whose thing is "revolving. . .alive," and another woman called "The Long Neck. . .alive," still another called "The Girl Without a Middle. . .alive," and several other "alives" who, it seems, survived electrocution, hanging, though presumably the biblical fates of stoning and beheading weren't considered worthy of midway display. Lined up to go into one of the Palace's "Main Entrances" is a man seemingly unaware he will soon be under contract—tiny of head, pigeon in the chest, and ballooned-out extravagantly in the middle. Madam Twisto will probably spin seeing him. He is not alone. That guy in glasses you always see coming out of peepshows and bumshows is with him—and several hundred others with forefinger upraised to catch the freaks on an Instamatic, "all alive"!

During its first days I came out to the Stampede when rain washed attendance away. The grandstand was new, all sorts of shifts and changes had been made since 1973's show. The result was little parking, a fair amount of inconvenience. Till more than 140,000 people turned up on closing day the Stampede seemed to be in deep trouble (as it was, attendance in 1974 was only 20,000 shy of the 1973 record—993,777). The new setup, good for horseracing, was, I found, far less suited to the rodeo events. Not till Paul Matte of the Stampede office sneaked me across the racetrack and I climbed into a TV tower just above the chutes was I able to see *the* Stampede. Behind those chutes sat the families, the friends of contestants, the rodeo aficionados as oblivious of the midway as the midway is of the rodeo.

These Calgarians and visitors know rodeo champions the way *Hockey Night in Canada* watchers have a legend on Bobby Orr, or Ken Dryden, or the guys in the "other league," Gordie Howe and Bobby Hull. Aficionados take it personally when the world champion bull rider, Bobby Steiner, doesn't compete in the 1974 Stampede. They want to know if it's because Bobby's hurt or because some other rodeo dares to compete on these dates with the Stampede. If it's the latter, they want to know if Steiner's absence doesn't downgrade the competing this year.

When they check down the program they look for the other "world" (*i.e.*, North American) champions, and, happily, find the champion of champions, Larry Mahan, of Dallas, Texas, on the premises. Mahan has been the All-Around champion five years in a row (six times in all), has won more money in a single year than any other competitor, and has won more money in total than any other competitor. Larry Mahan's presence more than makes up for Bobby Steiner's absence. The rodeo pushers call him, alas, "Mr. Supersaddle," and with a touch of Grand Old Opry refer to him as "the world's most winningest cowboy," but Larry Mahan doesn't need that breed of bull. At the 1974 Stampede he won the All-Around by winning the Bareback bronc championship and placing second in the bull-riding (won by a Saskatoon rider, Brian Claypool, ranked fifth in the "world" behind Bobby Steiner).

There's a great deal of controversy about rodeos. The rodeo people have set up their own "humane" society to take the heat off the charges made by various local, national and international branches of the Society for the Prevention of Cruelty to Animals. Watching the bareback bronc and bull-riding events, I wondered if anybody thought to include man among those animals. There is no way for someone to sit a horse or a bull for eight seconds (or ten, when that's called for) without taking a lot of cruel and unusual punishment. Every rider—successful or instantly thrown—suffers disorientation on touching ground. A sine wave passes through a man's body, not smoothly but powerfully, whiplashing both ends against the humped-up, bucked and belted middle. That kind of violence sends shocks against the brain pan as severe, it seems to me, as a succession of uppercuts on the chin of a boxer. A rider goes against an animal who may be familiar to him, or strange. If strange, regardless of what other riders have told him about the animal's rhythm, he must key on that rhythm in about a second, and then, instantly programmed, adapt what he has learned to the variations in the animal's tricks. Think of the difficulty one has trying to figure an electric maze of complexity and trickiness: a bucking surging bronc or wildly spinning bull of the championship class is far more difficult to figure than a maze, and eight seconds, which, as punishment, may seem a century, is, as time allowed for problem-solving, incredibly short.

Larry Mahan's formula for bull-riding is pure Plato:

"I try," he says, "to picture a ride in my mind before I get on the bull. Then I try to do it by the picture."

Professional cowboys have among their rodeo icons not only the great cowboys but the great animals of circuit history, the most famous of which, a Canadian horse named Midnight, is mentioned whenever the serious challenges of the sport come up. Midnight is buried in the grounds of the Cowboy Hall of Fame in Oklahoma City, Oklahoma, his grave marked by a plaque, "1910-1936," and Angus Cameron, perhaps the most famous of horse book editors and a frequent visitor to the Hall of Fame, tells me the greatest attraction there is Midnight's grave. Cowboys talk about Midnight and such famous bulls as Tornado as "athletes:" they characterize the animals as "honest," by which they mean nothing is held back, and boast of the bronc nobody could ride with almost the same enthusiasm they talk of those great animals someone eventually did stay on.

Transport, the horse Larry Mahan rode to win his bareback bronc riding championship was such an "athlete." To ride him, Mahan lay back like a swimmer trying to float a whipping, powerful, spine-snapping wave. From fifty feet away I could hear the cracking and lashing sounds of Mahan's body as Transport strained and humped to shoot him off—this above the crowd shouts and the announcer's amplifiers. At the eight-second signal two pickup men charged toward Transport and swept Mahan off the still-bucking back, dropped him, stumbling, dazed, rocking on his feet, while they chased and steered the bronc out of the arena into a narrow runway.

Events in a rodeo follow upon one another with the speed and smoothness of a well-managed three-ring circus. At the Stampede I was as impressed by those who make a rodeo work as I was by the contestants. These were the professionals who keep the stock moving into the pens and chutes, who do the saddling, who measure the lengths of braided manila rope needed in bull-riding and saddle bronc-riding, who raise and lower the pen gates, who time an animal's release, who, on a Stampede after-noon when horseracing punctuates the rodeo events, use the putting up of the swinging gates as a rhythmic pause in the largely uninterrupted con-tests they must manage. The mounted pickup men in the bronc-riding and the rodeo clowns in the bull-riding were other pros absolutely essential to the continuity and safety of the bronc- and bull-riding events. By either ac-cident or intent a bull could gore or trample a bucked-off rider, which means, of course, that the "clowns" in their 100-pound rubber barrels or running on cleated football shoes to divert the charging bulls are engaged in a serious and dangerous business. If, say, pickup men on horses tried to scoop up a fallen bull rider the horse would become a most vulnerable target. Therefore the clown operates on foot, always risking a stumble and a fall, and the almost certain injury that would follow. For this reason three clowns usually stand by for the bull-riding events. In the circus, clowns not only amuse but act as a diverting bridge between acts; in the rodeo the clown is an actor and participant. There could be no bronc- or bull-riding events without the pickup men and these clowns.

The rodeo, like a one-ring circus, aims at an illusion: that all contests dovetail, making the rodeo one continuous event, from the opening "Grand Parade" to the climactic bull-riding contest. The rodeo, like any other spectacle, structures its program, starts with "crowd-pleasers," leads into the main events—steer-wrestling, calf-roping, bareback and saddle bronc-riding, bull-riding—careful to intersperse "novice" and "boys" among the professional contests.

At the Stampede finale the Buffalo Ride, featuring young Canadian Indians, or pseudo-Indians mostly, served as "warm-up," "prelim," free-for-all show biz calculated to make an audience not only laugh but pay attention. In the insane confusion of buffalo charging, riders slipping and falling into the dirt, the crowd howled, egged on by the chortle and shout of the announcer. The Buffalo Ride and the Wild Cow Milking contest that followed, though connected to the rodeo, could as easily have been part of the midway hoke outside. The Buffalo Ride particularly, in which almost every contestant was tumbled, bumped, or fell staggering—running off, reeling, or limping—was something Nero's Roman compatriots might have enjoyed as a rather tame prelim for the bigger and better lion games that followed.

With the spectators still yowling and hooting like a studio audience at a TV participation show, the Buffalo Ride gave way to the Wild Cow Milking "fun," with the announcer's shouts even louder now, to encourage the aspiring hysterical. Only then, with the spectators ostensibly "delivered," did the rodeo proper begin, featuring "real" cowboys in a *real* contest directed to the *real* spectators in the rodeo seats behind *real* animals in their pens and chutes. Laughter stopped. Show biz disappeared. Everything, now, was between man and animal. Frequently a child's voice cut through, imploring a father or brother to be careful, or to "give 'im hell, Dad." During the boys' or novices' events women could be heard shouting, for the most part, *stay-on*, *stick-with-it*, *hang-in* encouragement. Nationalism touched the Stampede as it does most things Canadian: though the spectators wanted the big-time American rodeo contestants at the Stampede, they also wanted their Canadian heroes to knock them off.

In the first real rodeo event, bareback bronc-riding, the competition, curiously, fell into two groups—Canadian novices who hadn't scored *higher* than 138 in two previous short go-rounds (or heats), competitors who hadn't scored *lower* than 140. Yet even here, with little chance to beat the eventual winner, Mahan, Mel Hyland of Alberta cowboytown, Ponoka, the 1972 "world" saddle bronc champion, made a great try, actually outscoring Mahan on the short-go, 76-75. Every year, people in the stands told me, they look for signs that more Canadians are arriving as rodeo champions. If 1974 wasn't a good year for the bareback, it was an excellent year for the saddle bronc- and bull-riding events.

What Calgary saw were two young Saskatchewan competitors, eighteen-year-old Melvin Coleman, of Pierceland, and twenty-year-old Brian Claypool, of Saskatoon, win the saddle bronc- and bull-riding championships respectively. It was only Mel Coleman's first year as a non-novice competitor. A few old grizzled American cowboys grumbled that the judging seemed to favor Canadians but, for the most part, the results were conceived as fair. Brian Claypool, as I've already indicated, stood high among bull-riding competitors on the continent, so his victory wasn't all that surprising, though Coleman's, won in competition against such stars as Dennis Reiners and Marty Wood, was. Not only was Coleman young; this was his first try at a Stampede "North American" championship; in 1973 he was second in the *novice* competition.

"Hey," I hollered down from my tower platform at a cowboy who didn't look too happy when Coleman's high short-go score of 82 was announced, "what do you think of that?"

"He-e-ll," the man said in an accent I took for Texan, "they musta give him a little somethin' extra for wearing' that checker shirt."

A third Saskatchewan competitor, Richard Todd of Wood Mountain, had a superb short-go time of 4.2 in his last steer-wrestling try, actually beating the eventual champion, Tom Ferguson, the present "world" All-Around champ, by half a second, but in the aggregate and average lagged far behind Ferguson and another circuit star, Darryl Sewell.

Event followed event, each one settling a championship, each one meaning money. As usual, Larry Mahan's winnings put him in front of everybody else; but when one thinks of the punishment someone like Mahan has to absorb in order to win a total of, in Calgary, $7,468, it shivers the sports perspective. A successful rodeo rider will earn in a year what Johnny Miller or Jack Nicklaus walks off with winning a big stop on the golf tour—$50,000. Only a few top rodeo figures will earn in a year two-thirds of what Miller or Nicklaus get for coming out on top *twice*. No cowboy could hope to earn, in three or four years, the more than $300,000 Nicklaus and Miller have each won in their best tour years.

"We know it don't make sense," says Freckles Brown, a more or less retired rodeo cowboy, "get on another head o' stock, land on your shoulder, land on your head, pick yourself up, get on a rig, go another 900 miles, and get on another head o'stock. . ."

In the novice saddle bronc ride, a young Alberta rider, Tom Crowe, thrown from his mount before he knew he was on a "head o' stock," crashed to the ground, then crawled through the sunwarmed dirt to curl up like some hurt creature in the shade of the cement dugout under the grandstand stage. Stunned and huddled into himself, obviously hurting, Crowe spurned the stretcher bearers who raced out to help him. Cowboy macho. The code: *Walk off under your own legs, even if they is broke. Don't give no head o' stock the satisfaction o' knowin' he hurt you.* Shaky, doubled up, hobbling, Crowe made it out of the arena to much code applause, the spurned stretcher-bearers jogging beside him.

In the boys' steer-riding championship, though, the rodeo clown closest to the youngest, smallest contestant, Cam Bruce, snatched him off the steer's back at the horn, rather than risk the small boy being thrown that long fall from the animal roof. In the second half of the steer-riding, Daryl Schacher shot out of the chute, clinging two-handed (by the rules) as his steer bolted, smashing into the fence with Daryl still holding on tight, and everyone in the stands shouting. The clowns rushed in to pull Daryl free while other clowns chased the steer back through the runway. The result of it all? Daryl was given an official re-ride!

Sometimes the novices, disappointed, reacted like much younger boys. In the saddle bronc competition one competitor came in far ahead of everyone else but was penalized for a rule infraction on his final short-go, and assigned a zero. In a second the certain winner was turned into a loser. In disappointment and anger he began to cry, while his friends and fellow-competitors gathered to console him.

Only once—after the Buffalo Ride and the Wild Cow Milking show biz act—was anything in the arena arranged for Nero and his Romans, the Wild Horse Race. The rules called for several competing three men-with-a-wild-horse teams, each made up of:

1. a wild horse
2. an "ear man" who was supposed to bite the wild horse's ear in a Spockian touch intended to "distract and calm the animal"
3. the "shank man" who clings to the horse's shank while
4. the rider, or, one assumes, "ass man," tries to vault himself up into a saddle he himself has attached to the horse.

At the signal to begin, all aspiring riders try to saddle, mount, and then ride over a short designated "track," the first horse and rider to cross a white washed line being the winner.

While the announcer chuckled and confounded, while the tucked-up-in-the-stands spectators screamed and laughed, terror dominated the arena below. I saw it in the ear man's face, the shank man's spine, the aspiring rider's eyes—because his face tried hard to show *macho*, arrogance, pugnaciousness. Knee-bent the ear man cringed. Terror showed in the team ducked beneath a rearing horse's flailing hooves in fear that the wild horse, and animal retribution, would come crashing down. And greater terror, of being trampled by frightened, swerving animals bolted free of aspiring saddlers. Ear men and shank men hanging on as horse body slammed up against horse body, dragging neverseated riders through the dust spitting dirt and clutching at empty saddles. A few horses charged about aimlessly, saddles slung below their bellies like mailman's pouches. Heels dug in the dirt, captive heroes skidded by like water skiers, or startled farmboys trying to hang onto a plow behind Secretariat.

Loosed, horses struggled into an animal circle, a willed roundup full of nightmare Picasso images—teeth bared, streaming manes, frightened eyes, distended nostrils, taut vein-swollen necks, bodies shiny with sweat.

And what was it all for? The Emperor Nero, and many others in the stands, told the horses wouldn't kill anybody during their act, decided this was as good a time as any to go out for a hot dog and/or the men's room, and so missed the whole shebang. And those who run the midway "freak" show, interested in nothing *but* the Wild Horse Race, could now go back to their own exhibitionism, satisfied they had seen everything the rodeo had to offer.

Steer-wrestling and bull-riding slowly brought the rodeo back to the Stampede, and when those contests were over, so was the cowboy's Stampede—all but the chuckwagon races. But to see the chuckwagon races one had to leave the grandstand, wander the midway or casino areas for about three hours, spending, drinking, eating, and then, in order to watch the chuckwagons, pay another ticket's worth. The younger people around the Sun Tree wanted to see the chuckwagon races, they told me, but couldn't afford the price of another ticket. Some had already put out seven or eight dollars on little or nothing—without seeing any of the rodeo events they said they were most interested in seeing.

"It's all rip-off," an Edmonton girl told me. "This is supposed to be fun and we can't even make it into that grandstand. Why couldn't they have the rodeo and the chuckwagons all at once? Rip-off—just rip-off. Even this, that's free," she said, waving her hand at the Sun Tree, "this is supposed to be what young people want. It's insulting. It's the worst rip-off of all."

I left the Stampede grounds after the rodeo events, took a cab to a restaurant next to the Calgary Inn where a long line waited neatly to get in. Dates, twos, couples, all neat, all dressed up. I asked a couple what the line was all about.

"Cabaret," a young man said, beaming, "live entertainment."

He sounded as if he had just recently experienced the very opposite of live entertainment. Or, to put it another way, the Stampede midway.

When I got back to the Stampede the urgency of do-it-all-before-midnight-tolls had taken over. People were turning up for sweepstake draws, pots o' gold—that sort of thing. And the chuckwagon races.

From the very top of the grandstand I could see the racetrack, the stock pens, the stable area for racing horses, the river, everything now, in reddened sun tones, cast in the segment of the color spectrum that excludes anything blue. In the two symmetrical rodeo pens—one for horses, one for steers and calves—animal and earth and corral fence were all tinted brown, golden, orange. Everything was peaceful, serene—no hoke, no hype, no spiel, no violence, no show biz. The track, on which the chuckwagon race would begin, was in evening shade, but behind the pens the track lay in bright sunshine. Even as a recreation of something that might never have been, the chuckwagon race made it—the rig, the four horses, the hunched-forward driver, the tense outriders in helmets, cowboy hats or jockey caps getting ready to stow the stove and tent poles, mount, and race. Four wagons, everybody frozen except for the horses swishing tails at un-race-conscious flies.

All four teams broke at the start, inscribed their beautiful figure eights, then galloped onto the track, tails streaming, the drivers up and hollering, the outriders on their horses and out on the track in their race within the race. It took less than half an hour to run the four last heats of the chuckwagon finale and out of it emerged another young Canadian champion, Kelly Sutherland, 22, not only the grand winner but also the winner of the third spot, and a total of almost $11,500 out of a possible $67,000.

When the chuckwagon races ended, so, for many, did the Stampede. The midway was still open, the casino thrived, the rides went their appointed round, but the rodeo was gone. The year's peak flattened, the end of the circus that made the struggle for bread mean something special. At midnight the coach and horses were only pumpkin and mice—till summer '75.

A Northern Journal

From the diary of a journey in the late summer of 1968*

George Woodcock

Churchill: North from Thompson a land that from the air seems infinitely flat. Stunted taiga forest, lakes, yellow-green marshes with clumps of dead, grey trees, muddy slow rivers serpentining to Hudson's Bay. For a few miles out of Thompson, dirt roads, sawmills beside the rivers. Then the empty wilderness. Nearer to Churchill curious ice age formations: perfect circles of trees surrounding piles of whitish limestone rocks, accidental fabrications of ancient glaciers but regular enough to appear the creations of megalithic men. The circles are separated by dull green stretches of tundra. At Churchill, as we drive in from the airport, all the tiny trees, last scouts of the taiga, are one-sided, their seaward branches shaved by the wind of the Bay.

The coastline at Churchill. Ice-sculptured Henry Moore rocks, pools white with water crowsfoot, dwarf tart-fruited wild gooseberries hugging the crevices. A botanical frontier; the avens is arctic, but the fireweed is narrow-leaved, the southern species. We stand on the low summit at Cape Merry, looking across the estuary to the stone star of Prince of Wales Fort. The beluga whales are rolling in the heavy currents, their backs dazzlingly white against the cold blue of the water. At evening the Indians hunt them from canoes, with harpoon and rifle. They sell them to the cannery, $1 a foot length for whales up to ten feet, $1.25 a foot above that length; the skin will be canned as muktuk, the flesh sold to feed mink.

* "A Northern Journal" from *The Rejection of Politics* by George Woodcock. Used by permission of the author and New Press, 30 Lesmill Road, Don Mills, Ontario, Canada.

Churchill—six thousand people spread over five miles and as many subcommunities: an Indian village, an Eskimo village, a Métis slum of shacks—some built of crates and roofed with tentcloth, a ghetto of government officials at Fort Churchill, living in old barracks with utilidors and clubs, very sahib-like in a northern way, and the townsite itself, near to the docks and the railway.

The townsite: Hudson Square with the H.B.C., competing supermarket, wooden shed cinema, federal building and rival Oblate and Anglican missions tucked away in a straggle of side streets, among little wooden houses such as one finds in by-passed and decaying prairie towns; they are worn drab not by time but by eight months of winter. The railway has changed the way of life. Prices in the hotels are little more than in Winnipeg, and the cooking is better. H.B.C. is no longer a fur trade post, but a miniature department store. The highway will be a long way coming up from Thompson—the early seventies at least. But—with five miles of paved road going to nowhere—there are already many taxis, and even a motel. Permafrost makes some other facilities hard to get. A woman taxi driver tells me most houses have honey-buckets, and galvanized tubs filled by hand. "Perhaps you don't get as many baths as you'd like. But I was brought up on a farm. I'm used to it!"

The gravelly dustiness of Churchill. Off the one paved road, the houses are built beside frost-heaving dirt lanes. No gardens or lawns; even the baseball oval is rough, bare ground, so slow is growth here. Churchillians tell of the southerner who arrived in mid-February with golf-clubs. Point of the story is that he would have been just as outlandish at any season, since there will never be anything nearer to a green than a few tufts of mauve-sheened wild barley.

Two ships are standing beneath the grain elevators; one is Swiss. Later, in the Oblate's Eskimo Museum, three of the sailors come in and talk the harsh Schweitzerdeutsch of Basel. It is strange, at a port so far inside Canada, to hear voices from so far inside Europe. On the quay there are Volkswagens; nearest route from German ports to Winnipeg and Regina is via Hudson's Bay.

Most of the Eskimos in Churchill are in one way or another connected with the government and relatively well off. But this is really Indian country, as it was when Kelsey and Knight first came and the Indians and Métis have sure work only for three months of the year, when the ships are being loaded. A few have regular labouring jobs, some fish or hunt beluga in season, a few women work in the hotels, but most are unemployed and on welfare two thirds of the year. They accept their condition with a mingling of pleasure at not having to work—lacking our puritan ethic—and resentment at their second-class status. They hate the white man as the Eskimo do not—yet.

Polar bears are becoming urbanized. Last year seventy-three were counted in the neighbourhood of Churchill. Ten have been seen at a time at the garbage dump. An Indian was mauled recently.

Rankin Inlet: A long airstrip, stones and gravel, slashing across the tundra. No buildings, but a little crowd waits around the yellow panel wagon of the Department of Transport, the green pickup truck of the Arctic Research and Training Centre, and the H.B.C. tractor and trailer that takes the mail into the settlement. Everyone of consequence is there—the Administrator, Neil Faulkner, the H.B.C. manager, Vic Pearson, the Oblate missionary, Father Papillon, and Bob Williamson, the head of the research centre—three Englishmen and a Frenchman, typical of the arctic pattern, where Europeans have always fitted in better than native Canadians. We bump into Rankin Inlet over a hummocky dirt road, seated in the H.B.C. trailer among the mail. Ahead of us an Eskimo speeds on a skidoo over the stony, snowless ground.

The landscape. Low rocky hills, bare scanty growth of lichen, dwarf bushes, minuscule flowers. I walk out from the H.B.C. staff house, and in ten minutes pick a dozen different arctic plants still blooming in mid-August. On the hillside the great squat cylinders for the oil that keeps Rankin Inlet—this community of five hundred Eskimos, fifty whites—alive during winter and during summer for that matter, since the August temperature is still only in the forties. Above the oil tanks, on the crest of one of the hills, a manshaped Eskimo cairn: how old no one knows, for the people here are all strangers, gathered from many bands coming together after the great barren-land famines of twenty years ago. Stark and decaying, its corrugated iron rotting with the salt air; the tower of the nickel mine that brought them, now abandoned, still dominates the settlement. Below it gaudy pyramids of red and orange oildrums give Rankin Inlet its only colour. Out in the Inlet, the Eskimos, in powered canoes, race around the little vermilion ships of the Department of Transport, and a barge chugs in from Whale Cove down the coast, carrying muktuk for the cannery which a German immigrant operates at Rankin—the only private industrial plant on the whole western shore of Hudson's Bay. This year the annual H.B.C. boat has been delayed through running aground elsewhere in the Arctic, and the warehouse in the store echoes with emptiness. This is no longer the catastrophe it would have been in the days before the planes began to fly regularly into the Arctic, but air freight makes goods expensive, and this is a burden particularly on the Eskimo community, since most of the whites are government employees whose stores are brought in by the Department of Transport.

Rankin Inlet is one of the relatively fortunate places in the Arctic. The Eskimos do not like to be idle, and there is plenty of work: in summer construction, in winter the crafts centre; some Eskimos work at the H.B.C. store, some in the government office as clerks and interpreters. A few men fish and follow the whale in its season, but, though many were caribou hunters (and teenagers remember the life of the camps as part of their childhood) there are only half-a-dozen men in the settlement who still live off the barren land. They are older men. It is also older men who remember the traditions and, in the crafts centre, stop their work and sing songs for me to record. They are their own songs, personal property, inherited from their fathers. Okoktuk sings the song of the Hungry Camp; Erkuti sings the song of Caching the Meat. At Rankin the drum dances are no longer performed. We must wait for Baker Lake; there we may be lucky.

We try to probe for the social structure of Rankin Inlet. Among the whites it is obvious—the ladder of bureaucratic hierarchy, since more than eighty per cent are government employees, with the missionary, the H.B.C. people and Bob Williamson occupying honorary positions towards the top. About the Eskimos we know only what we are told, which is as much as most of the resident whites know since, like us, all but three speak no Eskimo. There is no tribal structure, since The People never banded together in more than extended family groups (rather like Hindu joint families), but in Rankin, where Eskimos from coastal settlements and inland camps came together, an undefined stratification has arisen, with the coast people—more prosperous in the past and more practised in the white men's ways—forming the upper stratum. Yet some of the celebrated artists, like Tiktak, are men from the barren land who once hunted the caribou.

The Eskimo here have their own community council, their own housing committee which assesses rents for the government-built houses, and men rise by intelligence and also by oratory, which is still greatly esteemed. But there are other men who, if not exactly powerful, are feared for reasons older than government-sponsored committees. These are the men still reputed to be shamans, who either practised in the past, or have received the 'gift' by descent. A young woman says there are three of them in Rankin Inlet; she refuses to name them. The white men say they no longer practise. The Eskimos evade answering when we ask this question. A missionary asserts that the Eskimos no longer *believe* in the powers of the shaman, but fear him in a precautionary way.

Sadie, sixteen, a girl from Rankin, says of Churchill: "What a big place! Once I got lost there!" One of the men has been to Montreal. "There were four of us, among all those people," he says. "We might have died, and nobody would have known."

9.45 p.m. The power station hooter. It is curfew time. By order of the Eskimo Community Council, all children under sixteen must be indoors.

Tiktak the carver. A man with a deep-lined mobile face who seems to be in his fifties but is not sure of his own age. He is partly crippled by a fall, so that, though he does some hunting still, he cannot go far from the settlement. A great humour, so that sometimes one feels it is a life of laughter that has creased his face. A shy giggle and oriental protestations of inadequacy when we praise his work. "I am a bad carver!" He has been carving only five years, and maintains that he still works without premeditation, taking the stone and letting the shape that is in it emerge. He wears a singlet, his wife a cotton frock like a prairie pioneer woman, but when he comes out to be photographed Tiktak puts on gumboots and a loud blue check jacket. A portrait of Trudeau hangs on his wall. He thinks the old life of the barren land was better than the new life. Caribou meat was better than store food, which he and his wife agree is 'too sweet'. Now, he says, he must work all the time to earn the money to live, because almost all his food is bought.

Caribou is still eaten raw in Rankin; so is polar bear. One bear, whose skin we see drying, was killed a few days ago, and still it is being eaten. Outside the Eskimo houses the flesh of arctic char turns mahogany brown as it dries in the air into food for the sleigh-dogs.

The Eskimo families all talk of children dead, suggesting high death rates in the past. They never know offhand the exact number of children they have had, but count slowly, turning down a top finger joint for each child. Is this bad memory? Or a lingering difficulty with numbers? Or perhaps some superstitious fear of being too exact? Half the families we meet have children adopted according to Eskimo custom.

Selina, a sophisticated little miss in a mini-skirt and open-work stockings who addresses us in English better than any other in the Eskimo village. We find she has been in Ottawa training as a nurse. She is looking forward to returning there. Does she intend to go back and work among her people? She would much prefer to go to Vancouver!

The white fox is the principal source of fur income at Rankin as elsewhere. It runs in a four-year cycle linked to that of the lemmings. This is a low year; Vic Pearson expects to gather no more than $8,000 worth to stack in the cool attic above the H.B.C. store. During the season only four or five trappers have been out full time, out of five hundred people.

In the south we have always believed Eskimos wilted in heat. In Rankin it is we who wilt, for all the Eskimo houses are extravagantly over-heated, to an average temperature of about 75°F.

Eskimos have no vocal way of signalling over long distances, like Swiss yodelling or Tibetan 'far-away singing'; they are so tuned to perceiving the slightest movement at a considerable distance that they communicate over great spaces by semaphore of the arms.

Motor toboggans are quickly replacing dog-sleighs; the R.C.M.P. now search with them, and there are less than half-a-dozen dog teams in Rankin. Similarly, canoes have replaced the kayak and the umiak, both of which have belonged for years to the museums and to history.

Northern prices. A good meal at the Hudson Hotel in Churchill costs $1.75. At the bunkhouse in Rankin it costs $5.00. An index of the difference between a community served by rail and one served only by air and the annual supply ship.

Baker Lake: Leaving Rankin Inlet, we fly over a scape so dotted with small pools there seems barely more land than water. A jigsaw of blues, buffs and browns—little rock visible—the smooth undulations of the tundra. Suddenly, grey-dun specks fan out beside a lake like a small explosion; a little herd of caribou, smaller than flies, scared by the plane.

Finally, we see the spread of Baker Lake, and the broad waving band of the Thelon River, cutting its silvery course through the tundra to the west. The first view of the settlement: white, red-roofed buildings of missions and stores strung along lakeshore, the lines of Eskimo huts behind them, the buff specks of tents spattered on the tundra beyond.

Wayne Sinclair, H.B.C. manager, meets the plane, with the administrator, and Father Choque in beret and mackinaw. We are to stay with him at the Oblate mission. It is a one-man establishment: tiny church, guest rooms, Father Choque's apartment, all under the same roof. Father Choque does everything, conducting services, keeping the house tidy, cooking, making bread, cutting and hauling ice for water from the lake in winter, helping with the problems of all the people who come to him (and by no means all from his flock), scanning the shore with his binoculars to identify arriving planes, and maintaining communication through short-wave radio with the missions in the rest of the north. He has been here since 1944, longer than any other man, white or Eskimo, in Baker Lake. When he first came, no Eskimos lived here. There were the Anglican and Oblate missions, the H.B.C. and R.C.M.P., and the Eskimos came only at certain seasons to trade. They lived on the barren land, in little groups of two or three related families, staying put in igloos during the winter. It was only at the beginning of the 1950's that some of them began to stay permanently in Baker Lake. In the past Father Choque would visit the people living on the land. He went in winter, by dog team. In summer they would be on the move, with their skin tents, and hard to find. "Those were good days," he says sadly.

Sound of gulls wailing: large grey and white gulls. The arctic terns hover like kestrels, drop with stone-like rapidity, and fly with beautiful sickle-winged grace. Small greyish birds flit over the tundra with undulating flight. This morning a falcon sat for an hour on an old sleigh on the shore. Rarely, white falcons are still seen.

I walk beyond the settlement on to the tundra, like a great dry sponge, or, even more, like a landscape of loofah: the tall lichens, pale grey and dull green, matting with alpine heather, blueberry, bearberry and a few ferns; the tiny leaves of the miniature shrubs already turning bright red and orange. In some places purple splashes of willow herb and yellow of arctic poppy and arnica. In the gullies going down to the lake are aged willows, two feet high, gnarled and twisted like bonzai trees.

White men are called Kabluna, which is said to mean eyebrow. Sometimes this is applied to Eskimos who have become more or less acculturated through government employment. Thus there are three groups in Baker Lake, the few acculturated and usually privileged ones, the equally few(and mostly elderly) men who try to sustain the old hunting life, and the great intermediate majority adopting much of the white way of life but with little purpose or direction as yet. A people on the way to alienation, but still a generation behind the Indians, and so not so hopeless and potentially explosive; but generations these days pass quickly. At present they accept too easily, with smiling helplessness, what is done for and to them. This is obviously more pleasant for everyone than the resentful sullenness of so many Indians. But is it more healthy? One gets the impression that, in relation to their numbers, the government is doing far more for the Eskimos than for the Indians—perhaps trying to assuage our general feeling of guilt for having neglected the Indians—but without much imagination or foresight, because bureaucrats still see Eskimos as *numbers*. The creativity and imaginativeness of the Eskimos are being only slightly utilized, and then often wrongly. Think of much Eskimo art, mechanically produced under dreary working conditions in government craft centres. Think also of the exploitation by official agencies, theoretically set up to aid Eskimos. We calculate that, on the average, through the triple markups before his work reaches a store 'outside', the Eskimo artist gets sixteen per cent to twenty per cent of the price for which one of his sculptures will eventually be sold. A white artist, selling a painting or sculpture through a gallery, gets sixty-six per cent!

An Eskimo woman, whose husband had received $200 a week before, went to the administrator for welfare. He asked what had happened to the $200. It had been spent on food, soap, and paraffin, she said. Surely not all of it! Well, there was also $60 for a bicycle. Her child had been unhappy because his friends had bicycles, so she could do nothing but buy him one. People on the barren land, where tokens were used in trading less than ten years ago, still have little sense of the 'value' of money, while they retain the old summer attitude of feast-or-famine (though they seem to have lost the providence that led them to set up caches of meat at the end of the autumn to tide over the winter). Consequence: they buy to the bottom of their pockets without thought of cost or value: imported sliced bread at 75¢ a loaf, small apples and oranges at 45¢ for two fruit. Even at such high air-freight prices, twenty-five cases each of apples and oranges vanished in half a day at the local store.

While the whites in Rankin and Baker Lake bake their own bread, the

Eskimos prefer bannocks of flour and lard, and eat great quantities of pilot biscuits.

August welfare at Baker Lake, $3,200. In winter it will average $7,000 to $8,000 a month, often at the rate of $200 a family. Now—in late summer— there are twenty Eskimo men in Baker Lake earning $400 to $500 on construction. In December, when the work is ended, most of them are expected to go on welfare.

In the Baker Lake area there is now only one family which still obstinately lives on the land, and five or six other families—out of six hundred people—go into camp during summer. It seems as though the last snowhouse was built last winter, and there will be no more.

Last year at Baker Lake twenty-seven children were born, an astonishing birthrate of forty-five per thousand. One woman in that year had her sixteenth child.

Sunday Services in the Arctic. Father Choque rings the mission bell in the morning, and with the single monotonous toll I am taken back fifty years, to the village church of my childhood, as in many ways the north returns one to a younger, more pristine age of man. The whites gather in Father Choque's little sitting room, with the geraniums blossoming in the window: the administrator's and school principal's families, some French Canadian and Irish summer workers, the Chinese nurse from Hong Kong wearing a mantilla of black lace. We troop together into the chapel, finding the back filled with Eskimos—but there are some Eskimos also who mingle with the whites in the front rows. Altogether there are less than fifty of us, but the small church is full. Father Choque, in green vestments that contrast with his daily mackinaw and beret, conducts mass in Latin, preaches in Eskimo and English. An elderly Eskimo plays the harmonium, the children alternately cry and sleep, a woman in front of me suckles her child during the sermon. One would have thought this simple but colourful ceremony not as alien to the Eskimo as the Low Anglican service at the other end of the village, but such matters seem to have been determined in the Arctic almost entirely by what church happened to arrive and build up loyalties first. In Baker Lake it is to the Anglican church that the people flock at evening along the insect-ridden lakeshore, and we have difficulty squeezing into a seat at the back of the church, which holds at least two hundred people. Immediately, when I have adjusted my tape recorder and can begin to take notice, I am reminded of the missionary churches of south India, for the women and girls are on one side of the aisle and the men and boys on the other, while the singing, as in the Syrian churches of Kerala, is unaccompanied by the organ. But through the open windows one sees not coconut groves, but the tundra, splashed with the purple of arctic willow herb, and the mosquitoes sail in from the hot night in clouds unimaginable in most parts of India. With too obvious appropriateness, the first hymn is "From Greenland's icy mountains to India's coral strand," sung lustily and unhesitatingly, like all the other hymns; the Eskimos are well trained, since there are services on Tuesday and Thursday nights as well, lest Satan find for idle hands some evil. Much of the service is conducted by the old Eskimo catechist, who wears a medallion on a red ribbon over his surplice. The missionary, who came direct from England four years ago with virtually no orientation, preaches in a halting Eskimo, to the accompaniment of much coughing and crying, while the older children play in the aisle with their plastic cars and aeroplanes and the adults assume a look of seemly and impenetrable boredom. One wonders how much more Christianity really is in the lives of the Eskimo—or most of them at least—than a routine in a life impoverished by the loss of the hunting pattern.

From the mission we can just see the white cross of the cemetery up on the hilltop behind the settlement. On the way there, climbing from the beach, we pass the one-room plywood boxes which the government first put up as Eskimo houses; the doors are all open to give ventilation. Around them water stinking of sewage stands in deep puddles, where the children play. Beyond this slum of modernization, the tents—widely spaced over the tundra—seem healthier and more appropriate to the Eskimo life; outside them the dogs, large, shaggy and dirty white, lie about at the end of their chains. (Unleashed dogs that wander through the settlement are shot, for fear of rabies, endemic among wolves and foxes in the barren land.) Higher up we pick our way between bogs white with cotton grass, sometimes jumping from one spongy tussock to the next. There are berries on the minute blueberry bushes, rather tasteless, and little mauvish mushrooms and puffballs. On higher levels, as we climb, pink bearberry flowers and large-cupped white heather. Also cushions of minuscule pinks. The cemetery lies on a rock platform to which one climbs through defiles between piled cubical rocks, which remind me of Inca ruins near Cuzco. The rocks are bright with green and orange map lichen. Above us now rises the white cross, tall and overbearing. The graves are stones piled over rough wooden boxes, with a small white wooden cross at the head of each, bearing English and Eskimo names of the occupant—Eskimo name in syllabics—and dates of birth and death. Many small stone piles suggest the high child death rate of the recent past. The Roman Catholics and the more numerous Anglicans are separated even in death by a no man's land of bare rock, empty except for two uncrossed graves. The R.C.'s have a stone monument to an Oblate Father who drowned when his sleigh went through the ice in the Back River; his body was never found. Anglicans have two monuments put up by the R.C.M.P. for Eskimo special constables. No white men are buried here.

From under the great cross, splendid views of little upland lakes set like turquoises in the undulating land, and Baker Lake itself; its hazy blue waters, golden sandbanks and yellow-green shores reminding one of

Titicaca, as the tundra in general reminds one inevitably of the Andean antiplano, one so far up in the north, the other so far up in the clouds, and therefore alike.

Talk with S., an old hunter and trapper, who carries sewn on his chest the number by which all Eskimos are recognized—like convicts—by the non-Eskimo-speaking officials who lord over them. He is sixty and this is his first summer off the land: his legs are letting him down, and there is work to be got with the Department of Transport. Normally he would go in September to kill and cache the caribou that would feed him and his dogs for the winter of trapping. He would take only tea and sugar (curiously Eskimos seem to feel no need of salt); tea and caribou would sustain him through the winter. Often the caribou would be eaten raw, though when willows were available for fuel he would try to cook once a day. If he ran out of tea, he would drink caribou broth instead. Fish he ate only in emergency; even arctic char, which seems to us so much of a delicacy, is regarded by Eskimos as fit only for dogs. S. trapped mainly white fox, with some wolf and wolverine; the best trapper in Baker Lake, he never went short even in the famine years, for he was able to go far on his own in search of game, relying on his knowledge of the land and a good rifle. He believes in having the best of both old and new worlds, boasts of possessing a dog team and two skidoos!

S. does not have much use for the missionaries, or for the new administrators, but he thinks there was good in the coming of 'the law'. Before 'the law' came, he says, the Eskimo hunters killed without discrimination, for the excitement, slaying from kayaks with spears and later guns when the caribou crossed the rivers, and keeping pace with the herds by laying their paddles on the backs of the swimming animals. Thus many beasts not needed for food were killed each season. Like most Eskimos and some white oldtimers, S. does not accept the view of the wildlife bureaucrats that it was a vast reduction of the herds that actually led to the great famines of the late 1940's and early 1950's. He believes the caribou merely showed their intelligence by not returning to places where their relatives had been killed indiscriminately and by changing their migration routes; he firmly believes vast herds still roam the remoter parts of the barren land. In the same way many Indians long refused to acknowledge the virtual destruction of the buffalo herds. But S. would not like to be compared with the Indians; like most Eskimos, he despises them.

S. does not like the present. He says the young men no longer know how to track or hunt a caribou, and the girls no longer learn to sew; even the Eskimo language, he complains, is declining, since the vocabulary narrows because non-hunters do not know the special terms applying to the hunt and to the hunted animals under special conditions, or even the words applying to snow and ice, which have different names in different circumstances. Like other Eskimos, he complains that the present government-controlled educational system, which keeps boys in school all winter and sends them away for two years' residential schooling in Churchill during adolescence, makes it virtually impossible for them to acquire hunting skills through apprenticeship in the barren land. He believes some way should be devised to enable modern knowledge to be imparted without losing the old ways. What, I wonder, would be the opinion of the Beatle-haired young motor cyclists who drive to nowhere every night along the dirt roads of the settlement?

The new school at Baker Lake, modern and as well-equipped as a school in the south, but clearly devised and operated on assumption that the educational needs of Eskimo children are the same as those of non-Eskimos. There is no hint that one is among a people with their own culture, a distinct way of life. I do not see a single word written in syllabics, or any suggestion that the Eskimo are a people with a great art and a unique tradition. The alphabet is taught by B for Bull and C for Cat in a land of Bears and Caribou. No Eskimo language is taught; even teaching of syllabics which the missionaries undertook is absent from government schools, probably because, like government officials, the teachers knew no Eskimo. Many Eskimo parents, worried by the situation, are teaching syllabics to the children in their homes. Inexperience of many arctic teachers, who often come on their first assignment, in effect spending their time learning rather than teaching.

In the North, interest in the outside world becomes less acute and events there seem more remote. There are no daily papers, no television, and radio programmes need patience to get regularly. Most people rely on weekly summaries like Time, and when the twice-weekly plane fails to bring such reminders, the ever existing feeling of a tenuous connection with the outside is increased. This is so even in summer, when transients are always passing through. It must be infinitely more so in the winter, when the supply of visitors dries up, and the planes sometimes do not come for weeks on end. Even the passing stranger finds himself taken up in the relative isolation of these little communities and curtained by it. It becomes a refreshing holiday from the world where the mass media have so deafeningly filled existence.

Our last night in Baker Lake. At 11 p.m. the phone rings in the H.B.C. house. The drum dance is on, the people are gathering, and we go along the dark sandy road to the I.O.D.E. Hall—the hall of the Eskimo community. A hundred people are seated around the bare hall. Most are Eskimos: the H.B.C. people are there as well, and some of the French Canadian construction workers, but none of the government people and the joke goes around the room that the Anglican missionary, who is very down on such things, will have a theme for his sermon next Sunday. Three old women, sitting together on one of the benches, are chanting shrilly as we enter; one is shrivelled to the tininess of a child, and the other two are swollen and enormous, but all wear shapeless berets and sealskin kamiks. The drum, about three feet across, lies in the middle of the floor; it is a single hoop of willow branch from the treeline down the Thelon River, on which is stretched a caribou skin, dampened with water to keep it taut. The five dancers, all middle-aged men wearing gum boots, sit together on another side of the hall from the women. After a few minutes one gets up and begins his performance. He holds the drum in his left hand by a short handle, and beats the rim—not the skin— with a short stick wrapped round with caribou skin, which gives a sharp resonant thud. He always beats upward, keeping the drum in constant motion and striking alternate edges as they come lowermost. At first he stands, bending his knees to the slow and tentative beats. Then the speed and the rhythmic vigour of the drumming increase, the women sing more loudly, the man begins to stamp, and to utter loud hoarse cries. Suddenly, it is all over, the drum is dropped, the man returns to his place, and we wait until the next man is ready. Even in this dingy hall, some of the magic remains to remind one of the days when this was a dance connected with the hunt; one dancer does a kind of pacing Russian dance, squatting low on his haunches, and then advancing on the audience with growls and menacing tread, suggesting the anger of the hunted bear. There is a great deal of clowning, to which the audience responds with delighted laughter; once a young woman gets up and does a parody of the men. When we return to the mission, along the cold starlit track at half past one, Father Choque is still up. As we drink a nightcap, he shakes his head reminiscently. The drum dance, he remarks, will never be as it was in the old days, held in mid-winter, in an igloo twenty feet across, with the beating and chanting echoing in the dome until it seemed as if the sky would fall.

Usually Destroyed[*]

Aldous Huxley

Our guide through the labyrinthine streets of Jerusalem was a young Christian refugee from the other side of the wall, which now divides the ancient city from the new, the non-viable state of Jordan from the non-viable state of Israel. He was a sad, embittered young man—and well he might be. His prospects had been blighted, his family reduced from comparative wealth to the most abject penury, their house and land taken away from them, their bank account frozen and devaluated. In the circumstances, the surprising thing was not his bitterness, but the melancholy resignation with which it was tempered.

He was a good guide—almost too good, indeed; for he was quite remorseless in his determination to make us visit all those deplorable churches which were built, during the nineteenth century, on the ruins of earlier places of pilgrimage. There are tourists whose greatest pleasure is a trip through historical associations and their own fancy. I am not one of them. When I travel, I like to move among intrinsically significant objects, not through an absence peopled only by literary references, Victorian monuments and the surmises of archaeologists. Jerusalem, of course, contains much more than ghosts and architectural monstrosities. Besides being one of the most profoundly depressing of the earth's cities, it is one of the strangest and, in its own way, one of the most beautiful. Unfortunately our guide was far too conscientious to spare us the horrors and the unembodied, or ill-embodied, historical associations. We had to see everything—not merely St Anne's and St James's and the Dome of the Rock, but the hypothetical site of Caiaphas's house and what the Anglicans had built in the 'seventies, what the Tsar and the German

[*] "Usually Destroyed" from *Adonis and the Alphabet* by Aldous Huxley, London (1956). Reprinted by permission of Chatto and Windus Ltd., and Mrs. Laura Huxley.

Emperor had countered with in the 'eighties, what had been considered beautiful in the early 'nineties by the Copts or the French Franciscans. But, luckily, even at the dreariest moments of our pilgrimage there were compensations. Our sad young man spoke English well and fluently, but spoke it as eighteenth-century virtuosi played music—with the addition of *fioriture* and even whole cadenzas of his own invention. His most significant contribution to colloquial English (and, at the same time, to the science and art of history) was the insertion into almost every sentence of the word 'usually.' What did he mean by it? The answer is, Nothing at all. What sounded like an adverb was in fact no more than one of those vocalized tics to which nervous persons are sometimes subject. I used to know a professor whose lectures and conversation were punctuated, every few seconds, by the phrase, "With a thing with a thing." "With a thing with a thing" is manifestly gibberish. But our young friend's no less compulsive 'usually' had a fascinating way of making a kind of sense—much more sense, very often, than the speaker had intended. "This area," he would say as he showed us one of the Victorian monstrosities, "this area" (it was one of his favourite words) "is very rich in antiquity. St Helena built here a very vast church, but the area was usually destroyed by the Samaritans in the year 529 after Our Lord Jesus Christ. Then the Crusaders came to the area, and built a new church still more vast. Here were mosaics the most beautiful in the world. In the seventeenth century after Our Lord Jesus Christ the Turks usually removed the lead from the roof to make ammunition; consequently rain entered the area and the church was thrown down. The present area was erected by the Prussian Government in the year 1879 after Our Lord Jesus Christ and all these broken-down houses you see over there were usually destroyed during the war with the Jews in 1948."

Usually destroyed and then usually rebuilt, in order, of course, to be destroyed again and then rebuilt, *da capo ad infinitum*. That vocalized tic had compressed all history into a four-syllabled word. Listening to our young friend, as we wandered through the brown, dry squalor of the Holy City, I felt myself overwhelmed, not by the mere thought of man's enduring misery, but by an obscure, immediate sense of it, an organic realization. These pullulations among ruins and in the dark of what once were sepulchres; these hordes of sickly children; these galled asses and the human beasts of burden bent under enormous loads; these mortal enemies beyond the dividing wall; these priest-conducted groups of pilgrims befuddling themselves with the vain repetitions, against which the founder of their religion had gone out of his way to warn them—they were dateless, without an epoch. In this costume or that, under one master or another, praying to whichever God was temporarily in charge, they had been here from the beginning. Had been here with the Egyptians, been here with Joshua, been here when Solomon in all his glory ordered his slaves in all their misery to build the temple, which Nebuchadnezzar had usually demolished and Zedekiah, just as usually, had put together again. Had been here during the long pointless wars between the two kingdoms, and at the next destruction under Ptolemy, the next but one under Antiochus and the next rebuilding under Herod and the biggest, best destruction of all by Titus. Had been here when Hadrian abolished Jerusalem and built a brand-new Roman city, complete with baths and a theatre, with a temple of Jupiter, and a temple of Venus, to take its place. Had been here when the insurrection of Barcochebas was drowned in blood. Had been here while the Roman Empire declined and turned Christian, when Chosroes the Second destroyed the churches and when the Caliph Omar brought Islam and, most unusually, destroyed nothing. Had been here to meet the Crusaders and then to wave them goodbye, to welcome the Turks and then to watch them retreat before Allenby. Had been here under the Mandate and through the troubles of 'forty-eight, and was here now and would be here, no doubt, in the same brown squalor, alternately building and destroying, killing and being killed, indefinitely.

"I do not think," Lord Russell has recently written, "that the sum of human misery has ever in the past been so great as it has been in the last twenty-five years." One is inclined to agree. Or are we, on second thoughts, merely flattering ourselves? At most periods of history moralists have liked to boast that theirs was the most iniquitous generation since the time of Cain—the most iniquitous and therefore, since God is just, the most grievously afflicted. Today, for example, we think of the thirteenth century as one of the supremely creative periods of human history. But the men who were actually contemporary with the cathedrals and Scholastic Philosophy regarded their age as hopelessly degenerate, uniquely bad and condignly punished. Were they right, or are we? The answer, I suspect is: Both. Too much evil and too much suffering can make it impossible for men to be creative; but within very wide limits greatness is perfectly compatible with organized insanity, sanctioned crime and intense, chronic unhappiness for the majority. Every one of the great religions preaches a mixture of profound pessimism and the most extravagant optimism. "I show you sorrow," says the Buddha, pointing to man in his ordinary unregenerate condition. And in the same context Christian theologians speak of the Fall, of Original Sin, of the Vale of Tears, while Hindus refer to the workings of man's home-made destiny, his evil karma. But over against the sorrow, the tears, the self-generated, self-inflicted disasters, what superhuman prospects! If he so wishes, the Hindu affirms, a man can realize his identity with Brahman, the Ground of all being; if he so wishes, says the Christian, he can be filled with God; if he so wishes, says the Buddhist, he can live in a transfigured world where Nirvana and Samsara, the eternal and the temporal, are one. But, alas—and from optimism based on the experience of the few, the saints and sages return to the pessimism forced upon them by their observation of the many—the gate is narrow, the threshold high, few are chosen because few choose to be chosen. In practice man usually destroys himself—but has done so up till now a little less thoroughly than he has built himself up. In spite of everything, we are still here. The spirit of destruction has been willing enough, but for most of historical time its technological flesh has been weak. The Mongols had only horses as transport, only bows and spears and butchers' knives for weapons; if they had possessed our machinery, they could have depopulated the planet. As it was, they had to be content with small triumphs—the slaughter of only a few millions, the stamping out of civilization only in Western Asia.

In this universe of ours nobody has ever succeeded in getting anything for nothing. In certain fields, progress in the applied sciences and the arts of organization has certainly lessened human misery; but it has done so at the cost of increasing it in others. The worst enemy of life, freedom and the common decencies is total anarchy; their second worst enemy is total efficiency. Human interests are best served when society is tolerably well organized and industry moderately advanced. Chaos and ineptitude are anti-human; but so too is a superlatively efficient government, equipped with all the products of a highly developed technology. When such a government goes in for usually destroying, the whole race is in danger.

The Mongols were the aesthetes of militarism; they believed in gratuitous massacre, in destruction for destruction's sake. Our malice is less pure and spontaneous; but, to make up for this deficiency, we have ideals. The end proposed, on either side of the Iron Curtain, is nothing less than the Good of Humanity and its conversion to the Truth. Crusades can go on for centuries, and wars in the name of God or Humanity are generally diabolic in their ferocity. The unprecedented depth of human misery in our time is proportionate to the unprecedented height of the social ideals entertained by the Totalitarians on the one side, the Christians and the secularist democrats on the other.

And then there is the question of simple arithmetic. There are far more people on the earth today than there were in any earlier century. The miseries, which have been the usual consequence of the usual course of nature and the usual behaviour of human beings, are the lot today, not of the three hundred millions of men, women and children who were contemporary with Christ, but of more than two and a half billions. Obviously, then, the sum of our present misery cannot fail to be greater than the sum of misery in the past. Every individual is the centre of a world, which it takes very little to transform into a world of unadulterated suffering. The catastrophes and crimes of the twentieth century can transform almost ten times as many human universes into private hells as did the catastrophes and crimes of two thousand years ago. Moreover, thanks to improvements in technology, it is possible for fewer people to do more harm to greater numbers than ever before.

After the capture of Jerusalem by Nebuchadnezzar, how many Jews were carried off to Babylon? Jeremiah puts the figure at four thousand six hundred, the compiler of the Second Book of Kings at ten thousand. Compared with the forced migrations of our time, the Exile was the most trivial affair. How many millions were uprooted by Hitler and the Communists? How many more millions were driven out of Pakistan into India, out of India into Pakistan? How many hundreds of thousands had to flee, with our young guide, from their homes in Israel? By the waters of Babylon ten thousand at the most sat down and wept. In the single refugee camp at Bethlehem there are more exiles than that. And Bethlehem's is only one of dozens of such camps scattered far and wide over the Near East.

So it looks, all things considered, as though Lord Russell were right—that the sum of misery is indeed greater today than at any time in the past. And what of the future? Germ warfare and the H-bomb get all the headlines and, for that very reason, may never be resorted to. Those who talk a great deal about suicide rarely commit it. The greatest threat to happiness is biological. There were about twelve hundred million people on the planet when I was born, six years before the turn of the century. Today there will probably be four thousand millions. At present about sixteen hundred million people are underfed. In the nineteen-eighties the total may well have risen to twenty-five hundred millions, of whom a considerable number may actually be starving. In many parts of the world famine may come even sooner. In his Report on the Census of 1951 the Registrar General of India has summed up the biological problem as it confronts the second most populous country of the world. There are now three hundred and seventy-five million people living within the borders of India, and their numbers increase by five millions annually. The current production of basic foods is seventy million tons a year, and the highest production that can be achieved in the foreseeable future is ninety-four million tons. Ninety-four million tons will support four hundred and fifty million people at the present sub-standard level, and the population of India will pass the four hundred and fifty million mark in 1969. After that, there will be a condition of what the Registrar General calls 'catastrophe.'

In the index at the end of the sixth volume of Dr Toynbee's *A Study of History*, Popilius Laena gets five mentions and Porphyry of Batamaea two; but the word you would expect to find between these names, *Population*, is conspicuous by its absence. In his second volume, Mr Toynbee has written at length on 'the stimulus of pressures'—but without ever mentioning the most important pressure of them all, the pressure of population on available resources. And here is a note in which the author describes his impressions of the Roman Campagna after twenty years of absence. "In 1911 the student who made the pilgrimage of the Via Appia Antica found himself walking through a wilderness almost from the moment when he passed beyond the City Walls.... When he repeated the pilgrimage in 1931, he found that, in the interval, Man had been busily reasserting his mastery over the whole stretch of country that lies between Rome and the Castelli Romani.... The tension of human energy on the Roman Campagna is now beginning to rise again for the first time since the end of the third century B.C." And there the matter is left, without any reference to the compelling reason for this 'rise of tension.' Between 1911 and 1931 the population of Italy had increased by the best part of eight millions. Some of these eight millions went to live in the Roman Campagna. And they did so, not because Man with a large M had in some mystical way increased the tension of human energy, but for the sufficiently obvious reason that there was nowhere else for them to go. In terms of a history that takes no cognizance of demographical facts, the past can never be fully understood, the present is quite incomprehensible and the future entirely beyond prediction.

Thinking, for a change, in demographic as well as in merely cultural, political and religious terms, what kind of reasonable guesses can we make about the sum of human misery in the years to come? First, it seems pretty certain that more people will be hungrier and that, in many parts of the world, malnutrition will modulate into periodical or chronic famine. (One would like to know something about the Famines of earlier ages, but the nearest one gets to them in Mr Toynbee's index is a blank space between Muhammad Falak-al-Din and Gaius Fannius.) Second, it seems pretty certain that, though they may help in the long run, remedial measures, aimed at reducing the birth-rate will be powerless to avert the miseries lying in wait for the next generation. Third, it seems pretty certain that improvements in Agriculture (not referred to in Mr Toynbee's index, though Agrigentum gets two mentions and Agis IV, King of Sparta, no less than forty-seven) will be unable to catch up with current and foreseeable increases in population. If the standard of living in industrially backward countries is to be improved, agricultural production will have to go up every single year by at least two and a half per cent, and preferably by three and a half per cent. Instead of which, according to the FAO, Far Eastern food production per head of population will be ten per cent less in 1956 (and this assumes that the current Five-Year Plans will be fully realized) than it was in 1938.

Fourth, it seems pretty certain that, as a larger and hungrier population 'mines the soil' in a desperate search for food, the destructive processes of erosion and deforestation will be speeded up. Fertility will therefore tend to go down as human numbers go up. (One looks up *Erosion* in Mr Toynbee's index but finds only Esarhaddon Esotericism and Esperanto; one hunts for *Forests*, but has to be content, alas, with Formosus of Porto.)

Fifth, it seems pretty certain that the increasing pressure of population upon resources will result in increasing political and social unrest, and that this unrest will culminate in wars, revolutions and counter-revolutions.

Sixth, it seems pretty certain that, whatever the avowed political principles and whatever the professed religion of the societies concerned, increasing pressure of population upon resources will tend to increase the power of the central government and to diminish the liberties of individual citizens. For, obviously, where more people are competing for less food, each individual will have to work harder and longer for his ration, and the central government will find it necessary to intervene more and more frequently in order to save the rickety economic machine from total breakdown, and at the same time to repress the popular discontent begotten by deepening poverty.

If Lord Russell lives to a hundred and twenty (and, for all our sakes, I hope most fervently that he will), he may find himself remembering these middle decades of the twentieth century as an almost Golden Age. In 1954, it is true, he decided that the sum of human misery had never been so great as it had been in the preceding quarter century. On the other hand, 'you ain't seen nuthin' yet.' Compared with the sum of four billion people's misery in the 'eighties, the sum of two billion miseries just before, during and after the Second World War may look like the Earthly Paradise.

But meanwhile here we were in Jerusalem, looking at the usually destroyed antiquities and rubbing shoulders with the usually poverty-stricken inhabitants, the usually superstitious pilgrims. Here was the Wailing Wall, with nobody to wail at it; for Israel is on the other side of a barrier, across which there is no communication except by occasional bursts of rifle fire, occasional exchanges of hand grenades. Here, propped up with steel scaffolding, was the Church of the Holy Sepulchre—that empty tomb to which, for three centuries, the early Christians paid no attention whatsoever, but which came, after the time of Constantine, to be regarded, throughout Europe, as the most important thing in the entire universe. And here was Siloam, here St Anne's, here the Dome of the Rock and the site of the Temple, here, more ruinous than Pompeii, the Jewish quarter, levelled, usually, in 1948 and not yet usually reconstructed. Here, finally, was St James's, of the Armenians, gay with innumerable rather bad but charming paintings, and a wealth of gaudily coloured tiles. The great church glowed like a dim religious merry-go-round. In all Jerusalem it was the only oasis of cheerfulness. And not alone of cheerfulness. As we came out into the courtyard, through which the visitor must approach the church's main entrance, we heard a strange and wonderful sound. High up, in one of the houses surrounding the court, somebody was playing the opening Fantasia of Bach's Partita in A minor—playing it, what was more, remarkably well. From out of the open window, up there on the third floor, the ordered torrent of bright pure notes went streaming out over the city's immemorial squalor. Art and religion, philosophy and science, morals and politics—these are the instruments by means of which men have tried to discover a coherence in the flux of events, to impose an order on the chaos of experience. The most intractable of our experiences is the experience of Time—the intuition of duration, combined with the thought of perpetual perishing. Music is a device for working directly upon the experience of Time. The composer takes a piece of raw, undifferentiated duration and extracts from it, as the sculptor extracts the statue from his marble, a complex pattern of tones and silences, of harmonic sequences and contrapuntal interweavings. For the number of minutes it takes to play or listen to his composition, duration is transformed into something intrinsically significant, something held together by the internal logics of style and temperament, of personal feelings interacting with an artistic tradition, of creative insights expressing themselves within and beyond some given technical convention. This Fantasia, for example—with what a tireless persistence it drills its way through time! How effectively—and yet with no fuss, no self-conscious heroics—it transfigures the mortal lapse through time into the symbol, into the very fact, of a more than human life! A tunnel of joy and understanding had been driven through chaos and was demonstrating, for all to hear, that perpetual perishing is also perpetual creation. Which was precisely what our young friend had been telling us, in his own inimitable way, all the time. Usually destroyed—but also, and just as often, usually rebuilt. Like the rain, like sunshine, like the grace of God and the devastations of Nature, his verbalized tic was perfectly impartial. We walked out of the courtyard and down the narrow street. Bach faded, a donkey brayed, there was a smell of undisposed sewage. "In the year of Our Lord 1916," our guide informed us, "the Turkish Government usually massacred approximately seven hundred and fifty thousand Armenians."

How
the Poor
Die*

George Orwell

In the year 1929 I spent several weeks in the Hôpital X, in the fifteenth arrondissement of Paris. The clerks put me through the usual third degree at
the reception desk, and indeed I was kept answering questions for some
twenty minutes before they would let me in. If you have ever had to fill up
forms in a Latin country you will know the kind of questions I mean. For
some days past I had been unequal to translating Reaumur into
Fahrenheit, but I know that my temperature was round about 103, and by
the end of the interview I had some difficulty in standing on my feet. At my
back a resigned little knot of patients, carrying bundles done up in colored
handkerchiefs, waited their turn to be questioned.

After the questioning came the bath—a compulsory routine for all
newcomers, apparently, just as in prison or the workhouse. My clothes
were taken away from me, and after I had sat shivering for some minutes
in five inches of warm water I was given a linen nightshirt and a short blue
flannel dressing gown—no slippers, they had none big enough for me,
they said—and led out into the open air. This was a night in February and I
was suffering from pneumonia. The ward we were going to was two hundred yards away and it seemed that to get to it you had to cross the
hospital grounds. Someone stumbled in front of me with a lantern. The
gravel path was frosty underfoot, and the wind whipped the nightshirt
round my bare calves. When we got into the ward I was aware of a strange
feeling of familiarity whose origin I did not succeed in pinning down till
later in the night. It was a long, rather low, ill-lit room, full of murmuring

voices and with three rows of beds surprisingly close together. There was a foul smell, fecal and yet sweetish. As I lay down I saw on a bed nearly opposite me a small, round-shouldered, sandy-haired man sitting half naked while a doctor and a student performed some strange operation on him. First the doctor produced from his black bag a dozen small glasses like wine glasses, then the student burned a match inside each glass to exhaust the air, then the glass was popped on to the man's back or chest and the vacuum drew up a huge yellow blister. Only after some moments did I realize what they were doing to him. It was something called cupping, a treatment which you can read about in old medical textbooks but which till then I had vaguely thought of as one of those things they do to horses.

The cold air outside had probably lowered my temperature, and I watched this barbarous remedy with detachment and even a certain amount of amusement. The next moment, however, the doctor and the student came across to my bed, hoisted me upright, and without a word began applying the same set of glasses, which had not been sterilized in any way. A few feeble protests that I uttered got no more response than if I had been an animal. I was very much impressed by the impersonal way in which the two men started on me. I had never been in the public ward of a hospital before, and it was my first experience of doctors who handle you without speaking to you or, in a human sense, taking any notice of you. They only put on six glasses in my case, but after doing so they scarified the blisters and applied the glasses again. Each glass now drew out about a dessert-spoonful of dark-colored blood. As I lay down again, humiliated, disgusted, and frightened by the thing that had been done to me, I reflected that now at least they would leave me alone. But no, not a bit of it. There was another treatment coming, the mustard poultice, seemingly a matter of routine like the hot bath. Two slatternly nurses had already got the poultice ready, and they lashed it round my chest as tight as a strait-jacket while some men who were wandering about the ward in shirt and trousers began to collect round my bed with half-sympathetic grins. I learned later that watching a patient have a mustard poultice was a favorite pastime in the ward. These things are normally applied for a quarter of an hour and certainly they are funny enough if you don't happen to be the person inside. For the first five minutes the pain is severe, but you believe you can bear it. During the second five minutes this belief evaporates, but the poultice is buckled at the back and you can't get it off. This is the period the onlookers enjoy most. During the last five minutes, I noted, a sort of numbness supervenes. After the poultice had been removed a waterproof pillow packed with ice was thrust beneath my head and I was left alone. I did not sleep, and to the best of my knowledge this was the only night of my life—I mean the only night spent in bed—in which I have not slept at all, not even a minute.

During my first hour in the Hôpital X I had had a whole series of different and contradictory treatments, but this was misleading, for in general you got very little treatment at all, either good or bad, unless you were ill in some interesting and instructive way. At five in the morning the nurses came round, woke the patients, and took their temperatures, but did not wash them. If you were well enough you washed yourself, otherwise you depended on the kindness of some walking patient. It was generally patients, too, who carried the bedbottles and the grim bedpan, nicknamed *la casserole*. At eight breakfast arrived, called army-fashion *la soupe*. It was soup, too, a thin vegetable soup with slimy hunks of bread floating about in it. Later in the day the tall, solemn, black-bearded doctor made his rounds, with an interne and a troop of students following at his heels, but there were about sixty of us in the ward and it was evident that he had other wards to attend to as well. There were many beds past which he walked day after day, sometimes followed by imploring cries. On the other hand if you had some disease with which the students wanted to familiarize themselves you got plenty of attention of a kind. I myself, with an exceptionally fine specimen of a bronchial rattle, sometimes had as many as a dozen students queuing up to listen to my chest. It was a very queer feeling—queer, I mean, because of their intense interest in learning their job, together with a seeming lack of any perception that the patients were human beings. It is strange to relate, but sometimes as some young student stepped forward to take his turn at manipulating you, he would be actually tremulous with excitement, like a boy who has at last got his hands on some expensive piece of machinery. And then ear after ear—ears of young men, of girls, of Negroes—pressed against your back, relays of fingers solemnly but clumsily tapping, and not from any one of them did you get a word of conversation or a look direct in your face. As a nonpaying patient, in the uniform nightshirt, you were primarily *a specimen*, a thing I did not resent but could never quite get used to.

After some days I grew well enough to sit up and study the surrounding patients. The stuffy room, with its narrow beds so close together that you could easily touch your neighbor's hand, had every sort of disease in it except, I suppose, acutely infectious cases. My right-hand neighbor was a little red-haired cobbler with one leg shorter than the other, who used to announce the death of any other patient (this happened a number of times, and my neighbor was always the first to hear of it) by whistling to me, exclaiming "Numero 43!" (or whatever it was) and flinging his arms above his head. This man had not much wrong with him, but in most of the other beds within my angle of vision some squalid tragedy or some plain horror was being enacted. In the bed that was foot to foot with mine there lay, until he died (I didn't see him die—they moved him to another bed), a little weazened man who was suffering from I do not know what disease, but something that made his whole body so intensely sensitive that any movement from side to side, sometimes even the weight of the bedclothes, would make him shout out with pain. His worst suffering was when he urinated, which he did with the greatest difficulty. A nurse would bring him the bedbottle and then for a long time stand beside his bed, whistling, as grooms are said to do with horses, until at last with an agonized shriek of *"Je pisse!"* he would get started. In the bed next to him the sandy-haired man whom I had seen being cupped used to cough up blood-streaked mucus at all hours. My left-hand neighbor was a tall, flaccid-looking young man who used periodically to have a tube inserted into his back and astonishing quantities of frothy liquid drawn off from some part of his body. In the bed beyond that a veteran of the war of 1870 was dying, a handsome old man with a white imperial, round whose bed, at all hours when visiting was allowed, four elderly female relatives dressed all in black sat exactly like crows, obviously scheming for some pitiful legacy. In the bed opposite me in the further row was an old bald-headed man with drooping moustaches and greatly swollen face and body, who was suffering from some disease that made him urinate almost incessantly. A huge glass receptacle stood always beside his bed. One day his wife and daughter came to visit him. At sight of them the old man's bloated face lit up with a smile of surprising sweetness, and as his daughter, a pretty girl of about twenty, approached the bed I saw that his hand was slowly working its way from under the bedclothes. I seemed to see in advance the gesture that was coming—the girl kneeling beside the bed, the old man's hand laid on her head in his dying blessing. But no, he merely handed her the bedbottle, which she promptly took from him and emptied into the receptacle.

About a dozen beds away from me was Numero 57—I think that was his number—a cirrhosis of the liver case. Everyone in the ward knew him by sight because he was sometimes the subject of a medical lecture. On two afternoons a week the tall, grave doctor would lecture in the ward to a party of students, and on more than one occasion old Numero 57 was wheeled in on a sort of trolley into the middle of the ward, where the doctor would roll back his nightshirt, dilate with his fingers a huge flabby protuberance on the man's belly—the diseased liver, I suppose—and explain solemnly that this was a disease attributable to alcoholism, commoner in the wine-drinking countries. As usual he neither spoke to his patient nor gave him a smile, a nod or any kind of recognition. While he talked, very grave and upright, he would hold the wasted body beneath his two hands, sometimes giving it a gentle roll to and fro, in just the attitude of a woman handling a rolling-pin. Not that Numero 57 minded this kind of thing. Obviously he was an old hospital inmate, a regular exhibit at lectures, his liver long since marked down for a bottle in some pathological museum. Utterly uninterested in what was said about him, he would lie with his colorless eyes gazing at nothing, while the doctor showed him off like a piece of antique china. He was a man of about sixty, astonishingly shrunken. His face, pale as vellum, had shrunken away till it seemed no bigger than a doll's.

One morning my cobbler neighbor woke me up plucking at my pillow before the nurses arrived. "Numero 57!"—he flung his arms above his head. There was a light in the ward, enough to see by. I could see old Numero 57 lying crumpled up on his side, his face sticking out over the side of the bed, and toward me. He had died some time during the night, nobody knew when. When the nurses came they received the news of his death indifferently and went about their work. After a long time, an hour or more, two other nurses marched in abreast like soldiers, with a great clumping of sabots, and knotted the corpse up in the sheets, but it was not removed till some time later. Meanwhile, in the better light, I had had time for a good look at Numero 57. Indeed I lay on my side to look at him. Curiously enough he was the first dead European I had seen. I had seen dead men before, but always Asiatics and usually people who had died violent deaths. Numero 57's eyes were still open, his mouth also open, his small face contorted into an expression of agony. What most impressed me, however, was the whiteness of his face. It had been pale before, but now it was little darker than the sheets. As I gazed at the tiny, screwed-up face it struck me that this disgusting piece of refuse, waiting to be carted away and dumped on a slab in the dissecting room, was an example of "natural" death, one of the things you pray for in the Litany. There you are, then, I thought, that's what is waiting for you, twenty, thirty, forty years hence: that is how the lucky ones die, the one who lives to be old. One wants to live, of course, indeed one only stays alive by virtue of the fear of death, but I think now, as I thought then, that it's better to die violently and not too old. People talk about the horrors of war, but what weapon has man invented that even approaches in cruelty some of the commoner diseases? "Natural" death, almost by definition, means something slow, smelly, and painful. Even at that, it makes a difference if you can achieve it in your own home and not in a public institution. This poor old wretch who had just flickered out like a candle end was not even important enough to have anyone watching by his deathbed. He was merely a number, then a "subject" for the students' scalpels. And the sordid publicity of dying in such a place! In the Hôpital X the beds were very close together and there were no screens. Fancy, for instance, dying like the little man whose bed was for a while foot to foot with mine, the one who cried out when the bedclothes touched him! I dare say *"Je pisse!"* were his last recorded words. Perhaps the dying don't bother about such things—that at least would be the standard answer: nevertheless dying people are often more or less normal in their minds till within a day or so of the end.

In the public wards of a hospital you see horrors that you don't seem to meet with among people who manage to die in their own homes, as though certain diseases only attacked people at the lower income levels. But it is a fact that you would not in any English hospitals see some of the things I saw in the Hôpital X. This business of people just dying like animals, for instance, with nobody standing by, nobody interested, the death not even noticed till the morning—this happened more than once. You certainly would not see that in England, and still less would you see a corpse left exposed to the view of the other patients. I remember that once in a cottage hospital in England a man died while we were at tea, and though there were only six of us in the ward the nurses managed things so adroitly that the man was dead and his body removed without our even hearing about it till tea was over. A thing we perhaps underrate in England is the advantage we enjoy in having large numbers of well-trained and rigidly disciplined nurses. No doubt English nurses are dumb enough, they may tell fortunes with tea leaves, wear Union Jack badges, and keep photographs of the Queen on the mantelpieces, but at least they don't let you lie unwashed and constipated on an unmade bed, out of sheer laziness. The nurses at the Hôpital X still had a tinge of Mrs. Gamp about them, and later, in the military hospitals of Republican Spain, I was to see nurses almost too ignorant to take a temperature. You wouldn't, either, see in England such dirt as existed in the Hôpital X. Later on, when I was well enough to wash myself in the bathroom, I found that there was kept there a huge packing case into which the scraps of food and dirty dressings from the ward were flung, and the wainscotings were infested by crickets.

When I had got back my clothes and grown strong on my legs I fled from the Hôpital X, before my time was up and without waiting for a medical discharge. It was not the only hospital I have fled from, but its gloom and bareness, its sickly smell and, above all, something in its mental atmosphere stand out in my memory as exceptional. I had been taken there because it was the hospital belonging to my arrondissement, and I did not learn till after I was in it that it bore a bad reputation. A year or two later the celebrated swindler, Madame Hanaud, who was ill while on re-mand, was taken to the Hôpital X, and after a few days of it she managed to elude her guards, took a taxi, and drove back to the prison, explaining that she was more comfortable there. I have no doubt that the Hôpital X was quite untypical of French hospitals even at that date. But the patients, nearly all of them working men, were surprisingly resigned. Some of them seemed to find the conditions almost comfortable, for at least two were destitute malingerers who found this a good way of getting through the winter. The nurses connived because the malingerers made themselves useful by doing odd jobs. But the attitude of the majority was: of course this is a lousy place, but what else do you expect? It did not seem strange to them that you should be woken at five and then wait three hours before starting the day on watery soup, or that people should die with no one at their bedside, or even that your chance of getting medical attention should depend on catching the doctor's eye as he went past. According to their traditions that was what hospitals were like. If you are seriously ill, and if you are too poor to be treated in your own home, then you must go into hospital, and once there you must put up with harshness and discomfort, just as you would in the army. But on top of this I was interested to find a lingering belief in the old stories that have now almost faded from memory in England—stories, for instance, about doctors cutting you open out of sheer curiosity or thinking it funny to start operating before you were prop- erly "under." There were dark tales about a little operating room said to be situated just beyond the bathroom. Dreadful screams were said to issue from this room. I saw nothing to confirm these stories and no doubt they were all nonsense, though I did see two students kill a sixteen-year-old boy, or nearly kill him (he appeared to be dying when I left the hospital, but he may have recovered later) by a mischievous experiment which they probably could not have tried on a paying patient. Well within living memory it used to be believed in London that in some of the big hospitals patients were killed off to get dissection subjects. I didn't hear this tale repeated at the Hôpital X, but I should think some of the men there would have found it credible. For it was a hospital in which not the methods, perhaps, but something of the atmosphere of the nineteenth century had managed to survive, and therein lay its peculiar interest.

During the past fifty years or so there has been a great change in the relationship between doctor and patient. If you look at almost any literature before the later part of the nineteenth century, you find that a hospital is popularly regarded as much the same thing as a prison, and an old-fashioned, dungeon-like prison at that. A hospital is a place of filth, torture, and death, a sort of ante-chamber to the tomb. No one who was not more or less destitute would have thought of going into such a place for treatment. And especially in the early part of the last century, when medical science had grown bolder than before without being any more successful, the whole business of doctoring was looked on with horror and dread by ordinary people. Surgery, in particular, was believed to be no more than a peculiarly gruesome form of sadism, and dissection, possible only with the aid of body-snatchers, was even confused with necromancy. From the nineteenth century you could collect a large horror-literature connected with doctors and hospitals. Think of poor old George III, in his dotage, shrieking for mercy as he sees his surgeons approaching to "bleed him till he faints"! Think of the conversations of Bob Sawyer and Benjamin Allen, which no doubt are hardly parodies, or the field hospitals in *La Débâcle* and *War and Peace*, or that shocking description of an amputation in Melville's *Whitejacket!* Even the names given to doctors in nineteenth-century English fiction, Slasher, Carver, Sawyer, Fillgrave, and so on, and the generic nickname "sawbones," are about as grim as they are comic. The anti-surgery tradition is perhaps best expressed in Tennyson's poem, *The Children's Hospital*, which is essentially a pre-chloroform document though it seems to have been written as late as 1880. Moreover, the outlook which Tennyson records in this poem had a lot to be said for it. When you consider what an operation without anaesthetics must have been like, what it notoriously *was* like, it is difficult not to suspect the motives of people who would undertake such things. For these bloody horrors which the students so eagerly looked forward to ("A magnificent sight if Slasher does it!") were admittedly more or less useless: the patient who did not die of shock usually died of gangrene, a result which was taken for granted. Even now doctors can be found whose motives are questionable. Anyone who has had much illness, or who has listened to medical students talking, will know what I mean. But anaesthetics were a turning point, and disinfectants were another. Nowhere in the world, probably, would you now see the kind of scene described by Axel Munthe in *The Story of San Michele*, when the sinister surgeon in top-hat and frock-coat, his starched shirtfront spattered with blood and pus, carves up patient after patient with the same knife and flings the severed limbs into a pile beside the table. Moreover, national health insurance has partly done away with the idea that a working-class patient is a pauper who deserves little consideration. Well into this century it was usual for "free" patients at the big hospitals to have their teeth extracted with no anaesthetic. They didn't pay, so why should they have an anaesthetic—that was the attitude. That too has changed.

And yet every institution will always bear upon it some lingering memory of its past. A barrack-room is still haunted by the ghost of Kipling, and it is difficult to enter a workhouse without being reminded of *Oliver Twist*. Hospitals began as a kind of casual ward for lepers and the like to die in, and they continued as places where medical students learned their art on the bodies of the poor. You can still catch a faint suggestion of their history in their characteristically gloomy architecture. I would be far from complaining about the treatment I have received in any English hospital, but I do know that it is a sound instinct that warns people to keep out of hospitals if possible, and especially out of the public wards. Whatever the legal position may be, it is unquestionable that you have far less control over your own treatment, far less certainty that frivolous experiments will not be tried on you, when it is a case of "accept the discipline or get out."

And it is a great thing to die in your own bed, though it is better still to die in your boots. However great the kindness and the efficiency, in every hospital death there will be some cruel, squalid detail, something perhaps too small to be told but leaving terribly painful memories behind, arising out of the haste, the crowding, the impersonality of a place where every day people are dying among strangers.

The dread of hospitals probably still survives among the very poor, and in all of us it has only recently disappeared. It is a dark patch not far beneath the surface of our minds. I have said earlier that when I entered the ward at the Hôpital X I was conscious of a strange feeling of familiarity. What the scene reminded me of, of course, was the reeking, pain-filled hospitals of the nineteenth century, which I had never seen but of which I had a traditional knowledge. And something, perhaps the black-clad doctor with his frowsy black bag, or perhaps only the sickly smell, played the queer trick of unearthing from my memory that poem of Tennyson's, *The Children's Hospital*, which I had not thought of for twenty years. It happened that as a child I had had it read aloud to me by a sick-nurse whose own working life might have stretched back to the time when Tennyson wrote the poem. The horrors and sufferings of the old-style hospitals were a vivid memory to her. We had shuddered over the poem together, and then seemingly I had forgotten it. Even its name would probably have recalled nothing to me. But the first glimpse of the ill-lit murmurous room, with the beds so close together, suddenly roused the train of thought to which it belonged, and in the night that followed I found myself remembering the whole story and atmosphere of the poem, with many of its lines complete.

Terms
and
Topics

TERMS

1. What is the meaning of the word *interview*? Does knowing the word's origins—its *etymology*—help you to understand its full meaning? (Your dictionary should provide the sources and histories of words as well as their definitions; if not, get a better dictionary, or consult an etymological dictionary.)

2. Distinguish between *journalism* and *journal*. What are the features of journalistic writing that make some people object to it? What are its advantages?

3. *Irony* Verbal irony consists in saying one thing and meaning another, usually with at least some humorous intent. If it is raining cats and dogs, and someone looks out the window and says, "It's a great day for a picnic!" everyone understands the intended meaning. Verbal irony that is lacking in wit or cleverness, that is particularly crude and obvious, or that is especially biting or brutal, is usually called *sarcasm*. There are other kinds of irony; for example *dramatic irony*, common in literature, is present when a character knows less about his circumstances than the audience does, or when expectations are aroused but not fulfilled. Irony always involves contrast.

4. *Mask* Another kind of irony is *Socratic irony*, so called because in Plato's dialogues Socrates characteristically pretends to be naive or ignorant in order to trap an opponent during an argument. In other words, figuratively speaking he wears a *mask* of innocence, though beneath it he is very wise indeed. Writers often put on such a mask, present a particular kind of image of themselves, adopt a *persona* or character other than their true or everyday one, in order to achieve cer-

tain rhetorical effects. An extreme and obvious example: In Browning's poem it is of course not Browning himself speaking but the Duke of Ferrara, the persona that Browning has assumed for the occasion of the poem. Interestingly, even the character the Duke presents could be considered a mask covering his true self. Could such a mask be useful for an interviewer as well as an interviewee?

TOPICS: On Individual Essays

SILVER DONALD CAMERON "Robertson Davies: The Bizarre and Passionate Life of the Canadian People"

1. If you have read any of Davies's Salterton novels (*Leaven of Malice, Tempest-Tost, A Mixture of Frailties*), do you find that his remarks about them change your view of them in any way?

2. Is there a "fossilized past" in your neighbourhood that is analogous to that which Davies finds around Peterborough?

3. Davies's style as recorded by Cameron is not exactly colloquial, but there is an informal, conversational flavour about it. Read some of Davies's own writing—nonfiction—and compare the style with what appears here. Are they very different? What specific differences can you point out?

4. In his introduction Cameron says that the Davies he talked with was not the Davies he had expected. From Davies's conversation, what kind of man do *you* think he is? Write a brief character sketch of him as he is revealed in the interview. Be prepared to point out where you think particular traits are revealed. Are any traits revealed involuntarily rather than directly, traits whose existence you infer by reading between the lines?

5. What is a "jester's bladder"? What is "etiology"? Does Davies's diction drive you to your dictionary with unusual frequency? Is this a good thing or a bad thing?

6. Davies remarks that Cameron, too, has "made a confession" (p. 100). What is it? Does Cameron, the interviewer, reveal anything further about himself, either directly or indirectly?

7. Explain in your own terms what you think Davies means when he says he is "religious" and when he says he is an "artist."

MARGARET LANE "The Ghost of Beatrix Potter"

1. Read, or reread, some of Beatrix Potter's better early works and try to reconcile their author's personality, insofar as you can infer it, with the character of Mrs. Heelis that peers out of Lane's memoir about not meeting her.

2. Do the details Lane provides make it believable that Mr. Heelis could have undergone so sudden and complete a turnabout in his attitude toward her inquiries?

3. Point out places where Lane reveals things about herself. Are any of these revelations implicit, indirect?

4. Are the details Lane mentions and quotes sufficient to support her statement that Mrs. Heelis's reply to her letter was "the rudest letter I have ever received?"

5. How would you characterize the tone of Lane's piece? On what grounds?

6. Compose a brief essay about not meeting someone.

7. Write a character sketch of someone you know only by hearsay, such as a grandparent who died before you were born.

JACK LUDWIG "The Calgary Stampede"

1. Note how much the vivid and unusual verbs and adjectives contribute to the scene Ludwig describes in his opening paragraph. Try your hand at writing a descriptive paragraph, first with no adjectives at all and with only quiet verbs, then again with the kind of imaginative verbs and adjectives Ludwig uses (but don't overdo it). Which is more effective?

2. Does Ludwig's overall attitude toward the Stampede seem to you to be favourable, unfavourable, or simply neutral? Point out several places in the essay that support your opinion.

3. Conduct several interviews with people engaged in some activity or event (a sporting event, such as a race or a golf tournament; a church bazaar or some other fund-raising enterprise; a reunion or some other kind of party). From whatever notes or tapes you collect, write up the event and its atmosphere, trying to portray it as seen through the eyes of the participants, but avoiding long stretches of quotation.

GEORGE WOODCOCK "A Northern Journal"

1. Note the economy and effectiveness—in the context of a journal—of the well-handled fragments, or minor sentences. Write a journal entry of your own in which you make use of such staccato fragments—but be careful not to overdo it. Would you want to use them in any other kind of writing? Try it and see.

2. Point out the different ways—some direct, some indirect—in which Woodcock contrives to contrast present and past. Can we be sure we know his own attitude toward the things he is reporting on? Does he ever state it explicitly, or does he remain objective, aloof?

3. Keep a daily journal for a period of two months or more. At the end of this time, look back over what you have written, and see what it reveals about yourself. Have you changed? How? Why? Try editing the entries in your journal to compose an essay similar to Woodcock's.

4. Has the word *Eskimo* changed its connotative meaning since Woodcock wrote his journal? Why is the term *Inuit* now used instead? Are there similar social variations among such words as those in the following groups, or are they of a different kind: African, black, Negro; Chinese, Asian, Oriental; Caucasian, paleface, white?

ALDOUS HUXLEY "Usually Destroyed"

1. It has now been a generation since Huxley wrote this essay. Consult some current sources of information to determine the accuracy of some of his predictions and those of others he mentions.

2. Is Huxley implicitly (or even explicitly) saying that we customarily go about looking at the history of mankind in the wrong way?

3. Comment on the structure of Huxley's essay. Obviously the title and the beginning and ending point up a principal theme, but much other matter comes in between. How is it ordered? What is its relevance to the rest?

4. Write a short essay in which you make use of some recurrent or choric phrase in the way Huxley does, repeating it throughout, sometimes with different effects, but building cumulatively to the end. The phrase might be a friend's comment that you can apply more broadly, or a slogan from advertising or politics, or any other phrase that—with a little thought—will yield greater significance and resonances than at first appear.

GEORGE ORWELL "How the Poor Die"

1. Characterize and explain the tone of Orwell's essay. What creates it? (Consider diction and sentence structure.) Does it seem appropriate to the subject matter? Why or why not?

2. Study the way Orwell's essay moves from the particular to the general, and then back and forth between them. How effective is this technique? What is the overall proportion of generalization to particular, concrete detail?

3. In a brief essay, describe the dehumanizing effects of some particular place—a doctor's or dentist's office, an automotive garage, the lobby of a building, a government liquor store, a supermarket, a locker room, an elevator, or some other such place you know from personal experience.

TOPICS: General and Comparative

1. Are journal writers honest with themselves? Or do they always write with another audience in mind? Is Davies really "confessional" when talking with Cameron? Silver Donald Cameron writes that the basic principle of interviewing is *listening*. Do you agree? Is the reader of an interview transformed into a listener? What other successful interviewing techniques can you think of? Why do they work?

2. Consider the openings of several of the essays in this section:

    (a) Lane refers immediately to irony. How ironic is her whole essay?

    (b) Huxley uses the word *labyrinthine*. How does this establish an idea that the essay as a whole will embroider? How does it relate to his comments on the relation between music and time?

    (c) Woodcock uses words like *flat, grey, empty, infinite*, and *perfect*. Do they establish a single tone or a more complex one? How functional are they?

    (d) How do Orwell's autobiographical details prepare the reader for his reflections on society?

3. Who or what do these essays reveal? What does Lane reveal about Lane, Ludwig about Ludwig? How does Orwell's essay reveal a whole society's inner structure?

4. Compare Woodcock's and Ludwig's use of sentence fragments. To what end do the fragments function? How does Ludwig's use of fragmented conversations set up the rhythm of his essay, and what connection is there between this rhythm and his notions about time? Compare Ludwig's essay with White's in Section I. Compare Ludwig's and Woodcock's works with the essays in section VI.

5. Try to record a conversation. Does it sound convincing and natural as you have it written down? How does a writer create the illusion of ordinary speech?

III
Writing
to
Persuade

In their daily lives, people are subject to hundreds of influences, from family and friends, churchmen and neighbours, reviewers and advertisers, employers and employees, publicists and politicians, fashion designers and faddists. The influences come openly or subliminally, deliberately or accidentally, in public and in private. They affect matters of taste and belief as well as matters of behaviour and fact. They are conveyed by deed and by word. Moreover, the reasons people change their minds are about as numerous as the changes themselves. Fear, shame, moral outrage, and emotional upheaval constitute some of the most potent weapons on which a would-be influencer can rely. Often the emotional influences masquerade as logical ones. People don't like to think that they have been swayed; they like instead to believe they have been convinced by logic. But how often are they? How often does a politician's appeal to order play upon fear, or an advertiser's image of normality induce a sense of envy? How often does a listener accept as logical only those ideas that confirm his existing prejudices, biases, beliefs? How often does the would-be influencer reveal his true intent?

The persuading essays collected here—examples of reviewing, polemical letter writing, political statement, argument, and feature journalism—all take contentious stances, sometimes for emotional reasons, sometimes out of a deep-seated intellectual commitment, sometimes for debate. They vary in tone. Some are solemn; some are witty; some are passionate; some are acid. None is neutral. And none is grey. Their styles are as individual as the styles of personal narratives: argument does not imply an absence of personality. Indeed, the overt presence of an authorial perspective often greatly aids a speaker in reaching and holding—and hence influencing—the members of an audience.

Argumentative techniques, however, do differ from narrative and descriptive techniques. Whereas narrative writers emphasize temporal organization and descriptive writers rely upon spatial organization, argumentative writers stress logical order. The make ample use of rhetorical questions, parallelism, and analogies; they frequently appeal to authority and experience; they assert cause and effect—and sometimes they do these things covertly or indirectly. In the hands of an argumentative writer, a topic becomes a thesis. Details of the commentary and the nature of the arrangement itself become evidence. Even the process of demolishing opponents and opponents' points of view helps bolster the position the writer has adopted. Unfortunately, logic sometimes gives way to empty (though still emotionally powerful) rhetoric and to logical fallacy. *Caveat emptor* applies in composition as well as in merchandising; the reader/listener/voter/customer must always beware. There are many questions a reader should ask: If a writer uses an analogy, is it enlightening or misleading? If he uses statistics, are they accurate and adequately based? If he appeals to an authority (whether the Bible, Aristotle, Science, Tradition, or the

Mayor), why does he do so? Is the "authority" truly authoritative? Is it relevant to the argument at hand? Is the language of the argument culturally biased, sexually biased, emotionally slanted? Is special pleading involved? Is the argument circular? Does the writer define his terms, document his sources? In short, does he prove his case?

The Latin tags that describe a number of familiar rhetorical strategies have become part of the English language; they are worth knowing, for they themselves are frequently used in debates, as part of a proof or a demolition. (Indeed, the Latin might be thought of as an implicit appeal to "authority.") Here are some of them:

a priori "from what comes before." A deductive process of reasoning that pursues, from cause to effect, the logical implications of given axioms or hypotheses. (Remember to ask if the "axioms" are accurate.)

a posteriori "from what comes after." An inductive process of reasoning that pursues an argument from effect to cause or from examples to principle. (Remember to ask if the cause or principle adduced is the only one possible.)

non sequitur "it does not follow." An illogical conclusion, often used jocularly in a humorous essay. (Remember to question a writer's use of *hence, thus, therefore,* and *because.*)

post hoc ergo propter hoc "after something, therefore because of it." An illogical assumption. (Remember that chronology isn't always synonymous with cause and effect.)

argumentum ad hominem "argument directed at the man." This diverts attention from the real subject to the character of an opponent in order to demolish the subject by discrediting the person.

argumentum ad populum "argument directed at the people." This appeals to crowd emotions rather than to logical decision; it usually employs a false distinction between "us" and "them."

Another term to know is *syllogism*, which refers to a structured set of premises in logical discourse. In a book entitled *Myth, Literature and the African World*, the Nigerian playwright Wole Soyinka attacks the concept of *Negritude* that others had postulated as a counter to racist European attitudes. His manner of argument is interesting for the way it makes use of syllogistic structures:

> The vision of Negritude should never be underestimated or belittled. What went wrong with it is contained in what I earlier expressed as the contrivance of a creative ideology and its falsified basis of identification with the social vision. This vision in itself was that of restitution and re-engineering of a racial psyche, the

establishment of a distinct human entity and the glorification of its long-suppressed attributes. (On an even longer-term basis, as universal alliance with the world's dispossessed.) In attempting to achieve this laudable goal however, Negritude proceeded along the route of over-simplification. Its re-entrenchment of black values was not preceded by any profound effort to enter into this African system of values. It extolled the apparent. Its reference points took far too much colouring from European ideas even while its Messiahs pronounced themselves fanatically African. In attempting to refute the evaluation to which black reality had been subjected, Negritude adopted the Manichean tradition of European thought and inflicted it on a culture which is most radically anti-Manichean. It not only accepted the dialectical structure of European ideological confrontations but borrowed from the very components of its racist syllogism.

By way of elaboration . . . we will now pose a pair of syllogisms from the racist philosophy that provoked it into being:

(a) Analytical thought is a mark of high human development. The European employs analytical thought. Therefore the European is highly developed.

(b) Analytical thought is a mark of high human development. The African is incapable of analytical thought. Therefore the African is not highly developed.

(For 'analytical thought' substitute scientific inventiveness etc.)

The dialectic progression in history of these two syllogisms need not be dwelt upon: the European is highly developed, the African is not, therefore etc. Slavery and colonialism took their basic justification from such palpably false premises. But the temper of the times (both the liberal conscience of Europe and the new assertiveness of the victims of Eurocentric dialectics) required a re-phrasing of premises and conclusions—preferably of course, even for liberal Europe, the conclusions only. Negritude strangely lent approval to this partial methodology, accepting in full the premises of both syllogisms and the conclusion of (a), justifying Sartre's commentary that the theoretical and practical assertion of the supremacy of the white man was the tacitly adopted thesis, and failing utterly to demolish it. The conclusion of (a) was never challenged, though attempts were made to give new definitions to what constitutes high development. The method there was to reconstruct (b) altogether, while leaving (a) intact. This was the initial error. Negritude did not bother to free the black races from the burden of its acceptance. Even the second premise of (a), 'The European employs analytical thought', is falsely posed, for it already implies a racial separatism which provides the main argument. Is the entire exercise not rendered futile if we substituted for this, 'Man is capable of analytical thought'? The Negritudinists did not; they accepted the battleground of Eurocentric prejudices and racial chauvinism, and moved to replace syllogism (b) with an amended version:

(c)   Intuitive understanding is also a mark of human development. The African employs intuitive understanding. Therefore the African is highly developed.

(For 'intuitive understanding' substitute the dance, rhythm etc.)

The dialectic progression which moved, logically enough, from this amendment, positing the attractive universality of Negritude, was based on (a) and (c), resulting in a symbiotic human culture—the black leaven in the white metallic loaf. How could the mistake ever have been made that the new propositions in (c) wiped away the inherent insult of (b), which was merely a development of the racist assumptions of (a)? They said, oh yes, the Gobineaus of the world are right; Africans neither think nor construct, but it doesn't matter because—voilà!—they intuit! And so they moved to construct a romantic edifice, confident that its rhythmic echoes would drown the repugnant conclusion of proposition (b), which of course simply refused to go away.[*]

[*] Reprinted from Wole Soyinka, *Myth, Literature and the African World*, London: Cambridge University Press, 1976.

How persuasive is Soyinka's argument?

A final word is necessary. Lest the foregoing points imply that reason explains everything, that passion proves nothing, and that all discoveries and judgments ought to be based on rigorous processes of logical thought, mention should be made of the *Eureka!* principle. When Archimedes leaped from his bath with a mathematical solution to the problem of displaced water, he undoubtedly had at least a glimmer of logical proof at the back of his mind. But sometimes reason is a servant rather than a leader. Sometimes the glimmer is a magnificent, unbidden leap of imaginative insight — and reason, then, can only trudge along after.

The Sound of...

The Sound of Music and The Singing Nun*

Pauline Kael

The Singing Nun will make you realize how good Fred Zinnemann's The Nun's Story was. Although the theme, the conflict and even the story line are similar, The Singing Nun reduces them to smiles, twinkles, banalities and falseness. It is almost a parody of The Nun's Story and, of course, without the courage of the conclusion of that earlier thoughtful, subtle film. Though The Singing Nun draws its ideas from The Nun's Story, its inspiration is obviously that movie phenomenon the trade press now refers to (very respectfully) as The Sound of Money. And perhaps to get at what goes on in a movie like The Singing Nun, we need to look at that phenomenon, which is so often called "wholesome" but which is probably going to be the single most repressive influence on artistic freedom in movies for the next few years.

The success of a movie like The Sound of Music makes it even more difficult for anyone to try to do anything worth doing, anything relevant to the modern world, anything inventive or expressive. The banks, the studios, the producers will want to give the public what it seems to crave. The more money these "wholesome" movies make, the less wholesome will the state of American movies be. "The opium of the audience," Luis Bunuel, the Spanish director, once said, "is conformity." And nothing is more degrading and ultimately destructive to artists than supplying the narcotic.

What is it that makes millions of people buy and like The Sound of Music—a tribute to "freshness" that is so mechanically engineered, so shrewdly calculated that the background music rises, the already soft focus blurs and melts, and, upon the instant, you can hear all those noses blowing in the theatre? Of course, it's well done for what it is: that is to say, those who made it are experts at manipulating responses. They're the Pavlovs of movie-making: they turn us into dogs that salivate on signal. When the cruel father sees the light and says, "You've brought music back into the house," who can resist the pull at the emotions? It's that same tug at the heartstrings we feel when Lassie comes home or when the blind heroine sees for the first time; it is a simple variant of that surge of warmth we feel when a child is reunited with his parents. It's basic, and there are probably few of us who don't respond. But it is the easiest and perhaps the most primitive kind of emotion that we are made to feel. The worst despots in history, the most cynical purveyors of mass culture respond at *this* level and may feel pleased at how tenderhearted they *really* are because they do. This kind of response has as little to do with generosity of feeling as being stirred when you hear a band has to do with patriotism.

I think it is not going too far to say that when an expensive product of modern technology like *The Sound of Music* uses this sort of "universal" appeal, it is because nothing could be safer, nothing could be surer. Whom could it offend? Only those of us who, *despite the fact that we may respond*, loathe being manipulated in this way and are aware of how self-indulgent and cheap and ready-made are the responses we are made to feel. And we may become even more aware of the way we have been *used* and turned into emotional and aesthetic imbeciles when we hear ourselves humming those sickly, goody-goody songs. The audience for a movie of this kind becomes the lowest common denominator of feeling: a sponge. The heroine leaves the nuns at the fence as she enters the cathedral to be married. Squeezed again, and the moisture comes out of thousands— millions—of eyes and noses.

And the phenomenon at the center of the monetary phenomenon? Julie Andrews, with the clean, scrubbed look and the unyieldingly high spirits; the good sport who makes the best of everything; the girl who's so unquestionably good that she carries this one dimension like a shield. The perfect, perky schoolgirl, the adorable tomboy, the gawky colt. Sexless, inhumanly happy, the sparkling maid, a mind as clean and well brushed as her teeth. What is she? Merely the ideal heroine for the best of all possible worlds. And that's what *The Sound of Music* pretends we live in.

Audiences are transported into a world of operetta cheerfulness and calendar art. You begin to feel as if you've never got out of school. Up there on the screen, they're all in their places with bright, shining faces. Wasn't there perhaps one little Von Trapp who didn't want to sing his head off, or who screamed that he wouldn't act out little glockenspiel routines for Papa's party guests, or who got nervous and threw up if he had to get on a stage? No, nothing mars this celebration of togetherness. Not only does this family sing together, they play ball together. This is the world teachers used to pretend (and maybe still pretend?) was the real world. It's the world in which the governess conquers all. It's the big lie, the sugarcoated lie that people seem to want to eat. They even seem to think they should feed it to their kids, that it's healthy, wonderful "family entertainment."

And this is the sort of attitude that makes a critic feel that maybe it's all hopeless. Why not just send the director, Robert Wise, a wire: "You win, I give up," or, rather, "We both lose, we all lose."

Yet there was a spider on the valentine: the sinister, unpleasant, archly decadent performance Christopher Plummer gives as the baron, he of the thin, twisted smile—my candidate for the man least likely to be accepted as a hero. Even the monstrously ingenious technicians who made this movie couldn't put together a convincing mate for Super Goody Two-Shoes. The dauntless heroine surmounts this obstacle: in the romantic scenes, she makes love to herself. And why not? We never believed for a moment that love or marriage would affect her or change her. She was already perfection.

Debbie Reynolds, as the character based on Soeur Sourire in *The Singing Nun*, is less than perfection. Her eyes are not so clear and bright, indeed they're rather anxious and, yes, almost bleary; and her singing isn't pure and pretty, it's sort of tacky and ordinary. So is the whole production. Henry Koster doesn't succeed even in making it very convincingly "wholesome." The religion is a familiar kind of Hollywood Christianity. The nuns are even more smiley and giggly—like a mush-headed schoolteacher's dream of ideally happy schoolchildren; Ricardo Montalban is a simperingly simple priest; and though Agnes Moorehead plays a nun like a witch, she is more than balanced by Greer Garson as the Mother Prioress. With her false eyelashes and her richly condescending manner, Greer Garson can turn any line of dialogue into incomparable cant. It's a gift, of a kind.

The people in *The Singing Nun* behave like the animals in a Disney movie: they are so cute and so full of little tricks. There are chintzy little pedagogical songs that are supposed to be full of *joy*, and there is Debbie's excruciating humility. "I have a lot to learn," she tells us; but we didn't need to be told. She gives up her singing career—which was giving her too much attention and adoration—in order to find her simple faith again. And so, at the end, we see her working as a nurse in Africa, posed like a madonna holding a Negro baby, surrounded by attentive, adoring Africans.... But then, of course, this movie is the kind of spiritual exercise in which the nuns say a little prayer for Ed Sullivan every day.

Why am I so angry about these movies? Because the shoddy falseness of *The Singing Nun* and the luxuriant falseness of *The Sound of Music* are part of the sentimental American tone that makes honest work almost impossible. It is not only that people who accept this kind of movie tend to resent work which says that this is not the best of all possible worlds, but that people who are gifted give up the effort to say anything. They attune themselves to *The Sound of Money*.

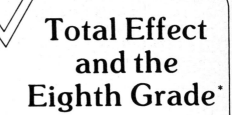

Total Effect and the Eighth Grade[*]

Flannery O'Connor

In two recent instances in Georgia, parents have objected to their eighth- and ninth-grade children's reading assignments in modern fiction. This seems to happen with some regularity in cases throughout the country. The unwitting parent picks up his child's book, glances through it, comes upon passages of erotic detail or profanity, and takes off at once to complain to the school board. Sometimes, as in one of the Georgia cases, the teacher is dismissed and hackles rise in liberal circles everywhere.

The two cases in Georgia, which involved Steinbeck's *East of Eden* and John Hersey's *A Bell for Adano*, provoked considerable newspaper comment. One columnist, in commending the enterprise of the teachers, announced that students do not like to read the fusty works of the nineteenth century, that their attention can best be held by novels dealing with the realities of our own time, and that the Bible, too, is full of racy stories.

Mr. Hersey himself addressed a letter to the State School Superintendent in behalf of the teacher who had been dismissed. He pointed out that his book is not scandalous, that it attempts to convey an earnest message about the nature of democracy, and that it falls well within the limits of the principle of "total effect," that principle followed in legal cases by which a book is judged not for isolated parts but by the final effect of the whole book upon the general reader.

I do not want to comment on the merits of these particular cases.

What concerns me is what novels ought to be assigned in the eighth and ninth grades as a matter of course, for if these cases indicate anything, they indicate the haphazard way in which fiction is approached in our high schools. Presumably there is a state reading list which contains "safe" books for teachers to assign; after that it is up to the teacher.

English teachers come in Good, Bad, and Indifferent, but too frequently in high schools anyone who can speak English is allowed to teach it. Since several novels can't easily be gathered into one textbook, the fiction that students are assigned depends upon their teacher's knowledge, ability, and taste: variable factors at best. More often than not, the teacher assigns what he thinks will hold the attention and interest of the students. Modern fiction will certainly hold it.

Ours is the first age in history which has asked the child what he would tolerate learning, but that is a part of the problem with which I am not equipped to deal. The devil of Educationism that possesses us is the kind that can be "cast out only by prayer and fasting." No one has yet come along strong enough to do it. In other ages the attention of children was held by Homer and Virgil, among others, but, by the reverse evolutionary process, that is no longer possible; our children are too stupid now to enter the past imaginatively. No one asks the student if algebra pleases him or if he finds it satisfactory that some French verbs are irregular, but if he prefers Hersey to Hawthorne, his taste must prevail.

I would like to put forward the proposition, repugnant to most English teachers, that fiction, if it is going to be taught in the high schools, should be taught as a subject and as a subject with a history. The total effect of a novel depends not only on its innate impact, but upon the experience, literary and otherwise, with which it is approached. No child needs to be assigned Hersey or Steinbeck until he is familiar with a certain amount of the best works of Cooper, Hawthorne, Melville, the early James, and Crane, and he does not need to be assigned these until he has been introduced to some of the better English novelists of the eighteenth and nineteenth centuries.

The fact that these works do not present him with the realities of his own time is all to the good. He is surrounded by the realities of his own time, and he has no perspective whatever from which to view them. Like the college student who wrote in her paper on Lincoln that he went to the movies and got shot, many students go to college unaware that the world was not made yesterday; their studies began with the present and dipped backward occasionally when it seemed necessary or unavoidable.

There is much to be enjoyed in the great British novels of the nineteenth century, much that a good teacher can open up in them for the young student. There is no reason why these novels should be either too simple or too difficult for the eighth grade. For the simple, they offer simple pleasures; for the more precocious, they can be made to yield subtler ones if the teacher is up to it. Let the student discover, after reading the nineteenth-century British novel, that the nineteenth-century American novel is quite different as to its literary characteristics, and he will thereby learn something not only about these individual works but about the sea-change which a new historical situation can effect in a literary form. Let him come to modern fiction with this experience behind him, and he will be better able to see and to deal with the more complicated demands of the best twentieth-century fiction.

Modern fiction often looks simpler than the fiction that preceded it, but in reality it is more complex. A natural evolution has taken place. The author has for the most part absented himself from direct participation in the work and has left the reader to make his own way amid experiences dramatically rendered and symbolically ordered. The modern novelist merges the reader in the experience; he tends to raise the passions he touches upon. If he is a good novelist, he raises them to effect by their order and clarity a new experience—the total effect—which is not in itself sensuous or simply of the moment. Unless the child has had some literary experience before, he is not going to be able to resolve the immediate passions the book arouses into any true, total picture.

It is here the moral problem will arise. It is one thing for a child to read about adultery in the Bible or in *Anna Karenina*, and quite another for him to read about it in most modern fiction. This is not only because in both the former instances adultery is considered a sin, and in the latter, at most, an inconvenience, but because modern writing involves the reader in the action with a new degree of intensity, and literary mores now permit him to be involved in any action a human being can perform.

In our fractured culture, we cannot agree on morals; we cannot even agree that moral matters should come before literary ones when there is a conflict between them. All this is another reason why the high schools would do well to return to their proper business of preparing foundations. Whether in the senior year students should be assigned modern novelists should depend both on their parents' consent and on what they have already read and understood.

The high-school English teacher will be fulfilling his responsibility if he furnishes the student a guided opportunity, through the best writing of the past, to come, in time, to an understanding of the best writing of the present. He will teach literature, not social studies or little lessons in democracy or the customs of many lands.

And if the student finds that this is not to his taste? Well, that is regrettable. Most regrettable. His taste should not be consulted; it is being formed.

Middlebrow*

Virginia Woolf

TO THE EDITOR OF THE "NEW STATESMAN"

Sir,

Will you allow me to draw your attention to the fact that in a review of a book by me (October) your reviewer omitted to use the word Highbrow? The review, save for that omission, gave me so much pleasure that I am driven to ask you, at the risk of appearing unduly egotistical, whether your reviewer, a man of obvious intelligence, intended to deny my claim to that title? I say "claim," for surely I may claim that title when a great critic, who is also a great novelist, a rare and enviable combination, always calls me a highbrow when he condescends to notice my work in a great newspaper; and, further, always finds space to inform not only myself, who know it already, but the whole British Empire, who hang on his words, that I live in Bloomsbury? Is your critic unaware of that fact too? Or does he, for all his intelligence, maintain that it is unnecessary in reviewing a book to add the postal address of the writer?

His answer to these questions, though of real value to me, is of no possible interest to the public at large. Of that I am well aware. But since larger issues are involved, since the Battle of the Brows troubles, I am told, the evening air, since the finest minds of our age have lately been engaged in debating, not without that passion which befits a noble cause, what a highbrow is and what a lowbrow, which is better and which is worse, may I take this opportunity to express my opinion and at the same time draw attention to certain aspects of the question which seem to me to have been unfortunately overlooked?

Now there can be no two opinions as to what a highbrow is. He is the man or woman of thoroughbred intelligence who rides his mind at a gallop

---

* From *The Death of the Moth and Other Essays* by Virginia Woolf. Reprinted by permission of the Author's Literary Estate and The Hogarth Press Ltd.

across country in pursuit of an idea. That is why I have always been so proud to be called highbrow. That is why, if I could be more of a highbrow I would. I honour and respect highbrows. Some of my relations have been highbrows; and some, but by no means all, of my friends. To be a highbrow, a complete and representative highbrow, a highbrow like Shakespeare, Dickens, Byron, Shelley, Keats, Charlotte Brontë, Scott, Jane Austen, Flaubert, Hardy or Henry James—to name a few highbrows from the same profession chosen at random—is of course beyond the wildest dreams of my imagination. And, though I would cheerfully lay myself down in the dust and kiss the print of their feet, no person of sense will deny that this passionate preoccupation of theirs—riding across country in pursuit of ideas—often leads to disaster. Undoubtedly, they come fearful croppers. Take Shelley—what a mess he made of his life! And Byron, getting into bed with first one woman and then with another and dying in the mud at Missolonghi. Look at Keats, loving poetry and Fanny Brawne so intemperately that he pined and died of consumption at the age of twenty-six. Charlotte Brontë again—I have been assured on good authority that Charlotte Brontë was, with the possible exception of Emily, the worst governess in the British Isles. Then there was Scott—he went bankrupt, and left, together with a few magnificent novels, one house, Abbotsford, which is perhaps the ugliest in the whole Empire. But surely these instances are enough—I need not further labour the point that highbrows, for some reason or another, are wholly incapable of dealing successfully with what is called real life. That is why, and here I come to a point that is often surprisingly ignored, they honour so wholeheartedly and depend so completely upon those who are called lowbrows. By a lowbrow is meant of course a man or a woman of thoroughbred vitality who rides his body in pursuit of a living at a gallop across life. That is why I honour and respect lowbrows—and I have never known a highbrow who did not. In so far as I am a highbrow (and my imperfections in that line are well known to me) I love lowbrows; I study them; I always sit next the conductor in an omnibus and try to get him to tell me what it is like—being a conductor. In whatever company I am I always try to know what it is like—being a conductor, being a woman with ten children and thirty-five shillings a week, being a stockbroker, being an admiral, being a bank clerk, being a dressmaker, being a duchess, being a miner, being a cook, being a prostitute. All that lowbrows do is of surpassing interest and wonder to me, because, in so far as I am a highbrow, I cannot do things myself.

This brings me to another point which is also surprisingly overlooked. Lowbrows need highbrows and honour them just as much as highbrows need lowbrows and honour them. This too is not a matter that requires much demonstration. You have only to stroll along the Strand on a wet winter's night and watch the crowds lining up to get into the movies. These lowbrows are waiting, after the day's work, in the rain, sometimes for hours, to get into the cheap seats and sit in hot theatres in order to see what their lives look like. Since they are lowbrows, engaged magnificently and adventurously in riding full tilt from one end of life to the other in pursuit of a living, they cannot see themselves doing it. Yet nothing interests them more. Nothing matters to them more. It is one of the prime necessities of life to them—to be shown what life looks like. And the highbrows, of course, are the only people who can show them. Since they are the only people who do not do things, they are the only people who can see things being done. This is so—and so it is I am certain; nevertheless we are told—the air buzzes with it by night, the Press booms with it by day, the very donkeys in the fields do nothing but bray it, the very curs in the street do nothing but bark it—"Highbrows hate lowbrows! Lowbrows hate highbrows!"—when highbrows need lowbrows, when lowbrows need highbrows, when they cannot exist apart, when one is the complement and other side of the other! How has such a lie come into existence? Who has set this malicious gossip afloat?

There can be no doubt about that either. It is the doing of the middlebrows. They are the people, I confess, that I seldom regard with entire cordiality. They are the go-betweens; they are the busybodies who run from one to the other with their tittle tattle and make all the mischief—the middlebrows, I repeat. But what, you may ask, is a middlebrow? And that, to tell the truth, is no easy question to answer. They are neither one thing nor the other. They are not highbrows, whose brows are high; nor lowbrows, whose brows are low. Their brows are betwixt and between. They do not live in Bloomsbury which is on high ground; nor in Chelsea, which is on low ground. Since they must live somewhere presumably, they live perhaps in South Kensington, which is betwixt and between. The middlebrow is the man, or woman, of middlebred intelligence who ambles and saunters now on this side of the hedge, now on that, in pursuit of no single object, neither art itself nor life itself, but both mixed indistinguishably, and rather nastily, with money, fame, power, or prestige. The middlebrow curries favour with both sides equally. He goes to the lowbrows and tells them that while he is not quite one of them, he is almost their friend. Next moment he rings up the highbrows and asks them with equal geniality whether he may not come to tea. Now there are highbrows—I myself have known duchesses who were highbrows, also charwomen, and they have both told me with that vigour of language which so often unites the aristocracy with the working classes, that they would rather sit in the coal cellar, together, than in the drawing-room with middlebrows and pour out tea. I have myself been asked—but may I, for the sake of brevity, cast this scene which is only partly fictitious, into the form of fiction?—I myself, then, have been asked to come and "see" them—how strange a passion theirs is for being "seen"! They ring me up, therefore, at about eleven in the morning, and ask me to come to tea. I go to my wardrobe and consider, rather lugubriously, what is the right thing to wear? We highbrows may be smart, or we may be shabby; but we never have the right thing to wear. I proceed to ask next: What is the right thing to say? Which is the right knife to use? What is the right book to praise? All these are things I do not know for myself. We highbrows read what we like and do what we like and praise what we like. We also know what we dislike — for example, thin bread and butter tea. The difficulty of eating thin bread and butter in white kid gloves has always seemed to me one of life's more insuperable problems. Then I dislike bound volumes of the classics behind plate glass. Then I distrust people who call both Shakespeare and Wordsworth equally "Bill" — it is a habit moreover that leads to confusion. And in the matter of clothes, I like people either to dress very well; or to dress very badly; I dislike the correct thing in clothes. Then there is the question of games. Being a highbrow I do not play them. But I love watching people play who have a passion for games. These middlebrows pat balls about; they poke their bats and muff their catches at cricket. And when poor Middlebrow mounts on horseback and that animal breaks into a canter, to me there is no sadder sight in all Rotten Row. To put it in a nutshell (in order to get on with the story) that tea party was not wholly a success, nor altogether a failure; for Middlebrow, who writes, following me to the door, clapped me briskly on the back, and said "I'm sending you my book!" (Or did he call it "stuff?") And his book comes — sure enough, though called, so symbolically, *Keepaway*, it comes. And I read a page here, and I read a page there (I am breakfasting, as usual, in bed). And it is not well written; nor is it badly written. It is not proper, nor is it improper; in short it is betwixt and between. Now if there is any sort of book for which I have, perhaps, an imperfect sympathy, it is the betwixt and between. And so, though I suffer from the gout of a morning — but if one's ancestors for two or three centuries have tumbled into bed dead drunk one has deserved a touch of that malady — I rise. I dress. I proceed weakly to the window. I take that book in my swollen right hand and toss it gently over the hedge into the field. The hungry sheep — did I remember to say that this part of the story takes place in the country? — the hungry sheep look up but are not fed.

But to have done with fiction and its tendency to lapse into poetry — I will now report a perfectly prosaic conversation in words of one syllable. I often ask my friends the lowbrows, over our muffins and honey, why it is that while we, the highbrows, never buy a middlebrow book, or go to a middlebrow lecture, or read, unless we are paid for doing so, a middlebrow review, they, on the contrary, take these middlebrow activities so seriously? Why, I ask (not of course on the wireless), are you so damnably modest? Do you think that a description of your lives, as they are, is too sordid and too mean to be beautiful? Is that why you prefer the middlebrow version of what they have the impudence to call real humanity?—this mixture of geniality and sentiment stuck together with a sticky slime of calves-foot jelly? The truth, if you would only believe it, is much more beautiful than any lie. Then again, I continue, how can you let the middlebrows teach *you* how to write?—you, who write so beautifully when you write naturally, that I would give both my hands to write as you do—for which reason I never attempt it, but do my best to learn the art of writing as a highbrow should. And again, I press on, brandishing a muffin on the point of a tea spoon, how dare the middlebrows teach *you* how to read—Shakespeare for instance? All you have to do is to read him. The Cambridge edition is both good and cheap. If you find *Hamlet* difficult, ask him to tea. He is a highbrow. Ask Ophelia to meet him. She is a lowbrow. Talk to them, as you talk to me, and you will know more about Shakespeare than all the middlebrows in the world can teach you—I do not think, by the way, from certain phrases that Shakespeare liked middlebrows, or Pope either.

To all this the lowbrows reply—but I cannot imitate their style of talking—that they consider themselves to be common people without education. It is very kind of the middlebrows to try to teach them culture. And after all, the lowbrows continue, middlebrows, like other people, have to make money. There must be money in teaching and in writing books about Shakespeare. We all have to earn our livings nowadays, my friends the lowbrows remind me. I quite agree. Even those of us whose Aunts came a cropper riding in India and left them an annual income of four hundred and fifty pounds, now reduced, thanks to the war and other luxuries, to little more than two hundred odd, even we have to do that. And we do it, too, by writing about anybody who seems amusing—enough has been written about Shakespeare—Shakespeare hardly pays. We highbrows, I agree, have to earn our livings; but when we have earned enough to live on, then we live. When the middlebrows, on the contrary, have earned enough to live on, they go on earning enough to buy—what are the things that middlebrows always buy? Queen Anne furniture (faked, but none the less expensive); first editions of dead writers—always the worst; pictures, or reproductions from pictures, by dead painters, houses in what is called "the Georgian style"—but never anything new, never a picture by a living painter, or a chair by a living carpenter, or books by living writers, for to buy living art requires living taste. And, as that kind of art and that kind of taste are what middlebrows call "highbrow," "Bloomsbury," poor middlebrow spends vast sums on sham antiques, and has to keep at it scribbling away, year in, year out, while we highbrows ring each other up, and are off for a day's jaunt into the country. That is the worst of course of living in a set—one likes being with one's friends.

Have I then made my point clear, sir, that the true battle in my opinion lies not between highbrow and lowbrow, but between highbrows and lowbrows joined together in blood brotherhood against the bloodless and pernicious pest who comes between? If the B.B.C. stood for anything but the Betwixt and Between Company they would use their control of the air not to stir strife between brothers, but to broadcast the fact that highbrows and lowbrows must band together to exterminate a pest which is the bane of all thinking and living. It may be, to quote from your advertisement columns, that "terrifically sensitive" lady novelists overestimate the dampness and dinginess of this fungoid growth. But all I can say is that when, lapsing into that stream which people call, so oddly, consciousness, and gathering wool from the sheep that have been mentioned above, I ramble round my garden in the suburbs, middlebrow seems to me to be everywhere. "What's that?" I cry. "Middlebrow on the cabbages? Middlebrow infecting that poor old sheep? And what about the moon?" I look up and, beyond, the moon is under eclipse. "Middlebrow at it again!" I exclaim. "Middlebrow obscuring, dulling, tarnishing and coarsening even the silver edge of Heaven's own scythe." (I "draw near to poetry," see advt.) And then my thoughts, as Freud assures us thoughts will do, rush (Middlebrow's saunter and simper, out of respect for the Censor) to sex, and I ask of the sea-gulls who are crying on desolate sea sands and of the farm hands who are coming home rather drunk to their wives, what will become of us, men and women, if Middlebrow has his way with us, and there is only a middle sex but no husbands or wives? The next remark I address with the utmost humility to the Prime Minister. "What, sir," I demand, "will be the fate of the British Empire and of our Dominions Across the Seas if Middlebrows prevail? Will you not, sir, read a pronouncement of an authoritative nature from Broadcasting House?"

Such are the thoughts, such are the fancies that visit "cultured invalidish ladies with private means" (see advt.) when they stroll in their suburban gardens and look at the cabbages and at the red brick villas that have been built by middlebrows so that middlebrows may look at the view. Such are the thoughts "at once gay and tragic and deeply feminine" (see advt.) of one who has not yet "been driven out of Bloomsbury" (advt. again), a place where lowbrows and highbrows live happily together on equal terms and priests are not, nor priestesses, and, to be quite frank, the adjective "priestly" is neither often heard nor held in high esteem. Such are the thoughts of one who will stay in Bloomsbury until the Duke of Bedford, rightly concerned for the respectability of his squares, raises the rent so high that Bloomsbury is safe for middlebrows to live in. Then she will leave.

May I conclude, as I began, by thanking your reviewer for his very courteous and interesting review, but may I tell him that though he did not, for reasons best known to himself, call me a highbrow, there is no name in the world that I prefer? I ask nothing better than that all reviewers, for ever, and everywhere, should call me a highbrow. I will do my best to oblige them. If they like to add Bloomsbury, W.C.1, that is the correct postal address, and my telephone number is in the Directory. But if your reviewer, or any other reviewer, dares hint that I live in South Kensington, I will sue him for libel. If any human being, man, woman, dog, cat or half-crushed worm dares call me "middlebrow" I will take my pen and stab him, dead.

Yours etc.,

VIRGINIA WOOLF.

Time on Our Hands*

Russell Lynes

Recently I discovered among some papers that my mother had stowed away in a deserted file a clipping from a magazine of the 1920s. It was headed "Schedule for a One-Maid House." The house, it said, "has seven rooms: a living-room, dining-room, porch, kitchen, maid's room and bath, three bedrooms, and two baths." The schedule starts with:

6:45 A.M. Wash and Dress

and ends with:

8:00 P.M. Plans for the evening will be adapted to the household convenience.

Bridget, if that was her name, was busy in the intervening hours with cleaning, cooking, bed-making, baking, and polishing silver and brass. Her respite came sometime between 1:30 and 3:00 P.M. when, according to the schedule, she was to "clear table, wash dishes, go to own room to rest, bathe, and change dress." At 3:00 she was back in the kitchen, "ready to answer door, etc."

Leisure was not much of a problem for Bridget at work in a one-maid house. Her schedule covers six days (on Saturday it says: "Bake cake for Sunday") and like everyone else she had Sunday as her only day off. (She doesn't seem to have had "maid's night out" on the customary Thursday.)

The familiar picture of the maid on her day off was of a girl dressed "fit to kill" on her way to meet her friends at church. The equally familiar picture of the man of the house was father asleep in a hammock buried under the Sunday paper. Leisure in those days was merely a restorative for work.

* "Time on Our Hands," *Harper's Magazine*, July 1958.

Now leisure has become work in its own right . . . and a worry to lots of earnest Americans.

Last year at the commencement exercises at New York University a clergyman said to the graduating class: "America can be undone by her misuse of leisure. Life is getting easier physically, and this makes life harder morally."

There are, of course, a great many professional and business men who wonder what all this talk about leisure is; somehow it is no problem to them—or so they think. There are also a good many women, especially young married women, who would give their heirlooms for a few minutes to themselves. They have only to wait.

But leisure is making some thoughtful people uneasy. In January the American Council of Churches met in Columbus to discuss the spare time of our increasingly urbanized populace. The Twentieth Century Fund is deep in an investigation of leisure and the University of Chicago is (with the help of Ford Foundation funds) making a study of the nature of leisure and how people use it. Corporations not only worry about the leisure of their employees; they do something about it. Schoolteachers and social workers and local politicians worry about it, about footloose youngsters, about long summer vacations for teen-agers, and about juvenile delinquency. City planners, safety experts, highway engineers watch the growing number of hours when families are not at work and feel they have to go somewhere. Where? To what extent is the boredom of leisure responsible for young drug addicts, for the common cold, for muggings on city streets?

Every new scientific development, whether it is aimed at saving our skins or washing our dishes, leads in one way or another to reducing still further the sweat of the public brow. The four-day week which looms on the immediate horizon (and which causes such consternation in the corporate breast) is, of course, less the product of labor's demands than of manufacturing genius. Machines not men have created the three-day weekend, and men are worried about what to do with it. Not long ago the Oil, Chemical, and Atomic Workers Union made a survey of its membership. It asked them ". . . if and when the Union enters a bargaining program for shorter hours" how would they like this additional leisure to be distributed? Would a housewife, for example, "want her husband at home three consecutive days?" Good question.

The attitude of many large corporations has been somewhat different. They have attacked the problem of employee leisure head on. They have provided all sorts of sports facilities, music clubs, theater groups, and bowling leagues. IBM has its own golf courses for its employees. Bell and Howell has baseball fields lighted for night games. Ford's River Rouge plant has an indoor shooting range, tennis courts, baseball diamonds (nine of them), and horseshoe pits. Corning Glass has its own museum, visiting repertory theater, and changing exhibitions, in addition to automatic bowling alleys, basketball courts, and dancing classes.

Business is not sentimental about the new leisure. "Many of these off-the-job or after-hours activities," the head of employee relations for General Motors has said, "have not only a therapeutic value, but can actually sharpen or increase employees' skills." And the President of Bell and Howell has said', "Everyone in the organization gains from a well-planned recreational program.

But these efforts to sponge up the ocean of the so-called leisure time which has engulfed us can only put a few drops in the bucket. The truth is that while the new leisure has come on us fairly gradually, it has found us not at all prepared. If we are to cope agreeably with it, we are going to have to change our minds about some shibboleths and even some rather basic beliefs. To do this, we need to understand what has happened to the pattern of our leisure and where it is likely to lead.

Leisure is not a new problem born of automation, but it is a new problem for a great many kinds of people who were never much concerned with it when Bridget was working her seventy- or eighty-hour week in the one-maid house. America has had a leisure class since the industrialization of our country began, and in the 1850s the art critic James Jackson Jarves complained in shocked tones of the number of scions of wealthy families who threw themselves into rivers because they were so bored that life seemed not worth living. (Mr. Jarves wanted to interest such young men in the arts as a suitable outlet for their energies and money.) These young men, whom we would call the idle rich, had on a large scale the same problem that nearly everybody in America has today on a small scale. In its simplest terms, the primary problem of leisure is how to avoid boredom.

We used to be more accomplished at being bored than we are today, or at least we seem to have taken boredom with better grace in the days of party calls and decorous parlor games. We assumed a high moral tone toward leisure, and in some respects this tone persists. "The devil finds work for idle hands," our parents said and shook their heads; and when they said, "All work and no play makes Jack a dull boy," they meant, of course, that Jack should work most of the time but not quite all of it. Primarily leisure was thought of as a way to get a man back on his feet so that after Sunday he could put in sixty or so productive hours from Monday through Saturday. Leisure for women (few women in those days had jobs) was something quite else—it was the custody of culture and good works. Women in their spare time were expected to cultivate the arts, foster the education of their children, and play the role of Lady Bountiful in the community.

It was a neat division of family functions and a tidy way of life. Father's leisure was restorative; mother's was extremely productive. But more has changed than just the roles of men and women; the whole complex machinery of leisure has changed.

Briefly the changes are these:

In the last few decades what had started about a century ago as a trickle of people from the country and small towns to the cities became a torrent. Cities filled like cisterns and overflowed into suburbs, and as we shifted from a predominantly agricultural economy to a predominantly industrial one, we changed the nature of much of our leisure from what might be called a natural one to an artificial one, from pleasures provided by nature to pleasures concocted by man. Ways of using leisure began to come in packages—in cars, in movies, in radios, and most recently in television sets, and what was once the sauce only for the city goose became the sauce for the country gander as well. City culture is now within easy reach of everyone everywhere and everyone has the same access to talent that only a few decades ago used to be reserved for the rich and the urbane.

During the time when we were changing from a rural to an urban culture, the length of the work-week fell from sixty hours or more to forty or thirty-five. Gradually the five-day week became an almost universal reality, and the four-day week is on the immediate horizon. With more leisure time, men have, quite naturally, taken on some of the household chores that only a short while ago they wouldn't have been caught dead at, and have assumed some of the cultural responsibilities which were once the domain of their wives. They have also, with time of their hands and cars at their disposal, turned again to many kinds of rural recreation . . . to fishing and hunting, especially, but also to sailing and skiing. The most solitary of all sports, fishing, is also the most popular of all sports with American men.

But the greatest assault on old patterns of leisure and on the shibboleths about devil's work for idle hands, has been industry's discovery that it needs the consuming time of workers as much as it needs their producing time. In an economy, geared as ours is to making life comfortable for everyone, it is essential to business that people have time to enjoy their comfort and to use up the things that make life comfortable.

A tremendous part of our production plant is committed to promoting leisure—to automobiles, to television sets, to time-saving gadgets, to sports equipment, and to hundreds of services which are unnecessary to life but which contribute to relaxed living. Our economy, in other words, is more and more involved with Time Off. Think of the industries, the purveyors of pleasure, that would collapse if we were to go back to the sixty-hour week. It looks as though we are far more likely (and not because of pressures from labor but the demands of technology and automation) to go to a twenty-eight hour week.

Urbanization, the shorter working day and week, and the changing roles of the sexes have, heaven knows, produced tremendous changes in the ways Americans live. But the premium put on the consuming time of the worker by our economic system presents us with a tidily packaged moral dilemma. When idleness is a public virtue, what becomes of the moral value of work? What are we going to substitute for the old adages on which we were brought up? What are we going to tell our children? What will happen to the economy if we go on saying that virtue is its own reward, that work is good for the soul, and that leisure is only a reward for toil? What happens to the Calvinist ethic?

This is a problem I would rather refer to a dilettante than to an economist or a clergyman or certainly to an engineer. The economist would consider it from the point of view of wealth, the clergyman of the after life, and the engineer of production. The dilettante can be counted on to look at it from the point of view of life, liberty, and especially the pursuit of happiness.

I would like to contend in all seriousness, at this moment when there is such a cry for engineers and when our theological seminaries are bursting at the doors, that what we need is more dilettantes. Compared with good dilettantes, good engineers and good clergymen are a dime a dozen. Every newspaper account of the engineering shortage is contradicted by another story of how big corporations are hoarding engineers the way people hoarded butter during the war. Recently, Dr. Robert J. Havighurst of the University of Chicago made it quite clear that the number of engineers and technologists being trained in our technical schools is more than adequate to our needs; the shortage, he said, is in good teachers. In the long run our civilization will be measured more accurately by our know-why than by our know-how.

It is probably because in the triumvirate of our ideals—life, liberty, and the pursuit of happiness—the last of these has always seemed to our Calvinist society rather naughty, that we have come to look down our noses at the dilettante. We have dismissed him as a trifler; we have despised him as a parasite on other people's work, the fritterer, the gadfly. But there was a time when the word dilettante was by no means the term of opprobrium it has become.

Originally *dilettante* meant a lover of the fine arts (it comes from the Latin word for delight) and it was used to distinguish the consumer from the producer. Its application spread beyond the arts in England, and in the eighteenth century the Society of the Dilettanti was a club of influential men interested not only in the arts but in the sciences and in archaeology. It meant the man of intellectual curiosity who devoted part of his time to the intelligent cultivation of the arts and sciences, to the resources of leisure and the satisfactions of the mind.

If you transplant the idea of the eighteenth-century dilettante from England to America, you discover that he was Thomas Jefferson and Benjamin Franklin—one a farmer who dabbled in architecture and introduced a new style to America, the other a printer who dabbled in natural science and flew a kite into a thunderstorm. You discover several others who got together and started a talkfest that became the Philosophical Society of Philadelphia, and others who, dabbling in the arts, somehow founded a string of distinguished museums across the nation and filled them with masterpieces, and, of course, a good many bad guesses. These men were dilettantes. There is no other word that fits them.

In the nineteenth century the word came on hard times. "The connoisseur is 'one who knows,' as opposed to the dilettante who "only thinks he knows'," said F. W. Fairholt in the 1850s. Fairholt, an antiquary who wrote among other things *A Dictionary of Terms in Art,* was, there is no question, a connoisseur, and like all experts he was impatient of non-scholars who pretended to the delights he reserved for himself and his kind. A connoisseur, he said, "is cognisant of the true principles of Art, and can fully appreciate them. He is of a higher grade than the amateur, and more nearly approaches the artists." In his definition of an amateur he puts the emphasis on his "skill" as a performer and his non-professionalism, just as we do today, and in his definition of the dilettante, while he acknowledges the seriousness of the original meaning of the word, he bemoans the dilettante's pretentiousness and his use of the arts for purposes of social climbing. He admits (as people who consider themselves connoisseurs today rarely admit, however far they may go in buttering up the dilettante for their own purposes) that the arts need the enthusiasm that the dilettante's support brings to them.

The trouble (and it is a trouble) is that, with the decline of the word *dilettante,* there is no word left to describe the enthusiast who is more serious than the fan, less knowledgeable than the connoisseur, and hasn't the skill that makes an amateur. (The amateur is, after all, basically a performer.) What we need in our society, I contend again, is more real dilettantes, and we need to extend the meaning of the word to many delights besides the arts and sciences.

The dilettante is just a consumer. He is a man who takes the pursuit of happiness seriously, not frivolously, and he works at it. He is part sensualist, part intellectual, and part enthusiast. He is also likely to be a proselytizer for those causes in which his interests are involved, and to be rather scornful of those people who do not take their pleasure seriously and who are passive instead of active in the cultivation of them. But whatever else he may be he is not lazy. He may or may not have a job that he finds interesting, but he does not use his leisure in a miscellaneous and undirected fashion. He knows what he wants out of life and will go to a lot of trouble to get it. Primarily, in Voltaire's sense, he wants to cultivate his own garden.

You will find dilettantes everywhere and in every aspect of our culture. I found one a few weeks ago driving a taxi in New York. He was a man in his early sixties.

"I only drive this hack three days a week," he said. "The other four days I go fishing. I like to fish and I'm pretty good at it."

By the time he had delivered me home I knew what he fished for at what times of the year, what bait he used and where and in what weather, and which were the best fishing boats and captains going out of New York harbor. I asked him what he did with all the fish he caught.

"I got a son-in-law runs a saloon," he said. "I give them to his customers."

Probably the most common and in some ways the most accomplished of American dilettantes is the baseball fan, though the national pastime is being crowded out of its position as top banana of entertainment these days by serious music. The baseball fan knows his subject with something very close to genuine scholarship. He is an expert in the minutiae of its history and understands the nuances and subtleties of its performance. He takes as much pleasure from the refinements of its details as from the outcome of any single game, and he enjoys the company of others with whom he can argue the relative virtues of performance and make comparisons with other similar situations. He demands skill on the field of a truly professional caliber, and he lets his displeasure with anything less be known in the most direct and uncompromising manner. He is, by and large, a less tolerant dilettante than the one whose interest is devoted to art, for his expert eye is less subject to changes in fashion. Unquestionably without him the standards of baseball would long since have gone to pot.

The simple fact is that the dilettante is the ideal consumer, not ideal, perhaps, from the point of view of those producers who would like their customers to accept their products with blind confidence, but ideal from the point of view of maintaining standards of quality . . . whether material or cultural. He takes his functions as a consumer seriously. He takes the trouble to know what he likes and to sort out the shoddy and the meretricious from the sound and reasonable. If he is a dilettante of music, for example, he demands the best performance from his record-player. He is unimpressed by an imitation mahogany cabinet in the Chippendale manner, but he knows that the components of his hi-fi equipment are the very best that he can afford. (He can, in fact, be credited with the very great improvement in mass-produced sound equipment; it was his interest in high-fidelity that spread the word to the general public and raised the level of public acceptance.)

We are likely to associate the dilettante only with the arts, which is one reason why he has such a bad name in America. In the rambunctious and expansive days of the nineteenth century when America was growing and fighting its way across the continent, toil was man's business; culture was left to women. So were most other refinements of life, and the arts were thought of as sissy and men who showed any interest in them as something less than virile. A man who didn't sleep through a concert or an opera was regarded with suspicion. It was only when a man retired from business that it was considered suitable for him to spend his money on art—not necessarily because he liked it or knew anything about it but because it gave him social prestige. Except in a few Eastern Seaboard cities, the arts were women's work, and there was no time and place for the dilettante.

The nature of our new-found leisure is rapidly changing the old stereotypes. The businessman who doesn't make some pretense at an interest in culture, who doesn't support the local symphony and museum, who isn't on the library board or out raising money for his college is looked upon as not doing his duty, much less serving his own interests. Babbitt isn't Babbitt any more. Babbitt is by way of becoming a dilettante. A lot worse things could happen to him. In no time at all being a dilettante will not be considered un-American.

The point at which the dilettante becomes an "expert" but not a "professional" is an indistinct one. Two successful businessmen who have, in their leisure time, become naturalists of considerable reputation are an officer of J. P. Morgan & Co., R. Gordon Wasson, who has recently produced an important book of original research on mushrooms, and Boughton Cobb, a textile manufacturer who is one of the world's leading authorities on ferns. A few years ago an ancient language known to scholars as "Minoan Linear B" that had had scholars completely at sea for years was "broken" by an English architect, Michael Ventris, for whom cryptanalysis was a leisure activity. These three men became experts, not professionals, dilettantes in the best sense, not amateurs.

Obviously not many men in any generation are going to be able to extend their leisure activities to such levels of distinction. But leisure without direction, without the satisfaction of accomplishment of some sort is debilitating to anyone brought up in an atmosphere, like ours, in which the virtues of work have been so long extolled and are so deeply imbedded in our mythology. The greatest satisfaction of the dilettante is not in doing but in discovering, in discriminating, and in enjoying the fruits of his knowledge and his taste.

There will, of course, always be those who can only find satisfaction in making something, the eternal do-it-yourselfers, the cabinetmakers, and needlepointers, and gardeners, and model builders, and rug hookers. These are the amateur craftsmen who often achieve professional competence. There are also those who will find their only satisfactions apart from work in sensuous pleasures, in sports, and food and drink, and love. The dilettante finds his satisfactions primarily in the mind. He is the ideal traveler, the perfect audience, the coveted reader, and the perceptive collector.

But he is not by any means necessarily a highbrow. Indeed the ideal dilettante is not. He may be a professional intellectual or he may not, but he does not pose as what he isn't. His tastes and his knowledge may well run to abstruse and esoteric things, to the dances of Tibet or the jewelry of pre-Columbian Mexico, but they may just as well run to the square dance and baseball cards. The dilettante of jazz, the man who knows the names of the instrumentalists in all of the great bands of the last thirty years, is as important a dilettante as the man who knows his Mozart by Kocchel numbers. It is genuine, not simulated, enthusiasm that counts. The function of the dilettante is to encourage a high degree of performance in whatever field of interest happens to be his, to be an informed, but by no means conventional, critic, and to be a watchdog. He must be both an enthusiast and an irritant who will praise what measures up to his standards and needle producers into doing as well as they know how, and better. He is an incorrigible asker of hard questions. He keeps controversy in our culture alive, and if he is sometimes proved to be dead wrong, he is at least never dead on his feet. He is the want-to-know-why man and the traditional anathema of the know-how man.

Several months ago I found myself in an argument, or the beginnings of one, in a radio interview with a well-known broadcaster. "Our colleges need to produce more and better trained men," he said, and I countered with the suggestion that they needed to produce better educated men. "We need experts," he said.

"We need dilettantes," I replied, and the word so surprised him that he gingerly changed the subject to safer ground.

I would like to change my position, but only slightly. What we need are trained men with the capacity for being dilettantes. There can be no argument with the fact that an industrialized society must have a great many highly trained men and women with specialized knowledge and skills. But in this country the consumers and the producers are the same people; all of us work both sides of the economic street. We are, the great majority of us, the part-time idle rich, and no nation, so far as I know, has ever found itself in such a position before. Ours is a society in which no man's nose need be permanently to the grindstone, and where every man is a potential dilettante.

We have thought of our know-how as our most exportable commodity, and when somebody else demonstrated, moon-fashion, a superior know-how, we took it as a blow to our "national prestige." In fact our most exportable commodity has been a cultural one, a way of life that balances work and leisure for almost everyone and distributes the fruits of labor with astonishing, if not complete, evenness. Our most effective know-how has been the production of leisure, a commodity filled with promise and booby traps. It is the engineer with his slide rule who knows how to produce leisure, but it is the dilettante who knows how to use it and make it productive.

It will be as dilettantes and consumers that we will, in the long run, determine the quality of our culture. We will determine not only the gadgets of our civilization but the fate of its arts as well. We will determine whether the pursuit of happiness has, after all, been worth it.

When does a dog outgrow his dog food?

It depends. On his age, his condition and importantly on what he's fed. As your dog goes through life, his nutritional needs change. <u>And no single dog food is designed to meet these changing needs the way the Cycle* dog foods can.</u>

For growing puppies, **Cycle 1** contains extra protein and vitamins; extra calcium for developing teeth and bones. All concentrated for a puppy's smaller stomach.

For dogs in their active years (ages 1 to 7), there's

Cycle 2. Specifically formulated with the correct balance of protein, vitamins and minerals to help them stay lively and alert.

Cycle 3 is made *with less fat and 20% fewer calories than the leading canned dog food.* To help the overweight dog return to his proper, healthy weight.

Finally, there's **Cycle 4.** Formulated for the special needs of the older dog. With extra calcium for his older

bones; and high-quality protein in an amount his aging kidneys can easily handle.

Every Cycle canned dinner comes in a choice of meaty flavors: chicken and beef. For a meal that's as satisfying as it is nutritious.

Remember: *your dog never outgrows the Cycle foods. There's one for each important stage in his life.*

Gaines

Cycle. Nutrition...for the life of your dog.

TEST <u>YOUR</u> HUSBAND.

Q. With chicken, I prefer: (check one)

☐ Mashed potatoes.
☐ Stove Top Stuffing.

We bet he'll choose Stove Top Stuffing.

Most men do.

Joe Prekup says, "Stuffing tastes a lot better than mashed potatoes. There's a lot more flavor to it and it complements the chicken better."

John Jackson says, "Stuffing really accents the taste of chicken. It adds more zest to the meal."

In a recent consumer test, over 62% of the husbands polled preferred Stove Top® Stuffing Mix to mashed potatoes with their chicken dinners.

No wonder. Toasty bread crumbs, real chicken flavor and the perfect balance of celery, onion, parsley and herbs make Stove Top irresistible.

We bet your husband will agree.

©General Foods Corporation 1977
Stove Top is a registered trademark
of the General Foods Corporation.

Art Martori says, "Stove Top tastes like stuffing my mother used to make."

INSTEAD OF POTATOES.

Tourists
We Lose Our Charm
Away from Home[*]

Bertrand Russell

It is an odd fact that, while we are all charming people when we are at home, most of us become horrid as soon as we travel abroad. English travellers in the United States frequently have made me blush by their arrogance, their wholly unfounded superciliousness and their blindness to the very important merits of American civilisation.

This foolish behaviour causes untravelled Americans to think far worse of the English than they deserve. The fact is that the average tourist, of whatever nation, views the life of a foreign country in its more trivial aspects and fails to display his own best qualities. This applies not only to European tourists but also to those from the Western Hemisphere, with the result that Europeans who have never left their own continent get a very false impression of Americans.

Speaking broadly and ignoring many exceptions, one may say that Americans come to Europe chiefly to find satisfaction for those parts of human nature which are least catered to in their own country. A degenerate Italian aristocrat with a name familiar in Renaissance history is more interesting to these Americans than Einstein. To Europeans, unless they are professional antiquaries, such an attitude is impossible, since they have to live in the present and, if possible, make Europe fit to live in. Nor do they observe that American interest in European historical survivals always is very discriminating.

A culture impregnated with history has a certain depth and solidity which may not be without value; but the mere survival of quaint costumes, titles and customs has only the superficial kind of interest that is exploited by Hollywood. No one likes to be the object of this kind of interest, and

[*] From *Mortals and Others*, ed. H. Ruja. Reprinted by permission of The Bertrand Russell Peace Foundation Ltd.

Europeans tend to be impatient of being regarded as picturesque though absurd relics.

There is another, less cultivated tourist, who seeks, chiefly in Paris, a loosening of the moral restraints to which he is subject when at home. He does not suspect that the Parisians have their own code and therefore does not know when he offends against it. But throughout his enjoyment the serious aspects of French life remain hidden from him.

It is a curious feature of American (and to some extent of British) civilisation that those who have created and maintained it seek for themselves, in their spare time, something differing from it as widely as possible. This does not apply, for example, to the civilisation of France. A Frenchman likes a foreign country in proportion as it resembles his own, and there is no feature of his own world from which he longs to escape. What is the reason for this difference?

My explanation is that the French have been thinking mainly of what was agreeable to themselves; while many Americans, and not a few British, under the influence of their lofty ethical standards, have been thinking mainly of what would be good for their neighbours. What is good for us is, alas, not always agreeable, though it is gratifying to think that we are producing what is good for others. Consequently the pleasure to be derived from American civilisation largely is the altruistic pleasure of reflecting upon the noble men and women it is producing, while for private delight countries based upon a less exalted morality are more agreeable. This is, I believe, the explanation of the curious paradox that even the most patriotic Americans seek out eagerly whatever is most different from what they approve in their own country.

24 August 1931

Power?*

V.S. Naipaul

The Trinidad Carnival is famous. For the two days before Ash Wednesday the million or so islanders—blacks, whites, the later immigrant groups of Portuguese, Indians, and Chinese—parade the hot streets in costumed "bands" and dance to steel orchestras. This year there was a twist. After the Carnival there were Black Power disturbances. After the masquerade and the music, anger and terror.

In a way, it makes sense. Carnival and Black Power are not as opposed as they appear. The tourists who go for the Carnival don't really know what they are watching. The islanders themselves, who have spent so long forgetting the past, have forgotten the darker origins of their Carnival. The bands, flags and costumes have little to do with Lent, and much to do with slavery.

The slave in Trinidad worked by day and lived at night. Then the world of the white plantations fell away; and in its place was a securer, secret world of fantasy, of Negro "kingdoms", "regiments", bands. The people who were slaves by day saw themselves then as kings, queens, dauphins, princesses. There were pretty uniforms, flags and painted wooden swords. Everyone who joined a regiment got a title. At night the Negroes played at being people, mimicking the rites of the upper world. The kings visited and entertained. At gatherings a "secretary" might sit scribbling away.

Once, in December, 1805, this fantasy of the night overflowed into the working day. There was serious talk then of cutting off the heads of some plantation owners, of drinking holy water afterwards and eating pork and dancing. The plot was found out; and swiftly, before Christmas, in the main Port of Spain square there were hangings, decapitations, brandings and whippings.

That was Trinidad's first and last slave "revolt". The Negro kingdoms

* From V. S. Naipaul, *The Overcrowded Barracoon* 1972. Reprinted by permission of Andre Deutsch Limited.

of the night were broken up. But the fantasies remained. They had to, because without that touch of lunacy the Negro would have utterly despaired and might have killed himself slowly by eating dirt; many in Trinidad did. The Carnival the tourist goes to see is a version of the lunacy that kept the slave alive. It is the original dream of black power, style and prettiness; and it always feeds on a private vision of the real world.

During the war an admiration for Russia—really an admiration for "stylish" things like Stalin's moustache and the outlandish names of Russian generals, Timoshenko, Rokossovsky—was expressed in a "Red Army" band. At the same time an admiration for Humphrey Bogart created a rival "Casablanca" band. Make-believe, but taken seriously and transformed; not far below, perhaps even unacknowledged, there has always been a vision of the black millennium, as much a vision of revenge as of a black world made whole again.

Something of the Carnival lunacy touches all these islands where people, first as slaves and then as neglected colonials, have seen themselves as futile, on the other side of the real world. In St Kitts, with a population of 36,000, Papa Bradshaw, the Premier, has tried to calm despair by resurrecting the memory of Christophe, Emperor of Haiti, builder of the Citadel, who was born a slave on the island. Until they were saved from themselves, the 6,000 people of Anguilla seriously thought they could just have a constitution written by someone from Florida and set up in business as an independent country.

In Jamaica the Ras Tafarians believe they are Abyssinians and that the Emperor Haile Selassie is God. This is one of the unexpected results of Italian propaganda during the Abyssinian war. The Italians said then that there was a secret black society called Niya Binghi ("Death to the Whites") and that it was several million strong. The propaganda delighted some Jamaicans, who formed little Niya Binghi play-groups of their own. Recently the Emperor visited Jamaica. The Ras Tafarians were expecting a black lion of a man; they saw someone like a Hindu, mild-featured, brown and small. The disappointment was great; but somehow the sect survives.

These islanders are disturbed. They already have black government and black power, but they want more. They want something more than politics. Like the dispossessed peasantry of medieval Europe, they await crusades and messiahs. Now they have Black Power. It isn't the Black Power of the United States. That is the protest of a disadvantaged minority which has at last begun to feel that some of the rich things of America are accessible, that only self-contempt and discrimination stand in the way. But in the islands the news gets distorted.

The media cannot make the disadvantages as real as the protest. Famous cities are seen to blaze; young men of the race come out of buildings with guns; the black-gloved hands of triumphant but bowed athletes are raised as in a religious gesture; the handsome spokesmen of protest make threats before the cameras which appear at last to have discovered black style. This is power. In the islands it is like a vision of the black millennium. It needs no political programme.

In the islands the intellectual equivocations of Black Power are part of its strength. After the sharp analysis of black degradation, the spokesmen for Black Power usually become mystical, vague, and threatening. In the United States this fits the cause of protest, and fits the white audience to whom this protest is directed. In the islands it fits the old, apocalyptic mood of the black masses. Anything more concrete, anything like a programme, might become simple local politics and be reduced to the black power that is already possessed.

Black Power as rage, drama and style, as revolutionary jargon, offers something to everybody: to the unemployed, the idealistic, the drop-out, the Communist, the politically frustrated, the anarchist, the angry student returning home from humiliations abroad, the racialist, the old-fashioned black preacher who has for years said at street corners that after Israel it was to be the turn of Africa. Black Power means Cuba and China; it also means clearing the Chinese and the Jews and the tourists out of Jamaica. It is identity and it is also miscegenation. It is drinking holy water, eating pork and dancing; it is going back to Abyssinia. There has been no movement like it in the Caribbean since the French Revolution.

So in Jamaica, some eighteen months ago, students joined with Ras Tafarians to march in the name of Black Power against the black government. Campus idealism, campus protest; but the past is like quicksand here. There was a middle-class rumour, which was like a rumour from the days of slavery, that a white tourist was to be killed, but only sacrificially, without malice.

At the same time, in St Kitts, after many years in authority, Papa Bradshaw was using Black Power, as words alone, to undermine the opposition. Round and round the tiny impoverished island, on the one circular road, went the conspiratorial printed message, cut out from a gasoline advertisement: *Join the Power Set*.

Far away, on the Central American mainland, in British Honduras, which is only half black, Black Power had just appeared and was already undermining the multi-racial nature of both government and opposition. The carrier of the infection was a twenty-one-year-old student who had been to the United States on, needless to say, an American government scholarship.

He had brought back news about the dignity of the peasant and a revolution based on land. I thought the message came from another kind of country and somebody else's revolution, and wasn't suited to the local blacks, who were mainly city people with simple city ambitions. (It was front-page news, while I was there, that a local man had successfully completed an American correspondence course in jail management.)

But it didn't matter. A message had come. "The whites are buying up the land." "What the black man needs is bread." "It became a phallic symbol to the black to be a log-cutter." It was the jargon of the movement, at once scientific-sounding and millenarian. It transcended the bread-and-butter protests of local politics; it smothered all argument. Day by day the movement grew.

Excitement! And perhaps this excitement is the only liberation that is possible. Black Power in these black islands is protest. But there is no enemy. The enemy is the past, of slavery and colonial neglect and a society uneducated from top to bottom; the enemy is the smallness of the islands and the absence of resources. Opportunism or borrowed jargon may define phantom enemies: racial minorities, "élites", "white niggers". But at the end the problems will be the same, of dignity and identity.

In the United States Black Power may have its victories. But they will be American victories. The small islands of the Caribbean will remain islands, impoverished and unskilled, ringed as now by a *cordon sanitaire*, their people not needed anywhere. They may get less innocent or less corrupt politicans; they will not get less helpless ones. The island blacks will continue to be dependent on the books, films and goods of others; in this important way they will continue to be the half-made societies of a dependent people, the Third World's third world. They will forever consume; they will never create. They are without material resources; they will never develop the higher skills. Identity depends in the end on achievement; and achievement here cannot but be small. Again and again the protest leader will appear and the millennium will seem about to come.

Fifty years ago, writing at a moment when Spain seemed about to disintegrate, Ortega y Gasset saw that fragmented peoples come together only in order "to do something tomorrow". In the islands this assurance about the future is missing. Millenarian excitement will not hold them together, even if they were all black; and some, like Trinidad and Guyana and British Honduras, are only half black. The pursuit of black identity and the community of black distress is a dead end, frenzy for the sake of frenzy, the self-scourging of people who cannot see what they will have to do tomorrow.

In *We Wish to be Looked Upon*, published last year by Teachers College Press, Vera Rubin and Marisa Zavalloni report on surveys of high-school students in Trinidad they conducted in 1957 and 1961, at a time of pre-independence, messianic optimism. (Eric Williams had come to power, suddenly and overwhelmingly, in 1956.) The students were asked to write at length about their "expectations, plans and hopes for the future".

Black: I would like to be a great man not only in music but also in sociology and economics. In the USA I would like to marry a beautiful actress with plenty of money. I would also like to be famed abroad as one of the world's foremost millionaires.

Black: In politics I hope to come up against men like Khrushchev and other enemies of freedom. I hope I will be able to overcome them with my words, and put them to shame.

Black: I expect to be a man of international fame, a man who by virtue of his political genius has acquired so much respect from his people that he will be fully capable of living in peace with his people.

Black: I want to be a West Indian diplomat. I would like to have a magnetic power over men and a stronger magnetic power over women. I must be very intelligent and quick-witted: I must be fluent in at least seven languages. I must be very resourceful and I must say the correct thing at the correct moment. With these qualities and a wonderful foresight and with other necessary abilities which I can't foresee, I would be able to do wonders for the world by doing wonders for my nation.

East Indian: I will write a book called the *Romance of Music and Literature.* I will make this book as great as any Shakespeare play; then I will return to India to endeavour to become a genius in the film industry.

East Indian: I want to develop an adventurous spirit. I will tour the earth by air, by sea, and by land. I shall become a peacemaker among hostile people.

East Indian: When I usually awake from my daydream, I think myself to be another person, the great scientific engineer, but soon I recollect my sense, and then I am myself again.

Coloured (mulatto): Toward the latter part of my life I would like to enter myself in politics, and to do some little bit for the improvement and uplift of this young Federation of ours.

Coloured: I am obsessed with the idea of becoming a statesman, a classical statesman, and not a mere rabble-rouser who acts impulsively and makes much ado about nothing.

White: I am going to apprentice myself to a Chartered Accountant's firm and then to learn the trade. When I want to, leave the firm and go to any other big business concern and work my way up to the top.

White: I want to live a moderate life, earning a moderate pay, slowly but surely working my way in the law firm, but I don't want to be chief justice of the Federation or anything like that...Look around. All the other boys must be writing about their ambitions to be famous. They all cannot be, for hope is an elusive thing.

White: By this time my father may be a shareholder in the company, I will take over the business. I will expand it and try to live up to the traditions that my father has built up.

Without the calm of the white responses, the society might appear remote, fantastic and backward. But the white student doesn't inhabit a world which is all that separate. Trinidad is small, served by two newspapers and two radio stations and the same unsegregated schools. The intercourse between the races is easier than inquiring sociologists usually find; there is a substantial black and East Indian middle class that dominates the professions. When this is understood, the imprecision of black and East Indian fantasy—diplomacy, politics, peacemaking—can be seen to be more than innocence. It is part of the carnival lunacy of a lively, well-informed society which feels itself part of the great world, but understands at the same time that it is cut off from this world by reasons of geography, history, race.

The sub-title of Rubin and Zavalloni's book is "A Study of the Aspirations of Youth in a Developing Society". But the euphemism is misleading. This society has to be more precisely defined. Brazil is developing, India is developing. Trinidad is neither undeveloped nor developing. It is fully part of the advanced consumer society of the West; it recognizes high material standards. But it is less than provincial: there is no metropolis to which the man from the village or small town can take his gifts. Trinidad is simply small; it is dependent; and the people born in it—black, East Indian, white—sense themselves condemned, not necessarily as individuals, but as a community, to an inferiority of skill and achievement. In colonial days racial deprivation could be said to be important, and this remains, obviously, an important drive. But now it is only part of the story.

In the islands, in fact, black identity is a sentimental trap, obscuring the issues. What is needed is access to a society, larger in every sense, where people will be allowed to grow. For some territories this larger society may be Latin American. Colonial rule in the Caribbean defied geography and created unnatural administrative units; this is part of the problem. Trinidad, for instance, was detached from Venezuela. This is a geographical absurdity; it might be looked at again.

A Latin American identity is also possible for Guyana and British Honduras. But local racial politics and servile prejudice stand in the way. The blacks of British Honduras, in their one lazy, mosquito-infested town, reject "Latinization" without knowing what they are rejecting. Until Black Power came along last year, the black flag of protest against Latinization was the Union Jack; and the days of slavery were recalled with pride as the days when blacks and their English owners, friends really, stood shoulder to shoulder against the awful Spaniards. The blacks, at the end of the day, see themselves as British, made in the image of their former owners, with British institutions; Latin Americans are seen as chaotic, violent, without the rule of law.

There is an irony in this. Because in these former British territories the gravest issue, as yet unrecognized, is the nineteenth-century Latin American issue of government by consent. These Caribbean territories are not like those in Africa or Asia, with their own internal reverences, that have been returned to themselves after a period of colonial rule. They are manufactured societies, labour camps, creations of empire; and for long they were dependent on empire for law, language, institutions, culture, even officials. Nothing was generated locally; dependence became a habit. How, without empire, do such societies govern themselves? What is now the source of power? The ballot box, the mob, the regiment? When, as in Haiti, the slave-owners leave, and there are only slaves, what are the sanctions?

It is like the Latin American situation after the break up of the Spanish Empire. With or without Black Power, chaos threatens. But chaos will only be internal. The islands will always be subject to an external police. The United States helicopters will be there, to take away United States citizens, tourists; the British High Commissions will lay on airlifts for their citizens. These islands, black and poor, are dangerous only to themselves.

Nobody Here but Us Dead Sheep*

William Zinsser

Nerve gas in Okinawa. Nuclear explosions in Nevada. Chemical Mace in the eyes. Every day it's something else in American life which strikes me as outlandish, but which evidently began in logic. I can no longer tell where we cross over from the normal to the insane.

I remember back in May seeing a picture of a tank and some infantrymen on the front page of the morning paper. I didn't bother to read the caption because it was the same combat picture of Vietnam that I've seen every other morning. But, it wasn't Vietnam—it was a college in North Carolina. A few days later I saw a photograph of several hundred soldiers standing guard in gas masks. They were in gas masks because a helicopter was poised overhead to spray chemicals. It was the University of California at Berkeley. In 1969 the incongruous becomes routine almost overnight.

I never knew, for instance, that the American Army has been storing nerve gas at its bases in other countries. The only way the Army lets us know about its nerve gas is to leak a little by mistake, as it did last month in Okinawa, briefly hospitalizing 24 men. Just routine deployment of deterrent power, the Pentagon said, explaining its policy on chemical weapons — nobody should be surprised.

Well, *I* was surprised. More surprised, actually, than the Okinawans, who suspected something last summer when 200 Okinawan children suffered skin burns while swimming at a beach 12 miles south of our 137th Ordnance Company's camp. The unusual still strikes them as unusual.

Not us. In the spring of 1968, 6,400 sheep dropped dead one week in

* *Life* 67, No. 8 (August 22, 1969).

Utah—a mortality rate not common in sheep-raising—fairly near the Army's chemical warfare testing center. Queried about this coincidence, the Army said it couldn't imagine what could have possibly happened to those sheep. Luckily, a few people felt that the sudden death of 6,400 sheep taunted the laws of zoology, and they kept bringing the matter up, clinging to reason amid denials that persisted for 14 months, until finally the official lies were turned into official truths—as happened when the Pentagon admitted that it knew exactly what happened to those sheep. A valve malfunctioned. The wind changed. So sorry.

Should we laugh or cry? We teeter every day on the edge of absurdity and think it is solid ground. Recently the Army decided to get rid of 27,000 tons of obsolete chemical and bacteriological weapons stockpiled at a base in the Rockies—including 2,660 tons of rockets and 12,322 tons of bomb clusters, all filled with nerve gas—by hauling the whole load across the country in railroad cars and dumping it in the ocean off New Jersey. A routine operation, perfectly safe.

The Army didn't think anything could happen to those weapons as they moved secretly across the country by train, bouncing 1,500 miles through American cities and towns where the populace lay sleeping, snug in the belief that it was only the night mail. But actually the Army doesn't even have responsibility while its cargo is on a train. That belongs to the railroad—and anything *can* happen. Just a few weeks ago a cargo of Army "ammunition propellant" exploded on a freight train as it passed through Noel, Mo., killing one resident, injuring 100, and damaging all the businesses and most of the homes in town.

Maybe this is what finally nudged the Senate into realizing that the Army could use some supervision, and, with any luck, the measure approved last week—to restrict the storage, transportation and use of chemical weapons—will provide it. We'll need the luck because we obviously can't count on logic. Remember the grotesque shipment of nerve gas across the country? Apparently only one person heard about it and found it grotesque—Representative Richard D. McCarthy, Democrat of New York, who said there must be a safer way to get rid of the stuff. There was. The Pentagon gave it a second thought and decided that it could neutralize the gases without moving them anywhere at all.

Then there's the funny story about the atomic tests in Nevada. Somehow it never occurred to me that a hydrogen bomb explosion would be a spectacle that tourists would want to see, like Cypress Gardens or Colonial Williamsburg. But then I came upon an article in the travel and resort section of the New York *Times*—nestled among the Caribbean cruises and Riviera nights—which said that the Atomic Energy Commission has decided to let sightseers observe large-scale atomic tests at its new test site 200 miles north of Las Vegas.

I was surprised to see this announcement made in the travel section. I could only take it to mean that our nuclear arsenal has somehow crossed over from the realm of American defense to the realm of American leisure: a fun facility for Dad, Mom and the kids. Undecided about your vacation? Already done Disneyland? Why not go to Nevada for the blasts?

Unfortunately, "Observers will not experience the blinding flashes, awesome fireballs and deafening roars of the early aboveground tests," the *Times* article explained. "But even at a distance of 12 miles an underground megaton shot produces an artificial earthquake that makes the ground shudder and seemingly heave a couple of feet, a shock that can knock a man off his feet. A spectacular curtain of dust, miles wide, is sent up from the desert floor. There is always a possibility that the huge caverns blasted underground may cause a spectacular surface cave-in. The principal unexpected thing that can happen is a venting of radioactive gas through unpredictable fissures in the ground."

Well, I've got to admit that as a tourist attraction it goes far beyond your average gator farm or monkey jungle. There's the whole new element of surprise. I mean, we all know that Old Faithful is going to erupt every 65 minutes. So what else is new? And at Disneyland everything is so clean—you simply don't have the possibility of a surface cave-in or a curtain of dust.

I assume the AEC will build a luxury motel out at the site. It should have a name that will look folksy on billboards—Atomland, or Nuclear Village—and convey the idea of a resort where the whole family can come and have a good time between explosions. It would be a shame, after all, to arrive on a Monday and catch an ordinary megaton shot with just a medium earthquake. By waiting around for another test, the family might see a really decent cave-in and get some funny pictures for the photo album ("Me and Mom in front of atom bomb hole—that's Dad on the ground"). It might even open some unpredictable fissures that would vent enough radioactive gas to show up on Bobby's toy Geiger counter, the one he bought at the New Hiroshima Boutique & Coffee Shoppe where he got those wonderful blastburgers.

Got time for one more joke? Let's look at the droll story of Chemical Mace. Several congressional committees recently learned that Mace, used by more than 4,000 police departments, can cause permanent injury.

Now comes the funny part. Sixteen months ago—in April, 1968—the Army made a "biological assessment" of Chemical Mace Mark IV on rabbits, monkeys and dogs and found that it "could cause scarring of the corneal surface and scarring of the skin." Surgeon General William Stewart therefore advised all state, county and city health officers that Mace could cause "more than transient effects to the exposed individual unless treatment is prompt."

Now anyone might think that all those public health officers would try to get a substance banned which can scar the corneas of the public whose health they are officering. But evidently they all thought it was somebody else's business, and it was not until this spring—a year later—that the matter came up before the Senate Subcommittee on Executive Reorganization. (Where have *they* been all these years?)

Why, Surgeon General Stewart was asked by a reporter, did he not recommend discontinuing the use of Mace?

"I think there was a misunderstanding," he replied, "that we have some authority to ban Mace." Translation: "Don't look at me, I'm only the Surgeon General." Besides, he said, he wasn't asked to evaluate Mace. He was only asked "what were the health effects and what do you do with people who are Maced?" He pointed out that the Public Health Service has no control over Mace as a weapon used by police departments, partly because it does not fit the definition of a drug.

This was disputed by former Food and Drug Commissioner James Goddard, who told the Senate subcommittee that Mace does indeed fit the definition of a drug "as altering in some way the structure or function of the human body." He cited reports of corneal scars, chemical burns and sharp rises in blood pressure—up to 100 points within seconds. I would have to say that it is a dangerous substance and it does have potential for causing blindness, according to the reports I have read, and to cause death.

"To the best of my knowledge, Mr. Chairman," Goddard added, "no police officer has sprayed Mace at a citizen and then immediately flushed the victim's eyes with cool water and rinsed his clothing."

Meanwhile the head of the Federal Trade Commission, Paul Rand Dixon, said that his agency is trying to halt the "deceptive advertising of chemical sprays being sold to the general public," but that the job requires some cooperation. "The commission deplores the fact that all interested government agencies were not informed of the results of the Army's tests. Without the free and complete exchange of such information, the enforcement of our laws in the protection of the public interests is virtually an impossible task."

Again, I don't know whether to laugh or cry at an executive organization so hopelessly in need of reorganizing. I'm too old to cry, but it hurts too much to laugh—mainly around the cornea.

What Psychiatry Can and Cannot Do[*]

Thomas S. Szasz

Psychiatry today is in the curious position of being viewed simultaneously with too much reverence and with undue contempt. Indeed, thoughtful Americans can be roughly divided between those who dismiss all forms of psychiatric practice as worthless or harmful, and those who regard it as a panacea for crime, unhappiness, political fanaticism, promiscuity, juvenile delinquency, and virtually every other moral, personal, and social ill of our time.

The adherents of this exaggerated faith are, I believe, the larger and certainly the more influential group in shaping contemporary social policy. It is they who beat the drums for large-scale mental health programs and who use the prestige of a massive psychiatric establishment as a shield of illusion, concealing some ugly realities we would rather not face. Thus when we read in the paper that the alcoholic, the rapist, or the vandal needs or will be given "psychiatric care," we are reassured that the problem is being solved or, in any event, effectively dealt with, and we dismiss it from our minds.

I contend that we have no right to this easy absolution from responsibility. In saying this I do not, as a practicing psychiatrist, intend to belittle the help that my profession can give to some troubled individuals. We have made significant progress since the pre-Freudian era, when psychiatry was a purely custodial enterprise.

However, our refusal to recognize the differences between medicine and psychiatry—that is, between deviations from biological norms, which we usually call "illness," and deviations from psychological or social norms, which we often call "mental illness"—has made it possible to popularize the simplistic clichés of current mental health propaganda. One of these, for instance, is the deceptive slogan "Mental illness is like any other illness." This is not true; psychiatric and medical problems are fundamentally dissimilar. In curing a disease like syphilis or pneumonia, the physician benefits both the patient and society. Can the psychiatrist who cures a "neurosis" make the same claim? Often he cannot, for in "mental illness" we find the individual in conflict with those about him—his family, his friends, his employer, perhaps his whole society. Do we expect psychiatry to help the individual—or society? If the interests of the two conflict, as they often do, the psychiatrist can help one only by harming the other.

II

Let us, for example, examine the case of a man I will call Victor Clauson. He is a junior executive with a promising future, a wife who loves him, and two healthy children. Nevertheless he is anxious and unhappy. He is bored with his job, which he believes saps his initiative and destroys his integrity; he is also dissatisfied with his wife, and convinced he never loved her. Feeling like a slave to his company, his wife, and his children, Clauson realizes that he has lost control over the conduct of his life.

Is this man "sick"? And, if so, what can be done about it? At least half a dozen alternatives are open to him: He could throw himself into his present work or change jobs or have an affair or get a divorce. Or he could develop a psychosomatic symptom such as headaches and consult a doctor. Or he could seek help from a psychotherapist. Which of these alternatives is the right one for him? The answer is not easy.

For, in fact, hard work, an affair, a divorce, a new job may all "help" him; and so may psychotherapy. But "treatment" cannot change his external, social situation; only he can do that. What psychoanalysis (and some other therapies) can offer him is a better knowledge of himself, which may enable him to make new and better choices in the conduct of his life.

Is Clauson "mentally sick"? If we so label him, what then is he to be cured of? Unhappiness? Indecision? The consequences of earlier, unwise decisions?

In my opinion, these are problems in living, not diseases. And by and large it is such problems that are brought to the psychiatrist's office. To ameliorate them he offers not treatment or cure but psychological counseling. To be of any avail, this process requires a consenting, co-operative client. There is, indeed, no way to "help" an individual who does not want to be a psychiatric patient. When treatment is imposed on a person, inevitably he sees it as serving not his own best interests, but the interests of those who brought him to the psychiatrist (and who often pay him).

Take the case of an elderly widow I will call Mrs. Rachel Abelson. Her husband was a successful businessman who died five years ago, bequeathing part of his estate of four million dollars to his children and grandchildren, part to charities, and one third to his wife. Mrs. Abelson has always been a frugal woman, whose life revolved around her husband. After he died, however, she changed. She began to give her money away —to her widowed sister, to charities, and finally to distant relatives abroad.

After a few years, Mrs. Abelson's children remonstrated, urging her to treat herself better, instead of wasting her money on people who had long managed by themselves. But Mrs. Abelson persisted in doing what she felt was "the right thing." Her children were wealthy; she enjoyed helping others.

Finally, the Abelson children consulted the family attorney. He was equally dismayed by the prospect that Mrs. Abelson might in this fashion dissipate all the funds she controlled. Like the children, he reasoned that if Mr. Abelson had wanted to help his third cousin's poverty-stricken daughters in Rumania, he could have done so himself; but he never did. Convinced that they ought to carry out the essence of their father's intention and keep the money in the family, the Abelson children petitioned to have their mother declared mentally incompetent to manage her affairs. This was done. Thereafter Mrs. Abelson became inconsolable. Her bitter accusations and the painful scenes that resulted only convinced her children that she really was mentally abnormal. When she refused to enter a private sanitarium voluntarily, she was committed by court order. She died two years later, and her will—leaving most of her assets to distant relatives— was easily broken on psychiatric grounds.

Like thousands of other involuntary mental patients, Mrs. Abelson was given psychiatric care in the hope of changing behavior offensive to others. Indeed, what was Mrs. Abelson's illness? Spending her money unwisely? Disinheriting her sons? In effect, recourse to psychiatry provided Mrs. Abelson's children with a socially acceptable solution for their dilemma, not hers. To an appalling degree, state mental hospitals perform a like function for the less affluent members of our society.

Out of all too many comparable cases, I will cite that of a man we may call Tim Kelleher, who worked steadily as a truck driver for forty years, supporting a wife and nine children. In his early sixties Kelleher found jobs getting scarcer. Now in his late seventies, he has not worked for over a decade. Since his wife died a few years ago, he has lived with one or another of his children.

For two years his daughter Kathleen, mother of four, has been caring for him. Because the old man has grown progressively senile and burdensome, Kathleen's husband wants to shift the responsibility to the other children, but they all feel they've done their share.

Mr. Kelleher's future depends on what his family decides to do with him. One of them may still be willing to take care of him, but, if not, he will be committed to a state mental hospital. His case will be diagnosed as a "senile psychosis" or something similar. More than a third of the patients now in our mental hospitals are such "geriatric" cases. This is how psychiatry meets a purely socioeconomic need.

If Mr. Kelleher or one of his children were even moderately wealthy, they could hire a companion or nurse to care for him at home, or they could place him in a private nursing home. There would be no need to label him a "mental patient" and confine him to a building he will never again leave, and where he will doubtless die within a year.

But, for the poor, the mental hospital is often the only way. Such is the plight of Mrs. Anna Tarranti (this is not her real name). At thirty-two—but looking ten years older—she has just been delivered of her seventh child. Her husband is a construction worker, sporadically employed, and a heavy drinker. After each of the last three babies was born, Mrs. Tarranti was so "depressed" that she had to stay in the hospital an extra week or more. Now she complains of exhaustion, cannot eat or sleep, and does not want to see her baby. At the same time she feels guilty for not being a good mother, and says she ought to die.

The fact is that Mrs. Tarranti is overwhelmed. She has more children than she wants, a husband who earns only a marginal living, and religious beliefs that virtually prohibit birth control. What should she do? She knows that if she goes home, she'll soon be pregnant again, a prospect she cannot endure. She would like to stay in the hospital, but the obstetrical ward is too busy to keep her long without a bona fide obstetrical illness.

Again psychiatry comes to the rescue. Mrs. Tarranti's condition is diagnosed as a "post-partum depression" and she is committed to the state hospital. As in the case of Mr. Kelleher, society has found no more decent solution to a human problem than confinement in a mental hospital.

In effect, psychiatry has accepted the job of warehousing society's undesirables. Such, alas, has long been its role. More than a hundred and fifty years ago, the great French psychiatrist Philippe Pinel observed, "Public asylums for maniacs have been regarded as places of confinement for such of its members as have become dangerous to the peace of society."[1]

---

[1] Pinel, P.: *A Treatise on Insanity* (1801, 1809), transl. by D. D. Davis, facsimile of the London 1806 edition (New York: Hafner Publishing Co., 1962), pp. 3-4.

III

Nor have we any right to comfort ourselves with the belief that in our enlightened age confinement in a mental institution is really the same as any other kind of hospitalization. For even though we show more compassion and understanding toward the insane than some of our forebears, the fact is that the person diagnosed as mentally ill is stigmatized—particularly if he has been confined in a public mental hospital. These stigmata cannot be removed by mental health "education," for the root of the matter is our intolerance of certain kinds of behavior.

Most people who are considered mentally sick (especially those confined involuntarily) are so defined by their relatives, friends, employers, or perhaps the police—not by themselves. These people have upset the social order—by disregarding the conventions of polite society or by violating laws—so we label them "mentally ill" and punish them by commitment to a mental institution.

The patient knows that he is deprived of freedom because he has annoyed others, not because he is sick. And in the mental hospital he learns that until he alters his behavior he will be segregated from society. But even if he changes and is permitted to leave, his record of confinement goes with him. And the practical consequences are more those of a prison than a hospital record. The psychological and social damage thus incurred often far outweighs the benefits of any psychiatric therapy.

Consider, for example, the case of a young nurse I will call Emily Silverman, who works in a general hospital in a small city. Unmarried and lonely, she worries about the future. Will she find a husband? Will she have to go on supporting herself in a job that has become drudgery? She feels depressed, sleeps poorly, loses weight. Finally, she consults an internist at the hospital and is referred to a psychiatrist. He diagnoses her trouble as a case of "depression" and prescribes "anti-depressant" drugs. Emily takes the pills and visits the psychiatrist weekly, but she remains depressed and begins to think about suicide. This alarms the psychiatrist, who recommends hospitalization. Since there is no private mental hospital in the city, Emily seeks admission to the state hospital nearby. There, after a few months, she realizes that the "treatment" the hospital offers cannot help solve her problems. She then "recovers" and is discharged.

From now on, Emily is no longer just a nurse; she is a nurse with a "record" of confinement in a state mental hospital. When she tries to return to her job, she will probably find it filled and that there are no openings. Indeed, as an ex-mental patient, she may find it impossible to obtain any employment in nursing. This is a heavy price to pay for ignorance, yet no one warned her of the hazards involved before she decided to enter the hospital for her "depression."

Because the therapeutic potentialities of psychiatry are consistently exaggerated and its punitive functions minimized or even denied, a distorted relationship between psychiatry and the law has evolved in our time.

Years ago some people accused of serious crimes pleaded "insanity." Today they are often charged with it. Instead of receiving a brief jail sentence, a defendant may be branded "insane" and incarcerated for life in a psychiatric institution.[2]

This is what happened, for example, to a filling-station operator I will call Joe Skulski. When he was told to move his business to make way for a new shopping center, he stubbornly resisted eviction. Finally the police were summoned. Joe greeted them with a warning shot in the air. He was taken into custody and denied bail, because the police considered his protest peculiar and thought he must be crazy. The district attorney requested a pretrial psychiatric examination of the accused. Mr. Skulski was examined, pronounced mentally unfit to stand trial, and confined in the state hospital for the criminally insane. Through it all, he pleaded for the right to be tried for his offense. Now in the mental hospital, he will spend years of fruitless effort to prove that he is sane enough to stand trial. If he had been convicted, his prison sentence would have been shorter than the term he has already served in the hospital.

IV

This is not to say that our public mental hospitals serve no socially useful purpose. They do, in fact, perform two essential—and very different—functions. On the one hand, they help patients recover from personal difficulties by providing them with room, board, and a medically approved escape from everyday responsibilities. On the other hand, they help families, and society, care for those who annoy or burden them unduly. It is important that we sort out these very different services, for unfortunately their goals are not the same. To relieve people annoyed by the eccentricities, failings, or outright meanness of so-called mentally disturbed persons requires that something be done *to* mental patients, not *for* them. The aim here is to safeguard the sensibilities not of the patient, but of those he upsets. This is a moral and social, not a medical, problem. How, for example, do you weigh the right of Mr. Kelleher to spend his declining years in freedom and dignity rather than as a psychiatric prisoner, against the right of his children to lead a "life of their own" unburdened by a senile father? Or the right of Mrs. Tarranti to repudiate overwhelming responsibilities, against her husband's and children's need for the services of a full-time

[2]Szasz, T.S.: *Psychiatric Justice* (New York: Macmillan, 1965).

wife and mother? Or the right of Mrs. Abelson to give away her money to poor relatives, against her children's claim on their father's fortune?

Granting that there can often be no happy resolution to such conflicts, there is no reason to feel that we are as yet on the right road. For one thing, we still tolerate appalling inequities between our treatment of the rich and the poor. Though it may be no more than a dimly grasped ideal, both medicine and law strive to treat all people equally. In psychiatry, however, we not only fail to approximate this goal in our practice; we do not even value it as an ideal.

We regard the rich and influential psychiatric patient as a self-governing, responsible client—free to decide whether or not to be a patient. But we look upon the poor and the aged patient as a ward of the state—too ignorant or too "mentally sick" to know what is best for him. The paternalistic psychiatrist, as an agent of the family or the state, assumes "responsibility" for him, defines him as a "patient" against his will, and subjects him to "treatment" deemed best for him, with or without his consent.

Do we really need more of this kind of psychiatry?

Terms
and
Topics

TERMS

1. All kinds of writing use *rhetorical devices*, though argument probably makes the greatest use of them. **Syllogism** is used in the introduction to this section, and **chiasmus** in the Note to the Reader. Here are a few other common rhetorical techniques:

    rhetorical question A question that does not expect an answer, because the answer is implicit in the question. Such a question is thus for rhetorical effect only.

    parallelism Parellel or repeated structure or phrasing for rhetorical effect.

    antithesis A balanced structure whose two halves contrast. Sometimes the two parts are like those of a chiasmus; sometimes they are parallel.

    analogy Reasoning from certain similarities between two things that they are alike in other respects as well. For example, if one begins by assuming that a country is like a business in certain ways, one could then conclude, by analogy, that the qualities of a good business manager are the qualities needed in the leader of a country. Not all analogies are logically sound. Is this one?

2. The Note to the Reader defined *metaphor* and *symbol*. Differentiate between *figurative language* and *rhetorical devices*. Is *paradox* (see Terms, section I), for example, a figure of speech or a figure of rhetoric? Is it, perhaps, a kind of *irony* (see Terms, section II)? Or is it in a way all three? Obviously all of these devices—and many more—are available to writers of prose. Can prose writers also make effective use of such figures of speech as **metonymy** and **synecdoche**? Can they use **rhyme**?

3. Must the terms **climax** and **anticlimax** be restricted to the plots of fiction or drama? Can a factual narrative essay also contain a climax or an

anticlimax, or both? How might a writer of an essay, whether argumentative or not, make use of climax or anticlimax? Is an anticlimax necessarily a bad thing?

4. *Topic* and *thesis* have been defined earlier (Terms, section I). Now differentiate between a **précis** and an **abstract**; between them and a **summary**; between a *summary* and a **conclusion**. Consider how the essays in this section begin and end.

5. How many kinds of **bias** can you think of? What is a **logical fallacy**?

6. **Denotation** and **connotation** are terms that are important to know and understand. *Denotation* is the literal, straightforward meaning of a word; *connotation* is what a word suggests or implies, sometimes by association of ideas or even of sound. For example, the words *fat, roly-poly, overweight, obese, chunky, heavy,* and *portly* all denote pretty much the same thing—but their connotations are quite different. Which do you think are negative? positive? neutral? What does *embonpoint* mean? What does it connote?

7. **Parody** Ridicule of a writer's style or of a specific work, either by exaggerated imitation of style or by straightforward imitation of style with the subject altered.

8. **Axiom** A self-evident truth or established principle. How does an axiom differ from an *assumption* or a *presumption*? Distinguish between a *hypothesis* and a *theory*. Is there any place for *conjecture* in argumentative writing?

TOPICS: On Individual Essays

PAULINE KAEL: "The Sound Of . . ."

1. At the end of the review Kael says that she is angry. Point out all you can find that makes her anger apparent throughout, long before she states it explicitly.

2. Are you convinced that these two movies are bad, and do you therefore not wish to see them? Or, if you have already seen one or both, do you agree with Kael's assessment?

3. Using the appropriate indexes and other aids that are in your library, look up others' reviews of these two films. Do any disagree substantially with Kael's opinions? If so, what are their reasons?

4. What should a review do? Who is it written for? Why might Kael's review appeal to—or alienate—particular kinds of readers?

5. Write a two- or three-page review of one or two movies or television programs you have seen recently that you feel are bad for other than obvious reasons—that is, *not* because of poor acting, script, direction, or photography, but because of their implicit assumptions or projected

values. Try to convince your readers, not that they won't be entertained, but that they shouldn't condone, foster, or submit themselves to such movies.

FLANNERY O'CONNOR "Total Effect and the Eighth Grade"

1. Judging from your own experience with fiction, do you agree or disagree with O'Connor's assertions?

2. Do you agree that a high-school student's taste, since it is in the process of being formed, should not be consulted? If so, at what point, if ever, should a student's taste be consulted?

3. Evaluate the logic of O'Connor's comparison of literature with algebra and irregular French verbs. Is the analogy sound, or could it be argued that literature is somehow different?

4. Write an essay in the form of a letter to a couple of cousins or other relatives two or three years your junior in which you tell them of several books you believe they should read, and why you believe they should. Would it be more difficult to tell them what they should not read?

VIRGINIA WOOLF "Middlebrow"

1. At what level would you locate your own brow? Do you agree with Woolf's various definitions and assertions?

2. Find at least half a dozen instances of irony in this piece, and explain how each works. Is Woolf at any point sarcastic, as opposed to merely ironic?

3. In a book of quotations, look up the line "the hungry sheep look up and are not fed," and read at least the whole passage of the work from which it comes. Does having done this help you understand Woolf's meaning? Can you find any other allusions and quotations in her letter?

4. Write a letter to a public figure or to a newspaper or magazine, protesting some statement or act or article that you feel strongly about. Use all the irony you can muster, and allow yourself at least one good burst of outright sarcasm. Consider actually sending the letter.

RUSSELL LYNES "Time on Our Hands"

1. Chart for a week the way you use your leisure time. Does the result tell you something about yourself that you were previously unaware of? Were you ever bored? Why? How do you think you might avoid being bored in the future?

2. Consider the ways in which the changing roles of women and men in recent years have affected how people think about and make use of leisure time.

3. Start by consulting several dictionaries, and then write an essay in which you define the terms *professional, expert, dilettante,* and *amateur* and carefully distinguish each one from the others. Support your definitions with concrete and specific examples and illustrations — as much as possible, ones from your own experience. Your definitions and distinctions, of course, may not agree with those of Lynes.

4. Write an argumentative essay attacking or defending one of the following assertions:

 (a) "The three developments that have most contributed to an increase in our leisure time — namely urbanization, industrialization, and computerization — are also the developments that have been most responsible for the relative lack of values in modern life."

 (b) "Life in North America is increasingly plagued by leisure time."

 (c) "For most people, leisure time is a problem because they hate to be alone."

BERTRAND RUSSELL "Tourists"

1. Is Russell's conclusion about American tourists convincing? Reconstruct, in something resembling syllogistic form, the steps that led him to his conclusion. Are the steps sound, or are there some logical leaps? Note the opening sentence of the third paragraph.

2. How many classes and subclasses of various nationalities, of their travelling or nontravelling, and of their attitudes and purposes, is Russell juggling in this brief essay? Are there more, or fewer, than you felt there to be during first reading? Were you able to follow it all clearly the first time through?

3. Paraphrase, in your own words, Russell's penultimate sentence.

4. What is your experience of tourists? In what other ways could they be classified? Write a short essay in which you argue for the superiority of one group or another.

V.S. NAIPAUL "Power?"

1. What is the point of the question mark after Naipaul's title? Is what it signifies echoed tonally anywhere in the essay?

2. What is a *cordon sanitaire?* Why has Naipaul chosen to use this phrase, when he could easily have conveyed the desired denotation in an English phrase? Was he seeking some particular *connotation?*

3. At one point (in the paragraph beginning "Fifty years ago...," p.191). Naipaul refers negatively to "the islands" and then, later in the same sentence, includes British Honduras—which is no island—in his

generalization. Is this playing fast and loose with the facts, or do you think it is mere carelessness? Does it undermine the validity of his statements?

4. Compare the attitudes of the blacks and other West Indians as described by Naipaul with those of the East Indians described by Mukherjee. Are there any noteworthy similarities or differences between them? If so, how do you account for them? An atmosphere of imminent cataclysm hangs over both essays; is it the same in each?

5. What is Naipaul trying to persuade his readers of? Does he seem to direct his essay toward any particular audience? How can you tell?

6. Write an essay on some manifestation of "power" in your community.

WILLIAM ZINSSER "Nobody Here but Us Dead Sheep"

1. What is the effect of Zinsser's statement in his opening paragraph that all the "insane" and "outlandish" things he mentions "evidently began in logic"—especially when, a few paragraphs later, he says that "we obviously can't count on logic"?

2. Come up with an adjective or two to describe Zinsser's tone; then cite specific passages to support your choice. Does Zinsser seem to you to adopt any kind of mask or persona? If so, how does it function?

3. What is the function of humour in this article? Is Zinsser serious when he refers to "one more joke"?

4. What audience is Zinsser addressing? Do you think his article would be a persuasive argument for one audience and not for another? Explain. In just what way can it be considered an argument at all?

5. Write an argument describing something going on in your vicinity that you think is patently absurd but that is nonetheless officially sanctioned. Try to use some irony and humour in the way Zinsser does.

THOMAS S. SZASZ "What Psychiatry Can and Cannot Do"

1. Why has Szasz provided fictitious names for the patients he describes as examples? If he didn't want to use real names, why not simply refer to Mr. A., Mrs. B., and so on?

2. Szasz's essay is much more obviously a formally structured argument than the other essays in this section. Analyze its structure by writing out the opening sentence of each paragraph (sometimes an opening word or two will be enough to reveal the structure and movement).

3. Compare Szasz's use of concrete illustration with that of Russell.

4. What rhetorical device does Szasz use in his final sentence? Is his conclusion effective for any other reason as well?

5. Construct a formal argument on some subject that you feel deeply about and about which you have some personal knowledge. Be sure to take into account the more likely points your opponents might raise.

TOPICS: General and Comparative

1. Look at several different kinds of magazines. What market does each appeal to? How does the advertising that appears in each magazine appeal to that market?
2. What makes a television commercial good or bad?
3. Write an argument for or against the control of advertising on television.
4. What different kinds of persuasion do the pieces in this section represent? Which persuade logically and which try to persuade emotionally? Russell calls his work an explanation; is it truly that, or does it display more of an argumentative stance? Pursue the ramifications of O'Connor's argument: can you propose an acceptable counter-argument?
5. Examine the technical methods of some of the essays in this section:
    (a) Kael and Zinsser both use irony. Zinsser writes of "the funny story"; what connection does he see between logic and the unreasonable? Unreasonable to whom? Is Kael ironic throughout or sometimes sarcastic? How can you distinguish? What is the effect of words and phrases like "twinkles," "operetta cheerfulness," " a spider on the valentine"? How does one use language to respond to a nonverbal experience, such as film (see Kael's essay), music (read Huxley's essay), or concrete poetry (read Colombo's essay)?
    (b) Woolf and Szasz both use sequences of examples. Are these cumulatively effective? Do they build to a climax or to an anti-climax? If Woolf's letter was never sent, why was it written? Why does Szasz use so many rhetorical questions?
    (c) Why does Naipaul begin his essay with an observation about Carnival? Why does he later call it "lunacy"? When he talks about bias in a culture, does he reveal a bias? Is his essay persuasive as well as explanatory?
    (d) Lynes uses a great many allusions and frequently appeals to authority. How effective are these in contributing to his argument? Do any unstated assumptions underlie his argument?
6. Write a paragraph or two of advertising copy for some fictitious product. Afterwards, write a brief analysis of the techniques you used. What kind

of reader were you aiming at? Try writing an ad for the same product for a markedly different audience.

7. Consider the argumentative points that Soyinka makes about race in the passage quoted in the introduction to this section. How relevant are his points to the comments on race made by Naipaul (Section III), Ellison, or McAuley (Section IV)?

8. "What we call justice derives from our uneasy recognition of a social paradox: that it is impossible to be fair, and possible only to enact the law." Discuss.

9. "Boredom is the source of more social disorder than malice is, just as fear is a greater source of prejudice than hate." Discuss.

10. "Brainwashing is another name for education." Write two essays, one arguing each side of this proposition. Then analyze your own argumentative techniques. In which essay are you more convincing? Why?

11. Write a political speech.

12. "There is no unemployment crisis. There is only a crisis in employers' imaginations. Greater flexibility in retirement age and greater use of part-time workers would resolve many of the problems young people currently face in obtaining jobs." Write a commentary on this view.

IV
Writing
to
Explain
and
Inform

In his essay in a book called *The Canadian Imagination*, Northrop Frye tells the story of a southern doctor travelling with an Inuit guide in the Arctic. When a blizzard blows up and they have to bivouac, the doctor panics and shouts aimlessly, "We are lost! We are lost!" The guide looks at him thoughtfully for a moment, and then observes: "We are not lost. We are here." Frye transforms the anecdote into a commentary on identity, probing the relation between geography and the imagination and exploring the force of the perspective one brings to the definition of cultural boundaries. Using an anecdote in this fashion, making it a functional part of a commentary rather than a simple narrative ornament, constitutes a characteristic feature of much expository writing. The expository writer's aim is to make a subject clear, to take a body of information and arrange the details so that they make sense, to answer the questions *how* and *why* as lucidly as possible: to explain things. A concrete anecdote often helps the process along.

Though exposition seems one of the most straightforward of prose forms, it is difficult to master, for an intelligent simplicity is an elusive goal. Some of the difficulties of explanation surface, for example, as soon as one tries to elucidate ostensibly simple things. It is a chastening exercise to try to explain, to someone who cannot distinguish right from left, how to put on a coat—and then to try to follow the directions exactly. Or to explain why three times four is twelve. To explain things adequately, expository writers must utilize internal definitions, helpful descriptions, comparisons, contrasts, analogies, anecdotal illustrations—in short, any techniques that will help clarify their subject.

Expository essays are also to a degree attempts to persuade. But because their essential aim is to explain, a reader primarily expects information from them. And however much he may appreciate an essayist's wit, grace, intelligence, and personality, he ultimately judges an expository essay by how much he has learned. As explanations, unclear recipes and inexact street directions alike prove unhelpful. The people who try to follow them may not get lost, but they will not know exactly what they are doing or where they are. Though such uncertainty might turn out to be productive, more often than not it simply proves confusing. What holds for simple explanations also holds for more complex analyses and more abstract subjects. Lack of clarity dulls one's ability to absorb information and discriminate among details; clear information, in whatever form it comes, can both stimulate and delight.

The essays that follow range in function and tone. There is a recipe, a piece of informative journalism, and a medical whodunit; there are magazine articles, informal reflections, and a formal cultural inquiry. As the subjects vary, so does the language. For Roueché and Thomas, a scientific vocabulary is a natural medium of expression; Yalden's essay, despite some pedagogical jargon, faces the complexities of education squarely; Galbraith defends the use of specialized occupational words. Authorial attitudes also vary, from Ellison's indirect subjectivity to McAuley's deliberate objectivity.

But this distinction raises the question of whether complete objectivity is ever possible. Most likely it is a stance never fully realizable, a quality of style never to be achieved. It is true that the reporter who strives for neutrality differs in many ways from the editorial writer who strives to persuade readers to embrace a particular social or political doctrine. The disinterested scientist and the academic investigator (neither of whom, it must be added, is likely to be uninterested) differ in many ways from the intellectual partisan. But the expository language of the scientist, like the argumentative language of the partisan, can also be slanted. It is open to misuse and subject to misinterpretation. It requires care. Even a formal researcher can distort matters in the process of communicating results, just as a writer who writes only out of his own experience may communicate personal biases of which he is unaware. Given such conditions, writers and readers both must sometimes be pleased if, after struggling to express or interpret an idea, they can know with a modest certainty where they stand.

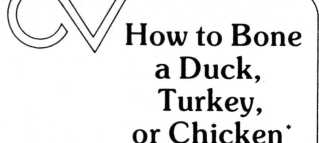

How to Bone a Duck, Turkey, or Chicken*

Simone Beck, Louisette Bertholle, and Julia Child

You may think that boning a fowl is an impossible feat if you have never seen it done or thought of attempting it. Although the procedure may take 45 minutes the first time because of fright, it can be accomplished in not much more than 20 on your second or third try. The object is to remove the flesh with the skin from the carcass bones without piercing the skin except at the back where the bird is slit open, and at the natural openings at the vent and neck. The skin is to serve as a container for the *pâté*. Laid flat on a board, the *pâté* mixture is heaped onto it, then the skin is folded over the *pâté* mixture and sewed in place. When baked in a *terrine* and unmolded, or baked in a crust, the sutures are on the bottom, and the *pâté* appears to be enclosed in an unbroken, browned casing—which is the skin. It is always an impressive sight. The important thing to remember is that the cutting edge of your knife must always face the bone, never the flesh, thus you cannot pierce the skin.

To begin with, cut a deep slit down the back of the bird from the neck to the tail, to expose the backbone. With a small, sharp knife, its edge always cutting against the bone, scrape and cut the flesh from the carcass bones down one side of the bird, pulling the flesh away from the carcass with your fingers as you cut. When you come to the ball joints connecting the wings and the second joints to the carcass, sever them, and continue down the carcass until you reach just the ridge of the breast where skin and

---

bone meet. Then stop. You must be careful here, as the skin is thin and easily slit. Repeat the same operation on the other side of the bird. By the time you have completed half of this, the carcass frame, dangling legs, wings, and skin will appear to be an unrecognizable mass of confusion and you will wonder how in the world any sense can be made of it all. But just continue cutting against the bone, and not slitting any skin, and all will come out as it should. When you finally arrive at the ridge of the breastbone on this opposite side, stop again. Then lift the carcass frame and cut very closely against the ridge of the breastbone to free the carcass, but not to slit the thin skin covering the breastbone. Chop off the wings at the elbows, to leave just the upper wing bones attached.

Then arrange this mass of skin and flesh on a board, flesh side up. You will now see, protruding from the flesh, the pair of ball joints of the wings and of the two second joints. Scrape the meat from the bones of the wings and pull out the bones. Repeat for the second joints, severing them from the ball joints of the drumsticks; the drumstick bones may be left in place if you wish. Discard any bits of fat adhering to the flesh, and the bird is ready to become a *pâté* or a galantine.

Methods in Language Teaching*

Janice Yalden

What do we mean by "methods" in language teaching? Do we mean a specific textbook that is used in a class? Do we mean certain kinds of drills and exercises? Are we referring to the practice of using only the language being learned, with English banned completely from the classroom? Or do we just mean that the teacher knows what he or she is doing? Usually we mean a little bit of all these things—especially the last. But basically, when we talk about a "method", what we have in mind is *an overall plan* for presenting, in a classroom, the language being studied. Such a plan should be based on a set of underlying assumptions about what language is; any method therefore must be consistent with the assumptions made by its creators. What the teacher does in order to implement the overall plan (after coming into the classroom, and saying "Bonjour", "Guten Tag", "Buenos días" or one of dozens of other possible greetings), is that he or she uses teaching *techniques* to get across a particular point, or reach a particular goal. These teaching techniques are the nuts and bolts of the language teaching profession—all the many tricks and drills and stratagems employed to help the student learn. There are hundreds of them; many a book has been written setting them out. The teacher—or the person designing a course—has to choose among them all, and he or she chooses according to the method which has previously been decided on in accordance with his or her beliefs about what language is and how best to teach it. We can see that there ought to be a progression, then, from *assumptions* to *overall plan (method)* to classroom *techniques*. Let us look at the principle methods used in language teaching, the ideas and assump-

*Janice Yalden, "Methods in Language Teaching," in *What's What for Children Learning French*, ed. Elaine Isabelle. Citizen's Committee on Children, 1978. Used by permission.

tions about language that form their basis, and also at how these methods
work out in practice.

The Grammar-Translation Tradition

There are two main currents of ideas about how we learn languages that
have given rise to two basic traditions in language teaching. From these
two traditions spring most of the methods used today. The older tradition
is probably the grammar-translation one. Latin and Greek were, along
with mathematics, the most important subjects of study for the educated
from ancient times until well into the nineteenth century. In the nineteenth
century, grammar was studied very carefully almost as though it were a
system of logic. Since it was believed that students could not understand
another language directly, languages were always translated into the
native language of the learner. Thinking about the language being learned
(the 'target' language) and about the native language was a process of continual switching back and forth; there was no attempt to break the
language barrier by "thinking" in the target language.

The Tradition of Direct Contact

Through the centuries there were many who criticized translation as a basis
for teaching languages. During and after the Renaissance, when national,
living languages were acquiring new importance and stature through the
emergence of national literatures, the criticism became louder, and direct
contact with the 'target' language was urged, on the grounds that it was
more natural, more like the way we learn our mother tongue. In this brief
article, however, we shall not try to trace styles in language teaching since
early times. What is of concern to us is the emergence of a new method
based on the scientific study of language combined with certain
psychological principles. This method began to receive its theoretical
framework in the early years of this century from men who shared the
belief that in foreign language teaching, primacy should be given to the
spoken language. Their point of departure was diametrically opposed to
that of the advocates of the grammar-translation approach. They believed
that the student must function, from the beginning, *directly* in the foreign
language, without going through the medium of the native tongue. The
Direct Method, as it is now known, goes back to the end of the nineteenth
century, when Wilhelm Viëtor in Germany, then François Gouin in
France, later M.D. Berlitz (whose *Berlitz Method* was published in 1907 in
New York), Henry Sweet and Harold Palmer in England (whose work was
published between 1899 and about 1922) and many others in Europe and
America all advocated thorough training in the spoken language, the study

of phonetics,* and aural comprehension and discrimination training. Their ideas had initially a great deal of influence in Europe, though due to the lack of properly trained teachers and a conservative desire to cling to familiar grammar-translation methods, the spread of the Direct Method was limited.

In the United States and Canada similar problems led to retention of the 'classical' method of language training (through grammar and translation) in the early part of the century; in 1929, a very lengthy study was published of the results of experimentation in the U.S. and Canada. The Coleman Report, as it is known, stated that since most students spent only a couple of years studying a language in school, training designed to produce efficiency in reading was the most desirable that should be provided. This advice was very widely followed for quite some time.

A New Influence:
The Contributions of Structural Linguistics

Leonard Bloomfield, an American linguist, published in 1933 a book called simply *Language* in which he upheld very strongly the idea that the spoken language comes first, both in teaching and in linguistic analysis. (His work, and the work of his followers, is known as "Structural" linguistics, and with it came a new concept of language teaching.) Although his main concern was the study of languages and not teaching them, a great many linguists became involved in the teaching of languages in the '40s, when the United States Armed Forces wanted to teach unusual languages to a large number of soldiers, and needed good, efficient materials with which to do so. The American Council of Learned Societies adopted in 1941 a training program called the Intensive Language Program, which was unusual in that linguists for the first time were put in charge of the language-learning process. They developed a view of language teaching which was very different from what had been classroom practice before the war. The central idea here was that of language as a system of speech habits. Three main principles governed the teaching in this program: that students should be taught first to speak the foreign language they were learning; that the linguists who were preparing teaching materials should use as a basis the spoken language; and that in teaching, before introducing the written language, phonetic transcription would be used, at least in the early stages. A very different thing indeed from translation of literary prose passages, learning parts of speech and memorizing lists of vocabulary. Of the various language training programs carried out during the war, the Intensive Language Program and its descendants were those which can be said to

---

* *Phonetics:* the study of speech processes, including how we articulate sounds. Phonetics has many applications, including phonetic transcription, a system of symbols which can be used to write down the sounds of any language.

have been the forerunners of the 'audio-lingual' method. The results obtained were much publicized, even exaggerated in the press; many principles of the Intensive Language Program were adopted after the war, especially in colleges.

'Rule learning' (the key to the grammar-translation method) was now looked on with horror by the proponents of the new approach; repetition of model sentences was the basic exercise in the new method developed by the structuralists. For those unfamiliar with this type of exercise, here is an example in English—the teacher utters the first model sentence, the students repeat it; the teacher then gives a verbal "cue," and the students must then repeat the model sentence, substituting the "cue" word in the appropriate place, and making any necessary changes.

Teacher: This is a table.
Students: This is a table.
Teacher: House
Students: This is a house.
Teacher: Houses
Students: These are houses.
Teacher: Chair
Students: This is a chair.
Teacher: That
Students: That is a chair.
Teacher: Those
Students: Those are chairs, etc., etc.

This is known as a "substitution" drill; there are many variations, but the technique remains essentially one of repetition with small changes. To construct these drills, the writer of teaching materials must have a very good knowledge of the basic "sentence patterns" of the foreign language he is working with, so as to be able to prepare a great many pattern drills of various kinds. Repetition of these drills, it was thought, would make the student give automatic responses to certain stimuli or cues, and thus develop in him the potential ability to converse freely.

Pattern drills as a basic exercise were enthusiastically adopted by the language-teaching profession, especially since there was now available a marvellous new teaching tool, the tape recorder. This machine was ideal for pattern practice. It could take over from the teacher the drudgery of repetitious drills without ever itself becoming weary. The student received all the advantages of being exposed to a variety of voices in the 'target' language (the language he wanted to learn), and in addition could record his own voice, replay what he recorded, and thus in theory be able to correct his own errors. Batteries of tape recorders were installed in specially designed classrooms which were outfitted with individual booths, and thus the language laboratory was born. Next, under the National Defence

Education Act passed in 1958, thousands and thousands of dollars of federal government funds were spent in the United States outfitting schools and colleges with increasingly complex and sophisticated language laboratories. Research studies were launched comparing results obtained using one type of installation with those obtained with another. But no research at all was done on the effectiveness of 'software' (that is, the material which was being recorded: types of exercises, and so on). Publishers produced ever larger 'packages' of teaching materials: textbook, teacher's manual, tape recordings, laboratory manuals for the students' use, etc.

A Second Major Influence:
Psychology and Language Teaching

Although the linguists had developed their teaching materials for use in the Intensive Language Program long before the appearance of B.F. Skinner's book, *Verbal Behaviour*, the psychological theories expressed in it have been used to give support to language teaching methods which grew out of the postwar experience. The argument seemed to be that human beings acquired and used language in a way not essentially different from that in which rats could be taught to go through a maze: that is, that through being given certain stimuli and through being rewarded for a correct response and punished for an incorrect one, they would acquire certain patterns of behaviour. This idea of human language as a set of acquired skills and patterns of behaviour has had a very profound influence both on techniques used in language teaching and on the construction of reading materials.

The Audio-Lingual Method—
A Descendant of Structural Linguistics

Psychology and linguistics had come together in their respective approaches to language. Certain assumptions (based on this union) concerning language learning were therefore made by those who developed new language-teaching materials in the '50s. These have been expressed as follows:

1. that learning a foreign language implies the mechanical formation of new habits and skills;
2. that the only really natural approach is to teach oral skills (listening and speaking) first and then later on reading and writing;
3. that (instead of being given an explanation of grammar and then some exercises to work on which are structured around the point just learned) the student should work out for himself the grammar of structures he encounters for the first time, before being given an explanation; i.e. analogy is better than analysis;
4. that a full understanding of cultural background is necessary in learning a language.

Certain characteristics of the "audio-lingual" method follow from the above ideas about how a second language is learned. These are: that items are presented and learned first in their spoken form and only later on presented in their written form; that the scientific analysis of contrasts between the learner's language and the foreign language underlies preparation of teaching materials; that much emphasis is placed on 'over-learning' of language patterns through use of the pattern drill; and that "real life" situations should be simulated as much as possible in the process of second-language learning.

It is these principles which lie behind the preparation and use of materials for the teaching of French at all levels such as *Ici on Parle Français* (Kerr, Nemni and Séguinot), *Cours Structuré* and *Le Français International* (Vinay and Rondeau), *Le Français Partout* (multiple authorship, published by Holt, Rinehart & Winston), *Écouter et Parler* (Coté, Levy and O'Connor), the *A-LM Materials* (published by Harcourt, Brace and World) and so on. These and other texts like them are designed for introduction at various levels: some are programs prepared for use from Kindergarten through high school, others represent a much shorter sequence for later introduction (Grade 7 or 8, even 9 and 10). But they all rest on the same principles. Although textbooks such as *Cours Moyen de Français* which rely on translation as a main exercise and present the grammar before the student does exercises based on such presentation are still in use, there is no doubt that the books and materials now in use in the majority of primary and secondary schools in all language courses, are audio-lingual.

Descendants of the Grammar-Translation Tradition

The grammar-translation tradition has produced few offspring. It continued for many years into this century untouched and unchanged. As a matter of fact, it is still alive. There is one heir, however: the COGNITIVE-CODE view or approach.

In 1966, John B. Carroll, a very well known psychologist at Harvard, in an article entitled "Research on Teaching Foreign Languages" (1963), speaks of there being two major theories of language learning: "one may be called the audio-lingual habit theory, the other, the cognitive code-learning theory". The first has been discussed above; the second theory is one which holds that, although a speaker does not have to think much about a second language during "the communicative process", i.e. when he is talking or listening, reading and writing, this is not true during the learning of that second language. During the learning process, the student must comprehend the meaning of words and forms he is using; since the spoken and the written language are both representations of the same language system, practice in both is necessary—separate training in both is also necessary. Since this theory is relatively new, it is as yet not as highly developed as the audio-lingual one, though articles and books are appearing with increasing frequency explaining and supporting it. There are as yet very few textbooks based on it. (Since it is not a straight return to grammar-translation, it cannot be considered that texts which used Latin-based explanations of grammar and translation as their main exercise are based on the 'cognitive' method.) However, some publishers advertise, claiming that their latest texts represent the 'perfect balance' between the audio-lingual and the cognitive approaches which indicates that the 'cognitive approach' is a real contender in the field today.

Descendants of the Classical Direct Methods:
Audio-Visual and Others

In CLASSICAL BERLITZ practice, the most famous of all the Direct Methods, the teacher uses actions and objects to show the meaning of the words, phrases and sentences he is teaching—or modelling, as some prefer to state it. No reading is used for some time. There are several modern methods which are in this tradition. SITUATIONAL TEACHING is one we hear of today, in which meaning is conveyed by creating a situation which will indicate to the learner what is going on. No use is made of the native language. THE SILENT WAY, developed by Caleb Gattegno, is a recent addition to this family. In it, the teacher uses colored rods and talks about them in the target language only. He encourages students, once they have learned a few basic phrases, to do most of the talking, hence the method's name.

From 1954 to 1956, a new method for teaching French to adult learners was very carefully worked out in France by Guberina and Rivenc at the École Normale Supérieure de St. Cloud just outside Paris. The results of their work are known internationally; *Voix et Images de France*, and many other courses for children and adults in several languages are based on the principles they elaborated. This method, known as AUDIO-VISUAL, like the audio-lingual one bases its materials on an extensive analysis of the spoken language. In teaching, its point of departure and chief goal are fluency and naturalness in speech. The exercises used are different from those used in the audio-lingual method: they are based on accurate and frequent repetition of whole sentences which have been carefully constructed to lead the student from the most basic structures in the spoken language to more complex ones (i.e., they require faithful repetition *without modification*, unlike the pattern drills). Filmstrips are used to teach meaning and the students have books with pictures corresponding to the filmstrips in them with which they practice basic structures. This use of pictures is the major innovation of these and other audio-visual methods. Teaching of reading and writing is completely delayed until the student has a thorough mastery of all the sounds and basic structures in the language, a technique which is sometimes, but not necessarily always, used in courses taught by audio-lingual methods.

New Additions to the Family

There are a couple of innovations in methods which represent a change in points of view on the language learning and teaching task. We could call these "counselling" or "psychiatric" views. One is called COMMUNITY LANGUAGE LEARNING, and was recently developed by Charles Curran in the U.S. The techniques used are like those in a counselling situation. Students sit in a small circle, and tell the teacher (counsellor), in their native language, what they want to say. He then prompts them and the other students also help. The student thus "picks up" the language, but decides himself what he wants to talk about, which has a motivational advantage. The community language learning method is not as yet much in use in this country.

The other innovation comes from Bulgaria, where Dr. Georgi Lozanov has elaborated the SUGGESTOPEDIC method. Students hear all material, in the target language, once around, then a second time while relaxing to soft music in a seance-like state, then finally they act out what they are saying. This method is being used in Canada, though so far is not very widely spread.

The IMMERSION teaching used in bilingual education can be considered a new addition to the family, with obvious attachments to the Direct Method tradition. What's different about immersion is that relatively little attention is given to teaching the language as a formal subject, but a great deal of attention is paid to teaching through the language, and having learners develop as quickly as possible the ability to communicate effectively.

How Do You Choose?

"Is there any 'best' method?" is a question which is frequently asked. When audio-lingual teaching was at its height in the '60s, it was generally felt that the 'best' method had indeed been found. But even then, there was a lack of confidence in some quarters that this was so. As early as 1948, results of studies had been published which cast doubt on the ability of 'aural-oral' (audio-lingual) methods to produce native-like fluency in the students, and it was becoming apparent that the audio-lingual method did not automatically teach reading skills. In spite of the fact that students claimed to be more highly motivated by an oral approach, it was found that many began to lose interest as they found themselves confronted with endless drill sessions. In 1960, the results of a study by Wallace Lambert and Leon Jakobovits were published which demonstrated that the subjects involved began to lose their grasp on the meaning of words after many repetitions. Another study conducted at the University of Colorado contrasting the achievements of two groups, one taught by the traditional method and the other audio-lingually, showed that the differences were so small as to suggest that it did not matter which method was used. And in 1970, the results of a study called the Pennsylvania Project appeared. A wave of discussion and self-examination within the foreign language teaching profession had begun; the result has been that no longer are there many who would still support all the tenets of the audio-lingual position. The idol had feet of clay: students were indeed learning what they were taught to do in class and in the laboratory—but they were unable to make the transition to free, creative speech. They could only repeat what they had memorized.

In the '60s, largely as a result of the influence of the linguist Noam Chomsky and others who agree with him, thinking has changed greatly concerning language; the emphasis has shifted away from looking at the behaviour of human beings in order to find out what language is and toward a closer look at language itself, in order to discover the clues. Chomsky, in 1966, made a number of statements concerning language which show how his view differs from Skinner's. For example, he said that language was not a "habit structure", a phrase much used by behaviourists; that "repetition of fixed phrases is a rarity"; that "ordinary linguistic behaviour characteristically involves innovation, formation of new sentences and new patterns in accordance with rules of great abstractness and intricacy." In an interview in 1968 (reported in *The Listener*, May 1968) he said with specific reference to language teaching: "My own feeling is that from our knowledge of the organism of language and of the principles that determine language structure one cannot immediately construct a teaching programme. All we can suggest is that a teaching programme be designed in such a way as to give free play to those creative principles that humans bring to the process of language learning, and I presume to the learning of anything else." Nevertheless, psychological and linguistic theory by this time had become the twin pillars of foreign language methodology—the majority of publications on language teaching and learning all reflect this duality of approach, despite Chomsky's repeated claims that neither discipline is yet sufficiently well developed to provide a solid basis for a theory of language teaching.

Other Factors

The best approach to the 'methods' problem today would seem to be to acknowledge that there is no best method—only methods which are best *within a given framework*. What makes up the framework within which the choice has to be made? A large number of factors in fact have to be taken into account. Some are linguistic ones: what language are we teaching? What is the native language of the learners? How much of the target language do we want to teach at any given time, or in any given course? What 'level' are our students at—are they beginners, or are they somewhere along the way to full fluency? Some factors are psychological: what attitudes do students have toward the target language and its speakers? Toward language learning in general? Are they well-motivated? Are they interested in the speakers of the other language? Do they want to use the other language in their work? How old are they? Much could be written on this question alone; suffice it to say here that no evidence has yet been produced to show that you can't learn another language at *any* time in life. What matters is how you go about it—and what your goals are. It may be that Eric Lennenberg, the biologist, is right: that there is a critical age for acquiring your first language, and so you cannot expect to acquire or learn a second one the same way because of age differential. But even this is in doubt. Anyway, people go on learning languages both ways: by simply being exposed to them *and* by classroom practice. The combinations are infinitely variable, and work in different ways in different settings.

Economic factors often of course also influence choice of method for classroom use. Class size, laboratory equipment, whether you can afford an audio-visual method or not—these and many other practical considerations are brought to bear on the problem. In fact, language teaching is now an interdisciplinary field—the whole process from designing a method to final testing of the students—and it requires more and more highly trained personnel to do the job. Whether it will get them depends on the importance attached to second-language acquisition today.

Three Sick Babies*

Berton Roueché

Dr. Paul M. Taylor, an assistant professor of pediatrics at the University of Pittsburgh School of Medicine, left his office on the first floor of Magee-Womens Hospital, an affiliate of the medical school, and climbed the stairs to the premature-baby nursery, on the second floor. It was twenty minutes to eleven on the morning of July 12, 1965, a Monday, and this was his regular weekday round. He was, in a way, attending physician to all the babies in the nursery. Two pediatric residents were waiting for him in the gown room. That, too, was as usual, and while Dr. Taylor scrubbed and disinfected his hands and got into a freshly laundered gown, they gave him the customary nursery news report. The weekend had been generally uneventful. All but one of the twenty-six babies in the nursery were progressing satisfactorily. The exception was one of the smallest—a twenty- five-day-old two-and-a-half-pound boy. He was in Room 227. Dr. Taylor nodded. He knew the one they meant. Well, early that morning, just after midnight, a nurse had noted that his breathing was unusually slow and his behavior somewhat apathetic. The resident on duty, seeing these signs as suggestive of septicemia, had treated the baby with penicillin and kanamycin, but he still looked and acted sick. It was probable that he would soon need artificial respiration. Meanwhile, the usual samples (blood, stool, mucus, spinal fluid) had been taken and sent along to the laboratory for culture and analysis.

Dr. Taylor heard his residents' review with no more than natural interest. Serious illness in a premature nursery is not an unusual occurrence, and a blood infection is only one of the many diseases that may afflict a premature baby during its first days of life. Trouble is inherent in the phenomenon of prematurity. For the truth of the matter is that premature birth is itself a serious affliction. A premature baby is a baby born in the seventh or eighth month of pregnancy. Its birth weight is largely determined by its relative prematurity, ranging from around two to five and a half pounds. The average term (or nine-month) baby weighs around seven pounds at birth, and it generally comes into the world alive and kicking. Premature babies begin life almost incapable of living. There is nothing more frail and fragile. Many of them are too meagerly developed to maintain normal body temperature. One in three requires immediate, and often prolonged resuscitation, and about the same number are unable to nurse, or even to swallow. Some of them are even unable to cry. All of them are exquisitely susceptible to all infection. Mental and neurological defects are also common in premature babies. One of the commonest of these is cerebral palsy. About half of all victims of the affliction are of premature birth. As recently as twenty-five years ago, most premature babies died. The technological innovations of the postwar era have greatly improved that record, but the mortality rate among newborn premature babies is still high. In even the best hospitals, some ninety percent of all two-pound babies die. So do about fifty percent of those weighing two to three pounds, around ten percent of those weighing three to four pounds, and between five and eight percent of those weighing four to five pounds. Such babies are simply too fetal to survive outside the womb. There are many causes of premature birth (including falls and blows), but most current investigators think that malnutrition is perhaps the most important cause. Prematurity would thus seem to be a socioeconomic problem, and this supposition is confirmed by statistics. The great majority of premature babies are born to women too poor to buy the nutritious food they need.

Dr. Taylor tied up the back of his gown and led the way through an inner door to the central nursing station of the nursery. Room 227 was the second room on the right. The sick baby was one of five babies being cared for there. He lay on his side in his incubator bassinet with a stomach feeding tube in his mouth, and he looked even sicker than the resident had said. There was nothing, however, that Dr. Taylor could do that hadn't already been done. He confirmed the resident's course of treatment and agreed that a respirator would probably soon be required, and then moved on to the other babies in that and the other rooms. They were all, as far as he could read the almost imperceptible manifestations of the premature, in their usual precarious but normal condition. At the end of his rounds, Dr. Taylor had lunch, and after lunch he occupied himself with his other professorial duties. Before leaving for home, he put in a call to the nursery for a report on the sick baby. The report was not comforting. The baby's condition had continued to worsen, and he had been moved to Room 229, which is reserved for babies needing constant scrupulous care. Later that evening, on his way to bed, he called the nursery again. The nurse who picked up the telephone was able to answer his question. The sick baby from Room 227 was dead.

Dr. Taylor's Tuesday-morning round was much like that of Monday. The residents' gown-room report included another sick baby. It also contained a post-mortem note on the baby from Room 227. The hospital laboratory had confirmed the general diagnosis of septicemia. A microbial culture had been grown from a sample of the baby's blood and identified as bacteria of the gram-negative type. It was one of some twenty-five species of bacteria (among them the causative organisms of typhoid fever, brucellosis, whooping cough, plague, and gonorrhea) that react negatively to the standard staining test devised in 1884 by the Danish bacteriologist Hans Christian Joachim Gram. A more specific identification was promised for the next day. Meanwhile, of course, the laboratory had been supplied with diagnostic samples from the second sick baby. This baby, also a boy, was one of the babies in Room 229. He was a term baby, three days old, but had been assigned to the premature nursery directly from the delivery room because he required artificial respiration and other intensive care. Dr. Taylor remembered the baby when he saw him. He had begun life with a severe aspiration pneumonia, stemming from an original inability to breathe, but that had been quickly controlled with penicillin, kanamycin, and dexamethasone. His trouble now was diarrhea. Diarrhea in a newborn baby is not a common complaint, and Dr. Taylor wondered if this attack might be a septic aftermath of the earlier pneumonia. But that was a question that only the laboratory could readily answer. There was no doubt about the treatment the baby was receiving. That seemed to be entirely satisfactory.

The Wednesday-morning gown-room news review contained three major items. One was that still another baby boy had become seriously ill overnight. The next item was a preliminary laboratory report on the second sick baby, which identified the cause of his diarrhea as a gram-negative bacillus. The third item was a more or less definitive laboratory report on the dead baby. After forty-eight hours of growth, the gram-negative bacteria cultured from his blood presented the colonial configuration, the fluorescent yellow-green pigmentation, and the spearmint odor generally characteristic of the type known as Pseudomonas aeruginosa.

Dr. Taylor went to Room 229 for a look at the new sick baby. He was nine days old and weighed about three pounds. His illness appeared to be a pneumonia. This illness had come on abruptly, but, like so many other premature babies, he had never been really well. He had been unable at birth to breathe spontaneously and had spent the first five or six days of his life in a respirator. It was obvious to Dr. Taylor that the baby's condition was grave. It seemed equally clear, however, that he was receiving the best of care, and a conventional course of penicillin and kanamycin had been started. Dr. Taylor left the nursery in an uneasy state of mind. His uneasiness had to do with Room 229 and the sudden string of serious illnesses there. He was afraid that they might be more than merely coincidental.

Dr. Taylor was not kept in suspense for long. One of his fears was confirmed that afternoon by a call from the resident then on duty in the nursery. He called to report that the new sick baby—the three-pound nine-day-old—was dead. His illness had lasted a scant eight hours. The next morning brought another confirmation. There was a final laboratory report on the first sick baby: the cause of his death was definitely Pseudomonas infection. There was a forty-eight-hour report on the second sick baby: the gram-negative bacteria grown from his blood had all the important characteristics of Pseudomonas aeruginosa. There was a twenty-four-hour report on the third sick baby: cultures grown from his blood had been identified as gram-negative bacteria. And that was too much for coincidence. It meant—it could almost certainly only mean—that a Pseudomonas epidemic had struck the premature nursery.

Pseudomonas aeruginosa is one of a group of gram-negative pathogens that have only recently come to be seriously pathogenic. Other members of this group include Escherichia coli and the several species of the Proteus and the Enterobacter-Klebsiella genera. Their rise to eminent virulence is a curious phenomenon. These microorganisms regularly reside in soil and water, and in the gastrointestinal tracts of most (if not all) human beings. Their presence in that part of the body is normally innocuous. Healthy adults are impervious to the thrust of such bacteria. The victims of Pseudomonas (and E. coli and Proteus and Enterobacter) infections are the very old, the very young, and the very debilitated (the badly burned, the postoperative, the cancerous), and in almost every case they have been receiving vigorous sulfonamide or antibiotic or adrenalsteroid therapy. Most antimicrobial drugs have little destructive effect on bacteria of the Pseudomonas group. Just the reverse, in fact. Their action, in essence, is tonic. In people rendered susceptible to the gram-negative pathogens by age or illness, the result of chemotherapy is the elimination not only of the immediately threatening pathogens but also of the natural resident bacteria that normally hold further incursions of Pseudomonas (or E. coli or Proteus or Enterobacter) in check. The virulence of Pseudomonas and its kind is thus a wry expression of perhaps the most beneficent accomplishment of twentieth-century medicine.

It is also cause for some alarm. "One of the great changes wrought by the widespread use of antibacterial agents has been the radical shift in the ecologic relations among the pathogenic bacteria that are responsible for the most serious and fatal infections," the *New England Journal of Medicine* noted editorially in July of 1967. "Whereas John Bunyan could properly refer to consumption as 'Captain of the Men of Death,' this title, according to Osler, was taken over by pneumonia in the first quarter of this century. During the last two decades, it has again shifted, at least in hospital populations, first to the staphylococcal diseases and more recently to infections caused by gram-negative bacilli. Most of the gram-negative organisms that have given rise to these serious and highly fatal infections are among the normal flora of the bowel and have sometimes been referred to as 'opportunistic pathogens.' . . . Before the present antibiotic era, some of them, like Escherichia coli, although they frequently caused simple urinary-tract infections, only occasionally gave rise to serious sepsis. . . . Strains of Proteus or Pseudomonas did so very rarely, and those of Enterobacter were not even known to produce infections in human beings before the introduction of sulfonamide drugs. Of great importance are the facts that most of these opportunistic pathogens are resistant to the antibiotics that have been most widely used, and that the infections they produce are associated with a high mortality." This mortality is anachronistically high. It is roughly that resulting from the common run of pathogenic bacteria some thirty years ago—in the days when the best defense against the many Men of Death was a strong constitution.

The most conspicuously troublesome of these ordinarily unaggressive pathogens is E. coli. It has been implicated in some ninety percent of the urinary-tract infections caused by members of this group, and it is responsible for many of the more serious cases of bacteremia, gastroenteritis, and pneumonia. It is not, however, the most opportunistic. The organism best equipped to take advantage of almost any chemotherapeutic opportunity is the Pseudomonas bacillus. Pseudomonas aeruginosa is all but invulnerable to the present pharmacopoeia. Only two antibiotics—polymyxin B and colistin—are generally effective against most Pseudomonas strains. Moreover, both must be used with great discretion to prevent severe kidney side reactions. Ps. aeruginosa is also distinctively lethal. Its mortality rate, as numerous recent outbreaks (including that in Pittsburgh in 1965) have shown, may run as high as seventy-five percent.

An investigation into the source of the Pseudomonas infections in the premature nursery at Magee-Womens Hospital was started by Dr. Taylor on Friday morning, July 16. A forty-eight-hour report from the laboratory had by then established as Ps. aeruginosa the gram-negative bacteria that had been cultured from the blood of the third sick baby, and the presence of an epidemic was now beyond dispute. The investigation began with a survey to determine the scope of the trouble. There were at that time, in addition to the surviving (or diarrheal) sick baby, twenty-eight babies in the nursery. Samples of nose, throat, and stool material were taken from each, to be dispatched to the laboratory for culture and analysis. Dr. Taylor saw this work well under way, and then walked down to his office and put in a call to a colleague named Horace M. Gezon, at the Graduate School of Public Health. Dr. Gezon (at the time professor of epidemiology and microbiology at the University of Pittsburgh Graduate School of Public Health and now chairman of the Department of Pediatrics at the Boston University School of Medicine) is an authority on hospital infections, and

Dr. Taylor wanted his help. Dr. Gezon had two immediate suggestions. One was that the investigators meet at the hospital the following morning for an exchange of information and ideas. The other was that Joshua Fierer, of the Allegheny County Health Department, be invited to join the investigation. Dr. Fierer (now a postdoctoral fellow in infectious diseases at the University of Pittsburgh Department of Medicine) was an Epidemic Intelligence Service officer assigned to Allegheny County by the National Communicable Disease Center, in Atlanta.

"Dr. Taylor called me on Friday afternoon," Dr. Fierer says. "I know it was Friday, because that's when all investigations seem to begin—at the start of the weekend. I knew Dr. Taylor. I had met him with Dr. Gezon back in March—on a Friday in March. There had an outbreak of diarrhea in the premature nursery that they thought might be a viral disease, and they called the county because we had the only virus-diagnostic laboratory in the area. That case turned out to be nothing to worry about. It got the three of us together, though, and I guess that was what brought me to mind when this new problem came up. I was delighted to be asked to participate. Pseudomonas is a very interesting organism these days. But I had to tell Dr. Taylor that I couldn't make the Saturday-morning meeting. Or, if I could, I'd be late. I had a firm commitment at the Pittsburgh Children's Zoo on Saturday morning. They had a chimpanzee out there with hepatitis.

"I got to the hospital, but I was more than late. It was after lunch, and the meeting was over and everybody had gone. I looked around the nursery, feeling kind of foolish, and said hello to the nurses, and they told me who had been at the meeting. There were six in the group, including Dr. Taylor and Dr. Gezon. The others were the two residents, a study nurse of Dr. Gezon's, and an assistant professor of epidemiology at the School of Public Health named Russell Rycheck. Dr. Rycheck was a particular friend of mine. I went over to the school and looked him up, and he gave me a good report. The meeting had naturally concentrated on the nursery. The big question, of course, was: Where had the infection come from? How had Pseudomonas been introduced into the nursery? Well, Pseudomonas is a water-dwelling organism. It can live on practically nothing in the merest drop of water. That suggested water as the probable source of the trouble, and the nursery had plenty of such sources. There were thirty incubator bassinets equipped with humidifiers drawing on water reservoirs, and there were fourteen sinks—one in each of the ten baby rooms, three in the central nursing station, and one in the gown room. And then there were the usual jugs of sterile water for washing the babies' eyes and for other medicative purposes. Dr. Gezon arranged for water samples from every possible source. That included two samples from each sink—one from the drain and one from the aerator on the faucet. The screens that diffuse the water in an aerator can provide a water bug like Pseudomonas with an excellent breeding place. For good measure, he took a swab of the respirator used in the ward. Also, Dr. Rycheck said, Dr. Gezon arranged for throat and stool samples from the two residents and from all the nurses working in the premature nursery. And he had called another meeting for Monday morning. The laboratory findings would be ready for evaluation by then.

"I made the Monday meeting. The laboratory reports were presented, and then we tried to decide what they meant. The human studies made pretty plain reading. There were two sets—the nurses and residents, and the twenty-eight seemingly well babies in the nursery. The laboratory eliminated the nurses and residents as possible carriers. Their cultured specimens were all negative for Pseudomonas. The reports on the babies confirmed what I think most of us had already suspected. This was a real epidemic. Twenty-two of the babies were negative for Pseudomonas, but six were positive. They weren't clinically sick. They didn't show any symptoms. They were, however, infected with Ps. aeruginosa. Why they weren't sick is hard to say. There were several possible explanations. The best one was that their exposure was relatively slight and their natural defenses were strong—they hadn't been weakened by antibiotics. The results of the environmental studies were very interesting. But they were also rather confusing. They showed five sink drains and three of the bassinet reservoirs to be contaminated. Everything else was negative for Pseudomonas—the water jugs, the respirator, the faucet aerators, and the other drains and bassinets. The contaminated drains were in Room 207, Room 209, Room 227, an unoccupied room, and the gown room. The contaminated bassinets were in 224, 227, and 229. All the infected babies were associated with just two rooms. They were, or had been, in either Room 227—the room where the first baby took sick—or Room 229, where he died and where the two other babies became sick. There was a contaminated sink in Room 227, but the sink in 229 was clean. There was a contaminated bassinet reservoir in each room, but only one of the bassinets was, or had been, occupied by an infected baby. There were no infected babies in two rooms—Room 209 and Room 207—that had contaminated sinks, and none in Room 224, which had a contaminated bassinet. It was all very peculiar. We had a lot of contamination and we had a lot of infected babies, but there didn't seem to be any connection between the two. The only link we could think of was the nurses. The babies had no contact with each other. The bassinets were self-contained, and none of the babies shared any equipment or medication. The nurses might have carried the infection on their hands. They could do that without becoming infected themselves. Healthy adults don't succumb to Pseudomonas. But why did they carry it only to the babies in 227 and 229?

"The meeting ended on that unsatisfactory note. Dr. Gezon was as puzzled as the rest of us. But, of course, this puzzling point was only part of the investigation. We still had an epidemic to contain. We didn't understand the mechanics of its spread, but we did know what it was, and we thought we had enough information to bring it under control. We knew who was sick and we knew that the nursery was contaminated at eight specific sites. By Monday night, the nursery was as clean as Dr. Gezon and the nursery staff knew how to make it. All the sinks were scrubbed with sodium-hypochlorite disinfectant. The bassinet reservoirs were emptied and disinfected with an iodophor, and only those in use were refilled. As a further precaution, that water was to be changed every day. Certain nurses were assigned to take exclusive care of the infected babies. Also, in the hope of dislodging their infection, all the infected babies were placed on a five-day course of colistimethate given intramuscularly, and colistin sulphate by mouth. It wasn't necessary to isolate the infected babies. They were already isolated. And it was arranged that specimens be taken every day from all the babies in the nursery, and from all the sinks and bassinets and so on. That would give us a constant focus on the course of the epidemic.

"I didn't participate in the sanitation program. They didn't need me. I would have been an extra thumb. I went back to my office and back to the regular Health Department routine, but part of my mind was still out there at the nursery, and I got to thinking about something I'd read a few months before. It was a report in the *Lancet* about an outbreak of Pseudomonas in an English nursery that was traced to a catheter used to relieve throat congestion in the babies. The source of the trouble eluded detection for almost a year. What I particularly remembered about the report was a description of a new system of microbial identification. There are several different types of Ps. aeruginosa, and this report told how they could be differentiated by a laboratory procedure called pyocine typing. Pyocine typing makes use of the fact that certain strains of Pseudomonas will kill or inhibit the growth of other Pseudomonas strains, and it's a complicated procedure. Well, it occurred to me that pyocine typing might help to clarify our problem. It could at least tell us if all the sinks and all the bassinets and all the infected babies were infected with the same strain of Pseudomonas. I thought about it, and finally I called up Dr. Gezon. He saw the point at once. But, as I say, pyocine typing was then very new, and we didn't know where to turn for help. It could be that the system was being used only in England. We talked it over and decided that the best place to begin was at the Communicable Disease Center, in Atlanta. If anybody was doing pyocine typing in this country, the people there would certainly know. That was Monday evening. On Tuesday morning, I got on the phone to Atlanta and talked to one of my friends at CDC and asked him what he knew about something called pyocine typing. 'Pyocine typing?' he said, 'Why, Shulman is working on that right now. I'll switch you over to him.' Shulman was Dr. Jonas A. Shulman, and a fellow Epidemic Intelligence Service officer. He's now assistant professor of preventive medicine at Emory University. I described the case to him and asked him if he could help us out, and he was more than willing. He was eager. He wanted all the work he could get. So as soon as we finished talking I arranged for specimens of all our isolates to be air-mailed down to Atlanta. Pyocine typing takes about two days. Shulman might have something for us by Thursday.

"Before I left the hospital, I went around to the premature nursery. That *Lancet* paper was still on my mind. Not pyocine typing. What interested me now was the source of the outbreak it described—that contaminated catheter. I looked up one of the pediatric residents and asked him what went on in the delivery rooms. I was thinking about contaminated equipment that the babies might have shared. For example, did they use a regular aspirator? The resident said no. The aspirators they used were all disposable and were discarded after each use. What about the resuscitators? Did they have humidifying attachments? A humidifier would mean water, and a possible breeding place for Pseudomonas. Another no. The resuscitators used in the delivery rooms were simply bags and masks attached to an oxygen line from the wall. I asked a few more questions along those lines and got the same kind of answers, and gave up. This wasn't a case like the *Lancet* case. So I was back in the nursery again. But the more I thought about those contaminated sinks and bassinets the less convinced I was that they were the source of our trouble. I just couldn't see any plausible link between those particular sites and those nine particular babies. But if the answer wasn't a piece of contaminated equipment, what else could it be? A contaminated person? And then I got a thought— maybe a contaminated mother. It sounded only too possible. A contaminated mother could very easily transmit an infection to her baby in the course of its birth. Childbirth is not a very tidy process.

"The next question was: Which mother? I thought I could answer that. It had to be the mother of the second sick baby. Not the baby in whom the infection was first diagnosed. The significant case was the second Pseudomonas baby—the term baby who came into the nursery with pneumonia and then developed diarrhea. The first sick baby had been healthy until the day before his death. He had been healthy for over three weeks. So he was actually No. 2. It wasn't hard to reconstruct the possible course of events. The infection was introduced into the nursery by the term baby and then spread to the other babies by the nurses. Pseudomonas is a difficult organism. You can't wash it off your hands with a little soap and water, the way you can the staphylococcus bug. To get Pseudomonas off, you have to scrub and scrub and scrub. And it's also extremely resistant to most disinfectants. But what made the infected-mother theory really attractive was that it seemed to explain what the environmental theory left unexplained. It explained why the infected babies were concentrated in Room 227 and Room 229. Both of those rooms were intensive-care rooms, and there was very little traffic between them and the other rooms. However, it was just a theory. It was based on the supposition that the diarrheal baby's mother was a Pseudomonas carrier. So the next thing to do was find out. The first thing I found was that the baby had been discharged on Saturday, and that he and his mother were now at home. I got the address, and Dr. Taylor and the baby's pediatrician gave me the necessary permission. I went out to the house and introduced myself, and the mother was nice and cooperative, and I got the specimens I needed and took them back to the Health Department Lab.

"She wasn't a carrier. The preliminary laboratory report on my specimens was negative for Pseudomonas. That was the following day—Wednesday afternoon. But by then it didn't matter. We had something much more interesting to think about. The way it happened was this. I was in the nursery that afternoon, and one of the residents came over and told me they had another infected baby. New babies had been coming along every day, of course, and this one was a term baby born on Monday and sent up to the premature nursery for special care. He had had trouble breathing at birth, and had required extensive resuscitation in the delivery room. Well, a routine nasopharyngeal culture taken when he was admitted to the nursery had just been found to be positive for Pseudomonas. I looked at the resident and the resident looked at me. This was real news. That baby could not possibly have been infected in the nursery. The laboratory samples had been taken before he was even settled there. He could have been infected only in the delivery room. And there were just two possible sources of infection there. His mother was one, and the other was some piece of contaminated equipment. My guess was naturally the mother. I found out what room the new baby's mother was in, and made the necessary arrangements, and went up and took the standard nose, throat, and stool samples, and arranged for the hospital laboratory to culture them. When I got back to the nursery, Dr. Gezon was there talking to the resident, and I could tell from the look on his face that he had heard the news.

"The three of us went down to the delivery suite. We found the nurse in charge and told her what we were doing. She was terribly upset. It was most distressing to her to have us arrive in her domain on such a mission. But she was a good nurse and she cooperated perfectly. The room where the baby had been born was not in use, and she took us in and showed us around. There was a delivery table in the middle of the room, and a row of scrub sinks along the left-hand wall. On the opposite wall was a resuscitator of the type described to me the day before. It consisted of a rubber face mask and a rubber Emerson bag enclosed in a cellophane casing, and it looked very neat and clean. But something made me take it down for a closer look. There was a little dribble of water in the bottom of the Emerson bag. I showed it to Dr. Gezon, and he raised his eyebrows and passed it on to the resident. The resident took a sample of the water. There were five other rooms in the delivery suite, and luckily none of them were in use. We checked the resuscitator in every room, and every one was wet. The question was: How come? The nurse explained the delivery suite cleaning procedure. There was one central wash sink, where all delivery-room equipment was washed. Everything was washed after every use, and then sterilized by steaming in an autoclave. Including the resuscitators? No—of course not. They were made of rubber, and rubber can't stand that kind of heat. The resuscitators were washed with a detergent, rinsed with tap water, and left on the drainboard to dry. It was possible, the nurse said, that they were sometimes returned to the delivery rooms before they were completely dry. We asked to see the wash sink. We were all beginning to feel sort of elated. I know I was. And when we saw the sink, that just about finished us. The faucet was equipped with an aerator—a standard five-screen water-bug heaven.

"It *was* a water-bug heaven. The laboratory cultured Pseudomonas from the swab samples we took from the aerator. It also cultured Pseudomonas from five of the six resuscitator samples. You can imagine how the delivery-suite nurses felt when those reports came down. They were crushed. Dr. Gezon was able to reassure them, though. He didn't consider them guilty of ignorance. They assumed, like almost everybody else, that city drinking water is safe. It is and it isn't. It's perfectly safe to drink, but it isn't absolutely pure. This is something that has only recently been recognized. There are water bugs in even the best city water. The concentrations are much too low in ordinary circumstances to cause any trouble, but a dangerous concentration can occur in any situation—like that provided by an aerator—that enables the bugs to accumulate and breed. An aerator is a handy device, but you'd probably be better off letting the water splash. It's certainly a device that a hospital can do without.

"The laboratory gave us three reports in all. The third was on the mother of the new baby. They found her negative for Pseudomonas, and that was welcome news. A positive culture from her would have been an awkward complication. Because everything else was very satisfactory. The contaminated resuscitators seemed to explain the concentration of infected babies in Room 227 and Room 229. Seven of the ten infected babies—including the diarrheal baby and the two that died—had received at least some resuscitation in the delivery room, and it was reasonable to suppose that the three others had got their infection from the resuscitated babies by way of the nurses. There's plenty of evidence for that in the literature. I remember one report that showed that nurses' hands were contaminated simply by changing the bedding of an infected patient. It was Dr. Shulman, however, who finally pinned it down. His pyocine typing confirmed the circumstantial evidence at every point. Shulman did two groups of studies of us—one on the original material I sent him, and then another on the new infected baby and the delivery-suite material. The results of his studies were doubly instructive. They identified the delivery-room resuscitators as the source of the epidemic, and they eliminated the contaminated sinks and bassinets in the nursery. The different pyocine types of Pseudomonas aeruginosa are indicated by numbers. The Pseudomonas strain cultured from the delivery-suite aerator was identified as Pyocine Type 4-6-8. So were the isolates from the resuscitator bags. And so were those of all of the infected babies. Type 4-6-8 was also recovered from two pieces of equipment in the nursery, but I think we can safely assume that they had been contaminated indirectly from the same delivery-room source. They were a bassinet used by an infected baby and the sink in Room 227. The other contaminations in the nursery were a wild variety of types—6, 4-6, 6-8, 1-2-3-4-6-7-8, and 1-3-4-6-7-8. And where they came from wasn't much of a mystery. There was only one possible explanation. They came out of the water faucets, too."

That was the end of the formal investigation. It wasn't, however, the end of the trouble. The pockets of contamination in the sinks and elsewhere in the nursery and in the delivery suite were eliminated (and a system of ethylene-oxide sterilization set up for all resuscitation equipment), but the epidemic continued. In spite of the most sophisticated treatment (first with colistimethate and colistin sulphate, and then with colistin in combination with polymyxin B), the infected babies remained infected. Moreover, in the course of the next few weeks twelve new infections were discovered in the nursery. In two of the new victims, the infection developed into serious clinical illness. It was not until the middle of September, when the remaining infected babies were moved to an isolated ward in another part of the hospital, that the epidemic was finally brought under control.

Hospital infections of any kind are seldom easily cured. Pseudomonas aeruginosa is only somewhat more stubborn than such other institutional pathogens as Staphylococcus aureus and the many Salmonellae. These confined and yet all but unextinguishable conflagrations are, in fact, the despair of modern medicine. They are also, as it happens, one of its own creations. The sullen phenomenon of hospital infection is a product equally of medical progress and of medical presumption. It has its roots in the chemotherapeutic revolution that began with the development of the sulfonamides during the middle nineteen-thirties, and in the elaboration of new life-saving and life-sustaining techniques (open-heart surgery, catheterization, intravenous feeding) that the new antibacterial drugs made possible, and it came into being with the failure of these drugs (largely through the development of resistance in once susceptible germs) to realize their original millennial promise. Its continuation reflects a drug-inspired persuasion that prevention is no longer superior to cure. "In the midst of the development of modern antibacterial agents, infection has flourished with a vigor that rivals the days of Semmelweis," Dr. Sol Haberman, director of the Microbiology laboratories at Baylor University Medical Center, noted. "It would appear that the long sad history of disease transmission by attendants to the sick has been forgotten again."

Time-Travel: One-Way*

Isaac Asimov

In 1905, Albert Einstein advanced a new way of looking at the universe that seemed to transcend and subvert "common sense." It seemed a weird outlook indeed, one in which objects changed as they moved, growing shorter and more massive. In the new outlook, what one person would see and measure and swear to, another person would not. All our most cherished certainties seemed to dissolve.

The only consolation the average man could count on was that under ordinary circumstances, the new changeability was so small it could be ignored.

Suppose we begin, for instance, by constructing an imaginary freight train which, when standing still, is exactly one mile long and exactly one million tons in mass. If it were to chug past us at sixty miles an hour, and if we could make the necessary measurements accurately enough while it was moving, we would find that it had shortened by a ten-billionth of an inch and had become more massive by a hundred-thousandth of an ounce.

A person on the freight train, however, making the same measurements, would find the length and mass of the train unchanged. To him it would still be exactly one mile long and exactly one million tons in mass. In fact, as far as the man on the train was concerned, we ourselves (the observers watching the train) would be the ones who were slightly distorted in shape and mass.

But who in blazes is going to argue over billionths of inches and ounces? It might seem that a complicated new view of the universe involving such insignificant changes is scarcely worth the trouble.

Yet the changes are not always insignificant. Just a few years before

Einstein had advanced his theory, it had been found that radioactive atoms were shooting out tiny subatomic particles that traveled at velocities far greater than that of our imaginary freight train. The velocities of the subatomic particles were anywhere from 10,000 to 186,000 miles *per second*. For them, length and mass changed drastically; changed enough to notice and measure; changed enough so that it was impossible to ignore the matter. The old notion, then, of a universe in which length and mass were unaffected by motion had to be abandoned. Einstein's outlook had to be adopted instead.

Of course, if we imagine freight trains, or anything else, taking up velocities so great as to make changes in length and mass really noticeable, they will escape from the earth's gravitational field at once. We would find ourselves in outer space and, since that is so, we might as well imagine ourselves out there to begin with.

Let's imagine ourselves on a spaceship named A, which is 1,000 feet long and has a mass of 1,000 tons. Passing us, at 162,000 miles per second, is the sister ship, B, which was built to have the same length and mass as A.

As B passes us, we use some sophisticated device to measure its length and its mass and we find that it is only 500 feet long and has a mass of 2,000 tons. It has, in other words, halved its length and doubled its mass.

We at once radio B and tell them this, but B informs us that by their own measurements, it has not changed at all. In fact, as they passed us, they measured us and found that it was *we*, A, that was only 500 feet long and fully 2,000 tons in mass.

The ships change course, approach, and rest side by side. Measurements are made and both ships are found to be normal. Both are 1,000 feet long and 1,000 tons in mass.

Which set of measurements was correct? The answer is that all were. Measurements, remember, change with motion. To the crew of A, it seemed that B was flashing past in the forward direction at 162,000 miles per second; and to B it seemed that A was flashing past in the backward direction at 162,000 miles per second. Each observed the other moving at this particular velocity and each measured the other as half-length and double-mass. Once the ships were side by side, however, each would consider the other motionless and the measurements would revert to "normal."

If you still insist on asking, "But *did* ship A shorten or didn't it?" then consider that in making a measurement, you are not necessarily checking "reality." You are merely reading the setting of a pointer, and this setting can vary under different conditions.

Einstein's theory involves more than length and mass; it involves time as well. According to Einstein, everything on a moving object slows down. The pendulum of a clock in motion moves more slowly; the hairspring of a watch pulsates in more leisurely fashion. All motion slows.

But it is periodic motion that we measure time by; some regular vibration, pulsation, or beat. If all these motions by which we measure time slow down, then we have every right to say that time itself slows down.

To some people, this seems harder to swallow than Einsteinian changes in length and mass. Length and mass are, after all, changeable in some ways. We can make an object shorter by hammering it; we can make it lighter by letting some of its water content (assuming it has some) evaporate. But nothing we know can change the rate at which time moves. We take it for granted that the time rate is something immutable; something which, oblivious to all things, proceeds unalterably on its way.

And yet, Einstein's postulated change in time rate with motion has actually been measured. Even with velocities of a few inches per second, a physical phenomenon known as the Mössbauer effect (after its discoverer) enables us to measure the excessively minute changes in time rate. Again, though, subatomic particles offer us velocities great enough to make the change easily measurable and quite significant.

There is a particle called the mu-meson which lasts for two microseconds (a microsecond is a millionth of a second) before breaking down. At least, it lasts two microseconds if it is moving at moderate speeds. Sometimes, however, a mu-meson is formed high in the atmosphere by cosmic rays and, in the shock of creation, comes streaking downward toward earth's surface at a velocity of over 180,000 miles a second.

If the mu-meson retained a lifetime of two microseconds at that speed, it ought to have time to move only about 1700 feet. Since it is formed miles high in the atmosphere it should, therefore, never last long enough to reach us here on the earth's surface.

But it *does* reach us. A really fast mu-meson can travel three miles or more before breaking down. This can be explained by supposing that time slows down for it. It still lives two microseconds by its own reckoning, but these are now (according to an earth-bound observer) very slow microseconds that stretch out over twenty ordinary microseconds.

The change in time rate exhibited by the mu-meson exactly fits Einstein's prediction, and so we must accept time as not an immutable thing but as something with properties that depend on one's point of view.

Let's return to our spaceships A and B again, then. Once more, we suppose B to be flashing past A and we can further imagine that there is an instrument on board A which enables its crew to observe a clock on B for exactly one hour by A's clock.

The clock on B will seem slow to the observing crew, because B is moving. After one hour by A's clock, the clock on board B will have recorded a bit less than an hour. The faster B is moving, the slower its time rate and the less time will be recorded by B's clock as having elapsed.

There is a formula that can be used to work out the slowing of time rate with motion and its use yields the following table:

Velocity of B with Respect to A (miles/second by A's clock)	Time Elapsed on B's Clock After 1 Hour by A's Clock
1,000	59 min. 50 sec.
50,000	57 min. 47 sec.
100,000	52 min. 18 sec.
120,000	45 min. 54 sec.
140,000	39 min. 36 sec.
160,000	30 min. 40 sec.
170,000	24 min. 25 sec.
180,000	12 min. 13 sec.
185,000	7 min. 48 sec.
186,200	1 min. 50 sec.
186,282	no time at all

And what happens if B travels past A at a velocity greater than 186,282 miles per second? Does its clock register less than no time? Does it start going backward?

No! We can avoid the possibility of time traveling backward, for 186,282 miles per second is the maximum possible relative velocity that can be measured. That is the velocity of light in a vacuum and, according to Einstein's theory, that relative velocity cannot be exceeded by material objects.

But there is one thing we must not forget. The crew on A observes B flashing past in the forward direction, but the crew on B observes A flashing past in the backward direction. To each crew, it is the other ship that is moving. So if the crew of B measured the clock on board A they would find *that* clock, A's clock, to be running slow.

This is serious, much more serious than the disagreement on length and mass which was mentioned earlier. To be sure, if two ships got together after a length-mass experiment we could imagine their crews arguing:

"When you passed us, you were shorter and heavier than I was."

"No, no, when *you* passed *me, you* were shorter and heavier than *I* was."

"No, no—"

An argument such as this can't be settled and doesn't have to be. If an object shrinks to half its length and then returns to normal or if it doubles in mass and then returns to normal, its adventure leaves no mark. There is no trace left behind to show whether it shrank temporarily or not, or whether it grew temporarily heavy or not. Arguments over that are futile and therefore unnecessary.

But if the clock on one ship is running slower than the clock on the other ship, then, when the two ships get together, *the clocks ought to bear the record of that.* If the two clocks were synchronized at the start of the experiment, they should no longer be synchronized at the end.

Let's say that one clock, because of the slowing of its time rate, lost a total of one hour. Therefore, when the ships come together again, one clock should say 2:15 if the other says 3:15.

But which clock says which time? The crew on A swears that the clock on B was slow, while the crew on B swears just as vehemently that the clock on A was slow. Each group of men fully expects that the other clock will be one hour behind their own clock. Since both can't be right, this seems an insoluble dilemma, one that is commonly called the "clock paradox."

Actually, it isn't a paradox at all. If one ship just flashed by the other and both crews swore the other ship's clock was slow, it wouldn't matter which clock was "really" slow, because the two ships would separate forever. The two clocks would never be brought to the same place at the same time in order to be matched, and the clock paradox would never arise.

On the other hand, suppose the two ships *did* come together after the flash-past so that the clocks *could* be compared. In order for that to happen, something new must be added. At least one ship must accelerate; that is, change its velocity. If it is B that does so, it must travel in a huge curve, point itself back toward A and then slow down to the point where it could hang motionless next to A.

The action of acceleration spoils the symmetry of the situation. B changes its velocity not only with respect to A but also with respect to all the universe, all the stars and galaxies. The crew on B might insist their ship is remaining motionless and that it is A that is somehow moving and approaching them, but then they must also say that the entire universe is changing position with respect to their ship. The crew on A, however, sees only B change its velocity; the universe remains unchanged in velocity relative to A.

It is because B accelerates with respect to the entire universe (not merely with respect to A) that brings about a slowing of B's clock of a kind that all observers can agree on. When the two ships come together it is B's clock that will register 2:15 while A's will register 3:15.

If, on the other hand, B had kept speeding onward at unchanging velocity, while A suddenly accelerated in order to chase after it and catch up with it, that acceleration would have made it possible for all observers to agree that it was A's clock that was slowed.

This *effect*, whereby all observers can agree that it is the accelerated object that has undergone the slowing of the time rate, is called time-dilatation, and it has an application to the Space Age.

The nearest star, Alpha Centauri, is just about 4¼ light-years away, a distance that comes to 25,000,000,000,000 (twenty-five trillion) miles. And since the velocity of light is the ultimate speed limit, it might seem that a trip from here to Alpha Centauri can never take less than 4¼ years.

In actual fact, a spaceship cannot reach velocities approaching that of light except by a long and gradual acceleration so that for a considerable period of time it travels at much below the velocity of light and should therefore take considerably longer than 4¼ years to reach Alpha Centauri.

But thanks to time-dilatation, this is not quite so. Suppose the ship accelerates at 1 *g* (an acceleration at which the crewmen will experience a feeling of weight directed toward the rear of the ship equal to that which they feel here on the earth). The combination of acceleration and rapid velocity introduces a slowing of time rate upon which all observers can agree.

To us on the earth, ten years might elapse while the space ship is *en route*, but to the crew on board ship, measuring the time lapse with clocks that move more and more slowly as their velocity increases, only 3½ years will pass before they reach Alpha Centauri.

As they continue to accelerate and their velocity approaches that of light more and more closely (though never quite matching the velocity of light) the time-dilatation effect becomes greater and greater. The ship can then cover perfectly amazing distances in what seems a comparatively short time to the crew.

Remember, however, that the time-dilatation is taking place only on the ship; not on the earth which continues at its accustomed velocity and which experiences time in the usual fashion. The time lapse which is short for the slow-time men on shipboard is therefore long for the fast-time men on the earth.

This can be shown, dramatically, by means of the following table which applies to a ship traveling out from the earth at a continual acceleration of 1 *g*.

Destination	Time Lapse on ship (years)	Time Lapse on earth (years)
Alpha Centauri	3.5	10
Vega	7	30
Pleiades	11	500
Center of the Milky Way	21	50,000
Magellanic Clouds	24	150,000
Andromeda Galaxy	28	2,000,000

So we can picture our astronauts visiting not only other stars, but other galaxies, in a trip enduring a mere quarter century.

And this quarter century is not just a matter of clock measurement. It is not just the clock or other time-telling device that slows down on board an accelerating ship; *all* motion slows down. All atomic motion and, therefore, the rate of all chemical action, including that within an astronaut's body, slows down. Body chemistry proceeds at a slower rate. The mind thinks and experiences more slowly.

This means that under the effect of time-dilatation on the trip to the Andromeda Galaxy, the astronauts not only measure the time lapse as 28 years, but *experience* the time lapse as 28 years. What's more, their bodies age 28 years and no more, even though, in that same interval of time, two million years pass on earth.

Furthermore, this time-dilatation effect is something to which all observers can agree, so that if the astronauts were to return to earth, the earthmen of millions of years hence would have to admit that the astronauts had not aged more than a few decades.

This is the foundation of the "twin paradox." Suppose that a person heads out on a spaceship which accelerates steadily to high velocities, while his twin brother stays at home. The traveling brother gradually slows, comes to a halt, turns, speeds up and slows down again while returning to earth. Thanks to time-dilatation, he ages 10 years while his stay-at-home brother (along with everyone else on the earth) ages 40 years. When the traveler returns, he is 30 years younger than his twin brother.

Mind you, the traveler has *not* been rejuvenated, he has not grown younger. It is impossible for time to move backwards, and the traveler has simply aged less rapidly than he would if he had stayed put.

Nor has the traveler extended his life-span. If both he and his stay-at-home brother lived to a physiological age of 70, then the stay-at-home might die in the year (let us say) 2050, while the traveler survives to 2080. Still, though the traveler witnesses thirty years of events after his brother's death, he has not experienced thirty years more all told. While he was on his travels, he was experiencing only ten years while his stay-at-home brother was experiencing forty. Both would die with exactly seventy years of memories.

Even if the traveling brother had gone to Andromeda and back and had eventually died millions of years after his stay-at-home brother, both would have experienced just 70 years of life and memories.

Of course, there are experiences and experiences. There is something attractive about the thought of 70 years spent in moving out into space and back, touching the earth, let us say, at fifty-thousand-year intervals (earth-time). There is not only the experience of space-travel, but also the experience of what is virtually time-travel. Such a spacehopping astronaut would have the ability to witness mankind's future history vastly telescoped.

However, there is one drawback to this. Time-travel by way of the twin paradox is one-way only—toward the future. Once having set out along the road of time dilatation, you cannot repent, you cannot return. The century of your birth will be gone forever and there will be no going back.

Notes of a Biology-Watcher[*]
The Hazards of Science

Lewis Thomas

The codeword for criticism of science and scientists these days is *hubris*. Once you've said that word, you've said it all; it sums up, in a word, all of today's apprehensions and misgivings in the public mind—not just about what is perceived as the insufferable attitude of the scientists themselves but, enclosed in the same word, what science and technology are perceived to be doing to make this century, this near to its ending, turn out so wrong.

Hubris is a powerful word, containing layers of powerful meaning, which is a peculiar thing when you consider its seemingly trivial history in etymology. It turned up first in popular English usage as a light piece of university slang at Oxford in the late 19th century, with the meaning of intellectual arrogance and insolence, applicable in a highly specialized sense to certain literary figures within a narrow academic community. But it was derived from a very old word, and as sometimes happens with ancient words it took on a new life of its own, growing way beyond the limits of its original meaning. Today, it is strong enough to carry the full weight of disapproval for the cast of mind that thought up atomic fusion and fission as ways of first blowing up and later heating cities, as well as the attitudes that led to strip-mining, off-shore oil wells, Kepone, food additives, SST's, and the tiny spherical particles of plastic recently discovered clogging the waters of the Sargasso Sea.

The biomedical sciences are now caught up with physical science and technology in the same kind of critical judgement, with the same pejorative

[*] Lewis Thomas, "Notes of a Biology Watcher: The Hazards of Science" from *New England Journal of Medicine*, Feb. 10, 1977. Reprinted by permission of the author.

word. Hubris is responsible, it is said, for the whole biologic revolution. It is hubris that has given us the prospects of behavior control, psychosurgery, fetal research, heart transplants, the cloning of prominent politicians from bits of their own eminent tissue, iatrogenic disease, overpopulation and recombinant DNA. This last, the new technology that permits the stitching of one creature's genes into the DNA of another to make hybrids, is currently cited as the ultimate example of hubris. It is hubris for man to manufacture a hybrid, on his own.

This is interesting, for the word hybrid is a direct descendant of the ancient Greek word hubris. Hubris originally meant outrage; it was in fact a hybrid word from two Indoeuropean roots: *ud*, meaning out, and *gwer*, meaning rage. The word became *hydrida* in Latin, and was first used to describe the outrageous offspring from the mating of a wild boar with a domestic sow; these presumably unpleasant animals were, in fact, the first hybrids.

Since then the word hybrid has assumed more respectable meanings in biology, and also in literary and political usage. There have been hybrid plants and hybrid vigor, hybrid words and hybrid bills in parliament for several centuries. But always there has been a hidden meaning of danger, of presumption and arrogance, of risk. Hybrids are things fundamentally to be disapproved of.

And now we are back to the first word again, from hybrid to hubris, and the hidden meaning of two beings joined unnaturally together by man is somehow retained. Today's joining is straight out of Greek mythology: it is the combining of man's capacity with the special prerogative of the gods, and it is really in this sense of outrage that the word hubris is being used today. This is what the word has grown into, a warning, a code-word, a shorthand signal from the language itself: if man starts doing things reserved for the gods, deifying himself, the outcome will be something worse for him, symbolically, than the litters of wild boars and domestic sows were for the ancient Romans.

To be charged with hubris is therefore an extremely serious matter, and not to be dealt with by murmuring things about anti-science and anti-intellectualism, which is what many of us engaged in science tend to do these days. The doubts about our enterprise have their origin in the most profound kind of human anxiety. If we are right, and the critics are wrong, then it has to be that the word hubris is being mistakenly employed, that this is not what we are up to, that there is, for the time being anyway, a fundamental misunderstanding of science.

I suppose there is one central question to be dealt with, and I am not at all sure how to deal with it although I am certain about my own answer to it. It is this: are there some kinds of information leading to some sorts of knowledge, that human beings are really better off not having? Is there a limit to scientific inquiry not set by what is knowable but by what we ought to be knowing? Should we stop short of learning about some things, for fear of what we, or someone, will do with the knowledge? My own answer is a flat no, but I must confess that this is an intuitive response and I am neither inclined nor trained to reason my way through it.

There has been some effort, in and out of scientific quarters, to make recombinant DNA into the issue on which to settle this argument. Proponents of this line of research are accused of pure hubris, of assuming the rights of gods, of arrogance and outrage; what is more, they confess themselves to be in the business of making live hybrids, with their own hands. The mayor of Cambridge, Massachusetts, and the Attorney General of New York have both been advised to put a stop to it, forthwith.

It is not quite the same sort of argument, however, as the one about limiting knowledge, although this is surely part of it. The knowledge is already here, and the rage of the argument is about its application in technology. Should DNA for making certain useful or interesting proteins be incorporated into *Escherichia coli* plasmids, or not? Is there a risk of inserting the wrong sort of toxins, or hazardous viruses, and then having the new hybrid organisms spread beyond the laboratory? Is this a technology for creating new varieties of pathogens, and should it be stopped because of this?

If the argument is held to this level, I can see no reason why it cannot be settled, by reasonable people. We have learned a great deal about the handling of dangerous microbes in the last century, although I must say that the opponents of recombinant-DNA research tend to downgrade this huge body of information. At one time or another, agents as hazardous as those of rabies, psittacosis, plague and typhus have been dealt with by investigators in secure laboratories, with only rare cases of self-infliction of the investigators themselves, and none at all of epidemics. It takes some high imagining to postulate the creation of brand-new pathogens so wild and voracious as to spread from equally secure laboratories to endanger human life at large, as some of the arguers are now maintaining.

But this is precisely the trouble with the recombinant-DNA problem: it has become an emotional issue, with too many irretrievably lost tempers on both sides. It has lost the sound of a discussion of technologic safety, and begins now to sound like something else, almost like a religious controversy, and here it is moving toward the central issue: are there some things in science we should not be learning about?

There is an inevitably long list of hard questions to follow this one, beginning with the one that asks whether the mayor of Cambridge should be the one to decide, first off.

Maybe we'd be wiser, all of us, to back off before the recombinant-DNA issue becomes too large to cope with. If we're going to have a fight about it, let it be confined to the immediate issue of safety and security of the recombinants now under consideration, and let us by all means have regulations and guidelines to assure the public safety wherever these are indicated, or even suggested. But if possible let us stay off that question about limiting human knowledge. It is too loaded, and we'll simply not be able to cope with it.

By this time it will become clear that I have already taken sides in this matter, and my point of view is entirely prejudiced. This is true, but with a qualification. I am not so much in favor of recombinant-DNA research as I am opposed to the opposition to this line of inquiry. As a long-time student of infectious disease agents I do not take kindly the declarations that we do not know how to keep from catching things in laboratories, much less how to keep them from spreading beyond the laboratory walls. I believe we learned a lot about this sort of thing, long ago. Moreover, I regard it as a form of hubris-in-reverse to claim that man can make deadly pathogenic micro-organisms so easily. In my view, it takes a long time and a great deal of interliving before a microbe can become a successful pathogen. Pathogenicity is , in a sense, a highly skilled trade, and only a tiny minority of all the numberless tons of microbes on the earth has ever involved itself in it; most bacteria are busy with their own business, browsing and recycling the rest of life. Indeed, pathogenicity often seems to me a sort of biologic accident in which signals are misdirected by the microbe or misinterpreted by the host, as in the case of endotoxin, or in which the intimacy between host and microbe is of such long standing that a form of molecular mimicry becomes possible, as in the case of diphtheria toxin. I do not believe that by simply putting together new combinations of genes one can create creatures as highly skilled and adapted for dependence as a pathogen must be, any more than I have ever believed that microbial life from the moon or Mars could possibly make a living on this planet.

But, as I said, I'm not at all sure this is what the argument is really about. Behind it is that other discussion, which I wish we would not have to become enmeshed in. And I will tell you why.

I cannot speak for the physical sciences, which have moved an immense distance in this century by any standard, but it does seem to me that in the biologic and medical sciences we are still far too ignorant to begin making judgements about what sorts of things we should be learning or not learning. To the contrary, we ought to be grateful for whatever snatches we can get hold of, and we ought to be out there on a much larger scale than today's, looking for more.

We should be very careful with that word hubris and make sure it is not used when not warranted. There is a great danger in applying it to the search for knowledge. The application of knowledge is another matter, and there is hubris in plenty in our technology, but I do not believe that looking for new information about nature, at whatever level, can possibly be called unnatural. Indeed, if there is any single attribute of human beings, apart from language, that distinguishes them from all other creatures on earth, it is their insatiable, uncontrollable drive to learn things and then to exchange the information with others of the species. Learning is what we do, when you think about it. I cannot think of a human impulse more difficult to govern.

But I can imagine lots of reasons for trying to govern it. New information about nature is very likely, at the outset, to be upsetting to someone or other. The recombinant-DNA line of research is already upsetting, not because of the dangers now being argued about but because it is disturbing, in a fundamental way, to face the fact that the genetic machinery in control of the planet's life can be fooled around with so easily. We do not like the idea that anything so fixed and stable as a species line can be changed. The notion that genes can be taken out of one genome and inserted in another is unnerving. Classical mythology is peopled with mixed beings— part man, part animal or plant—and most of them are associated with tragic stories. Recombinant DNA is a reminder of bad dreams.

The easiest decision for society to make in matters of this kind is to appoint an agency, or a commission, or a subcommittee within an agency, to look into the problem and provide advice. And the easiest course for a committee to take, when confronted by any process that appears to be disturbing people or making them uncomfortable, is to recommend that it be stopped, at least for the time being.

I can easily imagine such a committee, composed of unimpeachable public figures, arriving at the decision that the time is not quite ripe for further exploration of the transplantation of genes, that we should put this off for a while, maybe until next century, and get on with other affairs that make us less uncomfortable. Why not do science on something more popular?

The trouble is, it would be very hard to stop once this line was begun. There are, after all, all sorts of scientific inquiry that are not much liked by one constituency or another, and we might soon find ourselves with crowded rosters, panels, standing committees, set up in Washington for the appraisal, and then the regulation, of research. Not on grounds of the possible value and usefulness of the new knowledge, mind you, but for guarding society against scientific hubris, against the kinds of knowledge we're better off without.

It would be absolutely irresistible as a way of spending time, and people would form long queues for membership. Almost anything would be fair game, certainly anything to do with genetics, anything relating to population control, or, on the other side, research on aging. Very few fields would get by.

The research areas in the greatest trouble would be those already containing a sense of bewilderment and surprise, with discernible prospects of upheaving present dogmas. I can think of several of these, two current ones in which I've been especially interested, and one from the remote past of 40 years ago.

First, the older one. Suppose this were the mid-1930's, and there were a Commission on Scientific Hubris sitting in Washington, going over a staff report on the progress of work in the laboratory of O.T. Avery in New York. Suppose, as well, that there were people on the Commission who understood what Avery was up to and believed his work. This takes an excess of imagining, since there were vanishingly few such people around in the 1930's, and also Avery didn't publish a single word until he had the entire thing settled and wrapped up 10 years later. But anyway, suppose it. Surely, someone would have pointed out that Avery's discovery of a bacterial extract that could change pneumococci from one genetic type to another, with the transformed organisms now doomed to breed true as the changed type, was nothing less than the discovery of a gene; moreover, Avery's early conviction that the stuff was DNA might turn out to be correct, and what then? To this day, the members of such a committee might well have been felicitating each other on having nipped something so dangerous in the very bud.

But it wouldn't have worked in any case, unless they had been equally prescient about bacteriophage research and had managed to flag down phage genetics before it got going a few years later. Science can be blocked, I have no doubt of that, or at least slowed down, but it takes very fast footwork.

Here is an example from today's research on the brain, which would do very well on the agenda of a Hubris Commission. It is the work now going on in several laboratories here and abroad dealing with the endorphins, a class of small polypeptides also referred to as the endogenous opiates. It is rather a surprise that someone hasn't already objected to this research, since the implications of what has already been found are considerably more explosive, and far more unsettling, than anything in the recombinant-DNA line of work. There are cells in the brain, chiefly in the limbic system, which possess at their surfaces specific receptors for morphine and heroin, but this is just a biologic accident; the real drugs, with the same properties as morphine, are the pentapeptide hormones produced by the brain itself. Perhaps they are switched on as analgesics at times of trauma or illness; perhaps they even serve for the organization and modulation of the physiologic process of dying when thc time for dying comes. These things are not yet known, but such questions can now be asked. It is not even known whether an injection of such pentapeptides into a human being will produce a heroin-like reaction, but that kind of question will also be up for asking, and probably quite soon since the same peptides can be synthesized with relative ease. What should be done about this line of research—or rather, what should have been done about it two or three years ago when it was just being launched? Is this the sort of thing we are better off not knowing? I know some people who might think so. But if something prudent and sagacious had been done, turning off such investigations at an early stage, we would not have glimpsed the possible clue to the mechanism of catatonic schizophrenia, which was published just this month from two of the laboratories working on endorphins.

It is hard to predict how science is going to turn out, and if it is really good science it is impossible to predict. This is in the nature of the enterprise. If the things to be found are actually new, they are by definition unknown in advance, and there is no way of foretelling in advance where a really new line of inquiry will lead. You cannot make choices in this matter, selecting things you think you're going to like and shutting off the lines that make for discomfort. You either have science, or you don't, and if you have it you are obliged to accept the surprising and disturbing pieces of information, even the overwhelming and upheaving ones, along with the neat and promptly useful bits. It is like that.

And even if it were possible to call most of the shots in advance, so that we could make broad selections of the general categories of new knowledge that we like, leaving out the ones we don't have a taste for, there would always be slips, leaks, small items of shattering information somehow making their way through. I have an example of this sort of thing in mind, a small item largely overlooked in its significance, a piece of news to match in importance, for what it tells us about ourselves and our relation to the rest of nature, anything else learned in biology during the past century. This is the astonishing tale—astonishing to my ears anyway—of the true nature of mitochondria and chloroplasts.

Between them, these organelles can fairly be said to run the place. They are, from every fair point of view, in charge. The chloroplasts tap the energy of the sun, and the mitochondria make use of it. Without them we might still have a world of microbes, but we could not have eukaryotic forms of life, nor metazoans, nor any of ourselves. Now, as it turns out, both of these can be viewed as living entities, organisms rather than organelles. The mitochondria live in our cells, and the chloroplasts in the cells of plants, as symbiotic lodgers. They replicate on their own, independently of nuclear division, with their own DNA and RNA, their own ribosomes, their own membranes, and these parts are essentially similar to the corresponding parts of bacteria and blue-green algae from which they are now believed to have descended. They are, in fairness, the oldest living inhabitants of the earth, and the least changed by evolution.

Well, this is the sort of knowledge I would call overwhelming, even overturning, in its implications. It has not yet sunk in, really, but when it does it is bound to affect our view of ourselves as special entities, as selves, in charge of our own being, in command of the earth. Another way to put it is that what we might be, in real life, is a huge collection of massive colonies of the most primitive kind of bacteria, which have adapted themselves for motile life in air by constructing around themselves, like a sort of carapace, all the embellishments and adornments of the modern human form. When you settle down to think a thought, you may think it is all your own idea, but perhaps it is not so. You are sharing the notion around, with more creatures than you could count in a lifetime, and they are the ones that turned the thought on in the first place. Moreover, there is more than a family resemblance, maybe even something like identity, between the mitochondria running your cells and those in control of the working parts of any cloud of midges overhanging a summer garden, or of seagulls, or the mouse in the basement, or all the fishes in the sea. It is a startling relationship, of such strange intimacy that none of us could have counted on before the facts began coming in. Would you prefer not to know about this? It is too late for that. Or would you prefer to stop it here and learn no more, leaving matters where they stand, stuck forever with one of the great ambiguities in nature, never to know for sure how it came out?

The only solid piece of scientific truth about which I feel totally confident is that we are profoundly ignorant about nature. Indeed, I regard this as a major discovery of the past 100 years of biology. It is, in its way, an illuminating piece of news. It would have amazed the brightest minds of the 18th-century enlightenment to be told by any of us how little we know, and how bewildering seems the way ahead. It is this sudden confrontation with the depth and scope of ignorance that represents the most noteworthy contribution of 20th-century science to the human intellect.

We are, at last, facing up to it. In earlier times, we either pretended to understand how things worked or ignored the problem, or simply made up stories to fill the gaps. Now that we have begun exploring in earnest, doing serious science, we are getting glimpses of how huge the questions are, and how far from being answered. Because of this, these are hard times for the human mind, and it is no wonder that we are depressed. It is not so bad being ignorant if you are totally ignorant; the hard thing is knowing in some detail the reality of ignorance, the worst spots and here and there the not-so-bad spots, but no true light at the end of the tunnel nor even any tunnels that can yet be trusted. Hard times, indeed.

But we are making a beginning, and there ought to be some satisfaction, even exhilaration, in that. The method works. There are probably no questions we can think up that can't be answered, sooner or later, including even the matter of consciousness. To be sure, there may well be questions we can't think up, ever, and therefore limits to the reach of human intellect that we will never know about, but that is another matter. Within our limits, we should be able to work our way through to all our answers, if we keep at it long enough, and pay attention.

I am putting it this way, with all the presumption and confidence that I can summon, to raise another, last question. Is this hubris? Is there something fundamentally unnatural, or intrinsically wrong, or hazardous for the species, in the ambition that drives us all to reach a comprehensive understanding of nature, including ourselves? I cannot believe it. I would seem to me a more unnatural thing, and more of an offense against nature, for us to come on the same scene endowed as we are with curiosity, filled to overbrimming as we are with questions, and naturally talented as we are for the asking of clear questions, and then for us to do nothing about it, or worse, to try to suppress the questions. This is the greater danger for our species, to try to pretend that we are another kind of animal, that we do not need to satisfy our curiosity, that we can get along somehow without inquiry and exploration, and experimentation, and that the human mind can rise above its ignorance by simply asserting that there are things it has no need to know. This, to my way of thinking, is the real hubris, and it carries danger for us all.

The Language
of
Economics[*]

John Kenneth Galbraith

Among the Social Sciences, and indeed among all reputable fields of learning, economics occupies a special place for the reproach that is inspired by its language. The literate layman regularly proclaims his discontent with the way in which economists express themselves. Other scholars emerge from the eccentricities of their own terminology to condemn the economist for a special commitment to obscurity. If an economist writes a book or even an article in clear English, he need say nothing. He will be praised for avoiding jargon—and also for risking the rebuke of his professional colleagues in doing so. And economists themselves, in their frequent exercises in introspection, regularly wonder whether they are making themselves intelligible to students, politicians and the general public. Committees are occasionally impaneled to consider their communication with the world at large. Invariably they urge improvement.

My purpose in this essay is to go into these charges and assess their substance. My ambition is to put a period, or at least semicolon, to this discussion. For I hope to show that the transgressions of the economists in transmitting their knowledge, though some must be conceded, are not remarkable. Some of the fault lies in the attitudes, including the insufficient diligence, of those who lead the attack. Some is in the sociology of the subject and is not wholly peculiar to economics.

The language of economics is commonly indicted on three different counts. It is of some importance that these charges, which often are mixed together, be kept separate. They are:

1. That the ideas and terminology of economics are complex and artificial and exceedingly confusing to the layman.
2. That economists are bad writers. And it is said that proficiency in obscure and difficult language may even enhance a man's professional standing.
3. That arcane concepts and obscure language are the symptoms of a deeper disorder. So far from seeking communication with the world at large, the tendency of economics is to divorce itself therefrom and construct an unreal universe of its own.

I shall take up these several charges in turn. Each calls for a progressively more detailed examination.

II

That economics has a considerable conceptual apparatus with an appropriate terminology cannot be a serious ground for complaint. Economic phenomena, ideas and instruments of analysis exist. They require names. No one can reasonably ask a serious scholar in the field to avoid reference to index numbers, the capital gains tax, the consumption function, acceleration effects, circular money flows, inflation, linear programming, the progressive income tax, the pure rate of interest or the European Common Market. Nor should he be expected to explain what these are. Education in economics is, in considerable measure, an introduction to this terminology and to the ideas that it denotes. Anyone who has difficulties with the ideas should complete his education or, following an exceedingly well-beaten path, leave the subject alone. It is sometimes said that the economist has a special obligation to make himself understood because his subject is of such great and popular importance. By this rule the nuclear physicist would have to speak in monosyllables.

A physician, at least in the United States, does not tell you that a patient is dying. He says that the prognosis as of this time is without significant areas of encouragement. The dead man becomes not that to his lawyer but the decedent. Diplomats never ask. They make representations. Economists have similar vanities of expression and an accomplished practitioner can often get the words parameter, stochastic and aggregation into a single sentence.[1] But it would be hard to prove that the working terminology of the subject is more pretentious or otherwise oppressive than that of jurisprudence, gynecology or advanced poultry husbandry. One indication that it is not is the speed with which the really important words and ideas—gross national product, compensatory fiscal policy, GATT, interna-

---

[1] Arcane terminology and esoteric concepts do play a certain role in the prestige system of the subject to which I shall return.

tional liquidity, product differentiation, balance of payments deficit—pass into general use.

I turn now to the quality of writing in economics.

III

Anyone who wished to contend that economists are bad writers is faced with the fact that no learned discipline unconnected with literature or the arts has had such distinguished ones. Everyone has his own test of good writing. I would urge a multiple test for economists in which particular excellence in one respect is allowed to offset lesser achievement in others.

Thus power and resourcefulness of language are important, as is purity of style. Style means that the writing is identified with personality—that it does not have the rigid homogeneity sometimes associated with scientific prose. Nor should it. Language has many dimensions. It does not convey meaning better or more accurately by being flat and colorless.

Good writing, and this is especially important in a subject such as economics, must also involve the reader in the matter at hand. It is not enough to explain. The images that are in the mind of the writer must be made to reappear in the mind of the reader, and it is the absence of this ability that causes much economic writing to be condemned, quite properly, as abstract.

Finally, I doubt that good economic writing can be devoid of humor. This is not because it is the task of the economist to entertain or amuse. Nothing could be more abhorrent to the Calvinist gloom which characterizes all scientific attitudes. But humor is an index of man's ability to detach himself from his subject and such detachment is of considerable scientific utility. In considering economic behavior, humor is especially important for, needless to say, much of that behavior is infinitely ridiculous.

The writing of an impressive number of English-language economists qualifies by these standards. At the head of the list, I would put the work of Adam Smith. In purity and simplicity of style, and certainty in his command of language, he is inferior to John Stuart Mill. But he is more resourceful than Mill and much more amused by his subject. Smith sensed that a trip into the pin factory to see the division of labor in operation would establish the importance of the phenomenon for good. Pins, "a very trifling manufacture," were also an excellent selection; had the product been more portentous it would have competed with the process by which it was made. In competition with pins, the division of labor could not be less than triumphant. Similarly a less amused man would have stressed the penchant of businessmen for getting together to fix prices. (A halfway decent modern scholar would have isolated an instinct for antisocial behavior.) The businessmen would then have defended themselves, not without indignation. As the men of influence and admitted respectability, their views would have prevailed; Smith would have been dismissed as anti-business. Or, more likely, he would have been ignored. Instead, in one brilliant sentence, he noted that, "People of the same trade seldom meet together, even for merriment and diversion, but the conversation ends in a conspiracy against the public, or in some contrivance to raise prices."[2] Though the tendency is wholly innocent and convivial, the impulse to wickedness is overpowering. Neither anger nor reproach is in order; only sorrow at the inability to resist an improper penny. So expressed, the indictment has never been lifted. To this day, in the United States at least, anyone observing an exchange of words between two competitors assumes it is costing the public some money. Those so engaged feel obliged to make some embarrassed comment to the same effect when they are finished. Such craftsmanship was far beyond the reach of Mill.[3]

Mill, of course, was a greatly talented writer, a standard by which others have long been judged. And to the list I would add the name of Thorstein Veblen. In one sense it is hard even to think of him in the same terms as Mill; his prose, unlike Mill's, is involuted and pretentious. One reads Veblen with the constant impression of a struggle for effect. But few men have ever so resourcefully driven home a point. What had always seemed commonplace and respectable became, after Veblen, fraudulent, ridiculous and (a favorite word of his) barbaric. This is high art. The American rich never recovered from the sardonic disdain with which Veblen analyzed their behavior. The manners of an entire society were altered as a result. After he made the phrase "conspicuous consumption" a part of the language, the real estate market in Newport was never again the same. What had been the biggest and best was henceforth the most vulgar. "Conspicuous leisure" made it difficult even for the daughters of the rich to relax. Their entertainment had thereafter to be legitimatized by charitable, artistic or even intellectual purpose or, at minimum, sexual relief. Here is Veblen's account of the effect of increasing wealth on behavior:

> . . . Since the consumption of these more excellent goods is an evidence of wealth, it becomes honorific; and conversely, the failure to consume in due quantity and quality becomes a mark of inferiority and demerit.
>
> This growth of punctilious discrimination as to qualitative excellence in eating, drinking, etc. presently affects not only the manner of life, but also the training and intellectual activity of the gentleman of leisure. He is no longer simply the successful, aggressive male—the man of strength,

[2]Adam Smith, *Wealth of Nations* (New York, Modern Library, 1937), p. 128.
[3]I have always been enchanted by another observation of Smith's: "The late resolution of the Quakers in Pennsylvania to set at liberty their negro slaves, may satisfy us that their number cannot be very great." Adam Smith, *Wealth of Nations*, Book 3 (New York: Modern Library, 1937), chapter 2.

resource, and intrepidity. In order to avoid stultification he must also cultivate his tastes, for it now becomes incumbent on him to discriminate with some nicety between the noble and the ignoble in consumable goods. He becomes a connoisseur in creditable viands of various degrees of merit, in manly beverages and trinkets, in seemly apparel and architecture, in weapons, games, dancers, and the narcotics. This cultivation of the aesthetic faculty requires time and application, and the demands made upon the gentleman in this direction therefore tend to change his life of leisure into a more or less arduous application to the business of learning how to live a life of ostensible leisure in a becoming way.[4]

The list of good if less than inspired writers—the elder Mill, Thomas Malthus, Henry George, Alfred Marshall and (subject to some reservations to be mentioned presently) John Maynard Keynes—is also an impressive one. So it would be difficult, on the general evidence, to find fault with the literary qualifications of the English-writing economists.

IV

Perhaps, however, this does not quite settle things. It will be said that when economists have gone to the technical heart of the matter, as did Ricardo in *Principles*, or as they have come up against the full complexity of modern economic problems, as did Keynes in *The General Theory*, they have become less than lucid and accessible. Some will surely think it significant that the best writer by my accounting was so nearly the first. Were Smith or Mill writing about the economy today, they would, it will be said, be either as incomprehensible or as condescending in their prose as their contemporaries.

This confuses the problem of complex exposition or scientific perception with bad writing. Ricardo's problems were no more difficult than those which were lucidly discussed by Malthus or Mill and he did not go into them very much more deeply. Ricardo's reputation as a bad writer is greatly deserved. He was, in addition, an unscientific one. His prose was awkward, uncertain and unpredictable as to meaning conveyed, and it was his habit to state strong propositions and then qualify them to possible extinction. His natural price of labor was such as to "enable laborers, one with another, to subsist and perpetuate their race." But within a page or two the application of this heroic (and historic) law was suspended in "improving" societies, of which contemporary England was obviously one as were all others to which he had relevance. The notion of subsistence was simultaneously enlarged to include conveniences, these being any luxuries

[4]Thorstein Veblen, *The Theory of the Leisure Class* (New York: Macmillan, 1912), pp. 74-75.

to which the worker had become or might become accustomed. And the population theory on which the proposition depended was modified to exclude Englishmen although it was deemed to have full force and effect for the Irish. This is neither good writing nor good scientific method. It is bad writing based on incomplete thought.

The writing in Keynes's *General Theory* justifies similar if somewhat less severe comment. Keynes has been widely acclaimed as a master of English prose. A good part of this applause has come from economists who are not the best of judges. Much of it approved his criticism of the Versailles Treaty, or Winston Churchill, or his pleasant memoirs on academic contemporaries. But the real test of a writer is whether he remains with a difficult subject until he has thought through not only the problem but also its exposition. This Keynes did not do. *The General Theory* is an acrostic of English prose. The fact that it was an important book should not cause anyone to say that it was well written. In a real sense it was not even finished. Though new, the ideas were not intrinsically more complex than those presented with competence by A. C. Pigou and a certain churchly eloquence by Alfred Marshall. Other writers—Mrs. Joan Robinson, Professors Hansen, Harris and Samuelson—turned Keynes's ideas into accessible English, thus showing that it could be done. A better writer—patience has a certain notoriety as a component of genius—would have done the job himself.[5] The ideas of *The General Theory* could have been stated in clear English.

The influence of this book, combined with its unintelligibility, does bring up another question. It is whether clear and unambiguous statement is the best medium for persuasion in economics. Here, I think, one may have doubts.

V

Had the Bible been in clear, straightforward language, had the ambiguities and contradictions been edited out and had the language been constantly modernized to accord with contemporary taste, it would almost certainly have been, or have become, a work of lesser influence. In the familiar or King James version it has three compelling qualities. The archaic constructions and terminology put some special strain on the reader. Accordingly, by the time he has worked his way through, say, Leviticus, he has a vested interest in what he has read. It is not something to be dismissed like a col-

---

[5]Those who think this underestimates the difficulty of the ideas with which Keynes was dealing will do well to notice the carelessness of his nontechnical expression in this volume. The following is from a summary of his position in an early chapter: "The celebrated optimism of traditional economic theory, which has led to economists being looked upon as Candides who, having left this world for the cultivation of their gardens, teach that all is for the best in the best of all possible worlds provided we will let well enough alone, is also to be traced, I think, to their having neglected to take account of the drag on prosperity which can be exercised by an insufficiency of effective demand." *The General Theory of Employment Interest and Money* (New York: Harcourt, Brace, 1936), p.33.

umn by Alsop or even Lippmann. Too much has gone into understanding it.

The contradictions of the Old Testament also mean that with a little effort anyone can find a faith that accords with his preferences and a moral code that is agreeable to his tastes, even if fairly depraved. In consequence, dissidents are not extruded from the faith; they are retained and accommodated in a different chapter.

Finally, the ambiguities of the Scriptures allow of infinite debate over what is meant. This is most important for attracting belief, for in the course of urging his preferred variant on a particular proposition, the disputant becomes committed to the larger Writ.

Difficulty, contradiction and ambiguity have rendered precisely similar service in economics. Anyone who has worked his way through Ricardo, Marx or Keynes needs to feel that he has got something for such an effort. So he is strongly predisposed to belief. Ricardo is sufficiently replete with qualification and Marx with contradiction so that the reader can also provide himself with the interpretation he prefers.[6] All three lend themselves marvelously to argument as to what they mean. Thousands read these authors less for wisdom than because of need to participate in a suitably impressive way in arguments over what they said.

The case of Keynes is especially interesting because prior to the publication of the immensely difficult *General Theory*, he had advocated its principal conclusion—fiscal policy as an antidote for depression—in clear English in both the United States and Great Britain. He had not been greatly influential. Then in *The General Theory* he involved economists in a highly professional debate on technical concepts and their interpretation. His practical recommendations were not central to this discussion. But the participants carried his practical program to Washington and Whitehall. Would a simple, clearly argued book such as later produced by (among others) Professor Alvin Hansen have been as influential? My reluctant inclination is to doubt it.

Yet ambiguity is a tactic which not everyone should try. Economists will seize upon the ill-expressed ideas of a very great man and argue over what he had in mind. Others had better not run the risk.

VI

So far I have been dealing with (by broad definition) classical rather than contemporary writing in economics. The time has come to consider the

[6]No great figure since Biblical times has lent himself to such varied interpretation as Marx. This arises partly from the manner of expression, partly from the contradiction inherent in some of the ideas and partly from the fact that so much of his work was uncompleted at his death and conflicts that might otherwise have been cleared up by revision or deletion were carried into print. It is for this reason that the interpretation and re-interpretation of Marx has been not a scholarly pursuit but a profession.

complex language and the difficult mathematics of the current contributions not only to *Econometrica* and *The Review of Economic Studies* but also of many of the articles in *The Economic Journal* and *The American Economic Review*. And here the question ceases to be purely one of language. These articles are obviously beyond the reach of the intelligent layman. Is it possible that they are also out of touch with reality and that it is the ambition of some scholars to construct a world of their own choosing and exclusive understanding? Doubt is not confined to noneconomists. Professor Samuelson, in his presidential address to the American Economic Association several years ago. noted that the three previous presidential addresses had been devoted to a denunciation of mathematical economics and that the most trenchant had encouraged the audience to standing applause. Once when I was in Russia on a visit to Soviet economists, I spent a long afternoon attending a discussion on the use of mathematical models in plan formation. At the conclusion an elderly scholar, who had also found it very heavy going, asked me rather wistfully if I didn't think there was still a "certain place" for the old-fashioned Marxian formulation of the labor theory of value.

What is involved here is less the language of economics than its sociology. Once this is understood, the layman can view what he does not understand with equanimity.

Professional economists, like members of city gangs, religious congregations, aboriginal tribes, British regiments, craft unions, fashionable clubs, learned disciplines, holders of diplomatic passports and, one is told, followers of the intellectually more demanding criminal pursuits, have the natural desire of all such groups to delineate and safeguard the boundary between those who belong and those who do not. This has variously been called the tribal, gang, club, guild, union or aristocratic instinct.

The differentiation of those who belong from those who do not is invariably complemented by a well-graded prestige system within the tribal group. And—a vital point—the two are closely interdependent. If the members of the tribal group are sufficiently conscious of the boundary that separates them from the rest of the world, the tribe becomes *the* world to its members. Its limits and the mental horizons of its members are coterminous. This means, in turn, that the prestige system of the tribe is the only one that has meaning to a member and it is all important. The most honorific position in the tribal group then becomes the most honorific position in the universe. If the school is all that counts, then the head boy is a person of the greatest possible grandeur. In the Barchester Close the eminence of the Bishop was absolute because no one took cognizance of the world beyond. Similarly those who are privileged to the secrets of the CIA or who work in the White House. In each case, everything within depends on the exclusion of what is without.

The prestige system of economics is wholly in accord with these principles. It assigns, and for good reason, the very lowest position to the man who deals with everyday policy. For this individual, in concerning himself with the wisdom of a new tax or the need for an increased deficit, is immediately caught up in a variety of political and moral judgments. This puts him in communication with the world at large. As such, he is a threat to the sharp delineation which separates the tribal group from the rest of society and thus to the prestige system of the profession. Moreover, his achievements are rated not by his professional peers but by outsiders. This causes difficulty in fitting him into the professional hierarchy and argues strongly for leaving him at the bottom. [7,8]

A very low position is also assigned to economists who, even though forswearing any interest in practical affairs, occupy themselves with related disciplines—urban sociology, education, the social causes of poverty or juvenile delinquency. The reason is the same. These men are also inimical to the tribal delineation for their achievements depend on the judgment of noneconomists and thus cannot be integrated into the established scale. They are assumed by their colleagues to be escaping the rigors of their own subject.

At the higher levels, economics divorces itself fully from practical questions and from the influence of other fields of scholarship with the exception of mathematics and statistics. One can think of the full prestige structure of the subject as a hollow pyramid or cone, the sides of which, though they are transparent and with numerous openings at the base. become increasingly opaque and impermeable as one proceeds to the apex. Positions near the apex are thus fully protected from external communication and influence. Work here is pure in the literal sense. Questions of practical application are excluded as also the influence of other disciplines. And this being so, tasks can be accommodated to the analytical techniques which the scholar wishes to use. These techniques may not be

---

[7]In the United States, at least, a similar disposition is made of members who, being good teachers, are accorded the approval of their students.

[8]Thus during his life Keynes was held in rather low regard. In his *History of Economic Analysis*, which he intended to be an authoritative view of professional precedence, Professor Schumpeter affirms this judgement and bases his disapproval on Keynes's unscholarly preoccupation with useful and practical matters. He condemns Ricardo on similar grounds.

At the time of his election to the United States Senate, Professor Paul Douglas had a very high position in the prestige system of the profession and, indeed, had just completed his term as President of the American Economic Association. While economists continued to take pride in his accomplishments, and especially welcomed his demonstration of the versatility of their craft, no grave professional importance could any longer be attached to his writing or his stand on technical issues. From being a leading economist, he became the leading economist in politics. This resolution of the matter, no doubt, is a sensible one. To fit a United States Senator into the prestige system of the profession would be very difficult. Better to compromise on purely nominal rank.

mathematical but the absence of extraneous practical considerations is conducive to mathematical techniques. Needless to say, communication is closely confined to those within the pyramid and advancement to higher levels within the pyramid is exclusively by the agency of the other occupants. The standards of accomplishment which lead to recognition are thus self-perpetuating. It is no criticism of this work that is unrelated to the real world. Such divorce is its most strongly intended feature.[9]

VII

It is not part of my present task to pass judgment on this prestige structure or to compare it with that of other learned disciplines. In a world where for pedagogic and other purposes a very large number of economists is required, an arrangement which discourages many of them from rendering public advice would seem to be well conceived. Otherwise there would be more such advice than could possibly be heard let alone used. Much of the discussion in the upper reaches of the pyramid is idle—economic models unrelated to reality are constructed, criticized, amended, on occasion commended and then, alas, completely forgotten. But, as often happens, there is no ready way of separating valueless work here from the possibly valuable and any effort to do so would be intrinsically damaging. And it is the good fortune of the affluent country that the opportunity cost of economic discussion is low and hence it can afford all kinds. Moreover, the models so constructed, though of no practical value, serve a useful academic function. The oldest problem in economic education is how to exclude the incompetent. A certain glib mastery of verbiage—the ability to speak portentously and sententiously about the relation of money supply to the price level—is easy for the unlearned and may even be aided by a mildly enfeebled intellect. The requirement that there be ability to master difficult models, including ones for which mathematical competence is required, is a highly useful screening device.[10]

What is clear from this brief excursion into the sociology of economics, and this is the matter of present importance, is how the intelligent layman or the scholar from another discipline should regard contemporary economic writing. Its relevance to the real world is not great. Much of it, and more

---

[9]This explains why professional economists of the highest standing often come forward with proposals—for the abolition of corporations or trade unions, the outlawing of oligopoly, the enforcement of free competition, therapeutic unemployment, cathartic deflation, elimination of central banks, ending of income taxes—of the most impractical sort with no damage whatever to their reputations. No store is set by ability to assess such measures in their political and social context. On the contrary, such preoccupation is discrediting.

[10]There can be no question, however, that prolonged commitment to mathematical exercises in economics can be damaging. It leads to the atrophy of judgement and intuition which are indispensable for real solutions and, on occasion, leads also to the habit of mind which simply excludes the mathematically inconvenient factors from consideration.

especially that exchanged in the upper levels of the pyramid, is not meant to be. So it may be ignored.[11] It being designed to exclude practical questions, there is no practical loss. It being designed to exclude the outside scholar, the outsider may safely take the hint. The work at the less prestigious lower edges, since it must take account of information from other disciplines and also take account of political reality, does not lend itself to highly technical and mathematical treatment. This is the part that is important to the outsider. While he may not find it easy, he is not excluded.

None of this excuses anyone from mastering the basic ideas and terminology of economics. The intelligent layman must expect also to encounter good economists who are difficult writers even though some of the best have been very good writers. He should know, moreover, that at least for a few great men ambiguity of expression has been a positive asset. But with these exceptions he may safely conclude that what is wholly mysterious in economics is not likely to be important.

---

[11] The layman may take comfort from the fact that the most esoteric of this material is not read by other economists or even by the editors who publish it. In the economics profession the editorship of a learned journal not specialized to econometrics or mathematical statistics is a position of only moderate prestige. It is accepted, moreover, that the editor must have a certain measure of practical judgement. This means that he is usually unable to read the most prestigious contributions which, nonetheless, he must publish. So it is the practice of the editor to associate with himself a mathematical curate who passes on this part of the work and whose word he takes. A certain embarrassed silence covers the arrangement.

We Are Men— What Are You?*

James McAuley

When the Spanish discoverers first appeared amongst the Caribbean islands, the native Indians took them to be visitants from the world of divine beings. Thus in Cuba, as Columbus reported, the Spaniards were greeted by people bearing gifts and singing for joy, believing that the people and ships came from heaven.[1]

Similar things happened on first contact in the Pacific islands. Captain Cook, for instance, was taken by the Sandwich islanders to be a god returning, and divine honours were paid to him. Swathed in red cloth, perched precariously on a rickety scaffolding some twenty feet high, Cook was addressed as Orono and offerings of pigs were made to him.[2]

In Tasmania, the Aborigines believed in a remote Island of the Dead named Tini Drini, situated in Bass Strait, where the departed lived a spirit-like form of existence. When the English came, England was assumed to be that remote island and the white invaders were the dead returning. Similar conceptions occurred in other parts of Australia.[3]

For Melanesia, the picture has been put together for us by that fine and sympathetic observer Codrington in his book *The Melanesians* (1891):

* From James McAuley, *The Grammar of the Real*. Melbourne: Oxford University Press (1975).

[1] See S. E. Morison, *Admiral of the Ocean Sea: a Life of Christopher Columbus* (2 vols, Boston, 1942), II, 121-2, and *The Journal of Christopher Columbus*, trans. C. Jane (New York, 1960), p. 54.

[2] J. C. Beaglehole (ed.), *The Journals of Captain Cook on his Voyages of Discovery*, vol.3 (Cambridge, 1967), pp. 505-6.

[3] E. A. Worms, 'Tasmanian Mythological Terms', *Anthropos LV* (1960), 1-16.

There are still natives in these islands who remember when a white man was first seen, and what he was taken to be. In the Banks' Islands, for example, the natives believed the world to consist of their own group, with the Torres Islands, the three or four northern New Hebrides, and perhaps Tikopia, round which the ocean spread till it was shut in by the foundations of the sky. The first vessels they remember to have seen were whalers, which they did not believe to come from any country in the world; they were indeed quite sure that they did not, but must have been made out at sea, because they knew that no men in the world had such vessels. In the same way they were sure that the voyagers were not men; if they were they would be black. What were they then? They were ghosts, and being ghosts, of necessity those of men who had lived in the world. When Mr. Patteson first landed at Mota, the Mission party having been seen in the previous year at Vanua Lava, there was a division of opinion among the natives; some said that the brothers of Qat had returned, certain supernatural beings of whom stories are told; others maintained that they were ghosts. Mr. Patteson retired from the heat and crowd into an empty house, the owner of which had lately died; this settled the question, he was the ghost of the late householder, and knew his home. A very short acquaintance with white visitors shews that they are not ghosts, but certainly does not shew that they are men; the conjecture then is that they are beings of another order, spirits or demons, powerful no doubt, but mischievous. A ghost would be received in a peaceful and respectful manner as European visitors have always in the first instance been received; a being not a living man or ghost has wonderful things with him to see and to procure, but he probably brings disease and disaster. To the question why the Santa Cruz people shot at Bishop Patteson's party in 1864, when, as far as can be known, they had not as yet any injuries from white men to avenge, the natives have replied that their elder men said that these strange beings would bring nothing but harm, and that it was well to drive them away; and as to shooting at them, they were not men, and the arrows could not do them much harm.[4]

The coastal peoples of New Guinea retain, in some cases at least, the memory of what their fathers thought when the white men first appeared. I have myself heard accounts from the people around Madang of the reaction to the appearance of the Russian scientist Miklouho-Maclay. They

[4]R. H. Codrington, *The Melanesians* (Oxford, 1891), pp. 11-12.

thought he might be Kilibob, the deity who founded their culture. And by a native of Kopat, at the mouth of the Sepik, I was given an instance of the alternative type of judgement: the white men had been taken to be evil spirits.

The men who have conducted exploratory patrols into the Central Highlands, which were penetrated only in the 1930s, also came across this strange mode of interpretation. Thus J. L. Taylor records in his report on the exploration of the Purari headwaters:

> In some villages I visited in this area we were regarded as people who had returned from the dead, some of the party being actually recognized as ones who had died in recent years. Scenes of great emotion and enthusiasm were witnessed as we passed through the villages, laughing or crying people rushing to caress or kiss or even touch the members of my party. The recognized ones were asked to stay and take their old places in the community. [5]

This of course involved native police and carriers; but it was the presence of the white men that set off the misunderstanding.

Certainly it did not take long for the people to realize that the Europeans were in fact living human beings. But even so an aura of the uncanny lingered about them. Where did they come from? Why had they no women? Look, too, at the strange forms of wealth and the supernormal powers they had somehow acquired. And too often their actions inspired fear and distrust. The German observer Richard Parkinson in his book *Dreissig Jahre in der Südsee* (Stuttgart, 1926) remarks that in all his years in the Bismarck Archipelago he found no substantiated case of a white man having been eaten when killed by cannibalistic natives. He believed that the usual reason given by natives, when asked, that the white man's flesh did not taste good, was an evasion, and thought that the real reason was that given by an old chief of the Shortland Islands: *Spirit belong all white man no good!* In general, the natives believed that by eating the slain, one incorporated in oneself something of his strength. In the case of the white man they may have feared to allow the white man's spirit to gain an influence over them.

It is not to be thought that these original encounters were between mythomanic savages and clear-eyed Europeans devoid of illusions. Certainly some of the early navigators were realistic enough to see that the savages were just ordinary men and women with the normal spread of vices and virtues, reason and stupidity, though formed in a different culture. Quiros and Cook could not understand everything they saw, and

---

[5]Unpublished report in the library of the Australian School of Pacific Administration, Sydney.

might misinterpret some things, but they did see straight through to the essential humanity of the primitives, and did not systematically misinterpret by applying some false preconception. But from the beginning there were others who did systematically misinterpret; and these ideological distortions split in two opposite directions.

Either the native was the Noble Savage, inhabitant of a primitive paradise uncorrupted by civilization; or he was a subhuman creature whose uncivilized state was due to a brutish inferiority of nature.

The first idea was taken up more enthusiastically by those back home. Thus it was the court humanist Peter Martyr who gave wide currency to the Golden Age version of the life of the Caribbean Indians, in writing up the discoveries of Columbus. Translated by Richard Eden into English, his idealization became an ingredient in Shakespeare's The Tempest.[6] This strain of myth-making had its greatest fortune in the eighteenth century when Diderot and other ideologues in Paris acclaimed Bougainville's discovery of the New Cythera, namely, Tahiti. They fabricated a vision of the paradise of Natural Man, having a good start from the enthusiastic accounts of Rousseauistically-inclined members of the expedition, such as Philibert de Commerson, who told of the delights of innocent sexuality and wrote: 'I can state that it is the only corner of the earth where live men without vices, without prejudices, without wants, without dissensions'.[7] The reservations of the realistic Bougainville were swept aside.

On the other hand, the notion of the natural brutishness and inferiority of the dark savage had more success amongst settlers on the spot, who had to grapple with the inadequacies of the native when faced with European demands, or who wanted a justification for enslaving or exterminating or otherwise mistreating the inhabitants. The Spanish settlers in the New World found it convenient to believe that the Indians were without souls and therefore without personal rights, until rebuked by the Bull of Paul III which affirmed the contrary and forbade the enslavement of the Indians.

The Christian belief in the spiritual equality and brotherhood of men as persons, and the scientific understanding of primitive forms of social and mental life, were slow in breaking through the twin distortions which idealized or debased the savage. Missionaries and scientists themselves fell victim to the prevailing prejudices. Thus the pseudo-theological idea that the black races were subject to the curse laid on Ham's posterity—that they should be hewers of wood and drawers of water forever—an idea born in rabbinical circles and taken over by Dutch Calvinists, also had quite a success amongst Catholic missionaries in Africa in the nineteenth century. And as late as the nineteen-thirties among scientists we find the en-

---

[6]Richard Eden, The Decades of the Newe Worlde (1555) and The History of Travayle in the West and East Indies (1577).

[7]Denis Diderot, Supplement au voyage de Bougainville (Geneva. 1955), p. 82.

tomologist Evelyn Cheesman writing as follows of the Papuans amongst whom she had travelled:

> I have given offence to missionaries by using such a word, but far the best attitude to take towards natives is to look upon them all as a superior kind of animal. We are just as responsible for their well-being, and they are just as deserving of kindness and justice at our hands. We can find them every bit as interesting and study them quite as well...[8]

Here also is one of the leaders of thought in France in the twentieth century, Julien Benda:

> The humanitarianism which holds in honour the abstract quality of what is human, is the only one which allows us to love *all* men. Obviously, as soon as we look at men in the concrete, we inevitably find that this quality is distributed in different quantities, and we have to say with Renan: 'In reality one is *more or less* a man, *more or less* the son of God...I see no reason why a Papuan should be immortal'.[9]

Had Renan or Benda spoken with the French missionaries who, at the time they were writing, were working amongst the same Papuans, their superficial levity might have been curbed.

So great, then, was the initial 'distance' between the men who encountered one another in different parts of the world in the last few centuries that the first conquest of knowledge had to be an acceptance of the most elementary fact: that they shared a common humanity. Not gods or demons or ghosts on one side; not specimens of Adamic innocence or mere anthropoids on the other: simply men on both sides. Primitive peoples often apply to themselves as a designation the word in their language which means 'men'. Thus when asked by the explorer the name of their tribe, their reply is: 'We are *men*'. But, as we have seen, their reply frequently has another implication. It means also: '*We* are men—what are *you*?' This for both sides has been the first question in anthropology.

Such a simple conquest of knowledge is even now by no means complete, either in theory or in practice.

In practice the human relations that exist in colour-stratified societies, where discrimination is practised on grounds of skin colour, indicate a partial failure of *effective* realization of our common humanity. The black man may not be subject to the curse of Ham; but does he feel any the less under a curse if the very skin he was born with is a permanent disqualification and badge of inferiority?

In theory, things are not satisfactory either. It is not the discredited

[8]Evelyn Cheesman, *The Two Roads of Papua* (London, 1935), p. 222.
[9]Julien Benda, *The Treason of the Intellectuals* (trans. R. Aldington, New York, 1969), p. 8.

race theories which we need bother with. The problem lies rather in a defect in our philosophical anthropology—that is, in the general theory of what constitutes the human person, as distinct from the particular inquiries pursued in empirical anthropology. Certain assumptions often present among social scientists tend, far more than they wish to admit, to deprive human oneness of its full meaning. I refer to the 'positivist' or 'scientistic' approach.

The lurking philosophical assumption is that the only kind of knowledge which is truly knowledge is that which can be physically verified by sense-observation. This usually goes hand in hand with the methodological assumption that the social sciences must take the methods of the physical sciences as their model. So we get attempts at creating a 'social physics', at imaging society as a kind of geometry, at dismissing everything from view that cannot be quantified or given statistical form. One result is the elimination in principle of what is specifically human: namely, the intellectuality of man, his free will, and his responsibility towards an objective order of moral truths.

In this view there is no such thing as a common humanity. There is no 'human nature', only the immense variety of observable human behaviours. One kind of behaviour has to do with the assertion, implicitly, of principles governing social life, of metaphysical beliefs, of what we queasily and slipperily like to call 'values'. But these assertions are all trans-empirical in thcir content: there is no way of establishing their truth or falsity by purely empirical observation: and so, on a positivist view, the only thing verifiable about them is that they *are* put forward; and the only problem is to *relate* them to the particular social circumstances which are their sufficient cause. For since they have no objective character as possible knowledge, they must be explained wholly as products of the social situation in which they occur.

So we come easily to a position of cultural and moral relativism. Principles, beliefs and values have no possible truth-content; they are validated only in the sense that they are the demands or conventions that arise in a particular society. But this means that there is no community of mankind with access (however fallible or imperfect) to objective principles of order which can be intellectually recognized and which are valid for all. If we praise or condemn what is done in another society we are merely imposing our socially-determined approvals and disapprovals. There is no common ethical measure between cultures: each constitutes a closed world.

This is not, let it be noted, the tradition in which our Common Law was formed. The basis of that tradition is the belief in a 'natural moral law', pre-existing and superior to the diverse enactments and conventions of men. When applied to the assertion of governmental authority over peoples of an alien culture this leads (a) to the assertion that there are some basic human rights and principles of conduct which are binding for all social systems and all governments, and (b) to an effort to distinguish between what is merely different and legitimately tolerable in the usages of other peoples and what is intolerable because contrary to natural law. It is this approach which is given expression, for instance, in the legislation of Australian New Guinea, where the *Laws Repeal and Adopting Ordinance* states:

> The tribal institutions, customs and usages of the aboriginal natives of the Territory shall not be subject to this Ordinance and shall, subject to the provisions of the Ordinances of the Territory from time to time in force, *be permitted to continue in existence in so far as the same are not repugnant to the general principles of humanity.*

The full consequences of the positivist and relativist approach, with its tendency to break up the reality of human oneness, frequently trouble those who adhere to it. They often fall into an honourable inconsistency rather than accept the logic of their position, speaking and acting *as if* there were after all cognizable moral truths of universal application founded in human nature as such. But others seek to maintain their relativism doggedly against all comers.

The cost of maintaining this position is to substitute for the human person in his fullness a psychophysical simulacrum, methodically deprived of rational dignity. When the primitive accosts such theorists he might well say: '*We* are men—what are *you*?' And the theorists might well say: 'We have no human nature in common with you, though we have important observable biological similarities and similar basic needs in respect of food, sex, breathing, micturition etc....We regard ourselves as socially-determined phenomena and do not pretend to any rational principles of order and conduct; for, as our great teacher Bertrand Russell says, man can exhibit a certain cleverness in choosing means to an end, but ends themselves are not susceptible of rational judgement, being determined by passion and prejudice. We intend by superior power and scientific means to dominate and change your lives, but we claim no rational justification for interfering with you.'

This is, so far, mainly a difficulty in the theoretical domain. But one wonders if it will not accumulate practical efforts, as theoretical positions tend to do. Meanwhile signs continually appear that among social scientists there is some realization of the uncomfortable dilemmas into which positivism thrusts its adherents. Thus an American scholar, William L. Kolb, has remarked that a good deal of current thinking takes a direction inimical to social freedom. 'Sociologists', he notes, 'have believed for some time that in order for a society to exist the members of that society must share a system of values'. Furthermore, it seems that it is necessary for at least most men in that society to believe that these values are objectively *true*, if society is to be satisfactorily maintained. But if the real truth is that none of such values can claim to be 'true', the sociologist is placed in an intolerable dilemma: 'To give all men access to this truth would be to destroy society, for men cannot know to be false what they must believe to be true'. The practical result would seem to be that most men should be denied access to this dangerous truth about the nature of their values. The final illumination must be confined to the initiate. Kolb goes on to indicate a way out of the dilemma:

> But perhaps the positivist can forsake his positivism. There is nothing in science that compels one to assert the subjective character of values... When the sociologist restores his belief in the objectivity of values while, at the same time, remaining humble about their final content, he rejoins the human race in its eternal quest. [10]

Whether we are going to see any mass movement towards rejoining the human race amongst social scientists tainted with positivism remains to be seen. It is rather more likely that when the sons of the Melanesian primitives shortly arrive at our universities they will be told by their teachers that only the choice of means can be rational, the choice of ends and principles being necessarily irrational. Let us hope they do not learn this lesson too thoroughly. Nihilism does not invariably take polite academic forms.

[10]William L. Kolb, 'Values, Positivism and the Functional Theory of Religion', *Social Forces* XXXI (1953), pp. 305-11.

Harlem
Is
Nowhere*

Ralph Ellison

One must descend to the basement and move along a confusing mazelike hall to reach it. Twice the passage seems to lead against a blank wall; then at last one enters the brightly lighted auditorium. And here, finally, are the social workers at the reception desks; and there, waiting upon the benches rowed beneath the pipes carrying warmth and water to the floors above, are the patients. One sees white-jacketed psychiatrists carrying charts appear and vanish behind screens that form the improvised interviewing cubicles. All is an atmosphere of hurried efficiency; and the concerned faces of the patients are brightened by the friendly smiles and low-pitched voices of the expert workers. One has entered the Lafargue Psychiatric Clinic.

This clinic (whose staff receives no salary and whose fee is only twenty-five cents—to those who can afford it) is perhaps the most successful attempt in the nation to provide psychotherapy for the under-privileged. Certainly it has become in two years one of Harlem's most important institutions. Not only is it the sole mental clinic in the section, it is the only center in the city where both Negroes and whites may receive extended psychiatric care. Thus its importance transcends even its great value as a center for psychotherapy: it represents an underground extension of democracy.

As one of the few institutions dedicated to recognizing the total implications of Negro life in the United States, the Lafargue Clinic rejects all stereotypes, and may be said to concern itself with any possible variations

between the three basic social factors shaping an American Negro's personality: he is viewed as a member of a racial and cultural minority; as an
American citizen caught in certain political and economic relationships;
and as a modern man living in a revolutionary world. Accordingly each patient, whether white or black, is approached dynamically as a being
possessing a cultural and biological past who seeks to make his way toward
the future in a world wherein each discovery about himself must be made
in the here and now at the expense of hope, pain and fear—a being who in
responding to the complex forces of America has become confused.

Leaving the Lafargue Clinic for a while, what are some of the forces
which generate this confusion? Who is the total Negro whom the clinic
seeks to know; what is the psychological character of the scene in which he
dwells; how describe the past which he drags into this scene, and what is
the future toward which he stumbles and becomes confused? Let us begin
with the scene: Harlem.

To live in Harlem is to dwell in the very bowels of the city; it is to pass a
labyrinthine existence among streets that explode monotonously skyward
with the spires and crosses of churches and clutter under foot with garbage
and decay. Harlem is a ruin—many of its ordinary aspects (its crimes, its
casual violence, its crumbling buildings with littered area-ways, ill-smelling
halls and vermin-invaded rooms) are indistinguishable from the distorted
images that appear in dreams, and which, like muggers haunting a lonely
hall, quiver in the waking mind with hidden and threatening significance.
Yet this is no dream but the reality of well over four hundred thousand
Americans; a reality which for many defines and colors the world. Overcrowded and exploited politically and economically, Harlem is the scene
and symbol of the Negro's perpetual alienation in the land of his birth.

But much has been written about the social and economic aspects of
Harlem; we are here interested in its psychological character—a character
that arises from the impact between urban slum conditions and folk sensibilities. Historically, American Negroes are caught in a vast process of
change that has swept them from slavery to the condition of industrial man
in a space of time so telescoped (a bare eighty-five years) that it is possible
literally for them to step from feudalism into the vortex of industrialism
simply by moving across the Mason-Dixon line.

This abruptness of change and the resulting clash of cultural factors
within Negro personality account for some of the extreme contrasts found
in Harlem, for both its negative and its positive characteristics. For if
Harlem is the scene of the folk-Negro's death agony, it is also the setting of
his transcendence. Here it is possible for talented youths to leap through
the development of decades in a brief twenty years, while beside them
white-haired adults crawl in the feudal darkness of their childhood. Here a
former cotton picker develops the sensitive hands of a surgeon, and men
whose grandparents still believe in magic prepare optimistically to become

atomic scientists. Here the grandchildren of those who possessed no written literature examine their lives through the eyes of Freud and Marx, Kierkegaard and Kafka, Malraux and Sartre. It explains the nature of a world so fluid and shifting that often within the mind the real and the unreal merge, and the marvelous beckons from behind the same sordid reality that denies its existence.

Hence the most surreal fantasies are acted out upon the streets of Harlem; a man ducks in and out of traffic shouting and throwing imaginary grenades that actually exploded during World War I; a boy participates in the rape-robbery of his mother; a man beating his wife in a park uses boxing "science" and observes Marquess of Queensberry rules (no rabbit punching, no blows beneath the belt); two men hold a third while a lesbian slashes him to death with a razor blade; boy gangsters wielding homemade pistols (which in the South of their origin are but toy symbols of adolescent yearning for manhood) shoot down their young rivals. Life becomes a masquerade, exotic costumes are worn every day. Those who cannot afford to hire a horse wear riding habits; others who could not afford a hunting trip or who seldom attend sporting events carry shooting sticks.

For this is a world in which the major energy of the imagination goes not into creating works of art, but to overcome the frustrations of social discrimination. Not quite citizens and yet Americans, full of the tensions of modern man but regarded as primitives, Negro Americans are in desperate search for an identity. Rejecting the second-class status assigned them, they feel alienated and their whole lives have become a search for answers to the questions: Who am I, What am I, Why am I, and Where? Significantly, in Harlem the reply to the greeting, "How are you?" is very often, "Oh, man, I'm *nowhere*"—a phrase revealing an attitude so common that it has been reduced to a gesture, a seemingly trivial word. Indeed, Negroes are not unaware that the conditions of their lives demand new definitions of terms like *primitive* and *modern, ethical* and *unethical, moral* and *immoral, patriotism* and *treason, tragedy* and *comedy, sanity* and *insanity*.

But for a long time now—despite songs like the "Blow Top Blues" and the eruption of expressions like *frantic, buggy* and *mad* into Harlem's popular speech, doubtless a word-magic against the states they name—calm in face of the unreality of Negro life becomes increasingly difficult. And while some seek relief in strange hysterical forms of religion, in alcohol and drugs, and others learn to analyze the causes for their predicament and join with others to correct them, an increasing number have found their way to the Lafargue Psychiatric Clinic.

In relation to their Southern background, the cultural history of Negroes in the North reads like the legend of some tragic people out of mythology, a people which aspired to escape from its own unhappy homeland to the apparent peace of a distant mountain; but which, in migrating, made some fatal error of judgment and fell into a great chasm of mazelike passages that promise ever to lead to the mountain but end ever against a wall. Not that a Negro is worse off in the North than in the South, but that in the North he surrenders and does not replace certain important supports to his personality. He leaves a relatively static social order in which, having experienced its brutality for hundreds of years—indeed, having been formed within it and by it—he has developed those techniques of survival to which Faulkner refers as "endurance," and an ease of movement within explosive situations which makes Hemingway's definition of courage, "grace under pressure," appear mere swagger. He surrenders the protection of his peasant cynicism—his refusal to hope for the fulfillment of hopeless hopes—and his sense of being "at home in the world" gained from confronting and accepting (for day-to-day living, at least) the obscene absurdity of his predicament. Further, he leaves a still authoritative religion which gives his life a semblance of metaphysical wholeness; a family structure which is relatively stable; and a body of folklore—tested in life-and-death terms against his daily experience with nature and the Southern white man—that serves him as a guide to action.

These are the supports of Southern Negro rationality (and, to an extent, of the internal peace of the United States); humble, but of inestimable psychological value,[1] they allow Southern Negroes to maintain their almost mystical hope for a future of full democracy—a hope accompanied by an irrepressible belief in some Mecca of equality, located in the North and identified by the magic place names New York, Chicago, Detroit. A belief sustained (as all myth is sustained by ritual) by identifying themselves ritually with the successes of Negro celebrities, by reciting their exploits and enumerating their dollars, and by recounting the swiftness with which they spiral from humble birth to headline fame. And doubtless the blasting of this dream is as damaging to Negro personality as the slum scenes of filth, disorder and crumbling masonry in which it flies apart.

When Negroes are barred from participating in the main institutional life of society they lose far more than economic privileges or the satisfaction of saluting the flag with unmixed emotions. They lose one of the bulwarks which men place between themselves and the constant threat of chaos. For whatever the assigned function of social institutions, their psychological function is to protect the citizen against the irrational, incalculable forces that hover about the edges of human life like cosmic destruction lurking within an atomic stockpile.

And it is precisely the denial of this support through segregation and discrimination that leaves the most balanced Negro open to anxiety.

Though caught not only in the tensions arising from his own swift

---

[1] Its political and economic value is the measure of both the positive and negative characteristics of American democracy.

history, but in those conflicts created in modern man by a revolutionary world, he cannot participate fully in the therapy which the white American achieves through patriotic ceremonies and by identifying himself with American wealth and power. Instead, he is thrown back upon his own "slum-shocked" institutions.

But these, like his folk personality, are caught in a process of chaotic change. His family disintegrates, his church splinters; his folk wisdom is discarded in the mistaken notion that it in no way applies to urban living; and his formal education (never really his own) provides him with neither scientific description nor rounded philosophical intepretation of the profound forces that are transforming his total being. Yet even his art is transformed; the lyrical ritual elements of folk jazz—that artistic projection of the only real individuality possible for him in the South, that embodiment of a superior democracy in which each individual cultivated his uniqueness and yet did not clash with his neighbors—have given way to the near-themeless technical virtuosity of bebop, a further triumph of technology over humanism. His speech hardens; his movements are geared to the time clock; his diet changes, his sensibilities quicken and his intelligence expands. But without institutions to give him direction, and lacking a clear explanation of his predicament—the religious ones being inadequate, and those offered by political and labor leaders obviously incomplete and opportunistic—the individual feels that his world and his personality are out of key. The phrase "I'm nowhere" expresses the feeling borne in upon many Negroes that they have no stable, recognized place in society. One's identity drifts in a capricious reality in which even the most commonly held assumptions are questionable. One "is" literally, but one is nowhere; one wanders dazed in a ghetto maze, a "displaced person" of American democracy.

And as though all this were not enough of a strain on a people's sense of the rational, the conditions under which it lives are seized upon as proof of its inferiority. Thus the frustrations of Negro life (many of them the frustrations of *all* life during this historical moment) permeate the atmosphere of Harlem with what Dr. Frederic Wertham, Director of the Lafargue Clinic, terms "free-floating hostility," a hostility that bombards the individual from so many directions that he is often unable to identify it with any specific object. Some feel it the punishment of some racial or personal guilt and pray to God; others (called "evil Negroes" in Harlem) become enraged with the world. Sometimes it provokes dramatic mass responses, and the results are the spontaneous outbreaks called the "Harlem riots" of 1935 and 1943.

And why have these explosive matters—which are now a problem of our foreign policy—been ignored? Because there is an argument in progress between black men and white men as to the true nature of American reality. Following their own interests, whites impose interpretations upon

Negro experience that are not only false but, in effect, a denial of Negro humanity (witness the shock when A. Philip Randolph questions, on the basis of Negro experience, the meaning of *treason*). Too weak to shout down these interpretations, Negroes live nevertheless as they have to live, and the concrete conditions of their lives are more real than white men's arguments.

And it is here exactly that lies the importance of the Lafargue Psychiatric Clinic—both as a scientific laboratory and as an expression of forthright democratic action in its scientific willingness to dispense with preconceived notions and accept the realities of Negro, i.e., *American* life. It recognizes that the personality damage that brought it into being represents not the disintegration of a people's fiber, but the failure of a way of life. For not only is it an antidote to this failure, it represents a victory over another of its aspects.

For ten years, while heading various psychiatric institutions, Dr. Wertham had fought for a psychiatric center in which Negroes could receive treatment. But whether he approached politicians, city agencies or philanthropists, all gave excuses for not acting. The agencies were complacent, the politicians accused him of harboring political rather than humanitarian motives; certain liberal middlemen, who stand between Negroes and philanthropic dollars, accused him of trying to establish a segregated institution. Finally it was decided to establish the clinic without money or official recognition. The results were electric. When his fellow psychiatrists were asked to contribute their services, Dr. Wertham was overwhelmed with offers. These physicians, all of whom hold jobs in institutions which discriminate against Negroes, were eager to overcome this frustration to their science; and like some Southern Negroes who consider that part of themselves best which they hide beneath their servility, they consider their most important work that which is carried out in a Harlem basement.

Here, in the basement, a frustrated science goes to find its true object: the confused of mind who seek reality. Both find the source of their frustrations in the sickness of the social order. As such, and in spite of the very fine work it is doing, a thousand Lafargue clinics could not dispel the sense of unreality that haunts Harlem. Knowing this, Dr. Wertham and his interracial staff seek a modest achievement: to give each bewildered patient an insight into the relation between his problems and his environment, and out of this understanding to reforge the will to endure in a hostile world.

Terms
and
Topics

TERMS

1. Investigate the art of **allusion** (see Terms, section I). Why do writers allude to literary, classical, biblical, or other subjects? Compare Ellison's allusions to popular culture with the wide range of allusions in Huxley's essay in section II. What allusions can you find in other essays? To what is Eiseley alluding when he refers to "Man Friday" (section I)? How effective are allusions, examples, and analogies (see Terms, section III) as strategies for making ideas clearer in an explanation?

2. *Satire* Ridicule of something, supposedly in order to reform it. *Satire* could also be applicable to section V, since it is often humorous. Or it could be applicable to section III, since it is a kind of criticism, or argument. Do any of the essays in this section (IV) use satire, even if only in small doses?

3. *Exposition* One of the four traditional modes of discourse (the other three being narration, description, and argument). In a literary context, *exposition* refers to the provision of essential data, the who-what-why-where-when of a story. The essential meaning is the same in both instances: providing information, explaining, *exposing* the facts.

4. What is *language?* Consult a variety of sources for definitions (dictionaries, encyclopedias, handbooks, linguistic glossaries, and the like). You will likely find a variety of definitions. Then write your own, incorporating in it what you think to be the essential elements.

5. *Jargon* Strictly speaking, the specialized language of a particular occupation. The term, however, is usually broadened to mean any artificially or unnecessarily complex, fuzzy, or wordy diction or style. (See quotation number 6, page 7.)

6. *Ambiguity* Multiple meaning. An *ambiguous* statement is one that can be understood in more than one way. *She struck the man with the stick*, for example, or *The sparrow looked longer than the owl*, can be understood in two different ways. Poets and other writers will sometimes purposely create ambiguity, thereby forcing the reader to juggle two appropriate meanings at once. Jargon and other sloppy uses of language, however, can produce unintentional and befuddling ambiguity. Look for ambiguity in the things you read—whether in this book or elsewhere, and whether creative or unintentional. In what kinds of essay is intentional ambiguity most likely to be found? Try composing some ambiguous sentences.

TOPICS: On Individual Essays

SIMONE BECK, LOUISETTE BERTHOLLE, AND JULIA CHILD "How to Bone a Duck, Turkey, or Chicken"

1. Are the instructions clear? With them in hand, could you approach the designated task with at least a small degree of confidence? How have the authors tried to overcome the natural diffidence of a novice? What have they done to keep the directions from sounding utterly dry and mechanical?
2. Is there anything about the description of the process that makes you view it as something less than appetizing?
3. Write a set of instructions for some process of similar complexity, first for a reader of your own age and experience, then again for a child of about nine.
4. If you know how to tie flies, write a brief (one or two pages) set of instructions on how to tie a particular kind—perhaps a Harger's Orange?

JANICE YALDEN "Methods in Language Teaching"

1. In her third paragraph, Yalden refers to "discrimination training." What does the phrase mean?
2. Yalden uses a great deal of passive voice in her essay. Was this necessary? Try rewriting a predominantly passive passage in the active voice.
3. Do you feel that you learn behaviour—language or otherwise—through a process of stimulus, response, and then either reward or punishment, like a rat going through a maze? Write a short essay in which you try to analyze just how you learned some particular skill. Does your experience support the behaviourist theory? Do you think the age of a learner could affect the success of the method used?

4. Write an essay in which you evaluate the method by which you learned —whether well or inadequately—a language other than your native one.

5. Has the teaching of mathematics undergone a similar change in methodology? Is mathematics another language?

6. Write an essay which, like this one, begins with a definition of one or more key terms.

BERTON ROUECHÉ "Three Sick Babies"

1. Notice how Rouaché begins his essay with narrative (though narrative that contains information or "exposition"), somewhat in the manner of a police story, and then, in the second paragraph, provides almost pure exposition, background information necessary for the reader to understand what is going on. Does this pattern continue, or does he switch to a different technique?

2. Does the technical terminology Rouaché uses from time to time annoy you or does it reassure you? Do you feel that you are learning something from it (or could if you took time to go to a medical dictionary), or that Rouaché is trying to snow you with medical jargon? Does his frequent repetition of the key terms make them easier to absorb, make them seem almost familiar after a while? Or does their strangeness cumulatively nag at you as you read?

3. Considering the lengthy quotation from Fierer and the other material Rouaché presents, does his essay differ significantly in kind from, say, Cameron's interview with Davies? Does Rouaché have greater control over what he reports?

4. After Dr. Fierer comes on the scene, Rouaché gives us almost straight direct quotation. What does this do to the sense of narrative flow already established? If it doesn't damage it, why not?

5. Is there implicit irony in Dr. Fierer's being delayed by "a chimpanzee...with hepatitis"? Is the effect heightened by this fact's being disclosed at the end of a paragraph?

6. The Communicable Disease Center (CDC) in Atlanta is now known as the Center for Disease Control (CDC). What do you suppose were the reason or reasons for the change in name (and for the retention of the initials)?

7. Does having read this essay make you feel less or more secure about the prospect of going into hospital someday? Do you think Rouaché had one or the other of these results in view? Compare his intent with that of Orwell. If you have had experience as a patient in a hospital, try writing an essay directed at a general audience in which you explain what it was

like. In line with the point of this section, try to make your *primary* purposes those of explaining and informing, rather than merely relating, describing, or revealing, and try to keep anything argumentative out of it altogether.

8. Write an informative essay in which you deliberately use a few highly technical and specialized terms that are familiar to you but are unlikely to be familiar to most of your classmates. Do not define or translate these terms, but repeat them, using them in such a way that their meanings become progressively clearer to a lay reader. (Look back at Haig-Brown's essay on fishing: could he have been more helpful with his specialized terms, or are they best handled as he has done? Would it depend on the audience?)

ISAAC ASIMOV "Time-Travel: One-Way"

1. After reading Asimov's essay, do you feel that you understand Einstein's theory of relativity any better than before? Does the use of trains and spaceships as examples help?

2. Explain Asimov's basic paradox ("one-way"), that "you can't go home again," so to speak. Why, in the terms he describes, could one *not* reverse one's trip, in time as well as direction?

3. Science-fiction writers often make use of the kind of data that Asimov (himself a science-fiction writer) tries to explain to us earthlings. If you are familiar with one or more works of science fiction of this kind, try to explain some of the technicalities to a non-fan.

4. How would you try to describe our world to a creature who had experienced only two dimensions? Is Asimov trying to describe a four-dimensional concept to prisoners of a mere three dimensions?

5. If you understand mathematics, write an essay in which you attempt to explain the binomial theorem to, say, someone who never finished high school. Think about the techniques you will use to try to make clear the abstract concepts involved.

LEWIS THOMAS "Notes of a Biology-Watcher"

1. Does Thomas write the way you would expect a scientist to write? How, or how not?

2. What does Thomas mean when he says that "the question about limiting human knowledge" is "too loaded" (p. 251)? If he thinks it is "too loaded," how can he later turn to a direct discussion of it and give an extended answer to it?

3. Do you feel legitimately included in the audience for Thomas's essay, or do you think he was writing for fellow scientists? Cite specific details to support your answer.

4. Clearly Thomas's essay is not only informative but also argumentative. Compare his rhetorical techniques with those of one or more of the other essays in this section that are written to persuade. Then compare them with the techniques of the essays in section III.

5. Thomas begins almost as if his main interest were in the history of the meanings of the words *hubris* and *hybrid*. Browse in a good standard dictionary—or perhaps in an etymological dictionary—until you find two or three words that are similarly related etymologically but whose current meanings do not, at first glance, appear related. Then write a short essay tracing the history of their meanings.

6. Imagine yourself a non-scientist member of a "Hubris Commission." Three cases are put before you. The first is that of a scientist who seems to be on the verge of converting lead into gold. How would you react? The second is that of a scientist experimenting with ants—enormously strong creatures for their size—in an attempt to breed larger ones to be used as "workhorses" and thus conserve energy. Should he be allowed to continue? In the third case, a parapsychologist claims to have proof that a human being, properly trained, can raise the temperature of objects hundreds of miles away. Should he be locked up? Write a brief for presentation to the committee on one of these cases.

7. Read Milton's *Paradise Lost*, Book VIII, lines 5-38, 66ff., 167-78, and Book XII, lines 553-87, and write an essay discussing the statements of Raphael, Michael, and Adam alongside those of Thomas.

JOHN KENNETH GALBRAITH "The Language of Economics"

1. Galbraith's essay is not simply exposition; it is also in large part an argument, as he makes clear at the outset. Analyze its argumentative structure.

2. Is part II, in its brevity, sufficient to accomplish its purpose? When does Galbraith return to the subject, as he promises in the footnote? Has he a purpose in thus separating this discussion, or is the separation a sign of weak organization?

3. "It is not enough to explain," claims Galbraith (part III, third paragraph). What basic principle of good writing does he then enunciate to make his point clearer? Test his writing and that of others in this book for their adherence to this principle.

4. In the next paragraph, Galbraith writes of humour. Is he humorous as he does so? Is he humorous elsewhere in the essay? Galbraith is here referring to writing about economics; does his point hold for other kinds of writing as well? Explain, in terms of other essays in this book. Are there times when humour would be out of place?

5. Explain in your own words what Galbraith finds so good about the two

statements he quotes from Adam Smith in part III (one in footnote 3).

6. In part V, is Galbraith's analogy between the Bible and economic writing clear and valid? If so, what does it suggest about modern economic theory? Is this a suggestion that Galbraith intended or would welcome?

7. Reread, closely, parts VI and VII. Is Galbraith being intentionally ironic in certain spots? If so, where did the irony begin? What is the final, overall tone of the essay? (See also question 2 above.)

8. Veblen may have dealt what he called "conspicuous consumption" a heavy blow, but it did not disappear. Write an essay on one or more kinds of conspicuous consumption in today's society. Or write a confessional essay (you may wish to try being ironically self-mocking) about conspicuous consumption's part in your own behaviour. Or write an argumentative essay in which you attempt to justify at least some forms of conspicuous consumption.

9. Write an essay anatomizing a passage of prose from a professional journal of one kind or another. Evaluate the necessity and effectiveness of the language and style of the passage.

JAMES McAULEY "We Are Men—What Are You?"

1. After the first two or three pages, McAuley's essay becomes increasingly difficult to follow. How do you account for this?

2. Were you surprised by the turn the essay took—by what, at the end, is clearly its point and purpose? Where does McAuley first state his real subject, and where his thesis?

3. Write an account of some contact between two races that you know about from personal experience. Use it to test the validity of McAuley's conclusions.

RALPH ELLISON "Harlem is Nowhere"

1. The pronoun *it* in the first sentence is given no "antecedent" until the very end of the paragraph. What is the effect of this opening technique?

2. Apply McAuley's generalizations—about white people's attitudes to other races—to the concrete realities described by Ellison. Do Ellison's points substantiate McAuley's ideas and thereby underline the seriousness of both their warnings?

3. What is the significance of the title of Ellison's essay?

4. Try to find internal evidence to support the theory that Ellison intends an implicit metaphorical connection between the clinic in a basement and an "underground" operation. And what of the "mazelike hall" that leads to the clinic?

5. Consider the essays by McAuley and Ellison in the light of what has happened since they were written. Drawing on some of these events, write a short essay assessing the validity of their assertions.

TOPICS: General and Comparative

1. Consider the variations in tone in the essays in this section. Galbraith is wry; McAuley is formal; Yalden tries to be academically neutral. What is the effect of each tonal choice? How objective is Ellison? Galbraith?

2. Three essays in this section strive to make specialized scientific topics clear to the layman. How, faced with the complexities of subjects like medicine, genetics, and relativity, do the writers manage to be clear? How does their use of a specialized technical vocabulary help them to be clear? How do they manage at the same time to communicate informally?

3. Galbraith tries to distinguish between the clarity of a necessary technical language and the ambiguity that much jargon creates. How effective is he? Is the distinction valid?

4. How does a research essay differ from an informal essay? Contrast McAuley's formality with Asimov's informality.

5. Explain the difference between a base-3 number system and a base-10 number system. Are there advantages to each?

6. Write a brief history of cartooning.

7. Write a letter to the editor explaining your position on a matter of current municipal interest.

8. Write an essay that interprets a body of statistics. Consider such topics as the differences in food costs from place to place, ethnic distribution in your area over a twenty-year span, or the spread and control of an epidemic disease.

9. Explain the differences between a diatonic scale, a 12-tone scale, a pentatonic scale, and a chromatic scale.

10. Explain how to make spaghetti sauce; how to fix the gears on a 10-speed bike; how to play soccer; how to get from Winnipeg to Thunder Bay; how to drink soup through a straw; how to tie shoes; how to fly a kite.

V
Writing
to
Amuse

In an essay called "Humour as I See It," published in 1916 in *Further Foolishness*, Stephen Leacock reflects characteristically on his own craft:

> Until two weeks ago I might have taken my pen in hand to write about humour with the confident air of an acknowl-edged professional. But that time is past. Such claim as I had has been taken from me. In fact I stand unmasked. An English reviewer writing in a literary journal, the very name of which is enough to put contradiction to sleep, has said of my writing, "What is there, after all, in Professor Leacock's humour but a rather ingenious mixture of hyperbole and meiosis?"
>
> The man was right. How he stumbled upon this trade secret I do not know. But I am willing to admit, since the truth is out, that it has long been my custom in preparing an article of a humorous nature to go down to the cellar and mix up half a gallon of meiosis with a pint of hyperbole. If I want to give the article a decidedly literary character, I find it well to put in about half a pint of paresis. The whole thing is amazingly simple.°

Writing humorously, he underlines the great difficulties that exist in writing about humour: the almost overwhelming impulse to become solemn, the easy reliance on categories of humorous techniques, the temptation to cap the humorist's jokes with other jokes that usually fall flat. There are good reasons why one should not write about the subject at all, but instead just sit back with humorous writing and enjoy it.

Yet humour often has serious implications, and writers of humour do use various techniques, and there is an art to good storytelling: all of these subjects are worthy of comment. Involved in good storytelling are such matters as a writer's control over intonation, his careful pacing, and his use of dramatic pauses. Because intonation is particularly important in a work striving to amuse, it is necessary for a writer to orchestrate a written work so that readers can adequately gauge the tone. The techniques of hyper-bole (exaggeration) and meiosis (understatement) will both work to this end. But not always. A writer, and even a speaker, must place some trust in a reader's or an audience's ability to adjust to changes in tone, and such trust is often betrayed. Humourless persons often fail to perceive the speaker's ironic tone or ironic intent. Responding literally is the surest way to kill the humour of a situation, and literal (often outraged) responses are usually out of all proportion to the original comment. "Letters to the Editor" columns frequently are filled with such misspent energy. And readers who fail to find a written work funny—if indeed it is funny—have

° From *Further Foolishness* by Stephen Leacock, reprinted by permission of The Canadian Publishers, McClelland and Stewart Limited, Toronto.

often, like those mistaken listeners, simply failed to *hear the voice*—to catch the cadence and intonations—of the speaker who transcribed his ironic observations onto the page.

We use several different terms when talking about events or things that amuse us, and they are always in danger of being confused. Here are some of them:

> **humorous** (How neutral a term is this?)
> **funny** (Why does this word imply both simple amusement and strangeness?)
> **ironic** (Are there any limits to this term?)
> **comic** (Has this term become codified by modern criticism?)
> **laughable** (Does this imply any humour at all?)
> **witty** (Does this imply intellectual enjoyment only?)
> **amusing** (Does this imply distant superiority?)
> **wry** (In what way does this suggest emotional release?)
> **sardonic** (Does this differ from *wry*?)
> **smart** (Is this a culturally biased word?)
> **whimsical** (Is this word socially biased?)
> **facetious** (Has this word become a slur?)
> **capricious** (How does this relate to humour or enjoyment?)
> **farcical** (Why is this word associated with drama?)
> **droll** (Does this word now sound oddly archaic?)
> **sarcastic** (What does this imply that *ironic* does not?)
> **satiric** (Is humour a necessary element here?)

There are other terms as well, all of which imply different variations of response. And we have to be careful to distinguish among these differences. People often confuse *sarcastic* (which means "flesh-tearing") with *ironic*, even though irony need not be aggressive. *Comic*, similarly, is synonymous with neither *ironic* nor *satiric*, nor even with *witty*. Whereas *wit* usually involves verbal cleverness (not necessarily with intent to amuse), *comic*—like some of the other terms on the list—can refer to visual incongruity rather than verbal, or in a much more general way to a genial acceptance of the complexities and possibilities of life.

When one tries to distinguish *comedy* from *irony* and *satire*—either in substance and intent or in form—other problems arise, and still more literary categories spring into being. Irony and sarcasm can be formal techniques in the context of satiric writing, which many critics think of as essentially reformative. So can innuendo; so can burlesque (the travesty of a literary form); so can parody (the travesty of a particular literary work). But irony can also refer to a whole attitude of human expectations, a shrugging resignation in the face of the difference between human desires and the way things are.

292 Writing to Amuse

To contemplate theories of humour is to encounter further disagreement. A number of theorists see wit, for example, as a kind of indirect savagery, and they define both satiric humour and humour of the farcical, slipping-on-a-banana-peel kind as psychological sublimation of violence. These writers stress the implicit viciousness of humorous writing. By contrast, someone like Leacock, who in "A, B, and C" expresses a sympathy (not unalloyed) for human fallibility, stresses how humour emerges from our awareness of the close relation between sorrow and joy. Some people call humour elitist or escapist; others claim that it is necessary for sanity, for survival, for openness, for flexibility, and for the ability to deal sensibly with reality. All of these are large claims, and perhaps no single theory adequately explains why people find things funny or why they laugh.

Whatever the impulse behind it, humorous writing—whether reformative or reflective in nature, whether sympathetic or angry—will work only when the writer carefully controls what he or she has to say. And often it is easier to perceive the intent than to appreciate the accomplishment. Thomas Chandler Haliburton, in his 1836 work *The Clockmaker*, notes that "When reason fails to convince, there is nothin' left but ridicule." But ridicule without respect for human nature, or without sensible argument demonstrating an alternative to whatever is being criticized, will rebound on the person doing the ridiculing. Uncontrolled invective, similarly, will appear frivolous and laughable—or else vicious, or simply embarrassing. Beerbohm, Murdoch, Mitford, and Thurber, conscious of the value of verbal precision, take language itself as their direct subject; indirectly, however, through literary burlesque and other techniques, they probe cultural values, social attitudes, and the idiosyncrasies of "national character." Variously acid and gentle, light-hearted and wry, they demonstrate how, by writing to amuse, authors can still communicate seriously, and how, by engaging their readers in an appreciation of human foibles, they can engage them also in the art of communication.

The English Aristocracy*

Nancy Mitford

The English aristocracy may seem to be on the verge of decadence, but it is the only real aristocracy left in the world today. It has real political power through the House of Lords and a real social position through the Queen. An aristocracy in a republic is like a chicken whose head has been cut off: it may run about in a lively way, but in fact it is dead. There is nothing to stop a Frenchman, German, or Italian from calling himself the Duke of Carabosse if he wants to, and in fact the Continent abounds with invented titles. But in England the Queen is the foundation of honours and when she bestows a peerage upon a subject she bestows something real and unique.

The great distinction between the English aristocracy and any other has always been that, whereas abroad every member of a noble family is noble, in England none are noble except the head of the family. In spite of the fact that they enjoy courtesy titles, the sons and daughters of lords are commoners—though not so common as baronets and their wives, who take precedence after honourables. (So, of course, do all knights, except Knights of the Garter, who come after the eldest sons and the daughters of barons, but before the younger sons.) The descendants of younger sons, who on the Continent would all be counts or barons, in England have no titles and sit even below knights. Furthermore, the younger sons and daughters of the very richest lords receive, by English custom, but little money from their families, barely enough to live on. The sons are given the same education as their eldest brother and then turned out, as soon as

* From *Noblesse Oblige*, edited by Nancy Mitford, London, England: Hamish Hamilton, 1956.

they are grown up, to fend for themselves; the daughters are given no education at all, the general idea being that they must find some man to keep them—which, in fact, they usually do. The rule of primogeniture has kept together the huge fortunes of English lords; it has also formed our class system.

There is in England no aristocratic class that forms a caste. We have about 950 peers, not all of whom, incidentally, sit in the House of Lords. Irish peers have no seats, though some Irish peers have a subsidiary U.K. peerage giving a seat; Scotch peers elect sixteen representatives from among themselves. Peeresses in their own right are not, as yet, admitted. Most of the peers share the education, usage, and point of view of a vast upper middle class, but the upper middle class does not, in its turn, merge imperceptibly into the middle class. There is a very definite border line, easily recognizable by hundreds of small but significant landmarks.

When I speak of these matters I am always accused of being a snob, so, to illustrate my point, I propose to quote from Professor Alan Ross of Birmingham University. Professor Ross has written a paper, printed in Helsinki in 1954 for the *Bulletin de la Société Néo-philologique de Helsinki* on "Upper Class English Usage." Nobody is likely to accuse either this learned man or his Finnish readers of undue snobbishness. The Professor, pointing out that it is solely by their language that the upper classes nowadays are distinguished (since they are neither cleaner, richer, nor better-educated than anybody else), has invented a useful formula: U (for upper class)-speaker versus non-U-speaker. Such exaggeratedly non-U usage as "serviette" for "napkin" he calls non-U indicators. Since "a piece of mathematics or a novel written by a member of the upper class is not likely to differ in any way from one written by a member of another class...in writing it is in fact only modes of address, postal addresses and habits of beginning and ending letters that serve to demarcate the class."...The names of many houses are themselves non-U; the ideal U-address is PQR where P is a place-name, Q a describer, and R the name of a county, as "Shinwell Hall, Salop." (Here I find myself in disagreement with Professor Ross—in my view abbreviations such as Salop, Herts, or Glos, are decidedly non-U. Any sign of undue haste, in fact, is apt to be non-U, and I go so far as preferring, except for business letters, not to use air mail.) "But," adds Professor Ross, "today few gentlemen can maintain this standard and they often live in houses with non-U names such as Fairmeads or El Nido." Alas!

He speaks of the U-habit of silence, and perhaps does not make as much of it as he might. Silence is the only possible U-response to many embarrassing modern situations: the ejaculation of "cheers"[1] before drink-

---

[1]See Evelyn Waugh, *Men at Arms*, pp. 40, 44. But then Mr. Crouchback is a saint.

ing, for example, or "it was so nice seeing you," after saying goodbye. In silence, too, one must endure the use of the Christian name by comparative strangers and the horror of being introduced by Christian and surname without any prefix. This unspeakable usage sometimes occurs in letters—Dear XX—which, in silence, are quickly torn up, by me.

After discoursing at some length on pronunciation, the professor goes on to vocabulary and gives various examples of U and non-U usage.

Cycle is non-U against U *bike*.

Dinner: U-speakers eat *luncheon* in the middle of the day and *dinner* in the evening. Non-U speakers (also U-children and U-dogs) have their *dinner* in the middle of the day.

Greens: is non-U for U *vegetables*.

Homes: non-U—"they have a lovely *home*"; U—"*they've* a very nice *house.*"

Ill: "I was *ill* on the boat" is non-U against U *sick*.

Mental: non-U for U *mad*.

Toilet paper: non-U for U *lavatory paper*.

Wealthy: non-U for U *rich*.

To these I would add:

Sweet: non-U for U *pudding*.

Dentures: non-U for U *False teeth*. This, and *glasses* for *spectacles*, almost amount to non-U indicators.

Wire: non-U for U *telegram*.

Britain: non-U for U *England* ("The country which had been lost to view as Britain re-appears as England." Lord Macaulay.)

Scottish: non-U for U *Scotch*. I have a game I play with all printers. I write Scotch, it appears in the proofs as Scottish. I correct it back to Scotch. About once in three times I get away with it.

Phone, Bye-bye and *Riding* (except a horse or a bicycle) are non-U indicators. The dreadful Bye-bye has been picked up by the French, and one hears them saying *Bon—alors bye-bye mon vieux*. It makes me blush for my country.

(One must add that the issue is sometimes confused by U-speakers using non-U indicators as a joke. Thus Uncle Matthew in *The Pursuit of Love* speaks of his *dentures*.)

Finally Professor Ross poses the question: Can a non-U speaker become a U-speaker? His conclusion is that an adult can never achieve complete success "because one word or phrase will suffice to brand an apparent U-speaker as originally non-U (for U-speakers themselves never make mistakes)." I am not quite sure about this. Usage changes very quickly and I even know undisputed U-speakers who pronounce girl "gurl," which twenty years ago would have been unthinkable. All the same, it is true that one U-speaker recognizes another U-speaker almost as soon as he opens his mouth, though U-speaker A may deplore certain lapses in the conversation of U-speaker B.

From these U-speakers spring the "sensible men of substantial means" who, as Bagehot observed in 1875, "are what we wish to be ruled by" and who still seem to rule our land. When the means of these sensible men become sufficiently ample they can very easily be ennobled, should they wish it, and join the House of Lords. It might therefore be supposed that there is no aristocracy at all in England, merely an upper middle class, some of whom are lords; but, oddly enough, this is not so. A lord does not have to be born to his position and, indeed, can acquire it through political activities, or the sale of such unaristocratic merchandise as beer, but though he may not be a U-speaker he becomes an aristocrat as soon as he receives his title. The Queen turns him from Socialist leader, or middle-class businessman, into a nobleman, and his outlook from now on will be the outlook of an aristocrat.

Ancestry has never counted much in England. The English lord knows himself to be such a very genuine article that, when looking for a wife, he can rise above such baubles as seize quartiers. Kind hearts, in his view, are more than coronets, and large tracts of town property more than Norman blood. He marries for love, and is rather inclined to love where money is; he rarely marries in order to improve his coat of arms. (Heiresses have caused the extinction as well as the enrichment of many an English family, since the heiress, who must be an only child if she is to be really rich, often comes of barren or enfeebled stock.) This unconcern for pedigree leads people to suppose that the English lords are a jumped-up lot, and that their families are very seldom "genuine" and "old." One often hears it said, "No Englishman alive today would be eligible to drive in the carriage of a King of France." "Nobody really has Norman blood." "The true aristocracy of England was wiped out in the Wars of the Roses." And so on.

There is some truth in all these statements, but it is not the whole truth. Many of our oldest families have never been ennobled. Some no longer hold peerages. The ancient Scrope family has, in its time, held the baronies of Scrope of Marsham and Scrope of Bolton, the earldoms of Wiltshire and of Sunderland, the sovereignty of the Isle of Man, but the head of the family is now Mr. Scrope. If he should be offered a peerage he would no doubt proudly refuse. The only existing families known to descend from knights who came over with William the Conqueror in time to fight at Hastings, the Malets, the Giffards and the Gresleys and (according to *Burke's Landed Gentry*, 1952) the DeMarris, are another case in point. Of the Norman knights who came during William's reign or later, some were never anything but country gentlemen, but some are the direct ancestors of modern peers: St John, Talbot, West, Curzon, Clinton, Grey, Seymour, St. Aubyn, Sinclair, Haig, and Hay, for instance. There are one hundred peers of England from before the Union (including Prince Charles, as Duke of Cornwall). All of them are descended in the female line from King Edward III, except possibly Lord Byron, though a little research would probably find him an Edward III descent. All peers, except barons, are officially styled "Cousin" by the Queen; as regards most dukes and earls this is not so much fiction as a distinct truth. Only twenty-six earls have been created in this century and they have all been great men like Lloyd George and Haig. (The Haigs have borne arms and lived at Bemersyde since the twelfth century but had never previously been ennobled.)

The dukes are rather new creations. When James I came to the throne there were no dukes at all, the high traitors Norfolk and Somerset having had their dukedoms attainted. They were both restored in 1660. Between 1660 and 1760, eighteen dukedoms were created. On the whole, Englishmen are made dukes as a reward for being rich or royal (four descend from bastards of Charles II), though dukedoms have sometimes been bestowed for merit. The oldest title is that of earl. Several medieval earldoms still exist. Sixty-five barons hold titles from before 1711. Three hundred and twenty-seven of the present-day peerages were created before 1800, 382 belong to families which have borne arms in the direct male line since before 1485 and which are therefore eligible, as far as birth is concerned, to be Knights of Malta.

But whether their families are "old" or "new" is of small account—the lords all have one thing in common: they share an aristocratic attitude to life. What is this attitude? The purpose of the aristocrat is to lead, therefore his functions are military and political. There can be no doubt of the military excellence of our noblemen. Two hundred and fourteen peers alive today have been decorated in battle or mentioned in despatches. The families of the premier duke and the premier earl of England hold the George Cross. In politics, including the unglamorous and often boring local politics, they have worked hard for no reward and done their best according to their lights.

The purpose of the aristocrat is most emphatically not to work for money. His ancestors may have worked in order to amass the fortune which he enjoys, though on the whole the vast riches of the English lords come from sources unconnected with honest toil; but he will seldom do the same. His mind is not occupied with money, it turns upon other matters. When money is there he spends it on maintaining himself in his station. When it is no longer there he ceases to spend, he draws in his horns. Even the younger sons of lords seem, in all ages, to have been infected with this point of view: there is nothing so rare as for the scion of a noble house to make a fortune by his own efforts. In the old days they went into professions—the Army, the Navy, diplomacy, and the Church—in which it is impossible to earn more than a living. Those who went to the colonies were administrators, they rarely feathered their nests—the great nabobs were essentially middle class. Nowadays younger sons go into the City, but I have yet to hear of one making a large fortune; more often they lose in unwise speculations what little capital they happen to own.

All this should not be taken as a sign that our lords are lazy or unenterprising. The point is that, in their view, effort is unrelated to money. Now this view has, to a large extent, communicated itself to the English race and nation with the result that our outlook is totally different from that of our American cousins, who have never had an aristocracy. Americans relate all effort, all work, and all of life itself to the dollar. Their talk is of nothing but dollars. The English seldom sit happily chatting for hours on end about pounds. In England, public business is its own reward, nobody would go into Parliament in order to become rich, neither do riches bring public appointments. Our ambassadors to foreign states are experienced diplomatists, not socially ambitious millionairesses.

This idiosyncratic view of money has its good side and its bad. Let us glance at the case history of Lord Fortinbras. Fortinbras is ruined—we are now in the 1930's. (All English noblemen, according to themselves, are ruined, a fantasy I shall deal with later, but Fortinbras really is.) He is not ruined because of death duties, since his father died when he was a child, before they became so heavy, but because he and his forbears have always regarded their estates with the eyes of sportsmen rather than of cultivators. It is useless for him to plead that the policy of cheap corn has been his downfall; an intelligent landowner has always been able to make money with prize cattle, racehorses, market gardens, timber, and so on. But Fortinbras's woods have been looked after by gamekeepers and not by woodmen, his farms have been let to tenants chosen for their tenderness towards foxes and partridges rather than for their agricultural efficiency. His land is undercapitalized, his cottagers live in conditions no better than those of their Saxon forbears, water and electric light are laid on in his stables but not in the dwellings of his tenantry. He has made various unwise speculations and lost a "packet" on the Turf. In short, he deserves to be ruined and he is ruined.

Now what does he do? He is young, healthy, and not stupid; his wife, the daughter of another peer, is handsome, bossy, and energetic. She is the kind of woman who, in America, would be running something with enormous efficiency and earning thousands. They have two babies, Dominick and Caroline, and a Nanny. Does it occur to either Lord or Lady

Fortinbras to get a job and retrieve the family fortunes? It does not. First of all they sell everything that is not entailed, thus staving off actual want. They shut up most of the rooms in their house, send away the servants (except, of course, Nanny), and get the Dowager Lady Fortinbras and her sister to come and cook, clean, dust, and take trays upstairs to the nursery. Old Lady Fortinbras is quite useful, and Lady Enid is a treasure. The Fortinbrases realize that they are very lucky, and if at heart they wish there were a mother's hall for the two old ladies to sit in of an evening, they never say so, even to each other. Fortinbras chops the wood, stokes the boiler, brings in the coal, washes the Morris Cowley, and drives off in it to attend the County Council and sit on the Bench. Lady Fortinbras helps in the house, digs in the border, exercises the Border terriers, and also does a great deal of committee work. They are both on the go from morning to night, but it is a go that does not bring in one penny. Their friends and neighbors all say, "Aren't the Fortinbrases wonderful?"

Comes the war. They clear the decks by sending Nanny and the children to an American couple, the Karamazovs, whom they once met at St. Moritz and who have sent them Christmas cards ever since. Fortinbras goes off with his territorials and Lady Fortinbras joins the A.T.S. Their war records are brilliant in the extreme, their energy, courage, and instinct for leadership have at last found an outlet, and in no time at all they both become generals. After the war they are not surprised to find themselves more ruined than ever. The Karamazovs, whose lives for several years have been made purgatory by Dominick, Caroline, and Nanny, especially Nanny, send in a modest bill for the schooling of the young people which Fortinbras has no intention of settling. It would seem unreasonable to pay for one's children to be taught to murder the English language and taught, apparently, nothing else whatever. Dominick, failing to get into Eton, has had to be sent to some dreadful school in Scotland. Besides, what did the Karamazovs do in the war? Nothing, according to Nanny, but flop in and out of a swimming pool. The Karamazovs come to England expecting to be thanked, feted, and paid, only to find that their friends have left for Northern Capitals.

Now the Fortinbrases are getting on, over fifty. Dominick having come of age, they have broken the entail and sold everything, very badly, as the house is full of dry rot and the farms are let to tenants who cannot be dislodged. However, a little money does result from the sale. They arrange a mews flat behind Harrods where, generals once again, they will continue to cook and wash up for the rest of their days. They both still sit on endless committees, Fortinbras goes to the House of Lords, they kill themselves with overwork, and have never, except for their Army pay, earned one single penny. "Aren't the Fortinbrases wonderful?" Well yes, in a way they are.

Now, while the Fortinbrases have the typical aristocratic outlook on money, the state of their finances is by no means typical. Most people, nowadays, take it for granted that the aristocracy is utterly impoverished, a view carefully fostered by the lords themselves. It takes a shooting affray, letting police and reporters into a country house, to remind the ordinary citizen that establishments exist where several men-servants wait on one young woman at dinner. There are still many enormous fortunes in the English aristocracy, into which income tax and death duties have made no appreciable inroads. Arundel, Petworth, Hatfield, Woburn, Hardwicke, Blenheim, Haddon, Drumlanrig, Alnwick, Stratfield Saye, Harewood, Knole, Knowsley, Wilton, Holkham, Glamis, Cullen, Cliveden, Highclere, Althorp, Mentmore—all vast houses—are still inhabited by lords who have inherited them, or by members of their families. This little list is a mere fraction of the whole. The treasures such houses contain are stupendous. When the Duke of Buccleuch came to visit the Louvre, the curator, who had been to England and seen the Duke's collection of French furniture, greeted him with the words: "I apologize for the furniture of the Louvre, M. le Duc."

Another English duke owns a collection of incunables second only to that formerly in the possession of the Kings of Spain, and more Grolier bindings than the Bibliothèque Nationale. A jeweller told me that out of the one hundred finest diamonds in the world, sixty are in English families. One could go on citing such instances indefinitely.

The English, so censorious of those foreigners (the French peasantry for instance) who do not pay their taxes as they should, have themselves brought tax evasion within legal limits to a fine art. Death duties can be avoided altogether if the owner of an estate gives it to his heir and then lives another five years. One agreeable result of this rule is that old lords are cherished as never before. Their heirs, so far from longing to step into their shoes, will do anything to keep them alive. Doctors and blood donors hover near them, they are not allowed to make the smallest effort, or to be worried or upset, and are encouraged to live in soft climates and salubrious spots.

The crippling effects of supertax also can be overcome in various ways by those who own large capital sums. The aristocrat can augment his fortune in many a curious manner, since he is impervious to a sense of shame (all aristocrats are: shame is a bourgeois notion). The lowest peasant of the Danube would stick at letting strangers into his house for 2s. 6d., but our dukes, marquesses, earls, viscounts, and barons not only do this almost incredible thing, they glory in it, they throw themselves into the sad commerce with rapture, and compete as to who among them can draw the greatest crowds. It is the first topic of conversation in noble circles today, the tourists being referred to in terms of sport rather than of cash—a sweepstake on the day's run, or the bag counted after the shoot.

"I get twice as many as Reggie, but Bert does better than me."

The baiting of the trap is lovingly considered.

"Mummy dresses up in her Coronation robes, they can't resist it."

"I say, old boy, look out—you don't want to pay entertainment tax."

"No, no—I've taken counsel's opinion."

"We've started a pets' cemetery—a quid for a grave, three quid for a stone, and a fiver if Daphne writes a poem for it."

Of course the fellow countrymen of people who will descend to such methods of raising cash imagine that they must be driven to it by direst need. The fact is they thoroughly enjoy it. Also it has become a matter of policy to appear very poor. The lords are retrenching visibly, and are especially careful to avoid any form of ostentation: for instance, only five of them saw fit to attend the last coronation in their family coaches. Coronets on luggage, motor-cars, and so on are much less used than formerly. Aristocrats no longer keep up any state in London, where family houses hardly exist now. Here many of them have shown a sad lack of civic responsibility, as we can see by looking at poor London today. At the beginning of this century practically all the residential part of the West End belonged to noblemen and the Crown. A more charming, elegant capital city would have been far to seek. To the Crown—more specifically, I believe, to King George V in person—and to two Dukes, Westminster and Bedford, we owe the fact that London is not yet exactly like Moscow, a conglomeration of dwellings. Other owners cheerfully sold their houses and "developed" their property without a thought for the visible result. Park Lane, most of Mayfair, the Adelphi, and so on bear witness to a barbarity which I, for one, cannot forgive.

The lords have never cared very much for London, and are, in this respect, the exact opposite of their French counterparts who loathe the country. But even where his country house is concerned, the English nobleman, whose forbears were such lovers of beauty, seems to have lost all aesthetic sense, and it is sad to see the havoc he often brings to his abode, both inside and out. His ancestors spent months abroad, buying pictures and statues, which he cheerfully sells in order to spend months abroad. Should one of his guests perceive that a blackened square of canvas in a spare bedroom is a genuine Caravaggio, that picture will appear at Christie's before you can say Jack Robinson, though there is no necessity whatever for such a sale. The Caravaggio buyer planted his estate with avenues and coppices and clumps of cedar trees. The Caravaggio seller fiddles about with herbaceous borders, one of the most hideous conceptions known to man. He never seems to plant anything larger than a flowering prunus, never builds ornamental bridges, or digs lakes, or adds wings to his house. The last nobleman to build a folly on his estate must have been Lord Berners and he was regarded as foolish indeed to do such a thing. The noble eccentric, alas, seems to be dying out. Lord Berners was one, another was the late Duke of Bedford, pacifist, zoologist, and a good man. One of the chapters of his autobiography, I seem to remember, was headed "Spiders I have known," and he tells of one spider he knew whose favorite food was roast beef and Yorkshire pudding. The great days of patronage, too, are over, though there are country houses which still shelter some mild literary figure as librarian. The modern nobleman cannot, however, be blamed for no longer patronizing art, music, and letters. Artists, musicians, and writers are today among the very richest members of the community and even an English aristocrat could hardly afford to maintain Mr. Somerset Maugham, M. Stravinsky, or M. Picasso as part of his establishment.

Voltaire very truly said that those who own are those who wish to own: this wish seems to have left the English lords. Divest, divest, is the order of the day.

The nobleman used to study a map of his estate to see how it could be enlarged, filling out a corner here, extending a horizon there. Nowadays he has no such ambitions; he would much rather sell than buy. The family is not considered as it used to be; the ancestors are no longer revered, indeed they are wilfully forgotten, partly perhaps from a feeling of guilt when all that they so carefully amassed is being so carelessly scattered. The dead are hardly mourned. "Far the best for him," the children say, cheerfully (so long, of course, as he has lived the requisite five years). Nobody wears black any more. The younger generation is no longer planned for, and there is a general feeling of "*après nous le déluge.*"

The instinct of the lords to divest themselves of age-long influence and rights extends to their influence and rights in the Church. Most of them are members of the Church of England; though there are forty-seven Roman Catholics with seats in the House of Lords. On the whole, the lords, in common with most of their fellow countrymen, have always regarded religious observance as a sort of patriotic duty. The Church is the Church of England and must be supported to show that we are not as foreigners are. A friend of mine voiced this attitude during the war: "Well, you know, I don't do firewatching or Home Guard and I feel one must do something to help the war, so I always go to Church on Sunday." I am sure he did not imagine that his prayers would drive back the German hordes; he went as a gesture of social solidarity. Hitherto, the livings of our Church have been the gift of landowners, who have generally chosen downright, muscular Christians of low Church leanings. "Don't want lace and smells in my Church." Zeal has always been frowned upon. As it is impossible to remove a parson once he is installed in his living, some of the most ringing rows of all time have been between the Manor and the Vicarage. Now, however, faithful to the spirit of divest, divest, the temporal lords are busily putting their livings at the disposal of their spiritual colleagues, the Bishops.

Many people think that this will lead to more lace, more smells, and more un-English zeal in the Church, and indeed greatly alter its character. Incidentally, the marriage customs of the peerage have lately become very lax. One peer in eight has divested himself of his wife, and foreigners notice that there are rather more duchesses than dukes in London society today.

As for the House of Lords which gives the English aristocrat his unique position, Lord Hailsham, himself an unwilling member, says that the majority of peers are voting for its abolition "with their feet," by simply neglecting their hereditary duties. It must be said that the number of regular attendants has never been very large, and the august chamber has always been characterized by an atmosphere of the dormitory if not of the morgue. This is distressing to an active young fellow like Lord Hailsham but it is nothing new. One of the merits of the Upper House has been to consist of a hard core of politicians reinforced now and then by experts, and only flooded out in times of crisis by all its members. These have hitherto proved not unrepresentative of public opinion. Now, however, it seems that it is hardly possible to get through the work, so small is the attendance.

Does this apparent abdication of the lords in so many different directions mean that the English aristocracy is in full decadence and will soon exist only like the appendix in the human body, a useless and sometimes harmful relic of the past? It would not be safe to assume so. The English lord has been nurtured on the land and is conversant with the cunning ways of the animal kingdom. He has often seen the grouse settle into the heather to rise and be shot at no more. He has noticed that enormous riches are not well looked on in the modern world and that in most countries his genius is extinct. It may be that he who for a thousand years has weathered so many a storm, religious, dynastic, and political, is taking cover in order to weather yet one more. It may be that he will succeed. He must, of course, be careful not to overdo the protective coloring. An aristocracy cannot exist as a secret society. Nor must he overdo an appearance of destitution. There is the sad precedent of George Neville who was deprived of his dukedom (Bedford) by act of Parliament because "as is openly known he hath not, nor by inheritance may have, any livelihood to support the name, estate and dignity. . . ."

But the English lord is a wily old bird who seldom overdoes anything. It is his enormous strength.

How Shall I Word It?*

Max Beerbohm

It would seem that I am one of those travellers for whom the railway bookstall does not cater. Whenever I start on a journey, I find that my choice lies between well-printed books which I have no wish to read, and well-written books which I could not read without permanent injury to my eyesight. The keeper of the bookstall, seeing me gaze vaguely along his shelves, suggests that I should take *Fen Country Fanny*, or else *The Track of Blood* and have done with it. Not wishing to hurt his feelings, I refuse these works on the plea that I have read them. Whereon he, divining despite me that I am a superior person, says 'Here is a nice little handy edition of More's *Utopia*' or 'Carlyle's *French Revolution*' and again I make some excuse. What pleasure could I get from trying to cope with a masterpiece printed in diminutive grey-ish type on a semi-transparent little grey-ish page? I relieve the bookstall of nothing but a newspaper or two.

The other day, however, my eye and fancy were caught by a book entitled *How Shall I Word It?* and sub-entitled 'A Complete Letter Writer for Men and Women'. I had never read one of these manuals, but had often heard that there was a great and constant 'demand' for them. So I demanded this one. It is no great fun in itself. The writer is no fool. He has evidently a natural talent for writing letters. His style is, for the most part, discreet and easy. If you were a young man writing 'to Father of Girl he wishes to Marry' or 'thanking Fiancée for Present' or 'reproaching Fiancée for being a Flirt', or if you were a mother 'asking Governess her Qualifications' or 'replying to Undesirable Invitation for her Child', or indeed if you were in any other one of the crises which this book is designed to alleviate,

* From *And Even Now* by Max Beerbohm, London: William Heinemann Ltd. (1920). Reprinted by permission of Mrs. Eva Reichmann.

you might copy out and post the specially-provided letter without making yourself ridiculous in the eyes of its receiver—unless, of course, he or she also possessed a copy of the book. But—well, can you conceive any one copying out and posting one of these letters, or even taking it as the basis for composition? You cannot. That shows how little you know of your fellow-creatures. Not you nor I can plumb the abyss at the bottom of which such humility is possible. Nevertheless, as we know by that great and constant 'demand', there the abyss is, and there multitudes are at the bottom of it. Let's peer down. . . . No, all is darkness. But faintly, if we listen hard, is borne up to us a sound of the scratching of innumerable pens—pens whose wielders are all trying, as the author of this handbook urges them, to 'be original, fresh, and interesting' by dint of more or less strict adherence to sample.

Giddily you draw back from the edge of the abyss. Come!—here is a thought to steady you. The mysterious great masses of helpless folk for whom *How Shall I Word It?* is written are sound at heart, delicate in feeling, anxious to please, most loth to wound. For it must be presumed that the author's style of letter-writing is informed as much by a desire to give his public what it needs, and will pay for, as by his own beautiful nature; and in the course of all the letters that he dictates you will find not one harsh word, not one ignoble thought or unkind insinuation. In all of them, though so many are for the use of persons placed in the most trying circumstances, and some of them are for persons writhing under a sense of intolerable injury, sweetness and light do ever reign. Even 'yours truly, Jacob Langton', in his 'letter to his Daughter's Mercenary Fiancée', mitigates the sternness of his tone by the remark that his 'task is inexpressibly painful'. And he, Mr. Langton, is the one writer who lets the post go out on his wrath. When Horace Masterton, of Thorpe Road, Putney, receives from Miss Jessica Weir, of Fir Villa, Blackheath, a letter 'declaring her Change of Feelings', does he upbraid her? No, 'it was honest and brave of you to write to me so straightforwardly and at the back of my mind I know you have done what is best. . . . I give you back your freedom only at your desire. God bless you, dear.' Not less admirable is the behaviour, in similar case, of Cecil Grant (14, Glover Street, Streatham). Suddenly, as a bolt from the blue, comes a letter from Miss Louie Hawke (Elm View, Deerhurst), breaking off her betrothal to him. Haggard, he sits down to his desk; his pen traverses the notepaper—calling down curses on Louie and on all her sex? No; 'one cannot say good-bye for ever without deep regret to days that have been so full of happiness. I must thank you sincerely for all your great kindness to me. . . . With every sincere wish for your future happiness,' he bestows complete freedom on Miss Hawke. And do not imagine that in the matter of self-control and sympathy, of power to understand all and pardon all, the men are lagged behind by the women. Miss

Leila Johnson (The Manse, Carlyle) has observed in Leonard Wace (Dover Street, Saltburn) a certain coldness of demeanour; yet 'I do not blame you; it is probably your nature'; and Leila in her sweet forbearance is typical of all the other pained women in these pages; she is but one of a crowd of heroines.

Face to face with all this perfection, the not perfect reader begins to crave some little outburst of wrath, of hatred or malice, from one of these imaginary ladies and gentlemen. He longs for—how shall he word it?—a glimpse of some bad motive, of some little lapse from dignity. Often, passing by a pillar-box, I have wished I could unlock it and carry away its contents, to be studied at my leisure. I have always thought such a haul would abound in things fascinating to a student of human nature. One night, not long ago, I took a waxen impression of the lock of the pillar-box nearest to my house, and had a key made. This implement I have as yet lacked either the courage or the opportunity to use. And now I think I shall throw it away.... No, I shan't. I refuse, after all, to draw my inference that the bulk of the British public writes always in the manner of this handbook. Even if they all have beautiful natures they must sometimes be sent slightly astray by inferior impulses, just as are you and I.

And, if err they must, surely it were well they should know how to do it correctly and forcibly. I suggest to our author that he should sprinkle his next edition with a few less righteous examples, thereby both purging his book of its monotony and somewhat justifying its sub-title. Like most people who are in the habit of writing things to be printed, I have not the knack of writing really good letters. But let me crudely indicate the sort of thing that our manual needs....

LETTER FROM POOR MAN
TO OBTAIN MONEY FROM RICH ONE

[*The English law is particularly hard on what is called blackmail. It is therefore essential that the applicant should write nothing that might afterwards be twisted to incriminate him.* —Ed.]

Dear Sir,

To-day, as I was turning out a drawer in my attic, I came across a letter which by a curious chance fell into my hands some years ago, and which, in the stress of grave pecuniary embarrassment, had escaped my memory. It is a letter written by yourself to a lady, and the date shows it to have been written shortly after your marriage. It is of a confidential nature and might, I fear, if it fell into the wrong hands, be cruelly misconstrued. I would wish you to have the satisfaction of destroying it in person. At first I thought of sending it on to you by post. But I know how happy you are in your domestic life; and probably your wife and you, in your perfect mutual trust, are in the habit of opening each other's letters. Therefore, to avoid risk, I would prefer to hand the document to you personally. I will not ask you to come to my attic, where I could not offer you such hospitality as is due to a man of your wealth and position. You will be so good as to meet me at 3.0 A.M. (sharp) to-morrow (Thursday) beside the tenth lamp-post to the left on the Surrey side of Waterloo Bridge; at which hour and place we shall not be disturbed.

I am, dear Sir,
Yours faithfully,
James Gridge.

LETTER FROM YOUNG MAN
REFUSING TO PAY HIS TAILOR'S BILL

Mr. Eustace Davenant has received the half-servile, half-insolent screed which Mr. Yardley has addressed to him. Let Mr. Yardley cease from crawling on his knees and shaking his fist. Neither this posture nor this gesture can wring one bent farthing from the pockets of Mr. Davenant, who was a minor at the time when that series of ill-made suits was supplied to him and will hereafter, as in the past, shout (without prejudice) from the house-tops that of all the tailors in London Mr. Yardley is at once the most grasping and the least competent.

LETTER TO THANK AUTHOR
FOR INSCRIBED COPY OF BOOK

Dear Mr. Emanuel Flower,

It was kind of you to think of sending me a copy of your new book. It would have been kinder still to think again and abandon that project. I am a man of gentle instincts, and do not like to tell you that 'A Flight into Arcady' (of which I have skimmed a few pages, thus wasting two or three minutes of my not altogether worthless time) is trash. On the other hand, I am determined that you shall not be able to go around boasting to your friends, if you have any, that this work was not condemned, derided, and dismissed by your sincere well-wisher, Wrexford Cripps.

LETTER TO MEMBER OF PARLIAMENT
UNSEATED AT GENERAL ELECTION

Dear Mr. Pobsby-Burford,

Though I am myself an ardent Tory, I cannot but rejoice in the crushing defeat you have just suffered in West Odgetown. There are moments when political conviction is overborne by personal sentiment; and this is one of them. Your loss of the seat that you held is the more striking by reason of the splendid manner in which the northern and eastern divisions of Odgetown have been wrested from the Liberal Party. The great bulk of the newspaper-reading public will be puzzled by your extinction in the midst of our party's triumph. But then, the great mass of the newspaper-reading public has not met you. I have. You will probably not remember me. You are the sort of man who would not remember anybody who might not be of some definite use to him. Such, at least, was one of the impressions you made on me when I met you last summer at a dinner given by our friends the Pelhams. Among the other things in you that struck me were the blatant pomposity of your manner, your appalling flow of cheap platitudes, and your hoggish lack of ideas. It is such men as you that lower the tone of public life. And I am sure that in writing to you thus I am but expressing what is felt, without distinction of party, by all who sat with you in the late Parliament.

The one person in whose behalf I regret your withdrawal into private life is your wife, whom I had the pleasure of taking in to the aforesaid dinner. It was evident to me that she was a woman whose spirit was well-nigh broken by her conjunction with you. Such remnants of cheerfulness as were in her I attributed to the Parliamentary duties which kept you out of her sight for so very many hours daily. I do not like to think of the fate to which the free and independent electors of West Odgetown have just condemned her. Only, remember this: chattel of yours though she is, and timid and humble, she despises you in her heart.

I am, dear Mr. Pobsbury-Burford,
Yours very truly,
Harold Thistlake.

LETTER FROM YOUNG LADY IN ANSWER TO INVITATION FROM OLD SCHOOL MISTRESS

My Dear Miss Price,

How awfully sweet of you to ask me to stay with you for a few days but how *can* you think I may have forgotten you for of course I think of you so very often and of the three ears I spent at your school because it is such a joy not to be there any longer and if one is at all down it bucks one up derectly to remember that *thats* all over atanyrate and that one has enough food to nurrish one and not that awful monottany of life and not the petty fogging daily tirrany you went in for and I can imagin no greater thrill and luxury in a way than to come and see the whole dismal grind still going on but without me being in it but this would be *rather* beastly of me wouldn't it so please dear Miss Price dont expect me and do excuse mistakes of English Composition and Spelling and etcetra in your affectionate old pupil,

Emily Thérèse Lynn-Royston.

ps, I often rite to people telling them where I was edducated and highly reckomending you.

**LETTER IN ACKNOWLEDGMENT
OF WEDDING PRESENT**

Dear Lady Amblesham,

Who gives quickly, says the old proverb, gives twice. For this reason I have purposely delayed writing to you, lest I should appear to thank you more than once for the small, cheap, hideous present you sent me on the occasion of my recent wedding. Were you a poor woman, that little bowl of ill-imitated Dresden china would convict you of tastelessness merely; were you a blind woman, of nothing but an odious parsimony. As you have normal eyesight and more than normal wealth, your gift to me proclaims you at once a Philistine and a miser (or rather did so proclaim you until, less than ten seconds after I had unpacked it from its wrappings of tissue paper, I took it to the open window and had the satisfaction of seeing it shattered to atoms on the pavement). But stay! I perceive a possible flaw in my argument. Perhaps you were guided in your choice by a definite wish to insult me. I am sure, on reflection, that this was so. *I shall not forget.*

Yours, etc.,
Cynthia Beaumarsh.

PS. My husband asks me to tell you to warn Lord Amblesham to keep out of his way or to assume some disguise so complete that he will not be recognised by him and horsewhipped.

PPS. I am sending copies of this letter to the principal London and provincial newspapers.

LETTER FROM . . .

But enough! I never thought I should be so strong in this line. I had not foreseen such copiousness and fatal fluency. Never again will I tap these deep dark reservoirs in a character that had always seemed to me, on the whole, so amiable.

On Pioneering*

Walter Murdoch

Hail, ye faithful, much-enduring readers!....But perhaps I had better explain. I spent a vacation recently in reading nearly three hundred Odes to Western Australia; and I wonder whether anybody ever spent a vacation in this way before, since the world began. I am now convalescent, thank you; except that I find a certain difficulty in not beginning sentences with "Hail!" the symptoms of odeshock have practically disappeared.

They mostly began with "hail" or "all hail" and many of them threw in an extra "hail" whenever their feelings got the better of them or the metre seemed to call for an extra syllable. They hailed everything and everybody; they hailed the country, they hailed the centenary, they hailed our wool, our wheat, our gold, our pearling industry, our wildflowers, the men of a century ago and the generations yet unborn. One of them exhorted his readers, at intervals, to "shout a loud hooray," and the variation was so pleasing that I felt inclined to take him at his word. Another invited us all to "shout and sing, and make the welkin blithely ring," but most of them were content with something less noisy than this. They were satisfied with hailing.

Of the earnest patriotism of these poets there can be no question; they have boundless faith in their land. We are a young people—"the debutante of nations," one of our singers calls us; and another, whose grammar is his servant, not his master, says, "the youngest of all thy fair sisters art thee"—and, being young, we are apt to be shy and to have too much respect for our elders. Our poets teach us a truer faith,

> Hail, beauteous land! hail, bonzer West Australia;
> Compared with you, all others are a failure.

That is the kind of thing, and it undoubtedly warms the cockles of the heart, though some may object to the rhyme—but then Western Australia is a puzzling name to fit into rhyme; one minstrel ingeniously solves the problem by turning it round:

> Hail, Groperland! Australia West!
> Of earth's fair places thou art best.

There is no doubt about the fervour of this; and most of these poems are fervid. We are the salt of the earth; other people are its scum. We inhabit the loveliest of lands; other countries are more or less blots on the landscape. Even the size of our State comes in for its meed of praise:

> Hail to Westralia!
> Hail to its bigness!
> Hail to its motto
> "Cygnis insignis."

We have done wonderful things—especially Lord Forrest, who comes into scores of odes; this, for instance is the country

> Where the purest water flows up-hill
> In accordance with Lord Forrest's will.

Wonderful man! wonderful country! wonderful poets! Hail, every one of you! All hail, in fact.

But what most of these bards praise most loudly and continuously is the character and achievements of the men of a century ago—the pioneers. So far as I am concerned, the net result is that I never want to hear another word about pioneers as long as I live. That being so, you may object, why write an essay about them?—but I hope this essay will turn out before it is done, not to be about the pioneers at all, but about a quite different subject. Anyhow, I am tired of them,

> Those souls of priceless rarity,
> Pioneers of our State,

who seem to have been physically almost as remarkable as they were in soul:

> Lean they were, with eyes aflame,
> These strong and sturdy men from hame.

"From hame" does not mean that they came from Scotland; it only means that the bard was bothered for a rhyme. (But what was the matter with "they came"?) When I try to discover from the odes what, exactly, these persons with flaming eyes and priceless souls did when they arrived, I get no very adequate account of their achievements. One poet does, indeed, endeavour to describe their doings with some exactness.

> They stopped at Mount Eliza,
> They camped beneath a tree,
> They said to one another,
> "This is good enough for me."

But I rather doubt the accuracy of this; the idiom has a too modern sound. It is wiser, perhaps, to keep to general statements, such as—

> They founded here a mighty State,
> On January 26th, 1828.

I suppose this is substantially true, though the poet seems to have antedated the event; and I suppose it is also true that they came to an inhospitable land, where—

> The native with his waddy, his boomerang and spear
> Held sway o'er its vast spaces by ignorance and fear.

And they got the better of him. At all events, whatever they did and whatever they were, it is in their honour that most of the odes beat the big drum.

> Then give to them the honour,
> For that they well deserve,
> And do your best endeavour
> To hand on the preserve.

By all means. Give them the honour they deserve; and give others the honour they, in their turn, deserve. The centenary celebrations are not to be arranged, I take it, for the glorification of the passengers on the *Parmelia* or of Thomas Peel's syndicate, but rather for public rejoicing that Western Australia has reached a certain stage in her journey—that she has survived the teething troubles (or weathered the storms, if that seems a more dignified way of putting it) of her first century; and for public thankfulness to whatsoever powers, human or divine, have guided her steps so far. Why anybody should pick out for special gratitude the men and women who happened to be the first on the spot it is a little difficult to see. We might as well go farther back and sing paeans of praise to the Angles and Saxons and Jutes, calling them souls of priceless rarity. Or why not sing hymns in honour of Adam, with eyes aflame, and also Eve, his beauteous dame?

The men and women who first came to settle in Australia were of British stock, and of an honourably adventurous strain. They came here to better their fortunes, lured by fantastic accounts of the country (Fraser's report dwelt on the "superiority of the soil"—and also on its "permanent humidity," a feature not conspicuous in my garden). Captain Stirling described it as "the land, out of all that I have seen in various quarters of the world, that possesses the greatest natural attractions." Vast tracts of this land were to be granted to each settler for next to nothing, and they were to cultivate cotton, tobacco, sugar and flax, to rear horses for the East Indian trade, and to establish large herds of cattle and swine for the supply of salt junk to His Majesty's shipping. They were to make fortunes easily and quickly. The land did not come up to their expectations, and they had but a thin time of it for many years after their arrival.

I do not wish to say a word against them; only, I do not see why special praise is due to them. They showed a spirit of adventure, which is the common birthright of our race—and of other races. They showed great courage in coming out to a remote and unknown world; courage, thank Heaven, is not an uncommon virtue. Are we not all born of women who have sailed gallantly into the perilous sea of marriage and faced death to bring us into the world? Everywhere in our country to-day, not only in remote and lonely places in the backblocks, but in the heart of our cities, too, men and women are confronting their fate with a high courage worthy of all honour. Those pioneers endured many hardships without whimpering; all praise to them for that; but why not praise also the innumerable persons who in our midst today are enduring hardships without whimpering, and who, because they do not whimper, are unhonoured and unsung? To single out the pioneers for special glorification is to libel humanity; it is to imply that virtue has been lost. The world is as full today as ever it was of the shining virtues of courage in danger and fortitude in adversity. Did the war show that our nation—or any nation—had lost its ancient hardihood? It is impossible to read the newspapers intelligently without being proud to belong to the indomitable human race; but the best examples do not get into the newspapers. They are to be found in all sorts of odd places; in the lonely bush and in the crowded slum; the heroic is everywhere at home.

Of course if, misled by the glamour of the past, you like to talk nonsense about the pioneers, and represent them as souls of priceless rarity stalking about with eyes aflame, I suppose no great harm is done. They were probably decent people, of average intelligence, fairly industrious and not without grit and resourcefulness; very like the normal Australian of to-day. The mistake made by the writers of some of these odes was to suppose that, to write poetry, you must talk nonsense. It is not so. Poetry and nonsense are incompatible. And this nonsense about pioneers gets, after a time, on one's nerves; hence this protest. The world is young; and we are all pioneers.

A, B, and C

The Human Element in Mathematics *

Stephen Leacock

The student of arithmetic who has mastered the first four rules of his art, and successfully striven with money sums and fractions, finds himself confronted by an unbroken expanse of questions known as problems. These are short stories of adventure and industry with the end omitted, and though betraying a strong family resemblance, are not without a certain element of romance.

The characters in the plot of a problem are three people called A, B, and C. The form of the question is generally of this sort:

"A, B, and C do a certain piece of work. A can do as much work in one hour as B in two, or C in four. Find how long they work at it."

Or thus:

"A, B, and C are employed to dig a ditch. A can dig as much in one hour as B can dig in two, and B can dig twice as fast as C. Find how long, etc., etc."

Or after this wise:

"A lays a wager that he can walk faster than B or C. A can walk half as fast again as B, and C is only an indifferent walker. Find how far, and so forth."

The occupations of A, B, and C are many and varied. In the older arithmetics they contented themselves with doing "a certain piece of work." This statement of the case, however, was found too sly and mysterious, or possibly lacking in romantic charm. It became the fashion to define the job more clearly and to set them at walking matches, ditch-digging, regattas, and piling cord wood. At times they became commercial and entered into partnership, having with their old mystery a "certain"

* From *Literary Lapses* by Stephen Leacock, reprinted by permission of The Canadian Publishers, McClelland and Stewart Limited, Toronto.

capital. Above all they revel in motion. When they tire of walking-matches —A rides on horseback, or borrows a bicycle and competes with his weaker-minded associates on foot. Now they race on locomotives; now they row; or again they become historical and engage stagecoaches; or at times they are aquatic and swim. If their occupation is actual work they prefer to pump water into cisterns, two of which leak through holes in the bottom and one of which is water-tight. A, of course, has the good one; he also takes the bicycle, and the best locomotive, and the right of swimming with the current. Whatever they do they put money on it, being all three sports. A always wins.

In the early chapters of the arithmetic, their identity is concealed under the names John, William, and Henry, and they wrangle over the division of marbles. In algebra they are often called X, Y, and Z. But these are only their Christian names, and they are really the same people.

Now to one who has followed the history of these men through countless pages of problems, watched them in their leisure hours dallying with cord wood, and seen their panting sides heave in the full frenzy of filling a cistern with a leak in it, they become something more than mere symbols. They appear as creatures of flesh and blood, living men with their own passions, ambitions, and aspirations like the rest of us. Let us view them in turn. A is a full-blooded blustering fellow, of energetic temperament, hotheaded and strong-willed. It is he who proposes everything, challenges B to work, makes the bets, and bends the others to his will. He is a man of great physical strength and phenomenal endurance. He has been known to walk forty-eight hours at a stretch, and to pump ninety-six. His life is arduous and full of peril. A mistake in the working of a sum may keep him digging a fortnight without sleep. A repeating decimal in the answer might kill him.

B is a quiet, easy-going fellow, afraid of A and bullied by him, but very gentle and brotherly to little C, the weakling. He is quite in A's power, having lost all his money in bets.

Poor C is an undersized, frail man, with a plaintive face. Constant walking, digging, and pumping has broken his health and ruined his nervous system. His joyless life has driven him to drink and smoke more than is good for him, and his hand often shakes as he digs ditches. He has not the strength to work as the others can; in fact, as Hamlin Smith has said, "A can do more work in one hour than C in four."

The first time that ever I saw these men was one evening after a regatta. They had all been rowing in it, and it had transpired that A could row as much in one hour as B in two, or C in four. B and C had come in dead fagged and C was coughing badly. "Never mind, old fellow," I heard B say, "I'll fix you up on the sofa and get you some hot tea." Just then A came blustering in and shouted, "I say, you fellows, Hamlin Smith has shown me three cisterns in his garden and he says we can pump them until tomorrow night. I bet I can beat you both. Come on. You can pump in your rowing things, you know. Your cistern leaks a little, I think, C." I heard B growl that it was a dirty shame and that C was used up now, but they went, and presently I could tell from the sound of the water that A was pumping four times as fast as C.

For years after that I used to see them constantly about town and always busy. I never heard of any of them eating or sleeping. Then owing to a long absence from home, I lost sight of them. On my return I was surprised to no longer find A, B, and C at their accustomed tasks; on inquiry I heard that work in this line was now done by N, M, and O, and that some people were employing for algebraical jobs four foreigners called Alpha, Beta, Gamma, and Delta.

Now it chanced one day that I stumbled upon old D, in the little garden in front of his cottage, hoeing in the sun. D is an aged labouring man who used occasionally to be called in to help A, B, and C. "Did I know 'em, sir?" he answered. "Why, I knowed 'em ever since they was little fellows in brackets. Master A, he were a fine lad, sir, though I always said, give me Master B for kindheartedness-like. Many's the job as we've been on together, sir, though I never did no racing nor aught of that, but just the plain labour, as you might say. I'm getting a bit too old and stiff for it nowadays, sir—just scratch about in the garden here and grow a bit of a logarithm, or raise a common denominator or two. But Mr. Euclid he use me still for them propositions, he do."

From the garrulous old man I learned the melancholy end of my former acquaintances. Soon after I left town, he told me, C had been taken ill. It seems that A and B had been rowing on the river for a wager, and C had been running on the bank and then sat in a draught. Of course the bank had refused the draught and C was taken ill. A and B came home and found C lying helpless in bed. A shook him roughly and said, "Get up, C, we're going to pile wood." C looked so worn and pitiful that B said, "Look here, A, I won't stand this, he isn't fit to pile wood to-night." C smiled feebly and said, "Perhaps I might pile a little if I sat up in bed." Then B, thoroughly alarmed, said, "See here, A, I'm going to fetch a doctor; he's dying." A flared up and answered, "You've no money to fetch a doctor." "I'll reduce him to his lowest terms," B said firmly, "that'll fetch him." C's life might even then have been saved but they made a mistake about the medicine. It stood at the head of the bed on a bracket, and the nurse accidentally removed it from the bracket without changing the sign. After the fatal blunder C seems to have sunk rapidly. On the evening of the next day, as the shadows deepened in the little room, it was clear to all that the end was near. I think that even A was affected at the last as he stood with bowed head, aimlessly offering to bet with the doctor on C's laboured breathing. "A," whispered C, "I think I'm going fast." "How fast do you think you'll go, old man?" murmured A. "I don't know," said C, "but I'm going at any rate."—The end came soon after that. C rallied for a moment and asked for a certain piece of work that he had left downstairs. A put it in his arms and he expired. As his soul sped heavenward A watched its flight with melancholy admiration. B burst into a passionate flood of tears and sobbed, "Put away his little cistern and the rowing clothes he used to wear. I feel as if I could hardly ever dig again."—The funeral was plain and unostentatious. It differed in nothing from the ordinary, except that out of deference to sporting men and mathematicians, A engaged two hearses. Both vehicles started at the same time, B driving the one which bore the sable parallelopiped containing the last remains of his ill-fated friend. A on the box of the empty hearse generously consented to a handicap of a hundred yards, but arrived first at the cemetery by driving four times as fast as B. (Find the distance to the cemetery.) As the sarcophagus was lowered, the grave was surrounded by the broken figures of the first book of Euclid.—It was noticed that after the death of C, A became a changed man. He lost interest in racing with B, and dug but languidly. He finally gave up his work and settled down to live on the interest of his bets.—B never recovered from the shock of C's death; his grief preyed upon his intellect and it became deranged. He grew moody and spoke only in monosyllables. His disease became rapidly aggravated, and he presently spoke only in words whose spelling was regular and which presented no difficulty to the beginner. Realising his precarious condition he voluntarily submitted to be incarcerated in an asylum, where he abjured mathematics and devoted himself to writing the History of the Swiss Family Robinson in words of one syllable.

Wild Bill
Hickok and
His Friends*

James Thurber

In one of the many interesting essays that make up his book called
'Abinger Harvest,' Mr. E. M. Forster, discussing what he sees when he is
reluctantly dragged to the movies in London, has set down a sentence that
fascinates me. It is: 'American women shoot the hippopotamus with
eyebrows made of platinum.' I have given that remarkable sentence a
great deal of study, but I still do not know whether Mr. Forster means that
American women have platinum eyebrows or that the hippopotamus has
platinum eyebrows or that American women shoot platinum eyebrows into
the hippopotamus. At any rate, it faintly stirred in my mind a dim train of
elusive memories which were brightened up suddenly and brought into
sharp focus for me when, one night, I went to see *The Plainsman*, a hard-
riding, fast-shooting movie dealing with warfare in the Far West back in the
bloody seventies. I knew then what Mr. Forster's curious and tantalizing
sentence reminded me of. It was like nothing in the world so much as certain sentences which appeared in a group of French paperback dime (or,
rather, twenty-five-centime) novels that I collected a dozen years ago in
France. *The Plainsman* brought up these old pulp thrillers in all clarity for
me because, like that movie, they dealt mainly with the stupendous activities of Buffalo Bill and Wild Bill Hickok; but in them were a unique fantasy, a special inventiveness, and an imaginative abandon beside which
the movie treatment of the two heroes pales, as the saying goes, into
nothing. In the moving from one apartment to another some years ago, I
somehow lost my priceless collection of *contes héroïques du Far-Ouest*,

but happily I find that a great many of the deathless adventures of the French Buffalo Bill and Wild Bill Hickok remain in my memory. I hope that I shall recall them, for anodyne, when with eyes too dim to read I pluck finally at the counterpane.

In the first place, it should perhaps be said that in the eighteen-nineties the American dime-novel hero who appears to have been most popular with the French youth—and adult—given to such literature was Nick Carter. You will find somewhere in one of John L. Stoddard's published lectures—there used to be a set in almost every Ohio bookcase—an anecdote about how an American tourist, set upon by *apaches* in a dark *rue* in Paris in the nineties, caused them to scatter in terror merely by shouting '*Je suis Nick Carter!* '. But at the turn of the century or shortly thereafter, Buffalo Bill became the favourite. Whether he still is or not, I don't know—perhaps Al Capone or John Dillinger has taken his place. Twelve years ago, however, he was going great guns—or perhaps I should say great dynamite, for one of the things I most clearly remember about the Buffalo Bill of the French authors was that he always carried with him sticks of dynamite which, when he was in a particularly tough spot—that is, surrounded by more than two thousand Indians—he hurled into their midst, destroying them by the hundred. Many of the most inspired paperbacks that I picked up in my quest were used ones I found in those little stalls along the Seine. It was there, for instance, that I came across one of my favourites, *Les Aventures du Wild Bill dans le Far-Ouest.*

Wild Bill Hickok was, in this wonderful and beautiful tale, an even more prodigious manipulator of the six-gun than he seems to have been in real life, which, as you must know, is saying a great deal. He frequently mowed down a hundred or two hundred Indians in a few minutes with his redoubtable pistol. The French author of this masterpiece for some mysterious but delightful reason referred to Hickok sometimes as Wild Bill and sometimes as Wild Bird. '*Bonjour, Wild Bill!* ' his friend Buffalo Bill often said to him when they met, only to shout a moment later, '*Regardez, Wild Bird! Les Peaux-Rouges!* ' The two heroes spent a great deal of their time, as in *The Plainsman*, helping each other out of dreadful situations. Once, for example, while hunting Seminoles in Florida, Buffalo Bill fell into a tiger trap that had been set for him by the Indians—he stepped onto what turned out to be sticks covered with grass, and plunged to the bottom of a deep pit. At this point our author wrote, ' "*Mercy me!*" *S'écria Buffalo Bill.*' The great scout was rescued, of course, by none other than Wild Bill, or Bird, who, emerging from the forest to see his old comrade in distress, could only exclaim, '*My word!* '

It was, I believe, in another volume that one of the most interesting characters in all French fiction of the Far West appeared, a certain Major Preston, alias Preeton, alias Preslon (the paperbacks rarely spelled anyone's name twice in succession the same way). This hero, we were told when he was introduced, 'had distinguished himself in the Civil War by capturing Pittsburgh,' a feat which makes Lee's invasion of Pennsylvania seem mere child's play. Major Preeton (I always preferred that alias) had come out West to fight the Indians with cannon, since he believed it absurd that nobody had thought to blow them off the face of the earth with cannon before. How he made out with his artillery against the forest skulkers I have forgotten, but I have an indelible memory of a certain close escape that Buffalo Bill had in this same book. It seems that, through an oversight, he had set out on a scouting trip without his dynamite—he also carried, by the way, cheroots and a flashlight—and hence, when he stumbled upon a huge band of redskins, he had to ride as fast as he could for the nearest fort. He made it just in time. 'Buffalo Bill,' ran the story, 'clattered across the drawbridge and into the fort just ahead of the Indians, who, unable to stop in time, plunged into the moat and were drowned.' It may have been in this same tale that Buffalo Bill was once so hard pressed that he had to send for Wild Bird to help him out. Usually, when one was in trouble, the other showed up by a kind of instinct, but this time Wild Bird was nowhere to be found. It was a long time, in fact, before his whereabouts were discovered. You will never guess where he was. He was 'taking the baths at Atlantic City under orders of his physician.' But he came riding across the country in one day to Buffalo Bill's side, and all was well. Major Preeton, it sticks in my mind, got bored with the service in the Western hotels and went 'back to Philadelphia' (Philadelphia appears to have been the capital city of the United States at this time). The Indians in all these tales—and this is probably what gave Major Preeton his great idea—were seldom seen as individuals or in pairs or small groups, but prowled about in well-ordered columns of squads. I recall, however, one drawing (the paperbacks were copiously illustrated) which showed two *Peaux-Rouges* leaping upon and capturing a scout who had wandered too far from his drawbridge one night. The picture represented one of the Indians as smilingly taunting his captive, and the caption read, '*Vous vous promenez très tard ce soir, mon vieux!* ' This remained my favourite line until I saw one night in Paris an old W. S. Hart movie called *Le Roi du Far-Ouest*, in which Hart, insulted by a drunken ruffian, turned upon him and said, in his grim, laconic way, '*Et puis, après?* '

I first became interested in the French tales of the Far West when, one winter in Nice, a French youngster of fifteen, who, it turned out, devoted all his spending money to them, asked me if I had ever seen a 'wishtonwish.' This meant nothing to me, and I asked him where he had heard about the wishtonwish. He showed me a Far West paperback he was reading. There was a passage in it which recounted an adventure of Buffalo Bill and Wild Bill, during the course of which Buffalo Bill signalled to Wild Bird 'in the voice of the wishtonwish.' Said the author in a parenthesis which at that time gave me as much trouble as Mr. Forster's sentence about the platinum eyebrows does now, 'The wishtonwish was seldom heard west of Philadelphia.' It was some time—indeed, it was not until I got back to America—before I traced the wishtonwish to its lair, and in so doing discovered the influence of James Fenimore Cooper on all these French writers of Far West tales. Cooper, in his novels, frequently mentioned the wishtonwish, which was a Caddoan Indian name for the prairie dog. Cooper erroneously applied it to the whip-poor-will. An animal called the 'ouapiti' also figured occasionally in the French stories, and this turned out to be the wapiti, or American elk, also mentioned in Cooper's tales. The French writer's parenthetical note on the habitat of the wishtonwish only added to the delightful confusion and inaccuracy which threaded these wondrous stories.

There were, in my lost and lamented collection, a hundred other fine things, which I have forgotten, but there is one that will forever remain with me. It occurred in a book in which, as I remember it, Billy the Kid, alias Billy the Boy, was the central figure. At any rate, two strangers had turned up in a small Western town and their actions had aroused the suspicions of a group of respectable citizens, who forthwith called on the sheriff to complain about the newcomers. The sheriff listened gravely for a while, got up and buckled on his gun belt, and said, '*Alors, je vais demander ses cartes d'identité!*' There are few things, in any literature, that have ever given me a greater thrill than coming across that line.

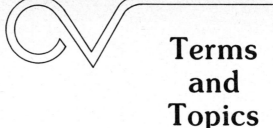

Terms
and
Topics

TERMS

1. *Meiosis* (see the introduction to this section) and *litotes* (see the Note to the Reader), two forms of understatement, are also kinds of *irony* (see Terms, section II). Is *hyperbole* (overstatement, exaggeration) also a kind of irony?

2. An essential ingredient of humour is *incongruity*. What is meant by this term?

3. Differentiate among the terms in each of the following groups: (a) witty, comic, humorous; (b) satiric, ironic, sarcastic; (c) parody, travesty, burlesque.

4. *Caricature* Exaggeration, whether in a picture or in words, of certain prominent features of the subject. If the features exaggerated are outstanding defects, caricature can be used to ridicule a subject.

5. Find out the meanings of *spoonerism* and *malapropism* and record several examples of each. Why are spoonerisms and malapropisms funny, whereas ordinary mistakes in the use of language are not?

6. *Innuendo* A usually derogatory suggestion or hint; an insinuation. Is an innuendo a kind of *allusion* (see Terms, section I), or not?

7. *Invective* Direct verbal abuse; vituperation. Explain the difference between invective and sarcasm. Can invective be called a kind of satire?

8. *Pun* Word play that depends on a word's having two different meanings or on two words having similar sounds but different meanings. For example, one could say of inflation that "it never reigns but it poors." Consult a good dictionary or glossary of literary terms to find out about the various kinds of puns. Puns are usually considered a product of wit; but wit is not always humorous. Are puns always humorous? A pun is a figure of speech. Can a pun also be a kind of allusion?

9. What do the terms *pacing* and *cadence* mean when applied to prose? Are they just other words for *rhythm*, or do they rather refer to certain *features* of rhythm?

TOPICS: On Individual Essays

NANCY MITFORD "The English Aristocracy"

1. What is "the rule of primogeniture"? If you believe in democracy and equal rights, do you think the rule is fair?
2. Since all of our first-class mail goes by air (supposedly) is there anything one could do to preserve the "U" method of not using air mail for personal correspondence?
3. Can you think of any circumstances in which you (whether U or not) customarily use "the U-habit of silence"?
4. What distinctions between pairs of words are you aware of in your own circle? Are they at all similar to the non-U against U terms cited in the essay?
5. How serious is Mitford in stating her personal opinions? Why, for example, should she consider herbaceous borders "one of the most hideous conceptions known to man"?
6. "I get twice as many as Reggie, but Bert does better than me." Does Mitford intend the grammatical error to be noticed?
7. What is the serious meaning behind Mitford's humorous description of the English aristocracy? Write a short essay in which you describe some group of people humorously, but with a serious underlying intent.

MAX BEERBOHM "How Shall I Word It?"

1. What mask or *persona* does Beerbohm adopt for the purpose of this essay? Analyze a number of sentences in order to point out significant characteristics of his style.
2. Write a letter of the sort you imagine Beerbohm to have found in the book of samples. Then rewrite it in the vein of the samples he himself offers.
3. Write a humorous short essay, also entitled "How Shall I Word It?" about the problems a writer might face when writing a letter to a relative asking for money, or a soft summer job, or . . .

WALTER MURDOCH "On Pioneering"

1. Have you recently suffered anything resembling the "odeshock" Murdoch refers to? "Adshock," perhaps, from perusing a few glossy magazines or spending an evening in front of the television set? Or "ed-shock," from reading too many Letters to the Editor in the newspaper?

Or "idshock," from overexposure to some fanatically Freudian friends? Write a short essay, in a vein similar to that of Murdoch's, satirizing something of this sort.

2. Murdoch ends by turning his satire into a serious statement about everyday human beings. Look around you, and write a brief essay praising some "unhonoured and unsung" people from everyday contemporary life. Perhaps you would also like to try your hand at composing an ode to them.

STEPHEN LEACOCK "A, B, and C"

1. By means of a humorous excess of imagination, Leacock makes fun of the apparent lack of imagination of those who set arithmetical problems. Examine your textbooks—especially those for sciences and social sciences—for instances of similar unimaginative sameness and dullness, and write a brief essay satirizing one of them.
2. Write a brief sketch in which you humorously impart life to—personify—some abstract concepts or labels, as Leacock has done in "A, B, and C." Perhaps some other mathematical concepts would do, or the symbols of certain elements or chemicals, or a few common acronyms. Use your imagination.
3. Write a narrative or descriptive paragraph of between 100 and 150 words entirely in monosyllables.

JAMES THURBER "Wild Bill Hickok and His Friends"

1. Analyze and discuss the various ways in which Thurber makes his piece funny. Pay attention to even the smallest details that contribute to the reader's amusement. How much of the humour depends on the phrases in French?
2. From your own experience—including your reading—find a subject having to do with cultural and linguistic mistranslation and misunderstanding, and write a humorous sketch about it. Aim, as Thurber does in his piece, not for the guffaw and the thigh-slapper, but for the gentler humour arising from the innocently erroneous and incongruous.

TOPICS: General and Comparative

1. How do writers of humour succeed in establishing a desired tone? Point out examples in the essays in this section.
2. Mitford uses a punning irony throughout her essay, and also uses understatement for a serious purpose. Point out examples of each. Examine Beerbohm's techniques of digression and burlesque, Murdoch's

satire, Thurber's opening understatement and exaggerated incidents, and Leacock's absurdly reductive intentional literal-mindedness. In what way does each of these writers rely on incongruity?

3. How have other essayists in this book used humorous techniques or established an ironic frame of reference? Consider the ironic understatement of MacLennan's essay in section I; the puns in the essays by Haig-Brown (section I) and Colombo (section VI); the exaggeration in the essay by Kael (section III); and the tone of the essays by Thomas and White (section I), Lane (section II), Morgan (section III), and Hornyansky (section VI).

4. Compare Mitford's, Beerbohm's, and Murdoch's attitudes toward language with those of Galbraith (section IV), Hornyansky, or Stein (section VI).

5. Is humour culturally biased?

6. Compare Leacock's use of caricature with that of Dylan Thomas or Margaret Lane. Compare it with Bharati Mukherjee's creation of *character*.

7. Picking terms from the list in the preface to this section and supplying whatever others you think useful, characterize the humour in each of the essays in this section. (You may well want to apply more than one term to each.)

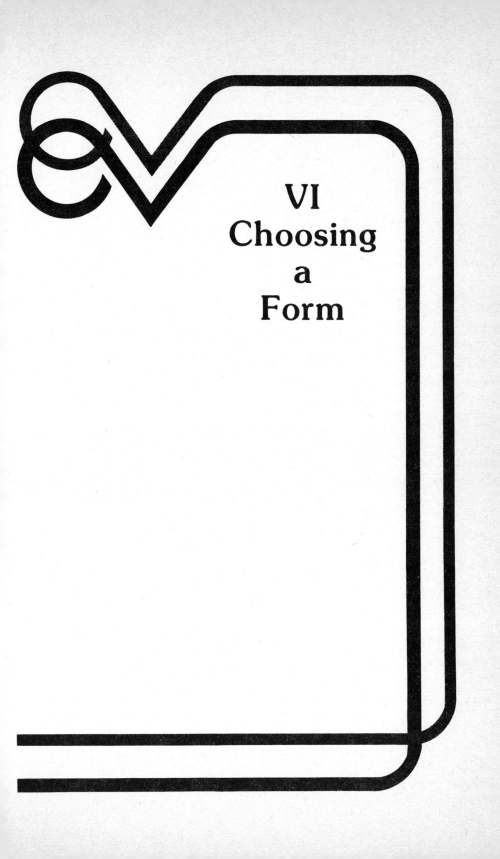

VI
Choosing
a
Form

The last section of this book contains three essays only, but they constitute a quite remarkable group. By turns expository and argumentative, they reveal the virtues (some would say vices) of a number of stylistic idiosyncrasies, and they therefore draw attention to the personality of literary form. Writing is not a mechanical act but a practised art, and the skilled writer to a degree invents his way into a new subject, breaking standard rules of order and syntax, developing other standards, honing fresh combinations of words and fresh ways to communicate. This observation does not mean that standards are pointless, that mechanics do not matter, or that every pretense at style should be tolerated. Indeed, Hornyansky's essay reads as a powerful tribute to the meanings that people should remember to respect in the words they use. Yet it is by no means stylistically staid. In method and in intent, it champions clarity and vigour together.

Other approaches to language and usage, possibly less conventional but not intrinsically more vital, emerge in the essays by Colombo and Stein. The concrete poems that Colombo discusses emphasize the power of language when actually seen-comprehended visually-as well as when decoded through the ordinary process we call "reading." (A novelist I know once asked me if I thought the word *castle* would be as interesting if it had no *t* in it; for him, it wouldn't, for lodged visually in the *t* were the crenellated walls and turrets of the castles of his imagination.) And in Stein's lecture there sounds another inflection of the art of communication: she relies heavily for her meaning on cadence and oral association. The reader of her essay has to think aurally. Voice matters. And the page, in a curious way, intervenes.

Everyone knows that words, whether lodged on the page or freed from it in some sort of utterance, have the capacity to convey meaning. But good writers also know that words are not the sole agency for conveying meaning, that good writing often borrows from other modes of expression for some of its finest effects. Music is one such mode, and there are also the visual arts, including film; and there is even mathematics. How the borrowing takes place is another question. It has become a commonplace for critics to praise "musical" and "cinematic" and "visual" literary styles—though it is not always easy to know what they mean. Or to recognize the criteria that elicit their praise. For example, critics laud rhythmic prose—and in this might be praising "musicality"—but they condemn overly apparent metrical patterns and disconcertingly obvious rhymes. Not all sound patterns prove laudable. Clearly it is the intrusiveness that bothers the critics, not the rhythm per se. They are uneasy whenever any single pattern of sound or structure takes over; they will be equally bothered by clusters of words ending in -*tion*, by strings of prepositional phrases, by unvarying sentence lengths, and by excessive alliteration. A good stylist, however, might still be able to take any one of these flaws and turn it, in a special context, into a stylistic strength.

Music has long been an obvious analogy for writers and critics to use. It has led them to think of rhythm as a product of movement and sound, providing ways to talk about the aural effects of language and ways to produce these effects on the page. More recently, film has provided a related analogy, one that adds the element of visual perspective to those of sound and movement, that transforms rhythm into a visual notion, and that makes *leitmotif*, for example, a visual as well as a musical technique. (Think of the sound patterns in Prokofiev's *Peter and the Wolf*; think of the light patterns in the film *Doctor Zhivago*.) And though there has not yet appeared a "scientific" ("mathematical"? Certainly not "formulaic"!) school of prose style, the division between the sciences and the art of writing is not necessarily greater than that between writing and the other arts. Science, indeed, may be among the most potent contributors to current stylistic change. Explications of entropy and quantum physics have already had some effect on literary style—most evident so far, perhaps, in interrupted, nonlinear fictional forms—and the influence might go further and deeper than many humanities-trained critics now realize.

But there remains a difficulty of interpretation and assessment. How can one validly distinguish between faddishness and creative experiment? For a conservative critic, there is no problem here, for there is no difference to be distinguished. But such an assertion is not one that many writers can accept. Casual reflection might suggest that *topic* determines *style*, and that to talk about a chaotic universe would require a kind of linguistic chaos. Yet even the essays collected here would say otherwise. Hornyansky, conservative by persuasion, is at least relaxed and idiomatic if not actually radical in style. And Stein, the most idiosyncratic stylist, is discussing what many would consider a commonplace. Possibly by refashioning the commonplace, her style freshens it as well. And though Colombo breaks into gimmickry for the sake of example, he is not chaotic. He has attempted, rather, to find a method that will communicate most aptly what he has to say.

The point is that writing depends on sound and sight and texture and movement as well as on grammar and syntax and vocabulary; the overall form an idea takes in speech and writing is as great a part of its meaning as the sum of the definitions that a reader or listener attaches to a series of separate words. Good writers, knowing enough about the ordinary rules of coherent discourse to know when to break them to gain an effect, choose their form. It is not accidental. It is personal.

Matters of time, taste, and fashion affect the distinctions we make among personal styles. Every writer, moreover, has to guard against defending quixotic notions and idiosyncratic styles simply on the grounds of "personality." Solipsism is not a literary virtue, if it is a virtue of any sort at all. And time often modifies the enthusiasms of fashion and taste. But over time, and transcending the individuality of style, the virtues of vitality and clarity persist. If writers begin with a subject to talk about and the intelligence to deal with it, then the two problems they face are these: how to present their subject so that it is fresh and alive, and how to make it clear. The trouble with an experimental style is that it often sacrifices clarity, and the trouble with a conventional style is that it often sacrifices vitality. The writer who claims, in the name of the other virtue, that he must make such sacrifices—that he can only be vital by being obscure, or only be clear by being conventional—is rationalizing, not excusing or explaining his act. Vitality and clarity are not mutually exclusive. Balance is all.

We know that poets, of all writers, compress the greatest possible meaning from the words they bring together, which might suggest that the kind of balance they achieve could prove instructive for essayists as well. We do not ask essay-writers to be poets. Yet many of the techniques poets use, once (and by some critics still) considered out of bounds for the essayist, have become widely acceptable in prose, and even praiseworthy. Puns, echoes, creative ambiguities, and the resuscitation of obscure or archaic meanings in the context of the contemporary and everyday: these are not the standard equipment of explication. Yet a stylist with a particular subject might find them appropriate. What is praiseworthy is a writer's ability to use any technical means to make a subject clearer than it was before, to help a reader understand it better. Experiments, of course, are not intrinsically more valuable than standard forms. Indeed, writing obscurely on the grounds that a subject is dense' and therefore requires it is as wrongheaded as assuming that a difficult idea can be made simple by ignoring its complexities.

Good writers do not make such mistakes. Instead, they address the problem they are trying to resolve. They neither underestimate its difficulty nor inflate it; they neither impose rigid and simplistic solutions upon it nor allow it to dissipate in clouds of generalization. They keep in mind, rather, that they must direct their words appropriately to the audience they want to reach. At the same time, they bring to their subject the range of their personal understanding and the force of their personal style. Good writers invest themselves in their words, and shape ideas the way they choose. They often make "unsafe" choices—choices that force readers to adjust their stylistic expectations. But often "safe" writers commit far more grievous assaults on the language: they uncritically adopt the evasive passive voice, as bureaucratese does; they equate length of word with height of style, and sound like a thesaurus in search of meaning; they elevate illiteracies into jargon (*to remediate, to input, to incrementalize*) in the apparent belief that arbitrary codification is equivalent to science; they confuse effusive writing with emotional commitment, pedantic writing with accuracy, mechanical and predictable writing with openness. Writers who follow such practices shirk their obligation to convey meaning. By contrast, good writers, who say what they mean and mean what they say, at once assert themselves validly and reach their chosen audiences. In the process of communicating, they call attention to the rewards to be gained, by writer and reader alike, from actually learning the craft.

Communicating through Form*

John Robert Colombo

What We Mean by Form

> Form follows function.
> Content has its own shape.
> "Good form" versus "bad form".
> Form versus content.
> Manner or matter.
> Substance or style.
> Formal, informal; material, immaterial.
> Chaos, cosmos; chance, control.
> Form as a vessel; content as a liquid.
> Freedom regardless of form; the freedom to conform.
> A matter, question, problem, possibility of form.
> The necessity of form; the irrelevancy of form.
> A formula; a formlessness.
> Transcendental form; immanent form.
> "The earth was without form."

These are only a few of the phrases we regularly use when we talk about form. There are many more, but most of these concepts cancel each other (if not themselves) out. The alleged dichotomy between form and content, which is one of the hoariest of metaphysical problems, has puzzled philosophers down through the ages, and there is no reason to believe that it will ever be solved. In fact, there is no reason to believe that it is even a "problem". Perhaps it is only an issue—a platform on which you take a

* From *A Media Mosaic*, ed. Walt McDayter, Holt, Rinehart & Winston of Canada Limited, 1971.

stand and defend it whether you actually believe in it or not. It has been argued, quite convincingly, that the words "form" and "content" have no meaning whatsoever.

One difficulty facing anyone making an inquiry into the meaning of form is that we think with words (or, at the very least, we formulate and communicate our thoughts using words to help us along). But like children with an unlimited supply of lettered blocks, we raise up immense and often shaky structures which spell out imponderables and then topple of their own weight. Some of these constructions have no obvious relation to reality and are of various orders of complexity.

At random: We can have pure forms that are antilogies, like the phrase "a formless form". We can have nonexistent things (about which we know a great deal), like "unicorns". We can have impossible things, like "phlogiston" and "sky hooks". We can have no-longer-existing things, like Napoleon I and the dodo. And we can have things like "god" and "angel" and "sin" and "grace", which may or may not have any objective meaning. Is our concept of form one of these? And if it is, which one?

No definition of "form" will be found in this essay. Everyone has his own rule-of-thumb meaning, and we all know we can recognize a single shape or a recurring pattern or an ordering principle when we see one. More general inquiries into form in reading matter are helped along by not narrowing down the concept but by expanding it as much as possible. Instead, what will be found in this essay are instances of infracted forms. Forms are not as much seen as over-seen. A form is exposed when another is imposed upon it, with a *moiré* screen. The patterned lines of such a screen, when placed over another pattern of lines, "generate" a third pattern. This is purely an optical illusion. The pattern does not exist, except perceptually, and what exists objectively are the two parents of that illusion, the two original patterns. The "third thing" is an interesting distortion, a child with a subjective existence only. This applies to many of the instances discussed in this essay.

Much modern art has the perception of pattern or the hunt for meaning as its organizing principle. As Paul Valery wrote, "I write half the poem, the reader writes the other half." There are numerous essays and books that discuss the serious arts, and the reader has only to turn to authors like Harold Rosenberg (*The Anxious Object* and *The Tradition of the New*) to fit many of these ideas into their proper perspective. But there are nooks and crannies that have not been swept clean and which, to my knowledge, have not been examined from the point of view of form and the new directions contemporary art is taking. The instances of violated forms I will be discussing are all literary and, in the main, poetic. But the inquiry could quite easily be extended to the other arts as well, music and painting and cinema in particular, and even into modern social concerns.

Art and the Environment

My starting point is that, strictly speaking, there is no content in art that is separate from the world. All art is entirely formal. By this I mean that art is an attitude to life and that the object of this attitude is life itself. To some extent, to be a human being one must be something of an artist. And to be an artist, one must work in the public, accessible world of people and their perceptions. At various times art has been other and different things. In fact, there is no single "art" but many "arts". At one point in history, art was craftsmanship and little more. The English word "art" derives from this sense of the artist as artisan or artificer. Art was something well done. At various other points in history, art (even the artist) was equated with expression, communication, madness, divine inspiration, problem-solving, information-accumulation, or what-have-you. Usually it was a number of these combined. Today it is perfectly possible for the artist to create works of art that are co-extensive with the world itself. It is, in a parallel fashion, perfectly possible for the art-fancier to react to the world as if it were a work of art itself. Was it Claes Oldenburg, the pop artist, who signed the southern-most tip of Manhattan Island, as he would a canvas, to "aesthetically claim" both this object and this way of seeing things?

With art so fully an attitude to life, everything that exists can be declared to be a work of art. Not all works are good ones, of course, but with this environmental approach as a background, it is possible to criticize one part of the ecology along aesthetic lines and retain some standard of objectivity. The Vancouver painter, Iain Baxter, photographs cityscapes and landscapes and then labels them. Bad views are marked "ART"—Aesthetically Rejected Things. Good views are stamped "ACT"—Aesthetically Claimed Things. Behind this seemingly facile gesture lies a deep and overwhelming idea: that the world itself is a single work of art. This is, at core, a religious notion. The world is not "the work of God" so much as the "the artwork of God". In a small way this has been recognized with landscapes. A brilliant sunset is called "a lovely Turner", a gentle countryside "a fine Constable". Nature imitates art, as Oscar Wilde observed, but in even more fundamental a sense than he imagined.

The "deep focus" of art may thus include all reaction, since nothing is exclusive to the aesthetic experience. The American composer, John Cage, has a composition called "4′ 33″" which is four minutes and 33 seconds of silence. He "performs" this composition at the keyboard. At the premiere, his audience was first surprised, then moved to irritation, and finally taken to a state of self-knowledge. The realization slowly dawned on those present that the random noises which accompany a musical concert in a hall—the shuffling of feet, coughing, etc.—are an accepted part of the auditory experience and can, as such, for a short while anyway, be contemplated singly.

This view, that art is co-extensive with the environment, that the artist is in a sense the "stage-manager of reality", is sometimes called Expanded Art.

It is close to the positions taken by Susan Sontag, with her stress on surface value and "against interpretation"; Andy Warhol, whose Campbell's soup labels are not representational so much as presentational; and Marshall McLuhan, who sees art as an anti-environment which exposes the invisible "wrap-around" of the environment. Expanded Art gives a rationale for such contemporary art movements as underground films, camp, happenings, environmental sculptures, endless paintings, interminable poems, sidewalk theatre, dance as movement, etc. Various phrases are commonly used to identify these contemporary artistic tendencies: Ecological Art, Environmental Art, Conceptual Art, Earth Art, and so on.

One of the pleasures of this new approach to art is that one can respond to a work (or a nonwork) on the simplest of levels. In fact, one's response is often joyous, and incredibly naive. It is like the nursery rhyme about the man and woman who live in Fife.

> In a cottage in Fife
> Lived a man and his wife,
> Who, believe me, were comical folk;
> For, to people's surprise,
> They both saw with their eyes,
> And their tongues moved whenever they spoke!
> When quite fast asleep,
> I've been told that to keep
> Their eyes open they could not contrive;
> They walked on their feet,
> And 'twas thought what they eat
> Helped, with drinking to keep them alive!

Reading Forwards, Backwards, Up or Down

One way in which we too are "comical folk" is that we accept all our conventions, and work within them. We seldom make fun of them, or if we do, we consider this "bad form". One convention of literacy in the Western world is that, without blinking or appearing to notice it, you are reading this page from the left-hand margin to the right-hand margin, moving from line to line in a downward direction. Why not read from right to left, as the Hebrews do? Or down rather than across, as the Chinese do? What difference does it make? Little, really, except that Westerners are inclined to "scan" the world in a similar fashion, and look at reality from left to right, from top to bottom, "placing" things in this total form. For the eye, focussed on the printed page, at least half of the movement is wasted effort. Our eyes "scan" across the page, taking in information, and then sweep back, disregarding the information that is available on the return leg of the round trip. The ancients, who read less than we do, were more concerned about this than we are, and some ancient inscriptions are carved into rock both forwards and backwards in alternate lines, just as a field is ploughed. The Greek word for "the turning of an ox" is *boustrophedon*, and

boustrophedonic writing is prose which appears in this backwards-and-for-
wards, continuous fashion. Strictly speaking, alternate "return" lines
should appear in a second set of characters in which the actual letter-forms
are reversed. (Many of these matters are discussed in Herbert Spencer's
The Visible Word [London: Lund Humphries, 1968].) But making do with
the standard set of characters, here are the first four lines of Lincoln's
"Gettysburg Address" in a boustrophedonic treatment.

> Fourscore and seven years ago our fathers brought forth
> dna ytrebil ni deviecnoc noitan wen a tnenitnoc siht no
> dedicated to the proposition that all men are created
> gnitset raw livic taerg a ni degagne era ew woN .lauqe

Why resurrect a form of writing as weird as boustrophedon? No one
practises it today. Since it was once a form of writing, at variance with our
own practice, why not reuse it if it can be made to serve a useful purpose?
What follows is a found poem (a free-verse arrangement of a passage of
someone else's prose) that has been given a semi-boustrophedonic treatment—"semi" because, given the difficulty the eye encounters when
forced to read a line backwards, the line has been arranged to be read in
the standard way but with the words in the backwards order. Thus only the
word order is boustrophedonic. One hold-over of this principle today is the
Hungarian custom of referring to an individual by his last name first. (In
English, this is customary only with alphabetical listings.) Thus, in
Hungarian, the former Prime Minister of Canada is "Diefenbaker John".
The found poem "Budapest" grew out of this convention.

BUDAPEST

> day present the to time that from
> from that time to the present day
> capital hungarian the of record the
> the record of the hungarian capital
> advance uninterrupted of one been has
> has been one of uninterrupted advance
> as such externals in merely not
> not merely in externals such as
> town the of reconstruction the slums of removal the
> the removal of slums the reconstruction of the town
> trade and industry communications of development the
> the development of communications industry and trade
> buildings public important of erection the and
> and the erection of important public buildings
> elevation physical and moral mental the in also but
> but also in the mental moral and physical elevation
> inhabitants the of
> of the inhabitants
> gain important another besides
> besides another important gain

statesman hungarian the of view of point the from
from the point of view of the hungarian statesman
improvement and increase progressive the namely
namely the progressive increase and improvement
population the of element magyar the of status of
of status of the magyar element of the population

The text of "Budapest" was given in—or taken from—the Eleventh Edition of the *Encyclopaedia Britannica*. The same 1911 edition supplies texts for the four found poems that follow. (They form part of a group, called *The Great Cities of Antiquity*, which treats each of 76 ancient cities mentioned in the *E.B.* in a characteristic style.) What is more appropriate for the capital of Japan than a (found) haiku?

KIOTO

Clear water
ripples everywhere
throughout the city.

For such a picturesque place as the capital of Thailand, only a delicate and romantic form like the (found) triolet would do.

BANGKOK

The climate has without a doubt
In occupation of Siam
Becoming king it was chosen
The climate has without a doubt
It was seized by the warrior
Become hotter and less humid
The climate has without a doubt
In occupation of Siam

Since the ancient capital of Persia, now Iran, is a closed book, archaeologically and historically, only a short poem is necessary. The entry in the *E.B.* begins and ends with the two words which open and close this brief poem. Luckily they happen to be evocative words.

PERSEPOLIS

Persepolis
ruins.

Two words are used to recreate the rise and fall of Persepolis, and only two words, united in a single graphic design, are needed to dramatize the fate of Pompeii in 79 A.D. This poem is both "found" and "concrete", and shows how Expanded Art can combine two modes of poetry and two types of art—graphics and poetry—to make a singleness of effect. (For those unused to "reading" this kind of poetry, the "X" might be seen as lava.)

POMPEII

X

V E S

U V I U S

P O M P E I I

X X X X X X X X X

Oddities of Shape

One difference between prose and poetry is that prose runs to the edge of the page and poetry does not. Purely typographical considerations play a large role in our appreciation of a passage of writing, and poets have occasionally given their poems typographical "shapes" consistent with the subjects or themes of their poems. The original inspiration might be derived from inscriptions in books and on monuments. "Emblematic poems" were popular in the late-sixteenth century, and the practice has persisted as a minor genre until our time. "Shaped whimseys" were very popular in the late-nineteenth century, and Carolyn Wells has collected a number of these in *A Whimsey Anthology* (New York: Charles Scribner's Sons, 1906). The ones reproduced here are oddities, perhaps, but Stéphane Mallarmé and Apollinaire both took the conceit and raised it from a curiosity to a cultural product. George Herbert, John Donne, Dylan Thomas, Edward Lear, John Hollander—all have tried their hand at "Shaped poems". "The Wine Glass" is based on Proverbs xxiii: 29-30.

THE WINE GLASS

Who hath woe? Who hath sorrow? Who
hath contentions? Who hath wounds
without cause? Who hath redness
of eyes? They that tarry long
at the wine! They that
go to seek mixed wine!
Look not thou upon the
wine when it is red,
when it giveth
its colour
in the
cup,
when it
moveth itself
aright.
At
the last it
biteth like a serpent
and stingeth like an adder!

"The Wine Glass" is a kind of collaboration between the author of Proverbs (said to be Solomon himself) and the anonymous nineteenth-century poet or designer or scribe who first gave the passage its picturesque shape. A characteristic of "Shaped poetry" is that it is impossible to read such poems without experiencing both a perception and an apperception. The reader experiences both the poem and his consciousness of experiencing the poem. Such experiments encourage self-awareness, self-consciousness. This response is close to the Distancing Effect discussed by the German playwright, Bertolt Brecht.

The following poem is an original, rhymed composition set in the shape of a sinister creature. A Stegomyia is a genus of mosquito, one variety of which carries Yellow Fever. Certainly the point of "The Stegomyia" is a moralistic one: Wash up, kiddies, or you will suffer!

THE STEGOMYIA

```
                    I
                    t
                    s

                    b
                    i
                    l
                    l

                   is
                  long
              and wick-
               ed, and
                   is
                 filled
             with deadly
  juice          and              you
needn't try    to dodge      it  for  it
  won't           be            any use;
                   it
                  will
                 chase
                you up
              and catch
               you and
            with woe will
            fill your cup;
            oh, the steg-
            omyia'll get
              you if you
             don't clean
                  up
                   !
```

Even if "Avoirdupois" is not strictly a poem, it is a fine example of the way in which an argument can be typographically visualized and given a concrete form. The poem could, as well, be presented orally. A stand-up comedian would give each line a different vocal emphasis—the lightness of the ashes, the monstrous size of the bill. The form seems to mirror the content. Or is it *vice versa?*

AVOIRDUPOIS

The length of this line indicates the ton of coal as dug by the miner.
This one indicates the ton shipped to the dealer.
The small dealer gets a ton like this.
This is the one you pay for.
This is what you get.
The residue is:
Cinders and
Ashes.
And this line will give you some conception of the size of the BILL.

Tricks and Teasers

Moving into the area of the poem-as-puzzle, we have "Greetings, in Season". The poem is more than the letters of the alphabet arranged in an aesthetically pleasing pattern. Examine the anonymous composition closely and you will find that a letter is missing. Which one? The point of the poem turns on a pun that identifies the missing letter. A clue: It's a Christmas greeting. (The answer is given at the end of this essay.)

GREETINGS, IN SEASON

A B C D E
F G H I J
K M N O P
Q R S T U
V W X Y Z

During the Victorian Era, versifiers by the hundreds tried their hands at typographical extravagances like "O I C". The title, and indeed the whole poem, must be sounded phonetically. These verses have to be "worked out". As constructions, they differ from rebuses only in that a rebus actually introduces a tiny picture of what the substituted word means, whereas a typographical poem uses symbols instead of signs.

O I C

I'm in a 10der mood today
& feel poetic, 2;
4 fun I'll just—off a line
& send it off 2 u.

I'm sorry you've been 6 O long;
Don't B disconsol8;
But bear your ills with 42de,
& they won't seem so gr8.

Perhaps the most unusual novel ever written is a book called *Gadsby*, published in 1939. The author was Ernest Vincent Wright, who subtitled his work "A Story of Over 50,000 Words Without Using the Letter E." The ingenious and industrious author decided to write a work which avoided the most common letter in the English alphabet—e. He tied down the e-key on his typewriter, and avoided "the" and "ed" endings and hundreds of other everyday words and phrases. He wrote what must be the longest lipogram ever created. (A lipogram is a work so constructed that a single letter has been consistently avoided.) Imagine the problems that Wright faced. Why, even this sentence alone contains six! David Kahn, in *The Code-Breakers: The Story of Secret Writing* (London: Weidenfeld and Nicholson, 1967), goes into further details about the significance of Wright's experiment, and he reproduces the opening paragraph:

> Upon this basis I am going to show you how a bunch of bright young folks did find a champion; a man with boys and girls of his own; a man of so dominating and happy individuality that Youth is drawn to him as is a fly to a sugar bowl. It is a story about a small town. It is not a gossipy yarn; nor is it a dry, monotonous account, full of such customary "fill-ins" as "romantic moonlight casting murky shadows down a long, winding country road". Nor will it say anything about twinklings lulling distant folds; robins carolling at twilight, nor any "warm glow of lamplight" from a cabin window. No. It is an account of up-and-doing activity; a vivid portrayal of Youth as it is today; and a practical discarding of that worn-out notion that " a child don't know anything".

Works which can be read every-which-way to yield differing meanings have been dubbed "Jesuitical verses". The work that follows is the "all-around platform", and was popular in the 1860s in the United States when the Secessionists and the Abolitionists were arguing it out. For the Secessionist view, read the first column down. For the Abolitionist view, read the second column down. For the Democratic platform, read everything all together.

THE PLATFORM
(Read down or across)

Hurrah for	The old Union
Secession	Is a curse
We fight for	The Constitution
The Confederacy	Is a league with hell
We love	Free speech
The rebellion	Is treason
We glory in	A free press
Separation	Will not be tolerated
We fight not for	The negro's freedom
Reconstruction	Must be obtained
We must succeed	At every hazard
The Union	We love
We love not	The negro
We never said	Let the Union slide
We want	The Union as it was
Foreign intervention	Is played out
We cherish	The old flag
The stars and bars	Is a flaunting lie
We venerate	The habeas corpus
Southern chivalry	Is hateful
Death to	Jeff Davis
Abe Lincoln	Isn't the Government
Down with	Mob law
Law and order	Shall triumph.

From works so formed that three points of view are simultaneously meaningful, it is not much of a leap to a work with a point of view that is logically impossible. "Resolutions Passed by the Board of Councilmen, Canton, Mississippi" pops up time and time again in different places. The former premier of Ontario, Mitch Hepburn, used to tell the same tale but in terms of a jail rather than a school. Here the form of the work is a series of mutually dependent propositions. The form of the syllogism is preserved, but the spirit is violated in intent.

1. Resolved, by this Council, that we build a new Jail.
2. Resolved, that the new Jail be built out of the materials of the old Jail.
3. Resolved, that the old Jail be used until the new Jail is finished.

Juggling the letters

Out of the twenty-six letters of the English alphabet, a million books could be constructed. Out of a half-a-dozen letters, what can be made? A word, a short phrase perhaps. With some juggling, the letters could be arranged and rearranged to make different words and phrases, different meanings. This accounts for the perpetual fascination of the anagram. An anagram is a word or phrase that has been transformed into another by the simple transposition of letters. For instance, "Evangelists" can be perversely rearranged without loss or substitution or addition of letters into "Evil's Agents".

Here are some others. "The Mona Lisa" may be altered into the following comment: "No hat, a smile."

To the anagramist, "Nova Scotia and Prince Edward Island" presents intriguing possibilities, including "The Canadian Provinces: Lands I Dread!"

Even the word "Anagrams" itself can be so treated. It becomes "Ars Magna", Latin for "Great Art."

Creating anagrams is a test of patience and wit. C. C. Bombaugh, in *Oddities and Curiosities of Words and Literature* (New York: Dover Publications, 1961), edited by Martin Gardner, takes anagrams a step further, into the area of magic squares, and writes:

> This word, Time, is the only word in the English language which can be thus arranged, and the different transpositions thereof are all at the same time Latin words. These words, in English as well as in Latin, may be read either upward or downward. Their signification as Latin words is as follows: Time—fear thou; Item—likewise; Meti—to be measured; Emit—he buys.

> TIME
> ITEM
> METI
> EMIT

A cousin of the anagram is the palindrome. In the anagram, the letters are reordered to create a different sense. In the palindrome, the letters are merely read backwards to repeat the same sense. This often results in such awkward English that the reader might confuse it initially with doubletalk. Take these two examples:

> Trash? Even interpret Nineveh's art.
> Red root put up to order.

Both sound preposterous, and as imponderable as the predictions of Nostradamus. Not all palindromes are laughable, for a few have a poetic quality that lends them memorability and has ensured their survival through the years. There is no basis for the following palindromes in the Bible, but there is a popular tradition that maintains the following conversation took place in Eden. Adam's first words to Eve were:

> Madam, I'm Adam.

And Eve's reply? This too is palindromial and has been preserved:

> Name no one man.

In the same fashion, Napoleon's last words—spoken in English!—are reputed to be:

> Able was I ere I saw Elba.

Thousands of palindromes have been written. There is something uncanny about them, almost magical.

Concrete Poetry

"The only unfortunate thing about concrete poetry," Emmet Williams once
said, "is the phrase concrete poetry. The word 'concrete' is misleading.
The stress should be on the word 'poetry'." Williams is the editor of *An Anthology of Concrete Poetry* (New York: Something Else Press, 1967) and a
world authority on the subject. Even he would balk at defining this fairly recent development in contemporary art. "The medium is the message"
might well have been coined to answer the question, "What is concrete
poetry?"

In any discussion of form in art, the work of the Brazilian poet Pedro
Xisto is of particular interest. The two examples of his work that follow
come from Xisto's *Logogrammes,* or word-forms, published in 1966.

At first glance, "Epithalamium II" looks like a corporate symbol. In
fact, it is a simple poem of great subtlety. It is also quite memorable and
mnemonic; once seen, it is unlikely to be soon forgotten. As well, Xisto's
poem has the virtues of brevity and wit. The theme of the poem is one's interpretation of it. The "h" can represent "he" or "homo", man. The "e"
can represent "Eve" or "elle". The "s" surely represents the uniting of the
two figures in a forceful yet graceful way. It is also a serpent, perhaps, and
is the poem "set" in the Garden of Eden? Together, the man and the
woman are united in a sexual union. Do they become a she? Is there a

female child of the union? Or is this another incarnation of the Eternal Feminine? Whatever the poet intended, all these (and many more) are valid readings of this simple-seeming concrete poem.

The second poem is a "logogram", and a splendid, classical one at that. The image is one of solid repose. It could be looked upon as many

* Concrete poem "Blues" by bpNichol. Used by permission of the author. (From New Direction in Canadian Poetry, Holt, Rinehart and Winston of Canada, Limited, 1971.)

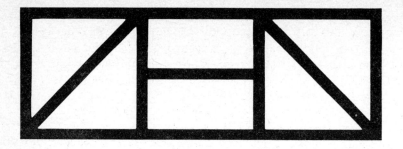

things, including an Art Deco design, a geometric construction, or rafters against a wall. In actual fact, the title of the poem is a dead giveaway. It is called "Zen", and this word can be traced continuously throughout the composition. Less is more.

David Kahn writes in *The Code-Breakers*:

> Three-quarters of English text is "unnecessary". English could theoretically express the same things with one-quarter its present letters if it were wholly non-redundant. A literary curiosity demonstrates graphically how a few letters carry most of the information of a text while the others are redundant.

DEATH AND LIFE

```
   cur    f    w       d       dis    and p
 A    sed iend rought eath     ease      ain.
   bles  fr   b      br    and           ag
```

A New Category for Artists

Today, in the West, the artist is regarded as now a craftsman, now a creator, but seldom as a realizer. Some of the newer art forms, like film, suggest that this new category of "realizer" should be created for the artist. In what way is a film director a creative artist? All the elements he works with—the script, the dialogue, the setting, the story, the actors, even the camera work—are the contributions of other individuals, often interpretative artists of the highest calibre. But with the *auteur*, or "author", theory, the director is the one who gives the film its final stamp. He imposes his personality on all its parts and makes them work together as a single whole—the artist is the "entrepreneur of reality", whose task it is to reveal aesthetic possibilities within situations or with objects not always of his own making.

The anthropologist Edmund Carpenter has described how the Eskimo sculptor does not carve his stone into the shape of a seal but, by cutting away, "releases" the seal from the stone. Chinese artists have made "natural stone paintings" which involve finding suitable rocks and then cutting them to reveal previously existing patterns. Perhaps the best-known Western expression of this search for a naturally satisfying form is the taste for driftwood. This is "low art", perhaps, and appropriate for living room tables and mantles. Found "high art" is the *objet trouvé*, the discovery of Dada that any object, taken from its original context and placed in another, acquires new and interesting aesthetic possibilities.

Word-plays like the ones that follow must be low on any artistic totempole. But if nothing else, these one-liners are interesting examples of juggled forms, "realized" possibilities. Placing one word within another is like injecting one form into another:

PREJEWDICE

Disguising a given formal order by giving it the trappings of another period is another way of having fun with forms. (This example comes from the first edition of the *Encyclopaedia Britannica*, 1768.)

Miffiffippi

Making a word reflexive—that is, making it comment upon itself—can be the operative device behind any number of word-plays:

CXNSXRSHXP

They can get quite short:

Ha!t

They can imitate natural objects:

mountAin

They can look pretty:

sn°w

Occasionally an innocent typo can subtly shift letters to bring home a different message:

UNITED STATES OF AMERCIA

This is not a misspelling of "AMERICA" but a way of drawing attention to the fact that the "CIA" is a part of American life and "deforms" the very symbol of the country. Finally, finding one complete word within another is a kind of punning that is especially appropriate in an essay on Expanded Art:

E(ART)H

So the search for form is an on-going process, and one that will never end—as long as there is a human being with an interest in art alive in the world. Man may think he imposes his "sense of form" on the world, but the chances are fifty-fifty that the world imposes its "sense of form" on him too.

---

* [Note. The poem "Greetings, In Season" is missing the letter L. There is no L. Noel.]

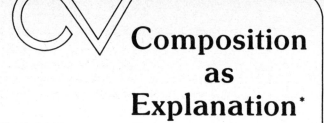

Composition
as
Explanation*

Gertrude Stein

There is singularly nothing that makes a difference a difference in beginning and in the middle and in ending except that each generation has something different at which they are all looking. By this I mean so simply that anybody knows it that composition is the difference which makes each and all of them then different from other generations and this is what makes everything different otherwise they are all alike and everybody knows it because everybody says it.

It is very likely that nearly every one has been very nearly certain that something that is interesting is interesting them. Can they and do they. It is very interesting that nothing inside in them, that is when you consider the very long history of how every one ever acted or has felt, it is very interesting that nothing inside in them in all of them makes it connectedly different. By this I mean this. The only thing that is different from one time to another is what is seen and what is seen depends upon how everybody is doing everything. This makes the thing we are looking at very different and this makes what those who describe it make of it, it makes a composition, it confuses, it shows, it is, it looks, it likes it as it is, and this makes what is seen as it is seen. Nothing changes from generation to generation except the thing seen and that makes a composition. Lord Grey remarked that when the generals before the war talked about the war they talked about it as a nineteenth century war although to be fought with twentieth century weapons. That is because war is a thing that decides how it is to be when it is to be done. It is prepared and to that degree it is like all academies it is not a thing made by being made it is a thing prepared. Writing and painting

* From *What Are Masterpieces?* by Gertrude Stein, London: Chatto and Winders Ltd. Reprinted by permission of David Higham Associates Limited.

and all that, is like that, for those who occupy themselves with it and don't make it as it is made. Now the few who make it as it is made, and it is to be remarked that the most decided of them usually are prepared just as the world around them is preparing, do it in this way and so I if you do not mind I will tell you how it happens. Naturally one does not know how it happened until it is well over beginning happening.

To come back to the part that the only thing that is different is what is seen when it seems to be being seen, in other words, composition and time-sense.

No one is ahead of his time, it is only that the particular variety of creating his time is the one that his contemporaries who also are creating their own time refuse to accept. And they refuse to accept it for a very simple reason and that is that they do not have to accept it for any reason. They themselves that is everybody in their entering the modern composition and they do enter it, if they do not enter it they are not so to speak in it they are out of it and so they do enter it; but in as you may say the non-competitive efforts where if you are not in it nothing is lost except nothing at all except what is not had, there are naturally all the refusals, and the things refused are only important if unexpectedly somebody happens to need them. In the case of the arts it is very definite. Those who are creating the modern composition authentically are naturally only of importance when they are dead because by that time the modern composition having become past is classified and the description of it is classical. That is the reason why the creator of the new composition in the arts is an outlaw until he is a classic, there is hardly a moment in between and it is really too bad very much too bad naturally for the creator but also very much too bad for the enjoyer, they all really would enjoy the created so much better just after it has been made than when it is already a classic, but it is perfectly simple that there is no reason why the contemporaries should see, because it would not make any difference as they lead their lives in the new composition anyway, and as every one is naturally indolent why naturally they don't see. For this reason as in quoting Lord Grey it is quite certain that nations not actively threatened are at least several generations behind themselves militarily so aesthetically they are more than several generations behind themselves and it is very much too bad, it is so very much more exciting and satisfactory for everybody if one can have contemporaries, if all one's contemporaries could be one's contemporaries.

There is almost not an interest.

For a very long time everybody refuses and then almost without a pause almost everybody accepts. In the history of the refused in the arts and literature the rapidity of the change is always startling. Now the only difficulty with the *volte-face* concerning the arts is this. When the acceptance comes, by that acceptance the thing created becomes a classic. It is a natural phenomena a rather extraordinary natural phenomena that a thing accepted becomes a classic. And what is the characteristic quality of a classic. The characteristic quality of a classic is that it is beautiful. Now of course it is perfectly true that a more or less first rate work of art is beautiful but the trouble is that when that first rate work of art becomes a classic because it is accepted the only thing that is important from then on to the majority of the acceptors the enormous majority, the most intelligent majority of the acceptors is that it is so wonderfully beautiful. Of course it is wonderfully beautiful, only when it is still a thing irritating annoying stimulating then all quality of beauty is denied to it.

Of course it is beautiful but first all beauty in it is denied and then all the beauty of it is accepted. If every one were not so indolent they would realize that beauty is beauty even when it is irritating and stimulating not only when it is accepted and classic. Of course it is extremely difficult nothing more so than to remember back to its not being beautiful once it has become beautiful. This makes it so much more difficult to realise its beauty when the work is being refused and prevents every one from realising that they were convinced that beauty was denied, once the work is accepted. Automatically with the acceptance of the time-sense comes the recognition of the beauty and once the beauty is accepted the beauty never fails any one.

Beginning again and again is a natural thing even when there is a series.

Beginning again and again and again explaining composition and time is a natural thing.

It is understood by this time that everything is the same except composition and time, composition and the time of the composition and the time in the composition.

Everything is the same except composition and as the composition is different and always going to be different everything is not the same. Everything is not the same as the time when of the composition and the time in the composition is different. The composition is different, that is certain.

The composition is the thing seen by every one living in the living they are doing, they are the composing of the composition that at the time they are living is the composition of the time in which they are living. It is that that makes living a thing they are doing. Nothing else is different, of that almost any one can be certain. The time when and the time of and the time in that composition is the natural phenomena of that composition and of that perhaps every one can be certain.

No one thinks these things when they are making when they are creating what is the composition, naturally no one thinks that is no one formulates until what is to be formulated has been made.

Composition is not there, it is going to be there and we are here. This is some time ago for us naturally.

The only thing that is different from one time to another is what is seen and what is seen depends upon how everybody is doing everything. This makes the thing we are looking at very different and this makes what those who describe it make of it, it makes a composition, it confuses, it shows, it is, it looks, it likes it as it is, and this makes what is seen as it is seen. Nothing changes from generation to generation except the thing seen and that makes a composition.

Now the few who make writing as it is made and it is to be remarked that the most decided of them are those that are prepared by preparing, are prepared just as the world around them is prepared and is preparing to do it in this way and so if you do not mind I will again tell you how it happens. Naturally one does not know how it happened until it is well over beginning happening.

Each period of living differs from any other period of living not in the way life is but in the way life is conducted and that authentically speaking is composition. After life has been conducted in a certain way everybody knows it but nobody knows it, little by little, nobody knows it as long as nobody knows it. Any one creating the composition in the arts does not know it either, they are conducting life and that makes their composition what it is, it makes their work compose as it does.

Their influence and their influences are the same as that of all of their contemporaries only it must always be remembered that the analogy is not obvious until as I say the composition of a time has become so pronounced that it is past and the artistic composition of it is a classic.

And now to begin as if to begin. Composition is not there, it is going to be there and we are here. This is some time ago for us naturally. There is something to be added afterwards.

Just how much my work is known to you I do not know. I feel that perhaps it would be just as well to tell the whole of it.

In beginning writing I wrote a book called *Three Lives* this was written in 1905. I wrote a negro story called *Melanctha*. In that there was a constant recurring and beginning there was a marked direction in the direction of being in the present although naturally I had been accustomed to past present and future, and why, because the composition forming around me was a prolonged present. A composition of a prolonged present is a natural composition in the world as it has been these thirty years it was more and more a prolonged present. I created then a prolonged present naturally I knew nothing of a continuous present but it came naturally to me to make one, it was simple it was clear to me and nobody knew why it was done like that, I did not myself although naturally to me it was natural.

After that I did a book called *The Making of Americans* it is a long book about a thousand pages.

Here again it was all so natural to me and more and more complicatedly a continuous present. A continuous present is a continuous present. I made almost a thousand pages of a continuous present.

Continuous present is one thing and beginning again and again is another thing. These are both things. And then there is using everything.

This brings us again to composition this the using everything. The using everything brings us to composition and to this composition. A continuous present and using everything and beginning again. In these two books there was elaboration of the complexities of using everything and of a continuous present and of beginning again and again and again.

In the first book there was a groping for a continuous present and for using everything by beginning again and again.

There was a groping for using everything and there was a groping for a continuous present and there was an inevitable beginning of beginning again and again and again.

Having naturally done this I naturally was a little troubled with it when I read it. I became then like the others who read it. One does, you know, excepting that when I reread it myself I lost myself in it again. Then I said to myself this time it will be different and I began. I did not begin again I just began.

In this beginning naturally since I at once went on and on very soon there were pages and pages and pages more and more elaborated creating a more and more continuous present including more and more using of everything and continuing more and more beginning and beginning and beginning.

I went on and on to a thousand pages of it.

In the meantime to naturally begin I commenced making portraits of anybody and anything. In making these portraits I naturally made a continuous present an including everything and a beginning again and again within a very small thing. That started me into composing anything into one thing. So then naturally it was natural that one thing an enormously long thing was not everything an enormously short thing was also not everything nor was it all of it a continuous present thing nor was it always and always beginning again. Naturally I would then begin again. I would begin again I would naturally begin. I did naturally begin. This brings me to a great deal that has been begun.

And after that what changes what changes after that after that what changes and what changes after that and after that and what changes and after that and what changes after that.

The problem from this time on became more definite.

It was all so nearly alike it must be different and it is different, it is natural that if everything is used and there is a continuous present and a beginning again and again if it is all so alike it must be simply different and everything simply different was the natural way of creating it then.

In this natural way of creating it then that it was simply different everything being alike it was simply different, this kept on leading one to lists. Lists naturally for a while and by lists I mean a series. More and more in going back over what was done at this time I find that I naturally kept simply different as an intention. Whether there was or whether there was not a continuous present did not then any longer trouble me there was or there was, and using everything no longer troubled me if everything is alike using everything could no longer trouble me and beginning again and again could no longer trouble me because if lists were inevitable if series were inevitable and the whole of it was inevitable beginning again and again could not trouble me so then with nothing to trouble me I very completely began naturally since everything is alike making it as simply different naturally as simply different as possible. I began doing natural phenomena what I called natural phenomena and natural phenomena naturally everything being alike natural phenomena are making things be naturally simply different. This found its culmination later, in the beginning it began in a center confused with lists with series with geography with returning portraits and with particularly often four and three and often with five and four. It is easy to see that in the beginning such a conception as everything being naturally different would be very inarticulate and very slowly it began to emerge and take the form of anything, and then naturally if anything that is simply different is simply different what follows will follow.

So far then the progress of my conceptions was the natural progress entirely in accordance with my epoch as I am sure is to be quite easily realised if you think over the scene that was before us all from year to year.

As I said in the beginning, there is the long history of how every one ever acted or has felt and that nothing inside in them in all of them makes it connectedly different. By this I mean all this.

The only thing that is different from one time to another is what is seen and what is seen depends upon how everybody is doing everything.

It is understood by this time that everything is the same except composition and time, composition and the time of the composition and the time in the composition.

Everything is the same except composition and as the composition is different and always going to be different everything is not the same. So then I as a contemporary creating the composition in the beginning was groping toward a continuous present, a using everything a beginning again and again and then everything being alike then everything very simply everything was naturally simply different and so I as a contemporary was creating everything being alike was creating everything naturally being naturally simply different, everything being alike. This then was the period that brings me to the period of the beginning of 1914. Everything being alike everything naturally would be simply different and war came and everything being alike and everything being simply different brings everything being simply different brings it to romanticism.

Romanticism is then when everything being alike everything is naturally simply different, and romanticism.

Then for four years this was more and more different even though this was, was everything alike. Everything alike naturally everything was simply different and this is and was romanticism and this is and was war. Everything being alike everything naturally everything is different simply different naturally simply different.

And so there was the natural phenomena that was war, which had been, before war came, several generations behind the contemporary composition, because it became war and so completely needed to be contemporary became completely contemporary and so created the completed recognition of the contemporary composition. Every one but one may say every one became consciously became aware of the existence of the authenticity of the modern composition. This then the contemporary recognition, because of the academic thing known as war having been forced to become contemporary made every one not only contemporary in act not only contemporary in thought but contemporary in self-consciousness made every one contemporary with the modern composition. And so the art creation of the contemporary composition which would have been outlawed normally outlawed several generations more behind even than war, war having been brought so to speak up to date art so to speak was allowed not completely to be up to date, but nearly up to date, in other words we who created the expression of the modern composition were to be recognized before we were dead some of us even quite a long time before we were dead. And so war may be said to have advanced a general recognition of the expression of the contemporary composition by almost thirty years.

And now after that there is no more of that in other words there is peace and something comes then and it follows coming then.

And so now one finds oneself interesting oneself in an equilibration, that of course means words as well as things and distribution as well as between themselves between the words and themselves and the things and themselves, a distribution as distribution. This makes what follow what follows and now there is every reason why there should be an arrangement made. Distribution is interesting and equilibration is interesting when a continuous present and a beginning again and again and using everything and everything alike and everything naturally simply different has been done.

After all this, there is that, there has been that that there is a composition and that nothing changes except composition the composition and the time of and the time in the composition.

The time of the composition is a natural thing and the time in the composition is a natural thing it is a natural thing and it is a contemporary thing.

The time of the composition is the time of the composition. It has been at times a present thing it has been at times a past thing it has been at times a future thing it has been at times an endeavour at parts or all of these things. In my beginning it was a continuous present a beginning again and again and again and again, it was a series it was a list it was a similarity and everything different it was a distribution and an equilibration. That is all of the time some of the time of the composition.

Now there is still something else the time-sense in the composition. This is what is always a fear a doubt and a judgement and a conviction. The quality in the creation of expression the quality in a composition that makes it go dead just after it has been made is very troublesome.

The time in the composition is a thing that is very troublesome. If the time in the composition is very troublesome it is because there must even if there is no time at all in the composition there must be time in the composition which is in its quality of distribution and equilibration. In the beginning there was the time in the composition that naturally was in the composition but time in the composition comes now and this is what is now troubling every one the time in the composition is now a part of distribution and equilibration. In the beginning there was confusion there was a continuous present and later there was romanticism which was not a confusion but an extrication and now there is either succeeding or failing there must be distribution and equilibration there must be time that is distributed and equilibrated. This is the thing that is at present the most troubling and if there is the time that is at present the most troublesome the time-sense that is at present the most troubling is the thing that makes the present the most troubling. There is at present there is distribution, by this I mean expression and time, and in this way at present composition is time that is the reason that at present the time-sense is troubling that is the reason why at present the time-sense in the composition is the composition that is making what there is in composition.

And afterwards.

Now that is all.

Is Your English Destroying Your Image?*

Michael Hornyansky

When I let it slip among ordinary company that I'm a professor of English, you can guess what the reaction is: "Oh-oh," they say with nervous smiles, "I'd better watch my language." No use explaining that I don't teach composition. If English professors hit the front page, or confront public awareness at all, it's not when they have had profound or brilliant ideas about literature, but when they are testily muttering that their latest crop of freshmen can neither read nor write. And the truth is, of course, that we are—we must be—concerned with language. It is the medium both of the works we study, and of our attempts to teach it. If language should decay far enough, the study of literature becomes difficult or impossible. I won't play for headlines by pretending this is the condition we have reached; but such a condition is at least imaginable, as things are going. So I worry a good deal about language, myself. And I think the most useful way to put my worries before you is to pursue that automatic reaction: "Oh-oh, I'd better watch my language."

It's a touchy area. People are as anxious about the impression their words make as they are about their clothes or their faces or their waistlines. If you catch someone in an error, he is mortified. If you suggest he doesn't speak well, you wound his vanity as sharply as if you claim he has no sense of humour. Sniping at other people's mistakes is a favourite sport of those who write letters to the *Globe and Mail*; and there are always other correspondents to jeer at the snipers. And even when there are no English

* "Is Your English Destroying Your Image" from *In the Name of Language* edited by Joseph Gold, 1975. Reprinted by permission of The Macmillan Company of Canada Limited.

teachers (official or amateur) within earshot, private citizens go on fretting over what words to use, and whether they're using them properly. I know of a group which spent hours wrangling over whether a certain person should be described as *responsible* for the task assigned to him, or whether that didn't seem to wag the finger at him needlessly. They finally settled on *accountable* instead—a word in fashion these days, but one which to my mind conveys a good deal less personal dignity and freedom than *responsible* does. That's how it often goes: the questions we're least certain about are the ones that arouse our stronger feelings. And when it comes to language, most of us are uncertain. The frequency of little check-up phrases in our normal speech—"you know? eh? like? see what I mean?"—is a symptom not so much of sloppiness, but of concern about whether we're getting through.

This is why I thought of offering some helpful hints. I don't aim to give you a lessson in grammar. Think of this chapter as an essay in linguistic psychology, not in rules. Remember my title: "Is your English destroying your image?" I put it that way not to be cute or disarming, but because that's the form our anxiety takes. I shall be asking not just what errors we make, but why we make them, and how they affect our view of each other; and after that, how to set about improving matters. To tell you that this is Right and that is Wrong (even if I had the confidence to do so) wouldn't be much help, anyway. Far better in the long run to try to understand why some things work and others don't—so we can judge for ourselves instead of carrying around a list of lapses. I say "we" because I talk for a living, and I am reminded daily of how my words can undermine rapport, or on good days virtually magic people into understanding me. I dare to advise you not because I'm a professor, but because I've been there, and I have some practical knowledge of what can go wrong and how to cure it.

If I am to write about mistakes in our use of language, I had best begin by establishing what makes a mistake—what standards to measure by. There are two possible misconceptions here. At one extreme is the idea of Correctness. Some people still hold to the notion that there is such a thing as Correct English: the King's English, possibly the Queen's, existing as a heavenly paradigm to which only educated people and professors have access. (Francophones are even more prone to think of Correct French, because they have an official Academy to act as its guardian and legislator; but as they are beginning to discover, their hopes are misplaced.) There are several reasons why this mystical notion won't do. One is that educated people—even teachers; even, heaven knows, Her Majesty—do not always speak well. How can we be certain when to follow them? Worse still, the belief that a correct pattern exists can become, in a curious way, a cause of errors: for the people who most firmly believe in the King's English are usually hazy about *what precisely it is*, and in their anxiety to be proper they lean over backwards, into slips that would not befall a more natural stance. No, the idea of Correct English has at best a social validity. By speaking like the Queen you may prove your loyalty and your place in society, but you do not exempt yourself from error. In fact 'there is no enduring pattern of correctness. As most people have come to realize, language changes, constantly and irresistibly—and correctness, if it's a workable idea at all, must change too. The purists are remembered as quaint defenders of the last ditch: like Jonathan Swift, rejecting the uncouth expression "mob," because all right-speaking people knew it should be *mobile vulgus*. (Swift also won a few, however. See Dwight Macdonald, *Against the American Grain*, Vintage, 1962, p. 323.) Or like the person who answers the telephone with "Hello: it is I, Clifton Webb."

At the other extreme is the notion that since language constantly changes, then anything goes—there are no rules at all, Usage is king. It will not be so easy to persuade you that this too is a misconception. The barometer of our times is set at Change. A recent letter to the *Globe* condemns the declared policy of Ontario's Minister of Education to return to the 3 R's: "[he] invites our children to take firm, confident steps backward into the future. Pity." (Ray MacLain, *Globe*, 25 Feb. 1975.) The CBC's news-readers, once modestly reliable (meaning they could be counted on to apologize for errors), have lost their supervisor of broadcast language, and now commit cheerfully such barbarisms as "It sounds like he's going to reform." This is the age of Humpty Dumpty, who claimed that words meant what he wanted them to mean; it was simply a question of who was to be master. You will recall what happened to Humpty Dumpty. But his fragmented soul is still with us: it lives on in the third edition of Webster's *New International Dictionary* (1961), which makes no attempt to distinguish acceptable usage from colloquial, slang, or illiterate. "If it is used, it is usage": that is Webster's principle in a nutshell—and a nutshell is where it belongs. To see the enterprise mercilessly analysed, read Dwight Macdonald's patient and savage review called "The String Untuned." (Reprinted in *Against the American Grain*, p. 289.)

Those who appeal to usage as the final arbiter seem to march under the banners of Life and Progress. In fact they are making a mystique of change, supposing that since it is normal it must also be good. Happily, the letter columns of the newspaper do feature other correspondents, who realize that change may be not growth but decay, and that mere growth is not always welcome, in language as in life.

> It is fatuous (publicists please note: this word does not yet
> mean stout or plump) to argue that the language is undergo-
> ing positive and dynamic change in the hands of our public
> figures. Only fools would unreservedly maintain so.
>
> (C.C.J. Bond, *Globe*, 17 Feb. 1975)

(I expect a later correspondent observed that it wasn't their *hands* but their mouths that did the damage.) Not all change is progress. Some of it has to be resisted, and when possible reversed. If the last ditch needs defending, I'll take my place alongside Sam Johnson:

> If the changes we fear be thus irresistible, what remains but to acquiesce with silence, as in the other insurmountable distresses of humanity? It remains that we retard what we cannot repel, that we palliate what we cannot cure.
>
> (Preface to the *Dictionary*)

That final sentence, by the way, is a grand example of how to project the image of Doctor Johnson.

But I don't think the situation's quite so desperate. One can take account of a flood without drowning in it or becoming flotsam. Call me Noah. I think that even for a language in flux, certain firm criteria can be proposed. They are based on this assumption: *that language is a means of giving a precise pattern to thought and feeling, and a means of conveying that pattern to other people.* I do not claim this is the only assumption possible. Language is commonly used for several other purposes. It is used to make up for, or disguise, the absence of thought, and to mask one's feelings; and it may communicate nothing more than a soothing assurance of togetherness. But for this purpose, as politicians (and some married couples) know, almost any noise will do: there is no question of Good Usage, or Correctness. Language can also be used deliberately to deceive. Here the question is skill, not usage. An assumption more likely to mislead us is one I've already alluded to: that language is above all a badge of social position. Here usage does matter. But which usage is socially acceptable (and that is the criterion, even though it may be called "proper"; for instance, there was a time not long ago when saying *ain't* and droppin' your final g's were the signals of aristocratic talk)—that is a question that varies rapidly with time and place, so that no general criteria can be proposed. One has to play it by ear, or find a member of the desired club who knows the passwords and is willing to tell, like Nancy Mitford or Henry Higgins.

My concern, however, is language that communicates thought and feeling—the kind I am trying to use now. This is where it makes some sense to apply standards of proper, or good, usage. And the standards I propose are these three: *Clarity, Impact,* and *Idiom.* (Not *correctness,* as you see, but bases upon which we can decide what *is* correct, or at least what is preferable.) *Is it clear? Does it hit home? Is it English?* These are the only reasonable standards I can find; and since they apply, so far as I can see, to a language at any time, they need not be surrendered under the pressure of change.

Clarity is of course what we aim at when we want to express thoughts with cool precision: easy to talk about, hard to achieve. It will govern our choice of words, the design of our sentences and arguments. It is the standard that causes Humpty Dumpty to fall, or at least to remain babbling to himself in a private lingo: for we all should know from experience that if we use words arbitrarily, instead of in their agreed senses, we will not make contact. Clarity also governs the gradual smoothing out of inflections (that is, variations in the form of a word according to its grammatical function, like *who/whose/whom*). Presumably it was in the interest of clarity that primitive tongues established remarkably complex systems of inflection (and of syntax generally); but as the history of our language shows, the complicated patterns that make French or German (or Latin) hard for us to learn have not proved necessary for speakers of English. Indeed, if clarity were our sole guide, we might wind up saying *he loves she*, or *you did hurt I*—in fact we're well on the way to that. But I proposed three standards, not one.

The second of them, *Impact*, is our aim when we want to persuade or impress rather than to inform; when instead of taking our cue from logicians or astronauts, we speak like witch doctors, advertising men, or poets. We know that by choosing certain words over others (not because they're more exact, but because they're fresh, arresting, expressive of likeness not essence) and by combining them in unexpected ways, we can charge our speech, and make it strike home as clarity alone would never do. We say, "John's a tiger." In point of literal fact, John is a featherless biped rather short on hair; but one simple and over-used metaphor conveys more about how he *strikes* us than would paragraphs of careful analysis. Again, however, impact by itself is not a sufficient guide. Without clarity squeezing the brakes, impact may run riot and collapse into nonsense or mumbo-jumbo— as poetry has been known to do, or advertising slogans, or slang. And there is no dull thud to compare with yesterday's impact: I mean, *lamp the frail with the solo cheater, will ya? Bro-ther, she just don't connect.* And neither do you, I imagine—though thirty years ago you would have followed me without trouble.

The mention of slang brings us at once to my third criterion, the tricky one: *Idiom*. I might have defined idiom as "the sense of linguistic fitness possessed by one who has grown up speaking a language"—I might have defined it so, if I hadn't learned better from experience. For I teach third- and fourth-generation Canadians who have spoken English (sort of, you know?) since the crib, yet who have no more sense of English idiom than a recent arrival from the Old Country.

You might suspect that under the mask of idiom I am actually dragging correctness in through the back door. Not so. By asking "Is it English?" I do not mean to ask, is it *proper* English—but whether it is English rather than Transylvanian or Tagalog. Thus, we accept as idiomatic "That's all right by me," but do not (yet) accept "By me you are lovely" (which is fine in German). This also demonstrates that idiom is not equivalent to usage: for there are some usages which although clear, and even fashionable for a while, are ultimately rejected as unidiomatic. By idiom in general, then, we mean the ground rules or *customs* of a particular language, developed over the centuries—no matter whether all its speakers know them or not. These rules (like those that distinguish Canadian football from the American and the British games) set limits to the ways in which a given language works, the kinds of "play" that are legitimate—limits that may have little connection with clarity or force; indeed, they almost set up an independent standard for clarity and force. I would suppose that idiom arises from the same motive as slang: a sense of clubbiness, of "the way we do things" (as against the way outsiders—aliens and foreigners—handle them). The difference is that in slang the club is narrower, the motive keener and more restless, so that fashions in slang change very swiftly—as I shall be noting later on. Idioms do change, but not too far and not too fast, for the club they signify is the main coherent body of speakers of a language; and the changes are not mindless accidents (as the proponents of Usage seem at times to suggest) but organic and adaptive. We may be able to explain why particular idioms arise; but they are unlikely to be logical or even grammatical, even in French. In short, idiom is the human side of language, balancing between the poles of emotion and reason (as we ourselves do). The idiomatic speaker recognizes that his language has a living identity. He will be so intimately acquainted with its every nerve and fibre that he knows instinctively how it prefers to behave, and will not force it into unnatural postures.

You see that these three standards of good usage are flexible, not absolute. I trust you will find them reasonable, not arbitrary. And you will realize that they work together in odd and unpredictable ways, so that we cannot apply them unimaginatively or with stickling accuracy. It should also be even clearer why I have chosen to discuss not "the mistakes we make in grammar," but (using the adman's idiom) the linguistic images we project: there are territories where grammar has little relevance. I shall assume that for the most part we *hope* to project the image of educated people—an image of clear thought, charged only with the emotion we consciously intend, and conveying by the way a perfect familiarity with the structure and temperament of our language. In short, the picture of people in control of themselves. But the fact is that we very easily go wrong, in the sense of transmitting unexpected and damaging pictures of ourselves, because our language is not wholly under our control. My main concern, therefore, will be the images we actually do project without intending them.

I'll start with a group of images that convey—well, I was going to say Ignorance, which has a nice honest ring to it; but it's not quite adequate, because in a way all the faulty images involve some ignorance. Let's try a few, and see what they have in common. First, the image of the Illiterate (the uneducated, the rube, the rough diamond). It is the most obvious, and should be the simplest to avoid; yet even in the guarded speech of Academe you may catch such expressions as *irregardless, equally as good as, a little ways further on, with regards to, anyways, most everyone.* I do not include in this category expressions which are linguistically O.K. but socially taboo, like *ain't.* I am pointing only at those which violate one or more of my three criteria, principally the test of clarity. For instance, *with regards to* is unclear because it's ambiguous; it belongs at the end of a let-ter—with regards to Auntie May, Uncle Harry, and Roger the dog—whereas *with regard to* is rather pompous but clear enough. A com-plaint about *how bad prisoners are treated* (on CBC Viewpoint, 17 March 1975) leaves us confused between bad prisoners and bad treatment. Or take the formula beloved of the newspaper reader: "Hey, I see where René Lévesque's been elected." *Where?* Well, in his constituency; where else?

These are the obvious errors, the ones that schoolteachers have ham-mered away at for years. Then why are they as common as ever? Partly carelessness, no doubt, and partly, yes, ignorance, for education of any kind is the perpetual caulking of a leaky boat. But I think there is another reason, much stronger than these: inverted snobbery, the wish not to seem better than anyone else. Illiteracy is an image often assumed for this pur-pose. When a mechanic reports that "she's runnin' real good," it takes a pretty stuffy professor to reply that "it is indeed running rather well." In-stead, with tact and democratic sympathy, he agrees that she sure is run-ning purty smooth, by the sound of her. For he knows that grammar varies inversely as virility; and that if you *continue on* down to the stadium, you'll find that nobody there plays well. He-men play *good.* In that quaint dream of pioneer society to which we North Americans so desperately cling, careful speech is the mark of the sissy or the dude or the schoolmarm (who isn't even a Real Woman until she takes off her glasses and drops her g's). Fluency is suspect, suggesting a flim-flam man at work: which is one reason why our politicians burble, haw, and drone.

As I shall bear witness, I have every sympathy with changing your tune to fit your environment. Boswell's memory of Dr. Johnson, address-ing a baffled stable-boy as if he were a meeting of the Royal Society, should be a warning to us all. By all means let us keep up the fiction that we're all simple country folk—if it makes us talk simply, it can't be all bad. But there are times in the real world when talking like Gary Cooper does not meet the necessities of the situation. Another risk: if we don't watch what we're doing, our assumed illiteracies may become chronic, and we'll find ourselves (at a Home and School meeting, say) unable to shift gears. For instance, in the past ten years it has become chic among fairly well-educated British journalists and authors to imitate the laxer kind of Americanism—at first in a campy way, half-sneering, but then trendily, and at last unconsciously. So that now you find columnists in the London *Observer* "spending money like it was going out of style" (as it is, of course; but the locution doesn't harmonize with the rest of their column), and authors, *veddy* conservative and precise by nature, striving for the Chandler image and descending to vilely un-British depths:

> This man had hooked her *helplessly*. Who now talked *like*
> he did and sometimes more wildly. (My italics)

That's from a thriller by William Haggard (*The Bitter Harvest*, Cassell, 1971, p. 142), whose normal style is literate and careful. By odd contrast, I find two American authors of fast, tough thrillers being surprisingly choosy. Ross Macdonald has his hero (Lew Archer, in *The Moving Target*) announce that he's the "new-type detective," and soften the illiteracy by carefully putting in the hyphen. John D. MacDonald (in the Travis McGee books) is liberal with illiteracies, but uses *horrid* either in the British slang sense or, it may be, in the original Latin sense.

All right: I've oversimplified the North American scene. Pioneer simplicity is not our only dream, or even the dominant one. We have a strong contrary tendency, to inflate and load down our language with impressive sonorities: to talk like judges and senators rather than cowboys. And for this too there is a trap. It's a subspecies of Illiteracy: call it the image of a *narrow education*—specifically, an education short on etymology in Latin, Greek, or even English. I am not saying educated people all ought to know Latin or Greek (though I opine wistfully that if they knew one or the other, preferably a bit of Latin, they would use English in a less wooden way). I am saying that when English words are imported from those tongues, it is useful to know what they've brought with them. The expression *continue on*, for example, occurs even in ivied towers; but it doesn't take a classical education to know that *continue* means to *go on*, not just *go*. The word *major* is generally believed to be a powerful synonym for *big* or *important* or *significant*, so that one hears visiting pundits speak continually of Very Major Problems. At the risk of offending them, let me spell it out: *major* began life as a Latin comparative, and the comparative flavour is still there—it means either *bigger* or *rather big*. And neither a "very bigger problem" nor a "very rather big" one makes much sense. Or take four common words which afford a handy test of a man's breadth of education: *phenomenon, criterion, stratum,* and *medium.* Two are Greek, two are Latin; and they behave accordingly when they become plural. Yet I have heard a respected literary scholar in a national broadcast refer to "an interesting phenomena"; to appreciate the full effect of this, imagine hearing it in the voice of W.C. Fields. *Criteria* and *strata* are likewise frequently used as if they were singular. They were not; they are not. And everyone these days knows (without pausing to think about it) that *a media* is something you communicate to the masses with. In fact there is only one Media: it's where the Medes came from.

Now I grant you there is a line past which this sort of objection becomes precious. But I think we ought to draw that line with care. For instance, the spelling (and pronunciation) *chaise lounge* is a peculiarly insensitive gaffe to allow ourselves in a country with Francophone leanings. And on our own monoglot ground, "between the three of us" should sound wrong (to the idiomatic ear) not because grammarians say so, but because *between* was once *bi tweyen*, or *by two*. "By two the three of us" becomes a study in vulgar fractions. Keep *between* for intimate moments *à deux*; it was made for you and me.

Pretentiousness in our speech is bedevilled by other dangers. Consider the image of Fogginess, shrouding the speaker who would like to make clear distinctions but has forgotten how. He says, "To me this is a semantic problem in that the confusion centres around a verbal misunderstanding." Sounds impressive at first; but there are three dead give-aways. *Semantic* is a favourite word with people who can't convey their meaning and want to shift the blame. *In that*, as my students seem to know by instinct, is a dandy way of implying a subtle connection when you are actually going to repeat the identical idea in different words. And *centres around*, as the critics have pointed out long ago, betrays a confusion in basic geometry. Nothing centres *around* anything. Things may *revolve around*, if they must, but if they centre at all, they centre *on*.

A frequent cause of fog is choosing the wrong word in a pair: *continual* for *continuous*, *differential* for *different*, *lie* for *lay*, and so on. (For a charmingly outdated list, see Fowler's *Dictionary of Modern English Usage* under "Pairs and Snares.") The normal result is haziness of outline, but at times it may be something more risky: "Oh, I was just laying around." One of Richard Needham's correspondents cripples his indignation with this kind of error:

> When the Government takes over Bell Canada—as *regret-fully* they will one day—does anyone seriously think that either service or costs will improve?
>
> (Needham, *Globe*, 25 Feb. 1975; my italics)

Regretfully imputes an emotion to the government which does it too much honour. And come to think of it, what does a cost do when it improves? *Nutritional*, much in people's mouths lately, is either ambiguous or an unnecessary variant of *nutritious*. And *disinterested* has virtually lost its useful idiomatic meaning of "impartial." I have had people tell me no thanks, they were disinterested in football—the perfect qualification for a referee, but I was looking for someone to use the other ticket. The most common confusion is that of *infer* with *imply*. I am quite aware that even a good dictionary gives *imply* as one meaning of *infer*. That simply proves you cannot always trust dictionaries. The words are so obviously meant for each other as opposites (the speaker *folding in* an extra meaning, the listener *taking it in*) that I mistrust the judgment of a person who mixes them up. Perhaps the most noticeable symptom of the foggy speaker, or woofer, is an addiction to *facts* and *factors*. He speaks of a *fact* when he means an opinion, a risk, or a possibility; and he says *factor* when he senses that something is important but doesn't know how or why. Allow me to offer you a brief cautionary tale about factors. Originally, you recall, factors were the men in charge of trading posts for the Hudson's Bay Company; but they proved to be such willing workers that when the Company retrenched, the factors went forth and multiplied—and became factotums.

Remember that I am speaking of inadvertent fogginess. Conscious or deliberate blurring of outlines belongs to propaganda. No doubt we condition ourselves to be its victims if we use, or even listen to without comment, such expressions as "the military *internationalization* of Arab oil" (proposed in a bloodless way by a U.S. commentator not long ago). Others have pointed out that the use of woolly abstractions (*defoliation* being one of the mildest) to disguise ugly particulars is one of the sorry consequences of the war in Vietnam. A senior American journalist (Edwin Newman, in *Strictly Speaking*, Bobbs-Merrill, 1974) has been so appalled by it as to cry out against the murder of the language; once *that* murder is accomplished, it makes others easier to excuse or condone. I think it is fair to describe this as the Nazification of English. It is the process that caused George Steiner virtually to give up on language altogether (see *Language and Silence*, Atheneum, 1967). I shall content myself with this brief reminder that the seemingly trivial effects which I am discussing do border on sombre realities; and that if I choose to play it light, that's because lightness makes for more clarity than does indignation.

Close kin to fogginess is the image of what appears to be the absent mind—which cannot remember how it started, three words ago. It goes to pieces over what the grammarian calls Agreement, because it forgets both the person and the number of what it was talking about. Try this: "Bell Canada refunds your money without question if you tell *them* you reached a wrong number." How many Bells are ringing here, and for whom? Or this advice from a TV golfer: "*a person* of short stature should take care in grasping *their* club. He *(or she)* should grasp *their* club firmly . . ." Who grasps whose club, exactly? Does the owner know? But I'm being unfair. The difficulty in both cases has to do with pronouns which won't do precisely the job we intend. For one thing, speakers of English feel the lack of a genuinely impersonal pronoun like *on* in French: the nearest we can come to *on dit* is "they say," or "it is said." Actually *on* derives from *homo*, the Latin word for *man*—just as the impersonal *man* in German is connected with the masculine *Mann*—but in French the derivation is so masked by time that I doubt if most French speakers recognize it. Our convention in English is that *he* does duty for both *he* and *she*, and can be used impersonally. Evidently this was felt to be awkward or misleading even before the voice of women was heard, and so it has been replaced by something even more awkward, the explicit *he or she,* or in some places *s/he*. English does have the alternative *one:* "one should grasp one's club..." But one hesitates to do much of this, largely because the British are prone to use *one* as a coy or playful self-effacement for *I* and *me.* Perhaps you recall the courtship of Princess Anne, when in interviews with the press Captain Phillips proved far too well-bred to draw attention to himself, and therefore became *oneself:* one belonged, one gathered, to the nation.... When the princess replied in kind, the two dear things practically faded from sight.

In such a cleft stick, what is the average speaker to do? I'd advise him to rely on *they,* and to avoid awkwardness by carrying the plural through: for instance "When you tell *them,* Bell Canada *refund* your money." Besides, it's good psychology to treat corporate entities like Bell or the government as plurals rather than monoliths; it helps remind us they're made of people, and can be reached. Another device is to stop being so impersonal, and use *you* instead: "If you're short, grasp your club." And try to stay out of ambiguous situations like "Everybody thinks they're in charge."

There are clearer test cases for this image (the absent or sieve-like mind). One is the formula so many people find irresistible, especially politicians talking to us on television: *as far as [X] is concerned...* By beginning the formula, one stands pledged to follow through, eventually, with the rest of it. But usually the windbag who starts out with a really big X, "*as far as* low-rental housing developments and their location within the metropolitan area within the foreseeable future, by which I mean until the next election, ah..."—well, such a man is lost. He's forgotten his launch platform, and we could wait for weeks without hearing a whisper of *concern.* Strip it down, and he's left with a silly dangle—"as far as housing." (If this is your problem, let me recommend some safe and easy alternatives, like *as for, as to, concerning,* or even *with regard to.* You might play it Edward G. Robinson style: "You wanna know about housing? Okay, I'll tell ya.") The other telltale habit is the mixed metaphor, as in "We promise to *harness* those *bottlenecks,*" or (to quote an Ontario cabinet minister) "One bad apple can give the whole thing a black eye." Perhaps it is too kind to blame these unconscious jokes on forgetfulness. A truer explanation may be that such speakers are totally deaf to metaphor, and largely deaf to wit as well. A *bad apple* no longer carries for them any memory of fruit, it's just a phrase filed under Crook or Rascal (in the same fashion, I suspect, as jokes are filed under subject headings and "injected" into their speeches at apt moments).

More seductive (and for the discriminating judge, more damaging) is the image of would-be elegance, which produces Genteelisms, like *between you and I*. A little grammar is a dangerous thing. The cause of trouble is something I've already mentioned: a misplaced faith in the King's English, a striving to be correct at any cost. The effect is the same as lifting one's pinkie at a formal teacup—exaggerated propriety, more ludicrous than honest ignorance. (The British used to have a word for such behaviour: *refained*. The Refained Speaker is so anxious not to sound like a Cockney—"the rine in Spine styes minely in the pline"—that he converts *all* his i's to a's; so he cannot even say *refined*.) The psychology of such errors is plain enough. Because one got scolded as a child for saying "Us kids are going to the store" or "Me and Jimmy got whipped," one assumes that *us* and *me* are always wrong. The result is Refained Grammar, like *between you and I*. Educated people, I suppose because they are conscious of having to set an example, are specially prone to this trick. I have heard my own colleagues say, "This report was prepared by Professor Perkins and I." If they reversed the order and said "by I, and Professor Perkins" they might notice the error—but they wouldn't do that, it would be impolite to put themselves first. Or take "you must be tolerant with *we* ordinary mortals": that came from an instructor in English. (No, an English department does not have faultless speakers; what makes it unusual is that the mistakes are more likely to be noticed.) A brilliant philosopher of my acquaintance will construct noble sentences rotten at the core: "Distinctions of this order are of major importance to he who cares about logic." *Him who cares about his image, I bid take note*. And then there is the *whom* problem, which the *New Yorker* used to love so well. "The lady in question, whom our informants advise us is known as Lou..." Whom is? Well, in my view *whom* is a booby trap. My advice is to drop it. It's on the way out, and the tactful speaker may avoid it even when it's technically correct. A question like "Whom do you mean?" really deserves the answer it gets from Pogo: "*Youm*, that's whom."

Now for a cluster of images which offend chiefly against Idiom. In doing so they also becloud clarity and muffle impact, for my three criteria intertwine so subtly that to hurt one is to hurt all. This fact strikes me as good presumptive evidence of having hit upon the right criteria.

The image which I confess most quickly riles me is that of the Pseudo-Immigrant—the speaker who blurs or disfigures the native idiom. The irony here, as I've already suggested, is that this speaker has known no other idiom since birth. *Genuine* foreigners who learn our language from the ground up can, of course, put him to shame—as Conrad and Nabokov have demonstrated for the written word. It is not always easy to decide what is idiomatically wrong, and what is merely illiterate or malaprop. What to do with this sentence, spoken by an old friend of mine: "We are enough individuals that we could never expect unanimity"? *Hein?* Does he mean, "There are so many of us that somebody is bound to vote No," or does he mean, "We're so different we'll never agree completely"? I suspect, but I can't be sure. What I do feel sure of is that he's not at home in the language. And that's what he has in common with the speaker who gets his meaning across but sounds all wrong: "If you would have broken that tackle, you may have gone all the way." A clear case of the conditional so *imperfect* as to be totally loused up; and a very common blooper among sports announcers and "colour commentators."

The most treacherous ground of all may be the use of prepositions, for it is here that English idiom hits a peak of unreason. Small wonder that they drive foreigners to despair; but a daily wonder that they also baffle a great many native high-school graduates, who speak of having *a preference to blondes* (or sometimes *an attraction for blondes*, lucky them), *an interest for snowmobiles* (let the finance company handle that one), or *an insight of the problem* (part of the problem being that they will spell "insight' with a C). And the chances are strong that they will compound the crime by leaning significantly on the faulty preposition: "an insight OF the problem." That's a habit they learn from their elders, who may choose the right prepositions but then try to project an image of profound deliberation by weighing them down: "I don't have detailed data ON that, Chief, but my office can get the figures FOR you." A clear and simple case of lead-swinging.

The pseudo-foreign flavour comes back strong with the unidiomatic choice of tenses, as in "Did you have dinner yet?" Did I have dinner yet: let a man ask me that but once, and his image by me is irreparably flawed. A host who understood English idiom (and human feelings) would ask, "Have you had dinner?"— by which he would delicately but unmistakably convey that there was (yet) more in the kitchen. By replying, "No, I haven't," I would likewise convey implicitly that although I had not dined up to that moment, I lived in hopes. That is what is so perfectly splendid about the Present Perfect. But our Alien wouldn't understand; in his world, I eat or I ate. And if I reply in the only language he knows, "No I didn't," it's all over and done with—dinner has fled, there is nothing but bleakness and starvation. I've *had it.*

This did-you-have-dinner-yet is the thin end of a great clumsy wedge. Pretty soon we'll be saying things like "Are you in this country since long?" and "Yes, my god, I was here since I am a child." It's full of rich ethnic flavour, no doubt, the stuff of which warm situation comedies are made, but it sticks in my craw. Why should I have these uncouth alien notions of time and sequence thrust upon me, when English idiom allows me to specify time within time, before time, and after time with infinite subtlety and satisfaction? Take for example this snatch of song from *Camelot:*

> If ever you would leave me,
> It wouldn't be in springtime.

I object to Mr. Lerner's lyrics because they warp idiom, and therefore wreak confusion. What he means, in his schmaltzy Transylvanian heart, is, "If ever you *should* leave me"—that is, it hasn't happened so far, and with luck it may not happen at all. But he says instead, "If ever you *would* ", which conveys something precise but quite different. To the idiomatic ear, it suggests a pitiable stretch of Time Past (*not* time to come), during which You were accustomed in a habitual and rather heartless way to leave Me—though not (one infers) for very long at a time, and never (one knows) between March and June. Given that opening clause, the verse ought really to unfold like this:

> If ever you would leave me
> I knew you had a reason—
> Like wishing to deceive me,
> Or wild duck's being in season.

Another form of idiom-smashing that attracts educated people is what I call Literalism. This is the habit of using a word for what it looks as if it should mean, rather than what idiom has brought it to mean. The most familiar example is *presently.* A man who asks me for a job, and says he is *presently completing* his thesis, already has one strike against him. Sure, to a foreign eye it appears to mean "at present." But as speakers of English we inherit the English genius for delay (as Samuel Johnson observes, "languages are the pedigree of nations"), and when we say "any moment now" we mean tomorrow. Once upon a time there was a good old four-letter word, *anon,* which meant *in one, at once;* but it soon became clear that you couldn't trust a tapster who said "anon, anon, sir," so somebody introduced the precise Latin word *presently* to mean *now,* and all was plain for a while. But the barman dragged his heels again, and *presently* became *some other time.* Now, if you want prompt action, you must specify *immediately,* or *on the double.* And if you mean *at present,* why not say it? It takes not one millisecond longer.

A slightly different case is presented by *momentarily* and *hopefully.* The idiomatic meaning—the only meaning given in a reliable Scottish dictionary, *Chambers's*—of *momentarily* is "for a moment, briefly," as in the poignant phrase, "momentarily she was mine; then, alas, she slipped through my fingers and was gone." (Feminist readers will substitute *he.*) So the fellow who says, with eyes aglow, "She will be mine momentarily," may be in for a big disappointment—and anyone who talks that way deserves it. He means *in a moment.* Other people abuse the word to mean *at the moment.* Thornton Wilder has even used it to mean *by the moment,* or *moment by moment*—and he does it in a stage direction, so there's no way out:

> The children lean forward and all watch the funeral in silence
> growing *momentarily* more *solemnized.*
> (*The Long Christmas Dinner*, Harper and Row, 1963, p. 95)

He wrote that in 1931. *Solemnized* is a bonus boner, which happily hasn't caught on. It will do fine as a reminder that if we wish to keep our language undefiled, we cannot always trust reputable authors.

As for *hopefully*, it appears to be a more recent immigrant from Germany by way of New York. But in German it was *hoffentlich*, and meant "hopingly": a detached, impersonal adverb that English hasn't invented yet—because English has other ways of being impersonal. If we want to say "hopingly" we can use *I hope, one hopes,* or even *it is to be hoped,* which ought to be impersonal enough for anybody. When we say *hopefully*, we mean in our idiomatic way that whoever is speaking or acting is *full of hope.* A famous example: "it is better to travel hopefully than to arrive." The man who tells us "She will be mine, hopefully, within the week (*ja*)" may thus be a decent modest fellow by German standards; but in English he's taking an awful lot for granted, for he implies that it's *she* who is so keen. And when the Hon. John Turner advertises in a British newspaper that his four children "require a kind and loving nannie [sic], *hopefully* with previous experience," any nanny worth her salt will perceive that it isn't only the children who need her help.

Momentarily, then, is misused through literalness and unawareness of idiom, as is *presently* (examples of what *Chambers's Dictionary* calls folk-etymology, or "popular unscientific attempts at etymology"). But the case of *hopefully* suggests an additional dimension, at least to my sensibilities. I connect it first with other personal adverbs misapplied in a general, impersonal way—*regretfully* instead of *regrettably*, maybe *pitifully* a while ago. What's happening here is the transfer of a private emotion to "the public sector," so that its source can no longer be traced. No wonder these usages prevail among businessmen and politicians. *Who* is full of hope, or regret, or pity? Not me, not you, not anyone: it has been shifted into a quality of the objective environment, as if there were a something, a process out there which had taken on sentience. Is it fanciful to connect this with other hints of personal abdication, such as is implied by *a decision-making process?* If a process can feel hope or regret, it can surely make decisions. And when decisions are made by a process, no single person can be held responsible; it *happens*, objectively and inexorably, like the march of history. No doubt, the original motive for the phrase was to imply (without promising) the breaking down of tyranny, the sharing of decisions by a number of persons (as in *participatory democracy*). In practice, however, both phrases are cop-outs, and in neither case does anything get decided or done. These are the phrases of people who have no policies, no self-reliance, no confidence—and who deserve none. The only way to bring about decisions and actions is to find some *person* who can *decide*, and *act*.

What disturbs me more than the standard lies and distortions of such propanganda language is this curious appearance of an inexorable process *out there*, because in common parlance we do not merely take part in a *decision-making process*, we are *plugged into it*. Immediately I am reminded of other locutions with the same metallic flavour: "This really turns me on, you know?" and, "Man, she turns me off" (which isn't an action by "her," exactly, nor yet a response by "me"). Who, or what, is speaking? *Where is the switch?* The image I detect here is Mechanism—half surrender to, half propitiation of the great, half-glimpsed machine which we half adore, half fear. By using the language of machines to describe our hopes, actions, reactions, by transferring to a humming external process what was once our private domain of striving, do we placate the Computer Politic, the World Machine, or do we program ourselves for sacrifice? Machines, as I understand them, have languages but no idioms. What I am expressing is not the modern fear that the robots are coming, but the fear that we are *robotizing, dehumanizing, depersonalizing* ourselves through words as ugly as the process they describe.

Another troublesome question under the general head of idiom has to do with the set of sub-idioms we call Slang. There are two opposite causes of concern: whether it is proper to use slang at all, or more commonly the question of *which* slang is fashionable or "in." The motive in both cases is *togetherness* (a piece of manufactured slang which never quite made it), the wish to confirm one's belonging to a group: in the first case the large group, the great club of all those who Speak Properly (and whose slang is called idiom); in the second case the small exclusive group, the tribe of the elite who share a secret attitude (and whose exclusiveness must be assured by continual changes in the password), like adolescents or pop musicians or anglers or astronomers. To those who ask the first question I reply cheerfully, "Yes, by all means use slang—if you know the risks." Those who worry about the second are not likely to ask me, because I am obviously no swinger; all the same, one or two of my random reflections may prove edifying.

Those who ask whether slang is permissible in polite society are really preoccupied with correctness, on which I've already offered my view. Applying my kind of standards, I would repeat that in our democratic, colloquial society you are more likely to be censured for using no slang at all. But of course there are risks in using it too. Some sober groups may find your flip ways unacceptable; argot that suits one milieu may draw sneers in another. My own preference for the simple and colloquial as salt to my discourse leads many of my colleagues to dismiss me as frivolous, unscholarly, simple-minded—a reflection to which I shall return. And slang of all kinds is in constant danger of not being clear, because impact, not clarity, presides at its birth. A current fad leans heavily but ambiguously on the simple word *to*. "To me, he's a wonderful person." (Great, but how does he behave to others?) "To the majority of immigrants, their perception of education is quite different from our own" (a spokesman for the Toronto Board of Education, quoted by Canadian Press, 17 Feb. 1975). Here *to* implies a perception *of a perception*. He means "most immigrants look on education in a way native Canadians don't," but he says, "most immigrants don't look at their perceptions as we would look at *their perceptions*"—which is true, perhaps, but not useful. A short way off is the modish use of *into*: "Yeah, I'm into the hard stuff," "I'm into medieval studies," "I'm into people." The obvious risk is that the literal meaning may overturn the slang one, as with the earnest boy who confides that he's really getting into girls now. Or take the curious American insistence on *human beings* as if they were a species of achievement. "Bruce is a superb human being," they affirm glowingly. (The hell you say; and here I was, expecting a stoat.)

This approaches the image of the Hopeless Square, who keeps treading on verbal land-mines because he is unaware of slang meanings. Scientific colleagues have complained to me of inexplicable merriment in their classes when they speak of a *crude model;* and we all recall the visiting Britisher who apologizes for *knocking up* his hostess at 2 a.m. Words like *cool* and *hot* have a perpetual but fluctuating slang sense: so that Marshall McLuhan's attempt to give them specific content with regard to the media runs into difficulties. The other way to look hopelessly square is to use argot that is out of date (or *old hat,* if you get me). For instance, a few years back *no way* was the all-purpose surfboard of the young, until like so many other passwords it sank from sight. But it did not quite disappear, for adults (in those days when youth could do no wrong) snatched at it eagerly, and have never let go—with the result that instead of being in the swim as they hoped, they are now quaintly stranded on an antique beach.

On the other hand, I observe with an agreeable sense of irony how the whirligig of time brings back the exile. *Groovy,* which I helped to bury 30 years ago, is suddenly alive and well. *Chap,* which in those early days was laughably British and probably a bit effeminate, is now a perfectly normal fella, even in New York. And although *gay* is at the moment unfit for any but its slang use, a fact I deplore, it seems possible that at last *queer* can be reinstated—and perhaps *fruit* as well.

One particular area which I would hesitate to call trendy in itself has undeniably provoked trendy convulsions in language: I mean of course the movement to liberate women. It took me a long time to realize that *consciousness raising* was not a phase of transcendental meditation but a specific manoeuvre in the feminist campaign. And I doubt that *chauvinism* will be fit for its original duty in my lifetime. But the silly edge of this argot shows when the new consciousness starts in on the unsexing of *métiers*. The *Globe* for Valentine's Day carried advertisements for "a Bodyman-woman, a Foreperson and, the most intriguing of all, a Parts man-woman." (Quoted in Letters, 18 Feb. 1975.) Richard Needham notes other transformations: cowboy into cattleperson, bus boy into dining-room attendant, governess into child mentor. Everyone keeps his own list. And because this kind of neurotic fiddling quickly invites a backlash, as we say, everyone keeps a list of put-downs. I have already demonstrated my impartiality, I hope, in various ways. So let me register my objection to the plague of *persons* where hateful sexist English reads *-man*. In *spokesman, chairman, barman,* and so on we don't even pronounce it "man," but "mun." I am reminded of a special British expression in which *person* is not neutral but insulting: "She's more of a *person*, really..." I am also reminded of the ultimate achievement in desexing language, the invention of a columnist that would replace *human* with the triumphant neuter *hu-person.* (And *Mädchen* is neuter, I recall. Do liberated Ger-persons object?)

Trendiness annoys me above all not merely because it is seductive and always has been, but because it seduces us back into the screwloose religion of change. The man who deplores a return to the 3 R's as a step back toward the cave is suffering from delirium *trendens.* He belongs to the McLuhanite fringe who scream that print is dead, the book is buried, and citizens of the global village must be expert in the new mysteries of film and tape and incantation. I never know how much to blame on the ancient sage himself, because I'm never sure what he means or how serious he is. But risking naiveté, let me suggest, to his disciples at least, that if the universe around the corner is electronic all the way, then we've got to find someone else who can write the *script,* and someone who can read it, and someone else who can use the camera properly (the emptiness of hand-held scriptless impromptu inaudible film happenings having at last registered on the most glazed watcher).

Are we lapsing into barbarism? Will we soon be unable to communicate except by coos and grunts and formulas? I don't really think so—though there are portents, dammit: such as my wife's hitchhiker, a braw school-leaver of nineteen, personable and polite. When she asked him to find out what was causing the noisy rattle he checked, diagnosed, and reported, "The uh thing...is, like...Uhhh..." Aghast, she conferred: did he mean the back door on the wagon was not properly shut? He heaved a great smiling sigh of relief. "Yuh," he said, having got through. No, what I fear is that well before that, we shall have lost touch with the past. That is the other purpose and glory of language, which the usage-mongers and the progress-peddlers and the flux-worshippers forget. The gift of my tongue does not merely enable me to "interrelate" with my contemporaries; it makes me a citizen of the entire human commonwealth, of an empire across time. I will not exchange that for a wilderness of global villages.

I remember that when I sang "We Three Kings" as a child I repeated the line, "Star with royal beauty *dight*," as generations of children had done before me. Later I learned with pleasure the ancient words to "This Endris Night." But I am hard put to excavate them now. Within one generation *dight* has vanished, replaced by "royal beauty *bright*." And in "Jingle Bells"—now sanctified as a *carol*, together with "Silver Bells"—who sings now of a one-horse open *shay?* (But it's still listed, glory be, in the *Dictionary of Canadian English* as a by-form of *chaise*.) How much longer before the only readers capable of grasping ancient documents (like *Sunshine Sketches of a Little Town* or *The Great Gatsby*) are eccentric antiquarians? You zealots of the flood, explain to me how it is that words can be preserved intact through the centuries, down the ringing grooves of change, and crumble only within our own half-life? I can guess. It is because, through the efforts of traditionalists and tories and purists who refused, God bless them, to believe that all our yesterdays were irrelevant, the barbarous babble current at any one time in the past was not allowed to prevail or prescribe. *Barbarous:* a good honest word. In Greek it meant "stammering," and they used it of foreigners' talk. We should know better. We know that stammering begins at home; and that barbarism begins inside the citadel.

To return, more calmly, from sermon to images. Let me round off my survey by asking what we should project, instead of all these inadvertent and regrettable images. I wonder how many readers will agree with my suggestion that there is no single answer, no proper image for all seasons. There is a whole range of good, desirable, effective impressions we can make with our words. It is our business to choose among them, and the one we choose should depend on the job we want to do and the audience we address. You can see the truth of this when it comes to accent. Only a very narrow-minded speaker would claim that the proper way to pronounce your English is the way they do it in Aburrdeen, or Suhhbiton, or Long Guyland, or Arnpryre. I propose quite seriously that the same is true for grammar, within limits, and above all for style. The style, or *register*, which you use to a bridge partner is not appropriate when you address a tax consultant or a bus driver—though each style may be free of errors. I remember a lady who taught grade nine, and told me of a boy who told her: "Look, I talk the way my father talks. What does my father *do?* He drinks. If I talked the way *you* talk, I'd get beat to a pulp." That boy was *right.* I suspect he was also clever enough to be leading a double or triple life by now, with a perfectly idiomatic language for each (as butlers used to do in England).

But let's take an example closer to hand. I wouldn't mind a small bet that some of you think there is such a thing as a Professorial Style—correct, dignified, formal, impressive, like a god talking. There is, of course; I've put in some examples of it myself, just to prove I can. But what I'd bet on is that you have a sneaky feeling that it's *the* proper style—that we should all aim to talk or write that way, and that when I depart from it (as I do) my image suffers. This is where people go wrong—professors most of all. That formal, god-like style is only too easy to reach; and if reached too often it becomes no style at all, but a disease. This is where Humpty Dumpty's remark does make sense. The question is who is to be master—you, or the style. A man at the mercy of his own style is as comic, and as much to be pitied, as a man at the mercy of drink. Your style ought to express *what you are,* and you are not the same person on all occasions, in every company. If you seem to be, you are a bore.

I see where I am heading. The image which I have really been deploring all along, an image which embraces all the unhappy ones I've described, is the image not of the Poor Boob, but of the Zombie. What I mourn over is not the mistakes, but the *numbness,* to every aspect of language, which they imply. I regret the sort of mind that measures sense by the syllable, and accepts as oratory flannel a yard wide. To such a mind, ideas expressed in a simple, playful way are (necessarily) simple and obvious ideas, not worth having. I regret likewise the mind that must cloak metaphors in prose, apparently believing that naked metaphor is indecent—the progeny of Knowlton Nash, those newsmouths that say "climb off his *legislative* high horse," or "this promises to become a *political* hot potato." I regret above all the mind insensitive to humour and wordplay of all kinds—not just the reflex groan at a bad pun, but the total inability to grasp a good one. I regret the mind which wears a superior smile when you play with a deliberate error (for instance, a friend of mine habitually says, "Oh, it was a congenital evening," and people exchange secret smiles because they think *he's* slipped). I regret, in sum, the mind to which all languages are dead languages, including its own.

Terms
and
Topics

TERMS

1. What is a concrete poem? What is meant by *concrete language*? (See the Note to the Reader.) Does a concrete poem have to use concrete language?

2. Distinguish between the words **simplistic** and **solipsistic**. How does *simplistic* differ from *simple*? How does *solipsistic* differ from *personal, private,* or *subjective*?

3. What is the difference between a **motif** and a **leitmotif**? What other terms, like *leitmotif*, has literary criticism adopted from the visual and plastic arts and from music?

4. **Alliteration** (repetition of the same sound at the beginning of words), **assonance** (similarity of vowel sounds within nearby words), **consonance** (similarity of consonant sounds within nearby words), **metre** (rhythmic beat of stressed syllables), and **rhyme** (the same or similar sound at the ends of words) are all common devices in poetry. How much can a writer of prose use such devices? Are there some kinds of essays in which a prose writer should avoid them all, others where they can be used in a limited way, and still others where they can be used with abandon? What are the differences between poetry and prose? Can you find any instances where it would be difficult, if not impossible, to label a particular piece of writing either poetry or prose? Try to write a paragraph of prose—perhaps descriptive of a scene or an action—in which you make deliberate use of alliteration, assonance, consonance, metre, and rhyme; are you tempted to think of it as poetry?

5. What do we mean by the term **reading**? What is the relation between reading and writing? Should a reader try to reproduce in himself the experience the writer had while writing? How important is it that a reader

"hear" an essay that is written down? Should a writer always read aloud something he has written? How can a reader learn to be conscious of *voice*? What account does a reader have to take of the appearance of an essay on the page? How can a reader "read" a concrete poem?

TOPICS: On Individual Essays

JOHN ROBERT COLOMBO "Communicating Through Form"

1. How could it possibly be argued that the words *form* and *content* "have no meaning whatsoever," as Colombo in his first paragraph says it has been?

2. Colombo says he will provide no definition of the word *form*. How does your dictionary define it? Try your own hand at defining it.

3. Advertising often follows and uses innovations in the arts. Can you find any ads that make use of the kind of "infracted forms" Colombo discusses?

4. Explain in your own words, with a concrete example, the difference between perception and apperception.

5. Take Colombo's hint and write an essay on "violated forms" of another kind, as for example in music, painting, photography, or movies. How could they exist also in "modern social concerns," as Colombo says they do?

6. Write a lipogram of at least one hundred words, avoiding one of the vowels. Then write one avoiding either *r*, *s*, or *t*.

7. Write a short paragraph in which each word contains an *a*; then one with each word having an *e*; an *i*; a *t*; an *o*; an *n*.

8. Compose a concrete poem.

GERTRUDE STEIN "Composition As Explanation"

1. Discuss the effect of the "constant recurring and beginning" Stein refers to and makes much use of. What has it to do with what she says about time?

2. Some of Stein's sentences at first sound like nonsense, but when read and reread and reread again and again they begin to make a kind of sense that would be impossible in more conventional sentences. Analyze two or three of her sentences to show how this happens.

3. Try to explain how *romanticism* and *war* function in this discussion of composition. What exactly does she mean by "composition"?

4. Some of the oddity of Stein's prose is due simply to the absence of conventional punctuation. Stein first delivered this essay as a lecture. Choose a likely paragraph of some length and read it aloud, slowly, several times. Does the oral delivery make it clearer? Try supplying the punctuation necessary to make it more like conventional writing.

5. Try your own hand at writing a paragraph that conveys the feeling of a "continuous present." Perhaps make it a "portrait," a description of someone you know well.

6. Stein uses the word *phenomena* as a singular noun. Is this deliberate, or a careless or carefree handling of the language?

7. How does Stein's essay force a reader to look closely at individual words and at the specific functions of parts of speech?

MICHAEL HORNYANSKY   "Is Your English Destroying Your Image?"

1. Compare several dictionaries to see what—if anything—they say about usage in the matter of such terms as *ain't, like* as a conjunction, *disinterested, due to, irregardless, good* as an adverb, *media, infer, hopefully, presently, momentarily.*

2. Do you agree that "lightness makes for more clarity than does indignation"? Why should this be so? Which would make for more *impact?* Is Hornyansky correct when he says that his three criteria are always subtly intertwined?

3. What is Hornyansky alluding to when he writes "A little grammar is a dangerous thing"?

4. Hornyansky doesn't refer to passive voice. Show how passive voice is often weak in the same way that such phrases as "a decision-making process" are weak.

5. Point out some of Hornyansky's own uses of slang and colloquialisms. Are they always effective?

6. From your everyday reading and listening, gather more words and phrases which create images of Fogginess and Mechanism.

7. Find some examples—perhaps in your textbooks—of the "Professorial" or "God-like" style that Hornyansky calls a "disease."

8. Can you think of any other "images" to add to those Hornyansky lists?

9. Keep a score-sheet for a week, recording the number of times you see or hear *hopefully* misused.

10. In his third paragraph, Hornyansky uses *magic* as a verb—which of course it isn't—and thus gets considerable vigour and freshness into his sentence. Compose half-a-dozen sentences using nouns as verbs, and another half-a-dozen using adjectives as verbs.

11. Do you agree that *whom* is best avoided? Construct a brief argument for its retention.

12. Write a persuasive essay either agreeing or disagreeing with Hornyansky's stand on "sexist English."

13. Write a short paragraph discussing some weakness or error of style in which you add to the point by purposely committing the error or weakness yourself. Then do the same to explain and demonstrate a stylistic or rhetorical strength.

TOPICS: General and Comparative

1. What use does Hornyansky make of anecdote? (Compare his essay with the essays in sections I, III, and IV.)

2. Find some examples of metaphor in current slang and in slang which has become out-of-date. Why do some slang words become accepted as part of standard vocabulary?

3. How many kinds of vocabulary can you find in the newspaper? How does editorial writing differ from sports writing? from news reporting? from commercial writing?

4. Read the legal transcript of a court trial, a chapter or more in a psychology textbook, a computer science journal, a few pages of *Hansard* or the Congressional *Debates,* or a professional paper in botany, zoology, or cliometrics. Analyze and assess the style you find. Characterize the language being used. Could it be simpler? Are there advantages or disadvantages to a technical language?

5. Look closely at the magazines displayed by a local newsstand. Are any of them aimed specifically at a teenage market? a male market? a female market? How can you tell? How is the layout—the whole combination of articles, pictures, letters, columns, advertising—designed to appeal to this market? Which magazines impart information? Which appeal to snobbishness or ambition? Which simply reinforce the status quo? What other kinds of appeal do they use?

6. Watch television closely for a week, and analyze the nature and the scheduling of the programming. What ages and interests do the programs appeal to? How effective is television as a means of communication and influence? Is it—or can it be—dangerous? Are there differences in quality or kind of programming from one channel to another?

7. In the next essay you write, make a conscious effort to introduce rhythm and sound patterns. How far dare you go? What considerations seem to determine how far you can go?

8. Choose a subject which interests you, such as athletics, home movies, blackberrying, Cézanne, dog shows, English kings, forensic medicine, snowmobiles, *Genesis*, whole numbers, sound waves, or seismography. First define your subject closely, narrowing it to a topic that can be handled in a short essay. Then cast yourself in a range of writer's roles, and write a series of short essays, say two or three pages each, all on the same subject, but varying in emphasis and approach as you alter your purpose and your audience in the following ways:

   (a) *Relate and describe.* Write a personal narrative which illustrates your involvement with the subject, but keep your emphasis on the subject rather than on yourself. Build descriptive elements into your story in such a way that they add to, but do not overpower, the narrative itself. Use some metaphoric language.

   (b) *Reveal.* Interview several people about your subject, taking notes. Then use some or all of your notes in an essay which explores the subject but also reveals aspects of personality—either your own or that of the person or persons who supplied the most striking perspective.

   (c) *Persuade.* Treat your subject argumentatively. Perhaps try to convince a reader of its virtues or shortcomings, or try to defend it against some attack which you can imagine being mounted against it. In any event, be sure to take into account what an opposing argument might say. If your subject is suitable, you might try writing an extended advertisement for it. Don't be afraid to use satire or irony if they are appropriate to your intentions.

   (d) *Explain and inform.* Explain some particular feature of your subject. Use descriptive and narrative elements if they help you to be clear about the point you are trying to elucidate, but keep them minimal. Do not let yourself be drawn into an argumentative stance; be as objective as possible.

   (e) *Amuse.* Treat your subject humorously. (Your central point can be serious, but the tone should be light.) Decide in advance which devices of humour will be appropriate to your purpose, but don't therefore automatically discard other promising ideas that inspiration gives you as you write.

When you have finished these essays, look back over them and consider the differences among them. To what audience does each essay appeal? Which essays are the most (and least) successful? Why? How and why have you varied their form? Have you been technically experimental? Where? Why? Now write one more essay, one in which you analyze your own writing style (as these five short essays reveal it) and explore how and why your style varies.

Notes on Authors and Sources

ADVERTISEMENTS. The *Gaines* ad appeared in *McCall's* (February 1978), and the *Stovetop* ad appeared in *Woman's Day* (27 March 1978).

ASIMOV, ISAAC (b. 1920). Russian-born American scientist and science fiction writer; author of over 100 novels, books of stories, and commentaries on aspects of science. "Time Travel: One-Way" appeared in *Is Anyone There?* (1967).

BECK, SIMONE AND LOUISETTE BERTHOLLE. See Julia Child.

BEERBOHM, SIR MAX (1872-1956). English novelist, essayist, and caricaturist, best known for his novel *Zuleika Dobson*. "How Shall I Word It?" is taken from his last volume of parodies, *And Even Now* (1920).

CAMERON, SILVER DONALD (b. 1937). Canadian freelance writer and founder of *The Mysterious East*; author of *Faces of Leacock* and other books, including *Conversations with Canadian Novelists* (1973), from which his interview with Davies is taken.

CHILD, JULIA. California-born chef and writer on culinary arts, and star of the television programme "The French Chef"; collaborated with French cooking teachers Simone Beck and Louisette Bertholle to produce *Mastering the Art of French Cooking* in 1965 (from which come the instructions on boning a fowl), and with Simone Beck to produce a second volume in 1970.

COLOMBO, JOHN ROBERT (b. 1936). Canadian poet, translator, and anthologist, compiler of *Colombo's Canadian Quotations*, and devotee of "found poetry." "Communicating Through Form" appeared in *A Media Mosaic*, ed. Walt McDayter, in 1971.

EISELEY, LOREN (1907-1977). American anthropologist; author of *The Firmament of Time*, *The Immense Journey*, and several other books on nature and modern life. "The Creature from the Marsh" is taken from *Night Country* (1971).

ELLISON, RALPH (b. 1914). American novelist (*Invisible Man*) and essayist. "Harlem Is Nowhere" appeared in his *Shadow and Act* (1964).

FORSTER, E.M. (1879-1970). English novelist and critic, best known for *A Passage to India*, *The Celestial Omnibus*, and *Aspects of Fiction*. "My Wood" appeared in *Abinger Harvest*, a collection of his essays, in 1936.

GALBRAITH, JOHN KENNETH (b. 1908). Canadian-born U.S. diplomat and economist; author of *The Scotch* and *The Affluent Society*. "The Language of Economics" appeared in *Fortune* magazine (December 1962), and was republished in *Economics, Peace & Laughter*, ed. Andrea D. Williams, in 1971.

HAIG-BROWN, RODERICK (1908-1976). English-born Canadian essayist, novelist, and magistrate; author of several books for children, including *Saltwater Summer*, and a number of books on the art of fishing, including *Fisherman's Fall* (1964), from which "Behind the Salmon" is taken.

HORNYANSKY, MICHAEL (b. 1927). Canadian folklorist, children's writer (*The Golden Phoenix*) and professor of English. His essay on usage appeared in *In the Name of Language!*, ed. Joseph Gold, in 1975.

HUXLEY, ALDOUS (1894-1963). English satirist, essayist, and novelist, long a United States resident; best known for his moral fable *Brave New World* and novels like *Point Counter Point* and *Island*. "Usually Destroyed" was collected in *Adonis and the Alphabet* (1956), called *Tomorrow and Tomorrow and Tomorrow* in the American edition.

KAEL, PAULINE (b. 1919). Widely-printed American film critic; author of *Kiss Kiss Bang Bang* (1968), in which her comments on *The Sound of Music* were collected, and other works, including *Going Steady* and *Reeling*.

LANE, MARGARET (b. 1907). English reporter, novelist, and biographer of Beatrix Potter, Edgar Wallace, Charlotte Brontë, and other literary figures. "The Ghost of Beatrix Potter" appeared in her *Purely for Pleasure* (1966).

LEACOCK, STEPHEN (1869-1944). Canadian humorist and professor of economics and political science; widely known as a humorous lecturer and as the author of *Sunshine Sketches of a Little Town* and other works. *Literary Lapses*, in which "A, B, and C" appeared, was first published in 1910.

LYNES, RUSSELL (b. 1910). American educator, ditor, and social commentator; author or *Highbrow, Lowbrow, Middlebrow* and *Domesticated Americans*, among other works. "Time on Our Hands" first appeared in *Harper's Magazine* in 1958.

LUDWIG, JACK (b. 1922). Canadian novelist, professor, and sports observer, now resident in New York; his works include a novel, *Above Ground*, and a book of essays, *Games of Fear and Winning* (1976), which included his comments on the Calgary Stampede.

McAULEY, JAMES (1917-1977). Australian poet and literary critic; author of *Under Aldebaran* and *A Vision of Ceremony*. His essay on New Guinea appeared in his *The Grammar of the Real* (1975).

MacLENNAN, HUGH (b. 1907). Canadian novelist (*Barometer Rising, The Watch That Ends the Night*) and essayist. "The Street-Car Conductor" appeared in his *Thirty and Three* (1955).

MITFORD, NANCY (b. 1904). English novelist and biographer, now resident in France; author of *Pigeon Pie, Voltaire in Love*, and other works, and editor of *Noblesse Oblige: An Enquiry into the Identifiable Characteristics of the English Aristocracy* (1956), from which her essay is taken.

MOOREHEAD, ALAN (b. 1910). Australian biographer and military writer, who has taken a special interest in the history of exploration. His works include *The White Nile, Cooper's Creek*, and *Darwin and the Beagle*. "A Pleistocene Day" is a chapter from *No Room in the Ark* (1959).

MUKHERJEE, BHARATI (b. 1940). Bengali-born Canadian novelist; author of *The Tiger's Daughter* and *Wife*. "Intimations" is part of the section she wrote for *Days and Nights in Calcutta*, an autobiographical account of a year in India which she wrote in collaboration with her husband Clark Blaise.

MURDOCH, WALTER (1874-1970). Australian newspaper essayist. "On Pioneering" appeared in *Speaking Personally* in 1930, and again in his *Collected Essays* in 1941.

NAIPAUL, V.S. (b. 1932). Trinidad-born novelist and travel writer, resident in England since 1950; author of *A House for Mr. Biswas, Guerillas*, and *An Area of Darkness*. "Power?" was collected in *The Overcrowded Barracoon* in 1972 after appearing in 1970 in *The New York Review of Books*.

O'CONNOR, FLANNERY (1925-1964). American novelist and short story writer; author of *Wise Blood* and *Everything that Rises Must Converge*. Her essay on education appeared in *Mystery and Manners*, ed. Sally and Robert Fitzgerald, in 1969.

ORWELL, GEORGE (1903-1950), pseud. of ERIC BLAIR. English novelist, essayist and cultural observer; author of *Animal Farm* and *1984*, and several collections of essays. "How the Poor Die" first appeared in *Now* in the 1940s, and was collected in his *Shooting an Elephant* (1950).

ROUECHE, BERTON (b. 1911). American medical journalist; author of *Eleven Blue Men, The Incurable Wound*, and other "narratives of medical detection." "Three Sick Babies" appeared in his *The Orange Man* in 1971.

RUSSELL, BERTRAND (1872-1970). English philosopher and mathematician, lecturer and controversial correspondent on a variety of topics. "Tourists," taken from *Mortals and Others* (1975), ed. Harry Ruja, was written in 1931 for the *New York American* as a regular literary page column.

STEIN, GERTRUDE (1874-1946). American writer, trained in psychology and medicine, who became a literary leader among the exiles who settled in Paris in the 1920s; author of *The Autobiography of Alice B. Toklas* and other works. "Composition as Explanation," first delivered as a lecture, was first published in 1926 in *What Are Masterpieces?*

SZASZ, THOMAS S. (b. 1920). American psychiatrist and author of *The Myth of Mental Illness, Ceremonial Chemistry*, and other books on psychiatry and public attitude. "What Psychiatry Can and Cannot Do" appeared in *Harper's Magazine* in 1964, and in his *Ideology and Insanity* (1970).

THOMAS, DYLAN (1914-1953). Welsh poet, scriptwriter (*Under Milk Wood*), and story writer. "Memories of Christmas" was first broadcast by the BBC Welsh Home Service in 1945 and printed in *The Listener*, and collected in *Quite Early One Morning* in 1954.

THOMAS, LEWIS (b. 1913). American medical doctor, director of the Memorial Sloan-Kettering Cancer Center in New York; author of *The Lives of a Cell*. His "Notes of a Biology-Watcher" appeared in the *New England Journal of Medicine*, 10 February 1977.

THURBER, JAMES (1894-1961). American cartoonist, humorist, journalist, and playwright, long a staff member of *The New Yorker*; among his works are *The Seal in the Bedroom* and *The Owl in the Attic*. "Wild Bill Hickok and His Friends" (also published as "The French Far West") appeared in his *Let Your Mind Alone* in 1937.

WHITE, E.B. (b. 1899). American poet, essayist, and letter writer; author of *Charlotte's Web* and other books for children as well as of numerous collections of essays and letters. "Once More to the Lake," written in 1941, appeared in *One Man's Meat* (1944) and was reprinted in *Essays of E.B. White* (1977).

WOODCOCK, GEORGE (b. 1912). Canadian poet, playwright, biographer, and travel writer; author and editor of over sixty books, including *Civil Disobedience, Anarchism*, and *Canada and the Canadians*. "A Northern Journal," the diary notes from a 1968 Arctic trip, appeared in 1972 in *A Rejection of Politics and Other Essays*.

WOOLF, VIRGINIA (1882-1941). English novelist and essay writer, best known for *To The Lighthouse, Mrs. Dalloway, The Waves*, and *A Room of One's Own*. "Middlebrow," written but never sent to *The New Statesman*, was printed in *The Death of the Moth* (1942).

YALDEN, JANICE M. Canadian professor of Spanish; "Methods in Language Teaching" is the revised and updated version of an essay that first appeared in *What's What for Children Learning French*, ed. Elaine Isabelle, in 1976.

ZINSSER, WILLIAM (b. 1922). American feature writer and teacher; author of *On Writing Well* and *Pop Goes America*. "Nobody Here But Us Dead Sheep" first appeared in *Life* magazine, 22 August 1969.